CHIEF
MODERN POETS
OF
BRITAIN AND AMERICA

A FIFTH EDITION OF

Chief Modern Poets of England and America

CHIEF
MODERN
POETS
OF
BRITAIN
AND
AMERICA

VOLUME I
Poets of Britain

Selected and Edited by
GERALD DEWITT SANDERS
JOHN HERBERT NELSON
M. L. ROSENTHAL

MACMILLAN PUBLISHING CO., INC.
New York
COLLIER MACMILLAN PUBLISHERS
London

Earlier editions entitled *Chief Modern Poets of England and America* copyright 1929, 1936, and 1943 and © 1962 by Macmillan Publishing Co., Inc. Copyright renewals 1957 and 1964 by Gerald DeWitt Sanders and John H. Nelson.

Library of Congress catalog card number: 78–90218

MACMILLAN PUBLISHING CO., INC.
866 THIRD AVENUE, NEW YORK, NEW YORK 10022

COLLIER-MACMILLAN CANADA, LTD.

PRINTED IN THE UNITED STATES OF AMERICA
Printing   20   21   22   Year   8   9
ISBN   0-02-405890-4

Credits and Acknowledgments

The editors are indebted to the publishers and agents and, in a number of instances, to the authors who are listed here for their generosity and cooperation in permitting us to reprint material for which they control the copyright. For these favors, we here record our thanks.

The Clarendon Press, Oxford: "Low Barometer" from *The New Verse of Robert Bridges* and "Johannes Milton, Senex" and "I Never Shall Love the Snow Again" from *The Shorter Poems of Robert Bridges* are reprinted by pemission of The Clarendon Press.

The Devin-Adair Co.: The poems from *Collected Poems* by Patrick Kavanagh, copyright © Patrick Kavanagh 1964, are reprinted by permission of the Devin-Adair Co.

The Dolmen Press, Ltd.: The poems by Austin Clarke and "In the Ringwood" and "Baggot Street Deserta" by Thomas Kinsella are reprinted by permission of The Dolmen Press, Ltd.

Doubleday & Company, Inc.: The poems by Robert Graves from *Collected Poems,* by Robert Graves, copyright 1955 by Robert Graves, are reprinted by permission of Doubleday & Company, Inc., and Cassell & Co., Ltd.

iv

E. P. Dutton & Co., Inc. The selections from *The Old Huntsman, Counter-Attack,* and *Picture-Show* by Siegfried Sassoon are reprinted by permission of E. P. Dutton & Co., Inc.

Faber and Faber, Ltd.: "On the Move" by Thom Gunn is reprinted by permission of Faber and Faber, Ltd., from *The Sense of Movement.*

Grove Press, Inc.: The poems by Edwin Muir from *Collected Poems 1921–1951,* copyright 1957, and *One Foot in Eden,* copyright 1956, are reprinted by permission of Grove Press, Inc

Harcourt, Brace & World, Inc.. The selections by William Empson from *Collected Poems,* copyright 1935, 1940, 1949 by William Empson, are reprinted by permission of Harcourt, Brace & World, Inc.

Harper & Row, Publishers: "The Committee" from *Pegasus and Other Poems,* copyright © 1957 by Cecil Day Lewis; the selections from *The Heart's Journey* by Siegfried Sassoon; "Hawk Roosting," "Pike," and "Lupercal" from *Lupercal,* copyright © 1959 by Ted Hughes; "An Otter" and "November," copyright © 1960 by Ted Hughes, from *Lupercal;* "Cadenza," copyright © 1966 by Ted Hughes; and "Song of a Rat—I, II, and III," copyright © 1967, from *Wodwo* by Ted Hughes, are reprinted by permission of Harper & Row, Publishers.

Holt, Rinehart and Winston, Inc.: The selections from *Last Poems* and *Complete Poems* by A. E. Housman, copyright 1922, © 1959 by Holt, Rinehart and Winston, Inc., copyright 1950 by Barclay's Bank, Ltd.; and selections from *Collected Poems, Down-adown-Derry, Memory and Other Poems, Motley and Other Poems, The Veil and Other Poems, Peacock Pie,* and *Poems for Children* by Walter de la Mare are reprinted by permission of Holt, Rinehart and Winston, Inc.

Houghton Mifflin Co.: Selections from John Betjeman's *Collected Poems,* copyright 1959, are reprinted by permission of and arrangement with Houghton Mifflin Company, the authorized publishers.

"For My Funeral" by A. E. Housman is reprinted by permission of the estate of the late A. E. Housman.

Alfred A. Knopf, Inc.: "A Country Walk," copyright 1967, 1968 by Thomas Kinsella is reprinted by permission of Alfred A. Knopf, Inc., from *Night Walker and Other Poems* by Thomas Kinsella.

"Lucy" and "A Robin" from *The Fleeting,* copyright 1933 by Walter de la Mare, are reprinted by arrangement with the author and with the consent of the publisher, Alfred A. Knopf, Inc.

Selections from *October and Other Poems* by Robert Bridges and from *More Poems* by A. E. Housman are reprinted by permission of Alfred A. Knopf, Inc.

D. H. Lawrence: "When I Went to the Circus," "Swan," "Willy Wet-Leg," and "When the Ripe Fruit Falls" from *Pansies,* published

"Futility," "Disabled," "Anthem for Doomed Youth," and "Strange Meeting" from Wilfred Owen, *Collected Poems,* © Chatto & Windus, Ltd., 1946, are reprinted by permission of New Directions Publishing Corporation.

"The Force That Through the Green Fuse," "Light Breaks Where No Sun Shines," "And Death Shall Have No Dominion," "After the Funeral," "Twenty-four Years," "A Refusal to Mourn the Death," "A Winter's Tale," "In My Craft or Sullen Art," "Ceremony after a Fire Raid," "Fern Hill," and "Altarwise by Owl Light" from Dylan Thomas, *Collected Poems,* copyright 1939, 1943, 1946 by New Directions Publishing Corporation, copyright 1952 by Dylan Thomas, are reprinted by permission of New Directions Publishing Corporation.

Ivan Obolensky, Inc: "Distinctions," "Paring the Apple," "Poem," "Farewell to Van Gogh," and "On the Hall at Stowey," by Charles Tomlinson, from *Seeing is Believing,* copyright 1958, are reprinted by permission of Ivan Obolensky, Inc.

Oxford University Press, Inc.: "The Summer Malison," "The Wreck of the *Deutschland,*" "Hurrahing in Harvest," "To R.B.," "As Kingfishers Catch Fire," and "Not, I'll Not, Carrion Comfort" from *Poems* of Gerard Manley Hopkins, fourth edition edited by W. H. Gardner and N. H. MacKenzie, © Society of Jesus 1967, are reprinted by permission of Oxford University Press, Inc.

"Snow," "Bagpipe Music," "Il Piccolo," "In Lieu," and "The Grey Ones" from *The Collected Poems* of Louis MacNeice, edited by E. R. Dodds, copyright © The Estate of Louis MacNeice 1966, are reprinted by permission of Oxford University Press, Inc.

Oxford University Press, London: "Return to Hinton" from *A Peopled Landscape* and "The Cavern" from *American Scenes* by Charles Tomlinson, published by Oxford University Press, are reprinted by permission of Oxford University Press.

Random House, Inc.: "Something Is Bound to Happen," "Petition," "As Well As Can Be Expected," "O Where Are You Going?" and "We All Make Mistakes" (*Poems*) W. H. Auden. Copyright 1934 by The Modern Library, Inc. Reprinted from *The Collected Poetry of W. H. Auden* by permission of Random House, Inc.

"Law Like Love," "September 1, 1939," "In Memory of W. B. Yeats," "Musée des Beaux Arts," and "The Capital" (*Another Time*) W. H. Auden. Copyright 1940 by W. H. Auden. Reprinted from *The Collected Poetry of W. H. Auden* by permission of Random House, Inc.

"The Quarry," "Now the Leaves Are Falling Fast," and "Fish in the Unruffled Lakes" (*On This Island*) W. H. Auden. Copyright 1937 by Wystan Hugh Auden. Reprinted from *The Collected Poetry of W. H. Auden* by permission of Random House, Inc.

"The Walking Tour" and "The Decoys" (*Poems*) W. H. Auden.

Preface to the Fifth Edition

British and American poetry of this century no longer needs defending. The age of Yeats has produced work equal in beauty and brilliance to that of any of the other great literary periods of our language. Rich in experimentation, this age has also been rich in the revitalization of poetic traditions. Moreover, throughout its tumultuous history there has run a quiet, pure stream of lyricism undefiled that has its source in the early beginnings of English poetry.

This anthology, intended for students, aims to give a balanced view of the many-sided modern achievement. The superb daring of a Pound or Eliot on the one hand, and the more conventionally contained power of a Frost or Stevens or Muir on the other, are, with many other contrasting values, essential to our poetic scene. Since its first, pioneering edition in 1929, *Chief Modern Poets of England and America* has sought to represent this scene in some depth by selecting a reasonable number of outstanding poets and giving enough of the best work of each to provide a meaningful context for any one poem. The advantages for study and appreciation over the usual anthology practice of providing a few feasts and a vast number of passing nibbles should, we hope, be clear.

In our selection of poets and poems, the primary standard has been excellence, with some attention to current informed opinion and to various further considerations useful to intelligent study. Thus the inclusion of Emily Dickinson and Gerard Manley Hopkins, though it violates the principle of representing only poets whose main achievement is of this century, seems necessary because they came into their own only in our age. They "lived before their time"—their poetry is more truly ours than that of many writers still living. Again, since Yeats so dominates the age, it is especially valuable to gain a ground sense of his development over a long career during which his whole method and way of thinking changed dynamically. Lawrence is significant not only in his own right but also because of his great influence on later poets, and it is historically important to see Auden as a spokesman of several moods of the 1930's and 1940's. Other poets, such as

Housman, Millay, and Betjeman, are figures of the age whose popular appeal—we speak of writing far above the level of the *merely* popular—is one real imperative. Our great regret is that although we provide a sampling of poets who have only recently come to the fore, our over-all purpose and our space limitations force us to exclude some whose work is comparable with that represented.

As in earlier editions, British and American writers appear separately. In each part, we print the poets in order of their birth and the poems in order of their first book publication, whose date we note after each poem. Hopkins and Dickinson were not, except insignificantly, pub-lished in their lifetimes, and so we have made an exception with them and arranged their work in the order, so far as can be determined, of composition. Where there are two dates, the first is that of composition, the second of original book publication. For a poem untitled by its author, we use the first line or opening phrase, placed in square brackets, as the title. When the author himself uses a first line as title, we follow him in the matter of quotation marks.

In general, our text is that of the most recent editions of the poets, although in some instances earlier versions seem preferable and have been retained. A notable example is Marianne Moore's "Poetry," a poem that like many others of hers has undergone considerable revision over the years. The version we use here is that of the *Collected Poems* (1951), which Miss Moore drastically alters in her *Complete Poems* (1967) by reducing it to the first three lines—though she does give the whole longer text in her notes at the back of the book, thus implying, perhaps, that she is teasing her readers by reminding them that she, after all, is mistress of her own work and quite free to balance *two* versions in the air if she wishes. Which is the better version? We choose the longer one, but at the same time accept the fact that the poetic process never really closes itself off, and that an understanding of this is essential to realizing what poems actually are.

W. H. Auden presents similar problems. As with Miss Moore, we find it a wrench to accept his omissions at times. Thus, in *The Collected Shorter Poems* (1966), he drops the eloquent original stanzas 2–4 in the third part of "In Memory of W. B. Yeats." He has, however, made some less debatable changes in the poem as well, and it would hardly do to treat his revisions selectively within a single piece. We do, though, for historical as well as critical reasons, retain a few poems he leaves out of his latest collection. For the same reasons, we have re-luctantly decided to use the text established by Thomas H. Johnson, as a result of his study of the manuscripts, for our Emily Dickinson selections. Although it seems likely that she would have revised her punctuation and capitalization for publication, this revision never in fact took place. Her mysterious dashes and eccentric capitals leave certain readings open that a more fixed system would obscure, and if that system is not hers, we do better to let every reader be his own interpreter. An anthology is, at best, a springboard to interest in a writer's whole development, and not a tyrannical reduction—this is the best teaching and studying hint we can give.

This obvious point of critical emphasis is one key to the problem of choosing the "best" versions of poems. Although a living poet will usually prepare and proofread his books with loving care, he does not always do so. If the poet is no longer living, of course, his text will be transmitted by someone who has taken on the task—perhaps his wife, perhaps another writer, perhaps a friend or a professional scholar or even some unnamed person. Recent years have seen a proliferation of new editions of varying dependability; one wonders whether earlier editions of certain poets did not, every so often, depend on insights or information that have simply vanished.

We have tried, in the light of these facts, to use intelligent judgment in preparing this edition. Sometimes we have thought it useful to choose an earlier version of a revised poem because of considerations like those provoked by Marianne Moore's "Poetry." Sometimes we have done so because an earlier version (or rejected poem) embodies qualities that first won the poet his recognition, though he himself may have turned against those qualities. We hope that the dates of first book publication provided after each of the poems, and the brief sections of bibliographical and biographical information after each volume, will help lead individual students to explore at least some poets in the perspective of their whole development.

Brief critical introductions precede the British and the American sections of this book. In each instance we intend the introduction neither as a definitive statement for the student nor an obstruction to the teacher, but merely as a series of suggestions toward rapport with the poets.

Contents

VOLUME I

Poets of Britain

Introduction: Modern British Poetry

Modern poetry in English has been strongly influenced by the French Symbolists of the last century and their predecessors. It shares with Mallarmé and Verlaine their interest in a psychologically evocative method and manner. It has been deeply affected by Rimbaud's way of thinking through images rather than through overt exposition. It is saturated with the ironies, the despair at modern civilization, and the personal alienation of Baudelaire, Laforgue, and others. It distrusts windiness and didacticism of every kind.

British poetry began in the 1890's to show the strong impress of the great French writers, though the work of that decade seems to us now somewhat affected and less than full-bodied in its preoccupation with "evil" and "Beauty" and the "Religion of Art." It was the age of Walter Pater, Oscar Wilde, and Arthur Symons, names we often associate with a pose of world-weary decadence. But the poets of the 'nineties were far more than mere poseurs. There was something very durable in their insights and preoccupations. William Butler Yeats, in his youth an outstanding poet of that period, stood until his death, in 1939, as a living link between its idiom and that of our century. He became, indeed, our most powerful single poetic voice. One of the chief reasons (and one of the most useful starting points for an understanding of his accomplishment) lay in his extension of the creed of the 'nineties that exalted aesthetic values over religious and moral ones. He used this creed to encompass the great philosophical, political, and doctrinal questions of the times, rather than to reject them and assert his own superiority as an artist to them.

Even without the French, the 'nineties had ample native precedent for their special kind of aestheticism. They had their own models in the lyricism, the spontaneity, the "magic" of Elizabethan poetry. They had also its rapid dramatic complexities, its cultivation of the conceit and other verbal pyrotechnics, and its brooding depths to study and imitate —though they left this task largely to a later generation, including the mature Yeats, to pursue. Again, they had behind them the pursuit of mystery, the imaginative flights, and the tragic sense of the gap be-

tween reality and the ideal of Blake and the great Romantics; and th
music of Tennyson, Swinburne, and the pre-Raphaelites was very muc
a part of their own apprenticeship. The classical economy and concen
tration of Housman and Bridges, whose poems are nevertheless highl
melodic, the beautiful strangeness of de la Mare, and the "songs" c
Auden are a few instances of the continuation into modern times c
well-established traditions. In general, our best contemporary poets hav
never lost touch with these traditions, however much they may hav
experimented with them in their several fashions.

The most drastic experimentation has been done by Americans, b
and large, rather than by British writers. Think of the revolution i
modern verse and it will be Eliot's The Waste Land or Pound's Cant
or the explosions of Cummings or Williams that first come to mind. Th
student may ponder this fact and come to many possible explanation
One of them, perhaps, is that the transition to the modern was a mor
gradual process in England; English poetry has grown naturally throug
several phases since the Renaissance, while American poetry had t
discover its own motives, language, and materials after a long sul
servience to English culture. Even the innovations of Gerard Manle
Hopkins, who lived entirely within the last century yet seems indi
putably modern, have their acknowledged antecedents in Anglo-Saxo
and Middle English poetry and in the versification of Milton's Samso
Agonistes.

Hopkins was a doubly "alienated" personality in that he was a Jesu
priest in a predominantly Protestant country and, at the same time,
man intensely responsive to sensory stimuli despite his ascetic vocation
When he became a candidate for priesthood, he renounced poetry fc
a number of years, until requested by his superiors to write about th
tragic incident described in "The Wreck of the Deutschland." Alway
especially intrigued by the paradoxes implicit in nature (see his ear
"Winter with the Gulf Stream"), he devoted this long elegy to th
mystery of Christian faith as well as to the heroism and pathos of th
nuns aboard the Deutschland. The internal struggle between the artist
bent and his spiritual discipline may well have entered this poem c
multiple conflict, as it entered the sonnet "The Windhover," in whic
the poet is amazed at himself for allowing the physical beauty an
power of a mere bird to stir him so, and as it entered the "terrible son
nets" he wrote toward the end of his life. "The Wreck of the Deutsch
land" argues that one must "stress" one's affirmation; the inner sel
must reach out toward Christ as the tall nun of the poem does, eage
to be put to the test of faith on which salvation depends. The argumen
is clearly related to Hopkins's "sprung rhythm" technique, whose pr
mary characteristic is the arrangement of stressed syllables in such a wa

that a special rhetorical emphasis is superimposed on the "normal" rhythm of a poem. It is easy, after reading Hopkins and Bridges side by side, to see why the latter poet, though for a long time Hopkins's faithful correspondent and the first editor of Hopkins's *Poems* (1918), felt constrained to temper his admiration with some harsh criticism of their "faults of taste" and "artistic wantonness."

Whatever the extravagances of Hopkins, however, they pointed the way to the future in all their essential aspects far more than the quieter perfectionism of Bridges. Though Yeats and Hardy were not directly influenced by "sprung rhythm," both developed ways of bringing the movement of common speech and impassioned argument into a supposedly conventional verse form. They thus, in effect, substituted that movement for the conventional one as the dominant element in their rhythm, while preserving the enormous advantages of the patterned structure of traditional verse. Hardy's close interest in and talent for catching the tones and data of ordinary life are as important to his poetry as to his fiction, and his ironic sense of human fate works with equal poignancy in both modes. He had a ready command of language and sound, if not a poetically rich one, and needed the ready-made molds of stanzaic form he employed to discipline his endlessly active contemplation of the surface of life. The driving artistic instinct that led Hopkins to allow himself to express his sensuousness and to try to justify it by finding all nature a proliferation of manifestations of the in-dwelling Divine Spirit forced him into some crucial formal inventions. Hardy has little to parallel this side of Hopkins. His is essentially a poetry of common sense, of a good man who hopes for the best but expects the worst. When he invents, it is by straining words to fit a set pattern amidst an active flow of ideas. Beyond that he cannot go very far. Thus, in *The Dynasts* all he can do is improvise a host of spirits who look down on the history of Napoleon's defeat by England and discuss it endlessly: a trite allegorical device whereby the Spirit of the Pities, the Spirit of the Years, the Spirit Ironical, and so on make Hardyesque speeches on the meaning of Fate and the possibilities of man. Hardy cannot be discounted. His great strength lay in his eye and ear for reality. He was a superb gossip in his poetry, which is full of the most vividly dramatic and revealing sketches. Moreover, he wrote some beautiful lyric poems and possessed a happy wit. But we are rarely free from his heavy-handed and gloomy pondering of the meaning of what he presents, as in Hopkins we are rarely free of the poet's doctrinal pressures.

Yeats tips the balance the other way. He is almost always more interested in the poetic possibilities of a theme or problem than in its literal meaning or solution, even when he is writing about Ireland's conflicts or dealing with his mystical conceptions of history and of personality. The difference may seem slight—after all, Yeats does present genuine issues and does advocate certain attitudes. But his method proved tremendously liberating. In a curious way the symbols of his poetry become at once more important than what they symbolize. For instance, "Leda and the Swan," "The Cat and the Moon," and "Crazy Jane Talks with the Bishop" can be accurately described as having to do, in the first, with the relationship between the human and the divine; in the second, between living, individual beings and the abstract cyclical process behind all existence; in the third, between the sacredness of the sexual principle and the assumptions of official religion. And they are very simple in their details, bold and clear in their statement, and compelling in their living, singing idiom. Even when Yeats gives us difficult and ambiguous ideas, there is usually a brilliantly lucid surface. But the symbols in these poems also have many further connotations, particularly in the light they throw on one another when placed in opposition. In Yeats's poetry we are taken again and again beyond the limits of the situation or picture he originally presents (Zeus ravishing Leda, a cat "dancing" in moonlight, a woman replying to a priest's reproaches) to a level of awareness with enormous emotional authority. His aim was to reach through to universal realizations rooted in the subconscious mind. There seems little doubt that Yeats's constant attempts to achieve this kind of awareness while keeping his writing vigorously immediate had a great deal to do with the steady increase of power that his later work shows.

Irish poetry after Yeats has thrived hardily, and its main directions may be glimpsed in the work of Austin Clarke, Patrick Kavanagh, and Thomas Kinsella. Clarke, a younger contemporary of Yeats, passed in his own idiosyncratic way through parallel phases of romantic lyricism and then a harsher, more direct realism. His later poems are bluntly critical of the Church and of the condition of the poor in his country; in a sense, they constitute a continuing denunciation, by an unpretentious prophet, of modern Ireland's neglect of the republican ideals that brought her to birth. Clarke's feeling for the daily atmosphere of Irish urban life, as well as for the essential physical and psychic landscape of Ireland, has encouraged younger poets to follow along his lines despite the ringing echoes of Yeats's great rhetoric. Kavanagh, too, has given voice to an appreciation, both loving and angry, of the precise nature of actual Irish life, but his basic material and attitude are more deeply rural, his criticism at once more exclusively anti-puritanical and more expansively raucous—when he lets go—than Clarke's. Kinsella's sensibility and methods are more sophisticated, with a more cosmopolitan orientation, than those of Clarke and

Kavanagh, yet he shares their local concerns at the same time. His *Wormwood* is a confessional sequence comparable in power, immediacy, and compression with Clarke's *Mnemosyne Lay in Dust*. Both works reveal the psychological preoccupations of modern poets everywhere, though they are saturated with Irish meanings.

To return to the broader scene once more, the name of Yeats so overshadows the poetry of modern Britain that it is impossible to think of other poets as comparably "great." One must go to Auden, forty-two years his junior, and to Thomas, seven years younger still, to find names in any sense rivaling his. Of the figures born before century's end, however, a number have written poetry of originality and relevance whose impact remains as effective as ever. John Masefield, it is true, cannot command the kind of recognition his *The Everlasting Mercy* once brought him, though his gift for story-telling and description in a swift, dramatic verse style should not be forgotten. And James Stephens, despite his fine ear for Irish folk-speech and his charm and immediacy and imagination, seems to have receded with that Celtic revival of which he was so much a part. But the war poems of Siegfried Sassoon and Wilfrid Owen remain in all their clear, bold pathos, and the "Georgian" countryside poetry of the former writer still retains its nostalgic realism that links his work with that of Robert Frost in the United States and of a number of Sassoon's fellow Englishmen who once comprised a notable literary movement. Most important, the work of Edwin Muir, Dame Edith Sitwell, Robert Graves, D. H. Lawrence, and Hugh MacDiarmid—though much of his best writing is in Scots—retains its intrinsic interest.

Dame Edith's poetry is especially attractive in its early period, when she experimented so joyously with synaesthesia (the mingling of sense effects, as in "the morning light creaks down again") or with a kind of half-whimsical, half-impressionistic incantatory verse not unlike that of Vachel Lindsay on occasion. Her success comes largely from her ability to compress into a single image a visual and an aural perception, and also from her sprightly pacing of rhythmic movement. Robert Graves at his best is not nearly so "stylized" as Dame Edith at hers, and by the same token he does not run her constant risk of affectation and preciosity. His work is an excellent example of poetry of the middle ground, at which in general the British are far more successful than the Americans. Without rising to great impassioned heights, without any dazzling explorations either of technique or sensibility, he gives us the idiom of a well-educated, humorous, forthright, nonconforming adult mind. The author of *Good-bye to All That*, an autobiography that reveals much about his psychologically scarifying experience of World War I, Graves is not insensitive to the subtleties of intense emotion, and he has a highly developed sense of awe and mystery. He is also the author of *The White Goddess*, and his poetry has many Romantic overtones to reflect this fact. He is extremely versatile—tender and delicate at one moment, bawdy at another—but mainly he is a richly gifted talker, full of anecdotes and specialized lore, who knows how to intrigue, amuse, and shock a listener.

Edwin Muir is perhaps the one modern British poet closest in mood to the Continent. A heavy fatalism pervades his writing—an ironic sense of the inability to break out of the trap of time that is close to Kafka and to Existentialism. Muir, with his slow yet compulsive rhythms, caught the terror of our age of totalitarianism and mass refugeeism with a terrible pathos. He felt in this age the defeat of Western humanism; history had become a nightmare in which the goals of man receded forever, and in which "the road" or "the journey" became more inescapably important than its destination. In Muir too we find some of the most poignant expression of a common modern theme, the betrayal of innocence by time and history. Muir's poetry provides a bitter contrast to that of D. H. Lawrence, who believed that the trap of the times could be broken by a kind of mystical shedding of the false self created by modern civilization. Lawrence, so alive to life's primal values, felt that they could be regained through the right kind of attunement with the physical universe. The key to this attunement was the realization of the true, unconscious self in the sexual relationship, but its object was not mere self-gratification but the discovery of the uniqueness of oneself and of other individual beings—in contrast to the blurring of all such distinctions by an impersonal civilization. Lawrence's empathy with birds, flowers, and other people made this conception a painfully real one to him, not an abstract proposition. Like Whitman, whose parallelism and general verse technique he obviously follows, he felt himself a prophet and a healer in his poems.

This motif of "rebirth" through attunement with the universe of nature, with its idealization of the life force and of the sexual principle and its implied program of a cultural revolution against the premises of the modern state, is shared by many writers. Hugh MacDiarmid (Christopher Grieve) gives the theme a specifically political turn, sometimes Marxian and sometimes Scottish Nationalist, in much of his poetry. His purest lyrical force, however, comes from sources beyond ideology that are similar to those moving Lawrence. The literary Scots, or Lallans, dialect in which some of his most beautiful work has been done—for instance, "O Wha's the Bride" and other poems in *A Drunk Man Looks at the Thistle* (1926)—has prevented his reputation from spreading as rapidly as it might have, but he has also written a great many poems in English.

Again, the early work of Auden is permeated with the spirit of Lawrence, albeit in a strange amalgam with Marxian and Freudian attitudes. "Rebirth" can mean social as well as personal rebirth, and it is interesting to see how Auden combines these ideas with the Christian idea of resurrection. He also follows out another of Lawrence's implications in his early work. If the self is unknown to us in a world like ours, one of the great sources of confusion and tragic error must be the ambiguity of our sense of identity. The theme is developed with great skill and compassion in "The Decoys." Another youthful influence was Hopkins, whose crowding of images and unusual employment of grammatical and syntactical elements to compress and give tension to his presentation can also be seen in the Auden of the early thirties. One reason for the influence would seem to be the attempt by both poets to reconcile purely private with larger, doctrinal perspectives. Another may be suggested by the word "doctrinal"—the need to assert a doctrine in the face of a world insisting on its denial is common to the Catholic English poet of the 1870's and 1880's and the English Leftist poet of the 1930's. The analogy is easy to push too far. After the Spanish Civil War Auden moved away from his earlier position to a more skeptically liberal politics strongly affected by a heavier religious emphasis and an existential mood, not unlike that of Muir, foreshadowed in the words that end his "Spain 1937":

> History to the defeated
> May say Alas but cannot help or pardon.

Auden, like Graves and Betjeman, has the ease and virtuosity of an accomplished man of letters, but he is also—more than they—capable of more extreme commitment and feeling than this characterization implies. He must be compared with Dryden and with Byron for his range and sudden depths. The names usually linked with his in the 'thirties are those of Stephen Spender, C. Day Lewis, and Louis MacNeice. These writers shared with him a sense of the historical moment that was sometimes as violent as a physical sensation. None has his bright, volatile, daring intelligence; but Spender, though he does not escape sentimentality, has values of exaltation and melody Auden never touches, and an open, almost naïve freedom of emotional statement he rarely allows himself. MacNeice has an easy, sometimes racy colloquialism and a zest for little details of experience and for talking about ideas that is engaging in itself. Day Lewis has a severity of form, and a surprisingly moving body of love poetry that shows a Metaphysical influence and yet is not at all derivative. All four poets shared a certain manner for a while—rather discursive, allusive and pointed at the same time. This is the aspect of their writing in the 'thirties that has become most dated and that Hugh MacDiarmid mocks in his

"British Leftish Poetry 1930–1940." The originality and significance of their several efforts to show "private faces in public places," as Auden once put it, remains.

The one poet of great power to emerge in England since the 'thirties was Dylan Thomas, who first gained recognition in that decade but came into his greatest popularity after World War II. Thomas's poetry was, with a few exceptions, thoroughly nonpolitical. In a sense it was nonintellectual, too, quite the opposite of the ideology-conscious Auden and of the almost completely cerebral William Empson, whose poetry puts his readers to work like students in a course on logic. (Actually, Empson is not at all devoid of feeling and sense perception: he has them, if not exactly in abundance, but unlike Thomas he gives little clue to his meanings until we have fathomed his literal thought.) Thomas is also very much the antithesis of John Betjeman, in recent years the most widely read modern English poet. Betjeman is extremely topical, very much concerned about what has happened to his country under the Welfare State and given to nostalgia for certain phases of her immediate past. He is an extraordinary writer of light verse and of a rather wry, usually charming, and occasionally very serious and touching verse of personal reminiscence. And occasionally he strikes a dark note and displays unexpected depths. But British poetry has not broken through the barriers of basically conventional virtuosity since Thomas stormed onto and off the contemporary scene.

Thomas can be compared more easily with the Americans Hart Crane and Robert Lowell than with any other British poet except Yeats at his most excited. His theme is essentially unvarying throughout his career—the terror of the nature of life, and his refusal to accept that terror. A thought that occurs to every sensitive child, that our birth is the beginning of our death, is the main theme with which Thomas struggles continually. The Crucifixion is thus the symbol of every life; we are all sacrificed to the mechanical and vital processes of nature, and we share our predicament with the lower orders of being, though we are unable to communicate the fact to them. To counter this tragic awareness, which is inseparable from human consciousness, Thomas repeatedly asserts his refusal to submit to it. "And death shall have no dominion," he shouts in one poem, and in another speaks of a communion of being, the "synagogue of the ear of corn" and the "round Zion of the waterbead," into which we enter joyously after death. He is strangely close to Lawrence in his identification of the sexual principle both as that which must be affirmed and as that which crucifies man. Yet there is none of the haranguing of Lawrence, nothing of his propagandism and prophecy, but simply the realization of the elementary conditions of life and his shouting that he will not allow it to be so. The wild proliferation of images, the endless inventiveness of a profusion of felicitous and suggestive phrasing, the sustained swelling of the music of the poems took audiences in England and America without a struggle.

Ted Hughes, Philip Larkin, Charles Tomlinson, and Thom Gunn are exemplars of the more promising recent developments in British verse. Hughes is generally acknowledged to be the English poet of greatest power since Thomas. He has cultivated a savage insistence on the ruthlessness of nature, both in his tightly structured animal poems and in more freely associative pieces such as "Lupercalia" and "Cadenza." A deep sense that man and nature are reciprocals of one another, that history is a tragic dimension of the deadly impersonality of nature, is imbedded in Hughes's poems. They may well be compared with those of his American wife, Sylvia Plath, for their extreme, anguished intensity. Indeed, all these poets except Larkin have been influenced, as has Thomas Kinsella, by American poetry and by residence in the United States. Though Larkin, in poems like "Dry-Point" and "Going," shares with Continental and American poets a long-standing interest in compressed, image-centered, evocative statement, his main direction is of another sort. It is that of the wry wit, the self-depreciatory clarity, and the sympathetic fatalism that mark his style as expressive of a dominant British postwar mood. Both Tomlinson and Gunn have assimilated certain originally American themes and experimental tendencies into a fundamentally British idiom and set of preoccupations.

Thomas Hardy
(1840–1928)

HAP

If but some vengeful god would call to me
From up the sky, and laugh: "Thou suffering thing,
Know that thy sorrow is my ecstasy,
That thy love's loss is my hate's profiting!"

Then would I bear it, clench myself, and die,
Steeled by the sense of ire unmerited;
Half-eased in that a Powerfuller than I
Had willed and meted me the tears I shed.

But not so. How arrives it joy lies slain,
And why unblooms the best hope ever sown?
—Crass Casualty obstructs the sun and rain,
And dicing Time for gladness casts a moan. . . .
These purblind Doomsters had as readily strown
Blisses about my pilgrimage as pain.   *(1866, 1898)*

NEUTRAL TONES

We stood by a pond that winter day,
And the sun was white, as though chidden of God,
And a few leaves lay on the starving sod;
        —They had fallen from an ash, and were gray.

Your eyes on me were as eyes that rove
Over tedious riddles of years ago;
And some words played between us to and fro
        On which lost the more by our love.

The smile on your mouth was the deadest thing
Alive enough to have strength to die;
And a grin of bitterness swept thereby
        Like an ominous bird a-wing. . . .

Since then, keen lessons that love deceives,
And wrings with wrong, have shaped to me
Your face, and the God-curst sun, and a tree,
      And a pond edged with grayish leaves. *(1867, 1898)*

THE SOULS OF THE SLAIN

The thick lids of Night closed upon me
    Alone at the Bill
    Of the Isle by the Race*—
Many-caverned, bald, wrinkled of face—
And with darkness and silence the spirit was on me
    To brood and be still.

No wind fanned the flats of the ocean,
    Or promontory sides,
    Or the ooze by the strand,
Or the bent-bearded slope of the land,
Whose base took its rest amid everlong motion
    Of criss-crossing tides.

Soon from out of the Southward seemed nearing
    A whirr, as of wings
    Waved by mighty-vanned flies,
Or by night-moths of measureless size,
And in softness and smoothness well-nigh beyond hearing
    Of corporal things.

And they bore to the bluff, and alighted—
    A dim-discerned train
    Of sprites without mould,
Frameless souls none might touch or might hold—
On the ledge by the turreted lantern, far-sighted
    By men of the main.

And I heard them say "Home!" and I knew them
    For souls of the felled
    On the earth's nether bord
Under Capricorn, whither they'd warred,
And I neared in my awe, and gave heedfulness to them
    With breathings inheld.

* The "Race" is the turbulent sea-area off the Bill of Portland, where contrary
tides meet.—AUTHOR'S NOTE.

Then, it seemed, there approached from the northward
　　　A senior soul-flame
　　　Of the like filmy hue:
　　And he met them and spake: "Is it you,
O my men?" Said they, "Aye! We bear homeward and hearthward
　　　To feast on our fame!"

"I've flown there before you," he said then:
　　　"Your households are well;
　　　But—your kin linger less
　　On your glory and war-mightiness
Than on dearer things."—"Dearer?" cried these from the dead then,
　　　"Of what do they tell?"

"Some mothers muse sadly, and murmur
　　　Your doings as boys—
　　　Recall the quaint ways
　　Of your babyhood's innocent days.
Some pray that, ere dying, your faith had grown firmer,
　　　And higher your joys.

"A father broods: 'Would I had set him
　　　To some humble trade,
　　　And so slacked his high fire,
　　And his passionate martial desire;
And told him no stories to woo him and whet him
　　　To this dire crusade!' "

"And, General, how hold out our sweethearts,
　　　Sworn loyal as doves?"
　　　—'Many mourn; many think
　　It is not unattractive to prink
Them in sables for heroes. Some fickle and fleet hearts
　　　Have found them new loves."

"And our wives?" quoth another resignedly,
　　　"Dwell they on our deeds?"
　　　—"Deeds of home; that live yet
　　Fresh as new—deeds of fondness or fret;
Ancient words that were kindly expressed or unkindly,
　　　These, these have their heeds."

—"Alas! then it seems that our glory
　　　Weighs less in their thought

Than our old homely acts,
And the long-ago commonplace facts
Of our lives—held by us as scarce part of our story,
And rated as nought!"

Then bitterly some: "Was it wise now
To raise the tomb-door
For such knowledge? Away!"
But the rest: "Fame we prized till to-day;
Yet that hearts keep us green for old kindness we prize now
A thousand times more!"

Thus speaking, the trooped apparitions
Began to disband
And resolve them in two:
Those whose record was lovely and true
Bore to northward for home: those of bitter traditions
Again left the land,

And, towering to seaward in legions,
They paused at a spot
Overbending the Race—
That engulphing, ghast, sinister place—
Whither headlong they plunged, to the fathomless regions
Of myriads forgot.

And the spirits of those who were homing
Passed on, rushingly,
Like the Pentecost Wind;
And the whirr of their wayfaring thinned
And surceased on the sky, and but left in the gloaming
Sea-mutterings and me.   (*December 1899, 1902*)

THE LACKING SENSE

SCENE.—*A sad-coloured landscape, Waddon Vale*

"O Time, whence comes the Mother's moody look amid her labours,
As of one who all unwittingly has wounded where she loves?
    Why weaves she not her world-webs to according lutes and tabors,
With nevermore this too remorseful air upon her face,
        As of angel fallen from grace?"

—"Her look is but her story: construe not its symbols keenly:
    In her wonderworks yea surely has she wounded where she loves.

The sense of ills misdealt for blisses blanks the mien most queenly,
   Self-smitings kill self-joys; and everywhere beneath the sun
      Such deeds her hands have done."

—"And how explains thy Ancient Mind her crimes upon her creatures
   These fallings from her fair beginnings, woundings where she loves
Into her would-be perfect motions, modes, effects, and features
   Admitting cramps, black humours, wan decay, and baleful blights,
      Distress into delights?"

—"Ah! knowest thou not her secret yet, her vainly veiled deficience,
   Whence it comes that all unwittingly she wounds the lives she loves
That sightless are those orbs of hers—which bar to her omniscience
   Brings those fearful unfulfilments, that red ravage through her zone
      Whereat all creation groans.

"She whispers it in each pathetic strenuous slow endeavour,
   When in mothering she unwittingly sets wounds on what she loves
Yet her primal doom pursues her, faultful, fatal is she ever;
   Though so deft and nigh to vision is her facile finger-touch
      That the seers marvel much.

"Deal, then, her groping skill no scorn, no note of malediction;
   Not long on thee will press the hand that hurts the lives it loves;
And while she plods dead-reckoning on, in darkness of affliction,
   Assist her where thy creaturely dependence can or may,
      For thou art of her clay."   (1902)

THE SUBALTERNS

    "Poor wanderer," said the leaden sky,
      "I fain would lighten thee,
    But there are laws in force on high
      Which say it must not be."

    —"I would not freeze thee, shorn one," cried
      The North, "knew I but how
    To warm my breath, to slack my stride;
      But I am ruled as thou."

    —"Tomorrow I attack thee, wight,"
      Said Sickness. "Yet I swear
    I bear thy little ark no spite,
      But am bid enter there."

—"Come hither, Son," I heard Death say;
    "I did not will a grave
Should end thy pilgrimage today,
    But I, too, am a slave!"

We smiled upon each other then,
    And life to me had less
Of that fell look it wore ere when
    They owned their passiveness.   (*1902*)

MUTE OPINION

I traversed a dominion
Whose spokesmen spake out strong
Their purpose and opinion
Through pulpit, press, and song.
I scarce had means to note there
A large-eyed few, and dumb,
Who thought not as those thought there
That stirred the heat and hum.

When, grown a Shade, beholding
That land in lifetime trode,
To learn if its unfolding
Fulfilled its clamored code,
I saw, in web unbroken,
Its history outwrought
Not as the loud had spoken,
But as the mute had thought.   (*1902*)

HIS IMMORTALITY

I saw a dead man's finer part
Shining within each faithful heart
Of those bereft. Then said I: "This must be
    His immortality."

I looked there as the seasons wore,
And still his soul continuously bore
A life in theirs. But less its shine excelled
    Than when I first beheld.

His fellow-yearsmen passed, and then
In later hearts I looked for him again;

And found him—shrunk, alas; into a thin
And spectral mannikin.

Lastly I ask—now old and chill—
If aught of him remain unperished still;
And find, in me alone, a feeble spark,
Dying amid the dark.   *(1899, 1902)*

THE LAST CHRYSANTHEMUM

Why should this flower delay so long
To show its tremulous plumes?
Now is the time of plaintive robin-song
When flowers are in their tombs.

Through the slow summer, when the sun
Called to each frond and whorl
That all he could for flowers was being done,
Why did it not uncurl?

It must have felt that fervid call
Although it took no heed,
Waking but now, when leaves like corpses fall,
And saps all retrocede.

Too late its beauty, lonely thing,
The season's shine is spent,
Nothing remains for it but shivering
In tempests turbulent.

Had it a reason for delay,
Dreaming in witlessness
That for a bloom so delicately gay
Winter would stay its stress?

—I talk as if the thing were born
With sense to work its mind;
Yet it is but one mask of many worn
By the Great Face behind.   *(1902)*

THE DARKLING THRUSH

I leant upon a coppice gate
When Frost was spectre-gray,

And Winter's dregs made desolate
    The weakening eye of day.
The tangled bine-stems scored the sky
    Like strings of broken lyres,
And all mankind that haunted nigh
    Had sought their household fires.

The land's sharp features seemed to be
    The Century's corpse outleant,
His crypt the cloudy canopy.
    The wind his death-lament.
The ancient pulse of germ and birth
    Was shrunken hard and dry,
And every spirit upon earth
    Seemed fervourless as I.

At once a voice arose among
    The bleak twigs overhead
In a full-hearted evensong
    Of joy illimited;
An aged thrush, frail, gaunt, and small,
    In blast-beruffled plume,
Had chosen thus to fling his soul
    Upon the growing gloom.

So little cause for carolings
    Of such ecstatic sound
Was written on terrestrial things
    Afar or nigh around,
That I could think there trembled through
    His happy good-night air
Some blessed Hope, whereof he knew
    And I was unaware   (*December 1900, 1902*)

THE COMET AT YELL'HAM

It bends far over Yell'ham Plain,
    And we, from Yell'ham Height,
Stand and regard its fiery train,
    So soon to swim from sight.

It will return long years hence, when
    As now its strange swift shine

Will fall on Yell'ham; but not then
On that sweet form of thine. *(1902)*

THE RUINED MAID

"O 'Melia, my dear, this does everything crown!
Who could have supposed I should meet you in Town?
And whence such fair garments, such prosperi-ty?"—
"O didn't you know I'd been ruined?" said she.

—"You left us in tatters, without shoes or socks,
Tired of digging potatoes, and spudding up docks;
And now you've gay bracelets and bright feathers three!"—
"Yes: that's how we dress when we're ruined," said she.

—"At home in the barton you said 'thee' and 'thou,'
And 'thik oon,' and 'theäs oon,' and 't'other'; but now
Your talking quite fits 'ee for high compa-ny!"—
"Some polish is gained with one's ruin," said she.

—"Your hands were like paws then, your face blue and bleak,
But now I'm bewitched by your delicate cheek,
And your little gloves fit as on any la-dy!"—
"We never do work when we're ruined," said she.

—"You used to call home-life a hag-ridden dream,
And you'd sigh, and you'd sock; but at present you seem
To know not of megrims or melancho-ly!"
"True. One's pretty lively when ruined," said she.

—"I wish I had feathers, a fine sweeping gown,
And a delicate face, and could strut about Town!"—
"My dear—a raw country girl, such as you be,
Cannot quite expect that. You ain't ruined," said she. *(1866; 1902)*

THE RESPECTABLE BURGHER

ON "THE HIGHER CRITICISM"

Since Reverend Doctors now declare
That clerks and people must prepare
To doubt if Adam ever were;
To hold the flood a local scare;

To argue, though the stolid stare,
That everything had happened ere
The prophets to its happening sware;
That David was no giant-slayer,
Nor one to call a God-obeyer
In certain details we could spare,
But rather was a debonair
Shrewd bandit, skilled as banjo-player:
That Solomon sang the fleshly Fair,
And gave the Church no thought whate'er,
That Esther with her royal wear,
And Mordecai, the son of Jair,
And Joshua's triumphs, Job's despair,
And Balaam's ass's bitter blare;
Nebuchadnezzar's furnace-flare,
And Daniel and the den affair,
And other stories rich and rare,
Were writ to make old doctrine wear
Something of a romantic air:
That the Nain widow's only heir,
And Lazarus with cadaverous glare
(As done in oils by Piombo's care)
Did not return from Sheol's lair:
That Jael set a fiendish snare,
That Pontius Pilate acted square,
That never a sword cut Malchus' ear;
And (but for shame I must forbear)
That ———— ———— did not reappear! . . .
—Since thus they hint, nor turn a hair,
All churchgoing will I forswear,
And sit on Sundays in my chair,
And read that moderate man Voltaire.   (1902)

From *IN TENEBRIS: II*

Considerabam ad dexteram, et videbam; et non erat qui cognosceret me. . . .
Non est qui requirat animam meam.—Psalms 142.

When the clouds' swoln bosoms echo back the shouts of the many and
    strong
That things are all as they best may be, save a few to be right ere long,
And my eyes have not the vision in them to discern what to these is
    so clear,
The blot seems straightway in me alone; one better he were not here.

The stout upstanders say, All's well with us; ruers have nought to rue!
And what the potent say so oft, can it fail to be somewhat true?
Breezily go they, breezily come; their dust smokes around their career,
Till I think I am one born out of due time, who has no calling here.

Their dawns bring lusty joys, it seems; their evenings all that is sweet;
Our times are blessed times, they cry: Life shapes it as is most meet,
And nothing is much the matter; there are many smiles to a tear;
Then what is the matter is I, I say. Why should such an one be
here? . . .

Let him in whose ears the low-voiced Best is killed by the clash of the
First,
Who holds that if way to the Better there be, it exacts a full look at
the Worst,
Who feels that delight is a delicate growth cramped by crookedness,
custom, and fear,
Get him up and be gone as one shaped awry; he disturbs the order here.
(1895–96, 1902)

From *THE DYNASTS*

THE FIELD OF TALAVERA

Talavera town, on the river Tagus, is at the extreme right of the fore-ground; a mountain range on the extreme left.

The allied army under Sir Arthur Wellesley stretches between—the English on the left, the Spanish on the right—part holding a hill to the left-centre of the scene, divided from the mountains by a valley, and part holding a redoubt to the right-centre. This army of more than fifty thousand all told, of which twenty-two thousand only are English, has its back to the spectator.

Beyond, in a wood of olive, oak, and cork, are the fifty to sixty thousand French, facing the spectator and the allies. Their right includes a strong battery upon a hill which fronts the one on the English left.

Behind all, the heights of Salinas close the prospect, the small river Alberche flowing at their foot from left to right into the Tagus, which advances in foreshortened perspective to the town at the right front corner of the scene as aforesaid. . . .

The hot and dusty July afternoon having turned to twilight, shady masses of men start into motion from the French position, come towards the fore-ground, silently ascend the hill on the left of the English, and assail the latter in a violent outburst of fire and lead. They nearly gain possession of the hill assailed.

CHORUS OF RUMOURS (aerial music)

Ten of the night is Talavera tolling:
Now do Ruffin's ranks come surging upward,
Backed by bold Vilatte's. Lapisse from the vale, too,
      Darkly upswells there!——

Downhill from the crest the English fling them,
And with their bayonets roll the enemy backward:
So the first fierce charge of the ardent Frenchmen
      England repels there!

Having fallen back into the darkness the French presently reascend in
yet larger masses. The high square knapsack which every English foot-
soldier carries, and his shako, and its tuft, outline themselves against the
dim light as the ranks stand awaiting the shock.

CHORUS OF RUMOURS

Pushing they spread, and shout as they reach the summit,
Strength and stir new-primed in their plump battalions:
Puffs of flame blown forth on the lines opposing
      Higher and higher.

There those hold them mute, though at speaking distance—
Mute, while the clicking flints, and the crash of the volley
Throw on the weighted gloom an immense distraction
      Pending their fire.

Fronting visages each ranksman reads there,
Epaulettes, and cheeks, and shining eyeballs,
(Called from the dark a trice by the fleeting panflash)
      Pressing them nigher!

The French again fall back in disorder into the hollow, and LAPISSE
draws off on the right. As the sinking sound of the muskets tells what has
happened the English raise a shout.

CHORUS OF PITIES

Thus the dim nocturnal voice of the conflict
Closes with the receding roar of the gun-fire.
Harness loosened then, and their day-long strenuous
      Strain unbending,

Worn-out lines lie down where they late stood staunchly—
Cloaks around them rolled—by the bivouac embers:

> There to pursue at dawn the dynasts' death-game
> Unto the ending!

The morning breaks. There is another murderous attempt to dislodge the English from the hill, the assault being pressed with a determination that excites the admiration of the English themselves.

The French are seen descending into the valley, crossing it, and climbing it on the other side under the fire of HILL's whole division, all to no purpose. In their retreat they leave behind them on the slopes nearly two thousand lying.

The day advances to noon, and the air trembles in the intense heat. The combat flags, and is suspended.

SPIRIT OF THE PITIES

> What do I see but thirsty, throbbing bands
> From these inimic hosts defiling down
> In homely need towards the little stream
> That parts their enmities, and drinking there!
> They get to grasping hands across the rill,
> Sealing their sameness as earth's sojourners.—
> What more could plead the wryness of the times
> Than such unstudied piteous pantomimes!

SPIRIT IRONIC

It is only that Life's queer mechanics chance to work out in this grotesque shape just now. The groping tentativeness of an Immanent Will . . . cannot be asked to learn logic at this time of day! The spectacle of Its instruments, set to riddle one another through, and then to drink together in peace and concord, is where the humour comes in, and makes the play worth seeing!

SPIRIT SINISTER

Come, Sprite, don't carry your ironies too far, or you may wake up the Unconscious Itself, and tempt It to let all the clockwork of the show run down to spite us! Where will be our theatre then, and where my enjoyment?

The drums roll, and the men of the two nations part from their comradeship at the Alberche brook, the dark masses of the French army assembling anew. SIR ARTHUR WELLESLEY has seated himself on a mound that commands a full view of the contested hill, and remains there motionless a long time. When the French form for battle he is seen to have come to a conclusion. He mounts, gives his orders, and the aides ride off.

The French advance steadily through the sultry atmosphere, the skirmishers in front, and the columns after, moving, yet seemingly motionless

Their eighty cannon peal out and their shots mow every space in the line
of them. Up the great valley and the terraces of the hill whose fame is at
that moment being woven, comes VILATTE, boring his way with foot and
horse, and RUFFIN's men following behind.

According to the order given, the Twenty-third Light Dragoons and the
German Hussars advance at a chosen moment against the head of these
columns. On the way they disappear.

SPIRIT OF THE PITIES

Why this bedevilment? What can have chanced?

SPIRIT OF RUMOUR

It so befalls that as their chargers near
The inimical wall of flesh with its iron frise,
A treacherous chasm uptrips them: zealous men
And docile horses roll to dismal death
And horrid mutilation.

SPIRIT OF THE PITIES

Those who live
Even now advance! I'll see no more. Relate.

SPIRIT OF RUMOUR

Yes, those pant on. Then further Frenchmen cross,
And Polish Lancers, and Westphalian Horse,
Who ring around these luckless Islanders,
And sweep them down like reeds by the river-brink
In scouring floods; till scarce a man remains.

Meanwhile on the British right SEBASTIANI's corps has precipitated itself
in column against GENERAL CAMPBELL's division, the division of LAPISSE
against the centre, and at the same time the hill on the English left is again
assaulted. The English are pressed sorely here, the bellowing battery tearing
lanes through their masses.

SPIRIT OF RUMOUR (continuing)

The French reserves of foot and horse now on,
Smiting the Islanders in breast and brain
Till their mid-lines are shattered. . . . Now there ticks
The moment of the crisis; now the next,
Which brings the turning stroke.

SIR ARTHUR WELLESLEY sends down the Forty-eighth regiment under
COLONEL DONELLAN to support the wasting troops. It advances amid those
retreating, opening to let them pass.

SPIRIT OF RUMOUR (continuing)
                                Then pales, enerved,
The hitherto unflinching enemy!
Lapisse is pierced to death; the flagging French
Decline into the hollows whence they came.
The too exhausted English and reduced
Lack strength to follow.—Now the western sun,
Conning with unmoved face both quick and dead,
Gilds horsemen slackening, and footmen stilled,
Till all around breathes drowsed hostility.
    Last, the swealed herbage lifts a leering light,
And flames traverse the field; and hurt and slain,
Opposed, opposers, in a common plight
Are scorched together on the dusk champaign.

The fire dies down, and darkness enwraps the scene.   (1908)

From THE DYNASTS, III, VI, viii

CHORUS OF THE YEARS

Yea, the coneys are scared by the thud of hoofs,
And their white scuts flash at their vanishing heels,
And swallows abandon the hamlet-roofs.

The mole's tunnelled chambers are crushed by wheels,
The lark's eggs scattered, their owners fled,
And the hare's hid litter the sapper unseals.

The snail draws in at the terrible tread,
But in vain; he is crushed by the felloe-rim;
The worm asks what can be overhead,

And wriggles deep from a scene so grim,
And guesses him safe; for he does not know
What a foul red flood will soak down to him!

Beaten about by the heel and the toe
Are butterflies, sick of the day's long rheum,
To die of a worse than the weather-foe.

Trodden and bruised to a miry tomb
Are ears that have greened but will never be gold,
And flowers in the bud that will never bloom.   (1908)

SHUT OUT THAT MOON

Close up the casement, draw the blind,
　Shut out that stealing moon,
She wears too much the guise she wore
　Before our lutes were strewn
With years-deep dust, and names we read
　On a white stone were hewn.

Step not out on the dew-dashed lawn
　To view the Lady's Chair,
Immense Orion's glittering form,
　The Less and Greater Bear:
Stay in; to such sights we were drawn
　When faded ones were fair.

Brush not the bough for midnight scents
　That come forth lingeringly,
And wake the same sweet sentiments
　They breathed to you and me
When living seemed a laugh, and love
　All it was said to be.

Within the common lamp-lit room
　Prison my eyes and thought;
Let dingy details crudely loom,
　Mechanic speech be wrought:
Too fragrant was Life's early bloom,
　Too tart the fruit it brought! *(1904, 1909)*

AFTER THE FAIR

The singers are gone from the Cornmarket-place
　With their broadsheets of rhymes,
The street rings no longer in treble and bass
　With their skits on the times,
And the Cross, lately thronged, is a dim naked space
　That but echoes the stammering chimes.

From Clock-corner steps, as each quarter ding-dongs,
　Away the folk roam
By the "Hart" and Grey's Bridge into byways and "drongs,"

Or across the ridged loam;
The younger ones shrilling the lately heard songs,
   The old saying, "Would we were home."

The shy-seeming maiden so mute in the fair
   Now rattles and talks,
And that one who looked the most swaggering there
   Grows sad as she walks,
And she who seemed eaten by cankering care
   In statuesque sturdiness stalks.

And midnight clears High Street of all but the ghosts
   Of its buried burghees,
From the latest far back to those old Roman hosts
   Whose remains one yet sees,
Who loved, laughed, and fought, hailed their friends, drank their toas
   At their meeting-times here, just as these!   *(1902, 1909)*

THE REMINDER

While I watch the Christmas blaze
Paint the room with ruddy rays,
Something makes my vision glide
To the frosty scene outside.

There, to reach a rotting berry,
Toils a thrush,—constrained to very
Dregs of food by sharp distress,
Taking such with thankfulness.

Why, O starving bird, when I
One day's joy would justify,
And put misery out of view,
Do you make me notice you!   *(1909)*

THE UNBORN

I rose at night, and visited
   The Cave of the Unborn:
And crowding shapes surrounded me
For tidings of the life to be,
Who long had prayed the silent Head
   To haste its advent morn.

Their eyes were lit with artless trust,
    Hope thrilled their every tone;
"A scene the loveliest, is it not?
A pure delight, a beauty-spot
Where all is gentle, true and just,
    And darkness is unknown?"

My heart was anguished for their sake,
    I could not frame a word;
And they descried my sunken face,
And seemed to read therein, and trace
The news that pity would not break,
    Nor truth leave unaverred.

And as I silently retired
    I turned and watched them still,
And they came helter-skelter out,
Driven forward like a rabble rout
Into the world they had so desired,
    By the all-immanent Will.   (*1905, 1909*)

THE MAN HE KILLED

"Had he and I but met
    By some old ancient inn,
We should have sat us down to wet
    Right many a nipperkin!

"But ranged as infantry,
    And staring face to face,
I shot at him as he at me,
    And killed him in his place.

"I shot him dead because—
    Because he was my foe,
Just so: my foe of course he was;
    That's clear enough; although

"He thought he'd 'list, perhaps,
    Off-hand like—just as I—
Was out of work—had sold his traps—
    No other reason why.

"Yes; quaint and curious war is!
You shoot a fellow down
You'd treat if met where any bar is,
Or help to half-a-crown."   *(1902, 1909)*

CHANNEL FIRING

That night your great guns, unawares,
Shook all our coffins as we lay,
And broke the chancel window-squares,
We thought it was the Judgment-day

And sat upright. While drearisome
Arose the howl of wakened hounds:
The mouse let fall the altar-crumb,
The worms drew back into the mounds,

The glebe cow drooled. Till God called, "No;
It's gunnery practice out at sea
Just as before you went below;
The world is as it used to be:

"All nations striving strong to make
Red war yet redder. Mad as hatters
They do no more for Christés sake
Than you who are helpless in such matters.

"That this is not the judgment-hour
For some of them's a blessed thing,
For if it were they'd have to scour
Hell's floor for so much threatening. . . .

"Ha, ha. It will be warmer when
I blow the trumpet (if indeed
I ever do; for you are men,
And rest eternal sorely need)."

So down we lay again, "I wonder,
Will the world ever saner be,"
Said one, "than when He sent us under
In our indifferent century!"

And many a skeleton shook his head.
"Instead of preaching forty year,"

My neighbour Parson Thirdly said,
"I wish I had stuck to pipes and beer."

Again the guns disturbed the hour,
Roaring their readiness to avenge,
As far inland as Stourton Tower,
And Camelot, and starlit Stonehenge. *(April 1914, 1914)*

WESSEX HEIGHTS

There are some heights in Wessex, shaped as if by a kindly hand
For thinking, dreaming, dying on, and at crises when I stand,
Say, on Ingpen Beacon eastward, or on Wylls-Neck westwardly,
I seem where I was before my birth, and after death may be.

In the lowlands I have no comrade, not even the lone man's friend—
Her who suffereth long and is kind; accepts what he is too weak to
   mend:
Down there they are dubious and askance; there nobody thinks as I,
But mind-chains do not clank where one's next neighbour is the sky.

In the towns I am tracked by phantoms having weird detective ways—
Shadows of beings who fellowed with myself of earlier days:
They hang about at places, and they say harsh heavy things—
Men with a wintry sneer, and women with tart disparagings.

Down there I seem to be false to myself, my simple self that was,
And is not now, and I see him watching, wondering what crass cause
Can have merged him into such a strange continuator as this,
Who yet has something in common with himself, my chrysalis.

I cannot go to the great grey Plain; there's a figure against the moon,
Nobody sees it but I, and it makes my breast beat out of tune;
I cannot go to the tall-spired town, being barred by the forms now
   passed
For everybody but me, in whose long vision they stand there fast.

There's a ghost at Yell'ham Bottom chiding loud at the fall of the night,
There's a ghost in Froom-side Vale, thin lipped and vague, in a shroud
   of white,
There is one in the railway train whenever I do not want it near,
I see its profile against the pane, saying what I would not hear.

As for one rare fair woman, I am now but a thought of hers,
I enter her mind and another thought succeeds me that she prefers;
Yet my love for her in its fulness she herself even did not know;
Well, time cures hearts of tenderness, and now I can let her go.

So I am found on Ingpen Beacon, or on Wylls-Neck to the west,
Or else on homely Bulbarrow, or little Pilsdon Crest,
Where men have never cared to haunt, nor women have walked with
   me,
And ghosts then keep their distance; and I know some liberty.

                                                    (1896, 1914)

THE YEAR'S AWAKENING

How do you know that the pilgrim track
Along the belting zodiac
Swept by the sun in his seeming rounds
Is traced by now to the Fishes' bounds
And into the Ram, when weeks of cloud
Have wrapt the sky in a clammy shroud,
And never as yet a tinct of spring
Has shown in the Earth's apparelling;
   O vespering bird, how do you know,
       How do you know?

How do you know, deep underground,
Hid in your bed from sight and sound,
Without a turn in temperature,
With weather life can scarce endure,
That light has won a fraction's strength,
And day put on some moments' length,
Whereof in merest rote will come,
Weeks hence, mild airs that do not numb,
   O crocus root, how do you know,
       How do you know?   (1910, 1914)

AT A WATERING-PLACE

They sit and smoke on the esplanade,
The man and his friend, and regard the bay
Where the far chalk cliffs, to the left displayed,
Smile sallowly in the decline of day.
And saunterers pass with laugh and jest—
A handsome couple among the rest.

"That smart proud pair," says the man to his friend,
"Are to marry next week. . . . How little he thinks
That dozens of days and nights on end
I have stroked her neck, unhooked the links
Of her sleeve to get at her upper arm. . . .
Well, bliss is in ignorance: what's the harm!"

(April 1911, 1914)

THE WALK

You did not walk with me
Of late to the hill-top tree
    By the gated ways,
    As in earlier days;
    You were weak and lame,
    So you never came,
And I went alone, and I did not mind,
Not thinking of you as left behind.

I walked up there to-day
Just in the former way;
    Surveyed around
    The familiar ground
    By myself again:
    What difference, then?
Only that underlying sense
Of the look of a room on returning thence. *(1914)*

"I FOUND HER OUT THERE"

I found her out there
On a slope few see,
That falls westwardly
To the salt-edged air,
Where the ocean breaks
On the purple strand,
And the hurricane shakes
The solid land.

I brought her here,
And have laid her to rest
In a noiseless nest
No sea beats near.
She will never be stirred

In her loamy cell
By the waves long heard
And loved so well.

So she does not sleep
By those haunted heights
The Atlantic smites
And the blind gales sweep,
Whence she often would gaze
At Dundagel's famed head,
While the dipping blaze
Dyed her face fire-red;

And would sigh at the tale
Of sunk Lyonnesse,
As a wind-tugged tress
Flapped her cheek like a flail;
Or listen at whiles
With a thought-bound brow
To the murmuring miles
She is far from now.

Yet her shade, maybe,
Will creep underground
Till it catch the sound
Of that western sea
As it swells and sobs
Where she once domiciled,
And joy in its throbs
With the heart of a child. (1914)

THE VOICE

Woman much missed, how you call to me, call to me,
Saying that now you are not as you were
When you had changed from the one who was all to me,
But as at first, when our day was fair.

Can it be you that I hear? Let me view you, then,
Standing as when I drew near to the town
Where you would wait for me: yes, as I knew you then,
Even to the original air-blue gown!

Or is it only the breeze, in its listlessness
Travelling across the wet mead to me here,
You being ever dissolved to wan wistlessness,
Heard no more again far or near?

Thus I; faltering forward,
Leaves around me falling,
Wind oozing thin through the thorn from norward,
And the woman calling. (*December 1912, 1914*)

AFTER A JOURNEY

Hereto I come to view a voiceless ghost;
    Whither, O whither will its whim now draw me?
Up the cliff, down, till I'm lonely, lost,
    And the unseen waters' ejaculations awe me.
Where you will next be there's no knowing,
    Facing round about me everywhere,
        With your nut-coloured hair,
And gray eyes, and rose-flush coming and going.

Yes: I have re-entered your olden haunts at last;
    Through the years, through the dead scenes I have tracked you;
What have you now found to say of our past—
    Scanned across the dark space wherein I have lacked you?
Summer gave us sweets, but autumn wrought division?
    Things were not lastly as firstly well
        With us twain, you tell?
But all's closed now, despite Time's derision.

I see what you are doing: you are leading me on
    To the spots we knew when we haunted here together,
The waterfall, above which the mist-bow shone
    At the then fair hour in the then fair weather,
And the cave just under, with a voice still so hollow
    That it seems to call out to me from forty years ago,
        When you were all aglow,
And not the thin ghost that I now frailly follow!

Ignorant of what there is flitting here to see,
    The waked birds preen and the seals flop lazily,
Soon you will have, Dear, to vanish from me,
    For the stars close their shutters and the dawn whitens hazily.

Trust me, I mind not, though Life lours,
   The bringing me here; nay, bring me here again!
     I am just the same as when
Our days were a joy, and our paths through flowers.   *(1914)*

THE PHANTOM HORSEWOMAN

Queer are the ways of a man I know:
     He comes and stands
     In a careworn craze,
     And looks at the sands
     And the seaward haze
     With moveless hands
     And face and gaze,
     Then turns to go ...
And what does he see when he gazes so?

They say he sees as an instant thing
     More clear than to-day,
     A sweet soft scene
     That once was in play
     By that briny green;
     Yes, notes alway
     Warm, real, and keen,
     What his back years bring—
A phantom of his own figuring.

Of this vision of his they might say more:
     Not only there
     Does he see this sight,
     But everywhere
     In his brain—day, night,
     As if on the air
     It were drawn rose bright—
     Yea, far from that shore
Does he carry this vision of heretofore:

A ghost-girl-rider. And though, toil-tried,
     He withers daily,
     Time touches her not,
     But she still rides gaily
     In his rapt thought

On that shagged and shaly
        Atlantic spot,
    And as when first eyed
Draws rein and sings to the swing of the tide.

                                    (*1913, 1914*)

NEAR LANIVET, 1872

There was a stunted handpost just on the crest,
        Only a few feet high:
She was tired, and we stopped in the twilight-time for her rest,
        At the crossways close thereby.

She leant back, being so weary, against its stem,
        And laid her arms on its own,
Each open palm stretched out to each end of them,
        Her sad face sideways thrown.

Her white-clothed form at this dim-lit cease of day
        Made her look as one crucified
In my gaze at her from the midst of the dusty way,
        And hurriedly "Don't," I cried.

I do not think she heard. Loosing thence she said,
        As she stepped forth ready to go,
"I am rested now.—Something strange came into my head;
        I wish I had not leant so!"

And wordless we moved onward down from the hill
        In the west cloud's murked obscure,
And looking back we could see the handpost still
        In the solitude of the moor.

"It struck her too," I thought, for as if afraid
        She heavily breathed as we trailed;
Till she said, "I did not think how 'twould look in the shade,
        When I leant back there like one nailed."

I, lightly: "There's nothing in it. For *you*, anyhow!"
        —"O I know there is not," said she . . .
"Yet I wonder . . . If no one is bodily crucified now,
        In spirit one may be!"

And we dragged on and on, while we seemed to see
    In the running of Time's far glass
Her crucified, as she had wondered if she might be
    Some day.—Alas, alas! *(1917)*

THE BLINDED BIRD

So zestfully canst thou sing?
And all this indignity,
With God's consent, on thee!
Blinded ere yet a-wing
By the red-hot needle thou,
I stand and wonder how
So zestfully thou canst sing!

Resenting not such wrong,
Thy grievous pain forgot,
Eternal dark thy lot,
Groping thy whole life long,
After that stab of fire;
Enjailed in pitiless wire;
Resenting not such wrong!

Who hath charity? This bird.
Who suffereth long and is kind,
Is not provoked, though blind
And alive ensepulchred?
Who hopeth, endureth all things?
Who thinketh no evil, but sings?
Who is divine? This bird. *(1917)*

THE OXEN

Christmas Eve, and twelve of the clock.
    "Now they are all on their knees,"
An elder said as we sat in a flock
    By the embers in hearthside ease.

We pictured the meek mild creatures where
    They dwelt in their strawy pen,
Nor did it occur to one of us there
    To doubt they were kneeling then.

So fair a fancy few would weave
  In these years! Yet, I feel,
If someone said on Christmas Eve,
  "Come; see the oxen kneel,

"In the lonely barton by yonder coomb
  Our childhood used to know,"
I should go with him in the gloom,
  Hoping it might be so. *(1915, 1917)*

THE FIVE STUDENTS

The sparrow dips in his wheel-rut bath,
  The sun grows passionate-eyed,
And boils the dew to smoke by the paddock-path;
  As strenuously we stride,—
Five of us; dark He, fair He, dark She, fair She, I,
    All beating by.

The air is shaken, the high-road hot,
  Shadowless swoons the day,
The greens are sobered and cattle at rest; but not
  We on our urgent way,—
Four of us; fair She, dark She, fair He, I, are there,
    But one—elsewhere.

Autumn moulds the hard fruit mellow,
  And forward still we press
Through moors, briar-meshed plantations, clay-pits yellow,
  As in the spring hours—yes,
Three of us: fair He, fair She, I, as heretofore,
    But—fallen one more.

The leaf drops: earthworms draw it in
  At night-time noiselessly,
The fingers of birch and beech are skeleton-thin,
  And yet on the beat are we,—
Two of us; fair She, I. But no more left to go
    The track we know.

Icicles tag the church-aisle leads,
  The flag-rope gibbers hoarse,

The home-bound foot-folk wrap their snow-flaked heads,
    Yet I still stalk the course—
One of us. . . . Dark and fair He, dark and fair She, gone.
    The rest—anon. *(1917)*

DURING WIND AND RAIN

They sing their dearest songs—
He, she, all of them—yea,
Treble and tenor and bass,
    And one to play;
With the candles mooning each face. . . .
    Ah, no; the years O!
How the sick leaves reel down in throngs!

They clear the creeping moss—
Elders and juniors—aye,
Making the pathways neat
    And the garden gay;
And they build a shady seat. . . .
    Ah, no; the years, the years;
See, the white storm-birds wing across!

They are blithely breakfasting all—
Men and maidens—yea,
Under the summer tree,
    With a glimpse of the bay,
While pet fowl come to the knee. . . .
    Ah, no; the years O!
And the rotten rose is ript from the wall.

They change to a high new house,
He, she, all of them—aye,
Clocks and carpets and chairs
    On the lawn all day,
And brightest things that are theirs. . . .
    Ah, no; the years, the years;
Down their carved names the rain-drop ploughs. *(1917)*

"FOR LIFE I HAD NEVER CARED GREATLY"

For life I had never cared greatly,
    As worth a man's while;

Peradventures unsought,
Peradventures that finished in nought,
Had kept me from youth and through manhood till lately
Unwon by its style.

In earliest years—why I know not—
I viewed it askance;
Conditions of doubt,
Conditions that leaked slowly out,
May haply have bent me to stand and to show not
Much zest for its dance.

With symphonies soft and sweet colour
It courted me then,
Till evasions seemed wrong,
Till evasions gave in to its song,
And I warmed, until living aloofly loomed duller
Than life among men.

Anew I found nought to set eyes on,
When, lifting its hand,
It uncloaked a star,
Uncloaked it from fog-damps afar,
And showed its beams burning from pole to horizon
As bright as a brand.

And so, the rough highway forgetting,
I pace hill and dale
Regarding the sky,
Regarding the vision on high,
And thus re-illumed have no humour for letting
My pilgrimage fail. (*1917*)

THE PITY OF IT

I walked in loamy Wessex lanes, afar
From rail-track and from highway, and I heard
In field and farmstead many an ancient word
Of local lineage like "Thu bist," "Er war,"
"Ich woll," "Er sholl," and by-talk similar,
Nigh as they speak who in this month's moon gird
At England's very loins, thereunto spurred
By gangs whose glory threats and slaughters are.

Then seemed a Heart crying: "Whosoever they be
At root and bottom of this, who flung this flame
Between kin folk kin tongued even as are we,

"Sinister, ugly, lurid, be their fame;
May their familiars grow to shun their name,
And their brood perish everlastingly." (*April 1915, 1917*)

IN TIME OF "THE BREAKING OF NATIONS"

(JEREMIAH 51:20)

Only a man harrowing clods
  In a slow silent walk
With an old horse that stumbles and nods
  Half asleep as they stalk.

Only thin smoke without flame
  From the heaps of couch-grass;
Yet this will go onward the same
  Though Dynasties pass.

Yonder a maid and her wight
  Come whispering by:
War's annals will fade into night
  Ere their story die. (*1915, 1917*)

AFTERWARDS

When the Present has latched its postern behind my tremulous stay,
  And the May month flaps its glad green leaves like wings,
Delicate-filmed as new-spun silk, will the neighbours say,
  "He was a man who used to notice such things"?

If it be in the dusk when, like an eyelid's soundless blink,
  The dewfall-hawk comes crossing the shades to alight
Upon the wind-warped upland thorn, a gazer may think,
  "To him this must have been a familiar sight."

If I pass during some nocturnal blackness, mothy and warm,
  When the hedgehog travels furtively over the lawn,
One may say, "He strove that such innocent creatures should come to no
    harm,
  But he could do little for them; and now he is gone."

If, when hearing that I have been stilled at last, they stand at the door,
   Watching the full-starred heavens that winter sees,
Will this thought rise on those who will meet my face no more,
   "He was one who had an eye for such mysteries"?

And will any say when my bell of quittance is heard in the gloom,
   And a crossing breeze cuts a pause in its outrollings,
Till they rise again, as they were a new bell's boom,
   "He hears it not now, but used to notice such things"? (1917)

"THE CURTAINS NOW ARE DRAWN"

(SONG)

The curtains now are drawn,
And the spindrift strikes the glass,
Blown up the jaggèd pass
By the surly salt sou'-west,
And the sneering glare is gone
Behind the yonder crest,
   While she sings to me:
"O the dream that thou art my Love, be it thine,
And the dream that I am thy Love, be it mine,
And death may come, but loving is divine."

I stand here in the rain,
With its smite upon her stone,
And the grasses that have grown
Over women, children, men,
And their texts that "Life is vain";
But I hear the notes as when
   Once she sang to me:
"O the dream that thou art my Love, be it thine,
And the dream that I am thy Love, be it mine,
And death may come, but loving is divine." (1913, 1922)

"ACCORDING TO THE MIGHTY WORKING"

When moiling seems at cease
   In the vague void of night-time,
   And heaven's wide roomage stormless
   Between the dusk and light-time,
   And fear at last is formless,
We call the allurement Peace.

Peace, this hid riot, Change,
    This revel of quick-cued mumming,
    This never truly being,
    This evermore becoming,
    This spinner's wheel onfleeing
Outside perception's range. *(1917, 1922)*

GOING AND STAYING

The moving sun-shapes on the spray,
The sparkles where the brook was flowing,
Pink faces, plightings, moonlit May,
These were the things we wished would stay;
    But they were going.

Seasons of blankness as of snow,
The silent bleed of a world decaying,
The moan of multitudes in woe,
These were the things we wished would go;
    But they were staying.

Then we looked closelier at Time,
And saw his ghostly arms revolving
To sweep off woeful things with prime,
Things sinister with things sublime
    Alike dissolving. *(1922)*

THE CONTRETEMPS

A forward rush by the lamp in the gloom,
  And we clasped, and almost kissed;
But she was not the woman whom
I had promised to meet in the thawing brume
On that harbour-bridge; nor was I he of her tryst.

So loosening from me swift she said:
  "O why, why feign to be
The one I had meant!—to whom I have sped
To fly with, being so sorrily wed!"
—'Twas thus and thus that she upbraided me.

My assignation had struck upon
  Some others' like it, I found.
And her lover rose on the night anon;

And then her husband entered on
The lamplit, snowflaked, sloppiness around.

"Take her and welcome, man!" he cried:
    "I wash my hands of her.
I'll find me twice as good a bride!"
—All this to me, whom he had eyed,
Plainly, as his wife's planned deliverer.

And next the lover: "Little I knew,
    Madam, you had a third!
Kissing here in my very view!"
—Husband and lover then withdrew.
I let them; and I told them not they erred.

Why not? Well, there faced she and I—
    Two strangers who'd kissed, or near,
Chancewise. To see stand weeping by
A woman once embraced, will try
The tension of a man the most austere.

So it began; and I was young,
    She pretty, by the lamp,
As flakes came waltzing down among
The waves of her clinging hair, that hung
Heavily on her temples, dark and damp.

And there alone still stood we two;
    She one cast off for me,
Or so it seemed: while night ondrew,
Forcing a parley what should do
We twain hearts caught in one catastrophe.

In stranded souls a common strait
    Wakes latencies unknown,
Whose impulse may precipitate
A life-long leap. The hour was late,
And there was the Jersey boat with its funnel agroan.

"Is wary walking worth much pother?"
    It grunted, as still it stayed.
"One pairing is as good as another
Where all is venture! Take each other,
And scrap the oaths that you have aforetime made." . . .

—Of the four involved there walks but one
  On earth at this late day.
And what of the chapter so begun?
In that odd complex what was done?
Well; happiness comes in full to none:
Let peace lie on lulled lips: I will not say. *(1922)*

"AND THERE WAS A GREAT CALM"

(ON THE SIGNING OF THE ARMISTICE, NOVEMBER 11, 1918)

There had been years of Passion—scorching, cold,
And much Despair, and Anger heaving high,
Care whitely watching. Sorrows manifold,
Among the young, among the weak and old,
And the pensive Spirit of Pity whispered, "Why?"

Men had not paused to answer. Foes distraught
Pierced the thinned peoples in a brute-like blindness,
Philosophies that sages long had taught,
And Selflessness, were as an unknown thought,
And "Hell!" and "Shell!" were yapped at Lovingkindness.

The feeble folk at home had grown full-used
To "dug-outs," "snipers," "Huns," from the war-adept
In the mornings heard, and at evetides perused;
To day-dreamt men in millions, when they mused—
To nightmare-men in millions when they slept.

Waking to wish existence timeless, null,
Sirius they watched above where armies fell;
He seemed to check his flapping when, in the lull
Of night a boom came thencewise, like the dull
Plunge of a stone dropped into some deep well.

So, when old hopes that earth was bettering slowly
Were dead and damned, there sounded "War is done!"
One morrow. Said the bereft, and meek, and lowly,
"Will men some day be given to grace? yea, wholly,
And in good sooth, as our dreams used to run?"

Breathless they paused. Out there men raised their glance
To where had stood those poplars lank and lopped,
As they had raised it through the four years' dance

Of Death in the now familiar flats of France;
And murmured, "Strange, this! How? All firing stopped?"

Aye; all was hushed. The about-to-fire fired not,
The aimed-at moved away in trance-lipped song.
One checkless regiment slung a clinching shot
And turned. The Spirit of Irony smirked out, "What?
Spoil peradventures woven of Rage and Wrong?"

Thenceforth no flying fires inflamed the gray,
No hurtlings shook the dewdrop from the thorn,
No moan perplexed the mute bird on the spray;
Worn horses mused: "We are not whipped to-day";
No weft-winged engines blurred the moon's thin horn.

Calm fell. From Heaven distilled a clemency;
There was peace on earth, and silence in the sky;
Some could, some could not, shake off misery:
The Sinister Spirit sneered: "It had to be!"
And again the Spirit of Pity whispered, "Why?" (1922)

THE FALLOW DEER AT THE LONELY HOUSE

One without looks in to-night
    Through the curtain-chink
From the sheet of glistening white;
One without looks in to-night
    As we sit and think
    By the fender-brink.

We do not discern those eyes
    Watching in the snow;
Lit by lamps of rosy dyes
We do not discern those eyes
    Wondering, aglow,
    Fourfooted, tiptoe. (1922)

THE SELFSAME SONG

A bird sings the selfsame song,
With never a fault in its flow,
That we listened to here those long
        Long years ago.

A pleasing marvel is how
A strain of such rapturous rote
Should have gone on thus till now
    Unchanged in a note!

—But it's not the selfsame bird.—
No: perished to dust is he. . . .
As also are those who heard
    That song with me. *(1922)*

FIRST OR LAST

(SONG)

If grief come early
Joy comes late,
If joy come early
Grief will wait;
  Aye, my dear and tender!

Wise ones joy them early
While the cheeks are red,
Banish grief till surly
Time has dulled their dread.

  And joy being ours
  Ere youth has flown,
  The later hours
  May find us gone;
    Aye, my dear and tender! *(1922)*

A DRIZZLING EASTER MORNING

And he is risen? Well, be it so. . . .
And still the pensive lands complain,
And dead men wait as long ago,
As if, much doubting, they would know
What they are ransomed from, before
They pass again their sheltering door.

I stand amid them in the rain,
While blusters vex the yew and vane;
And on the road the weary wain

Plods forward, laden heavily;
And toilers with their aches are fain
For endless rest—though risen is he.   (*1922*)

AN ANCIENT TO ANCIENTS

Where once we danced, where once we sang,
      Gentlemen,
The floors are sunken, cobwebs hang,
And cracks creep; worms have fed upon
The doors. Yea, sprightlier times were then
Than now, with harps and tabrets gone,
      Gentlemen!

Where once we rowed, where once we sailed,
      Gentlemen,
And damsels took the tiller, veiled
Against too strong a stare (God wot
Their fancy, then or anywhen!)
Upon that shore we are clean forgot,
      Gentlemen!

We have lost somewhat, afar and near,
      Gentlemen,
The thinning of our ranks each year
Affords a hint we are nigh undone,
That we shall not be ever again
The marked of many, loved of one,
      Gentlemen.

In dance the polka hit our wish,
      Gentlemen,
The paced quadrille, the spry schottische,
"Sir Roger."—And in opera spheres
The "Girl" (the famed "Bohemian"),
And "Trovatore," held the ears,
      Gentlemen.

This season's paintings do not please,
      Gentlemen,
Like Etty, Mulready, Maclise;
Throbbing romance has waned and wanned;
No wizard wields the witching pen

Of Bulwer, Scott, Dumas, and Sand,
    Gentlemen.

The bower we shrined to Tennyson,
    Gentlemen,
Is roof-wrecked; damps there drip upon
Sagged seats, the creeper-nails are rust,
The spider is sole denizen;
Even she who voiced those rhymes is dust,
    Gentlemen!

We who met sunrise sanguine-souled,
    Gentlemen,
Are wearing weary. We are old;
These younger press; we feel our rout
Is imminent to Aïdes' den,—
That evening shades are stretching out,
    Gentlemen!

And yet, though ours be failing frames,
    Gentlemen,
So were some others' history names,
Who trode their track light-limbed and fast
As these youth, and not alien
From enterprise, to their long last.
    Gentlemen.

Sophocles, Plato, Socrates,
    Gentlemen,
Pythagoras, Thucydides,
Herodotus, and Homer,—yea,
Clement, Augustin, Origen,
Burnt brightlier towards their setting-day,
    Gentlemen.

And ye, red-lipped and smooth-browed; list,
    Gentlemen;
Much is there waits you we have missed;
Much lore we leave you worth the knowing,
Much, much has lain outside our ken:
Nay, rush not: time serves: we are going,
    Gentlemen. *(1922)*

SNOW IN THE SUBURBS

Every branch big with it,
   Bent every twig with it;
Every fork like a white web-foot;
Every street and pavement mute:
Some flakes have lost their way, and grope back upward, when
Meeting those meandering down they turn and descend again.
   The palings are glued together like a wall,
   And there is no waft of wind with the fleecy fall.

A sparrow enters the tree,
   Whereon immediately
A snow-lump thrice his own slight size
Descends on him and showers his head and eyes,
    And overturns him,
    And near inurns him,
And lights on a nether twig, when its brush
Starts off a volley of other lodging lumps with a rush.

The steps are a blanched slope,
   Up which, with feeble hope,
A black cat comes, wide-eyed and thin;
    And we take him in. *(1925)*

ON THE PORTRAIT OF A WOMAN
ABOUT TO BE HANGED

Comely and capable one of our race,
Posing there in your gown of grace,
   Plain, yet becoming;
    Could subtlest breast
    Ever have guessed
What was behind that innocent face,
   Drumming, drumming!

Would that your Causer, ere knoll your knell
For this riot of passion, might deign to tell
   Why, since It made you
    Sound in the germ,
    It sent a worm

To madden Its handiwork, when It might well
    Not have assayed you,

Not have implanted, to your deep rue,
The Clytæmnestra spirit in you,
    And with purblind vision
        Sowed a tare
        In a field so fair,
And a thing of symmetry, seemly to view,
    Brought to derision!   (*January 6, 1923, 1925*)

Gerard Manley Hopkins
(1844–1889)

THE SUMMER MALISON

Maidens shall weep at merry morn,
And hedges break and lose the kine,
And field-flowers make the fields forlorn,
And noonday have a shallow shine,
And barley turn to weed and wild,
And seven ears crown the lodged corn,
And mother have no milk for child,
    And father be overworn.

And John shall lie, where winds are dead,
And hate the ill-visaged cursing tars,
And James shall hate his faded red,
Grown wicked in the wicked wars.
No rains shall fresh the flats of sea,
Nor close the clayfields' sharded sores,
And every heart think loathingly
    Its dearest changed to bores.   (*1865, 1930*)

WINTER WITH THE GULF STREAM

The boughs, the boughs are bare enough
But earth has never felt the snow.
Frost-furred our ivies are and rough

With bills of rime the brambles shew.
The hoarse leaves crawl on hissing ground
Because the sighing wind is low.

But if the rain-blasts be unbound
And from dank feathers wring the drops
The clogged brook runs with choking sound

Kneading the mounded mire that stops
His channel under clammy coats
Of foliage fallen in the copse.

A simple passage of weak notes
Is all the winter bird dare try.
The bugle moon by daylight floats

So glassy white about the sky,
So like a berg of hyaline,
And pencilled blue so daintily,

I never saw her so divine.
But through black branches, rarely drest
In scarves of silky shot and shine,

The webbed and the watery west
Where yonder crimson fireball sits
Looks laid for feasting and for rest.

I see long reefs of violets
In beryl-covered fens so dim,
A gold-water Pactolus frets

Its brindled wharves and yellow brim,
The waxen colours weep and run,
And slendering to his burning rim

Into the flat blue mist the sun
Drops out and all our day is done.   *(1871, 1918)*

THE WRECK OF THE DEUTSCHLAND

To the happy memory of five Franciscan Nuns, exiles by the Falk Laws, drowned between midnight and morning of Dec. 7th, 1875.

PART THE FIRST

Thou mastering me
God! giver of breath and bread;
World's strand, sway of the sea;
Lord of living and dead;
Thou hast bound bones and veins in me, fastened me flesh,
And after it almost unmade, what with dread,

Thy doing: and dost thou touch me afresh?
Over again I feel thy finger and find thee.

I did say yes
O at lightning and lashed rod;
Thou heardst me truer than tongue confess
Thy terror, O Christ, O God;
Thou knowest the walls, altar and hour and night:
The swoon of a heart that the sweep and the hurl of thee trod
Hard down with a horror of height:
And the midriff astrain with leaning of, laced with fire of stress.

The frown of his face
Before me, the hurtle of hell
Behind, where, where was a, where was a place?
I whirled out wings that spell
And fled with a fling of the heart to the heart of the Host.
My heart, but you were dovewinged, I can tell,
Carrier-witted, I am bold to boast,
To flash from the flame to the flame then, tower from the grace to the
grace.

I am soft sift
In an hourglass—at the wall
Fast, but mined with a motion, a drift,
And it crowds and it combs to the fall;
I steady as a water in a well, to a poise, to a pane,
But roped with, always, all the way down from the tall
Fells or flanks of the voel, a vein
Of the gospel proffer, a pressure, a principle, Christ's gift.

I kiss my hand
To the stars, lovely-asunder
Starlight, wafting him out of it; and
Glow, glory in thunder;
Kiss my hand to the dappled-with-damson west:
Since, tho' he is under the world's splendour and wonder,
His mystery must be instressed, stressed;
For I greet him the days I meet him, and bless when I understand.

Not out of his bliss
Springs the stress felt
Nor first from heaven (and few know this)

Swings the stroke dealt—
Stroke and a stress that stars and storms deliver,
That guilt is hushed by, hearts are flushed by and melt—
But it rides time like riding a river
(And here the faithful waver, the faithless fable and miss).

It dates from day
Of his going in Galilee;
Warm-laid grave of a womb-life grey;
Manger, maiden's knee;
The dense and the driven Passion, and frightful sweat:
Thence the discharge of it, there its swelling to be,
Though felt before, though in high flood yet—
What none would have known of it, only the heart, being hard at bay,

Is out with it! Oh,
We lash with the best or worst
Word last! How a lush-kept plush-capped sloe
Will, mouthed to flesh-burst,
Gush!—flush the man, the being with it, sour or sweet,
Brim, in a flash, full!—Hither then, last or first,
To hero of Calvary, Christ's feet—
Never ask if meaning it, wanting it, warned of it—men go.

Be adored among men,
God, three-numberèd form;
Wring thy rebel, dogged in den,
Man's malice, with wrecking and storm.
Beyond saying sweet, past telling of tongue,
Thou art lightning and love, I found it, a winter and warm;
Father and fondler of heart thou hast wrung:
Hast thy dark descending and most art merciful then.

With an anvil-ding
And with fire in him forge thy will
Or rather, rather then, stealing as Spring
Through him, melt him but master him still:
Whether at once, as once at a crash Paul,
Or as Austin, a lingering-out swéet skíll,
Make mercy in all of us, out of us all
Mastery, but be adored, but be adored King.

PART THE SECOND

"Some find me a sword; some
        The flange and the rail; flame,
Fang, or flood" goes Death on drum,
        And storms bugle his fame.
But wé dream we are rooted in earth—Dust!
Flesh falls within sight of us, we, though our flower the same,
        Wave with the meadow, forget that there must
The sour scythe cringe, and the blear share come.

        On Saturday sailed from Bremen,
        American-outward-bound,
    Take settler and seamen, tell men with women,
        Two hundred souls in the round—
O Father, not under thy feathers nor ever as guessing
The goal was a shoal, of a fourth the doom to be drowned;
        Yet did the dark side of the bay of thy blessing
Not vault them, the millions of rounds of thy mercy not reeve even
    them in?

        Into the snows she sweeps,
        Hurling the haven behind,
    The Deutschland, on Sunday; and so the sky keeps,
        For the infinite air is unkind,
And the sea flint-flake, black-backed in the regular blow,
Sitting Eastnortheast, in cursed quarter, the wind;
        Wiry and white-fiery and whirlwind-swivellèd snow
Spins to the widow-making unchilding unfathering deeps.

        She drove in the dark to leeward,
        She struck—not a reef or a rock
    But the combs of a smother of sand: night drew her
        Dead to the Kentish Knock;
And she beat the bank down with her bows and the ride of her
    keel:
The breakers rolled on her beam with ruinous shock;
        And canvas and compass, the whorl and the wheel
Idle for ever to waft her or wind her with, these she endured.

        Hope had grown grey hairs,
        Hope had mourning on,
    Trenched with tears, carved with cares,
        Hope was twelve hours gone;

And frightful a nightfall folded rueful a day
Nor rescue, only rocket and lightship, shone,
 And lives at last were washing away:
To the shrouds they took,—they shook in the hurling and horrible airs.

One stirred from the rigging to save
The wild woman-kind below,
 With a rope's end round the man, handy and brave—
He was pitched to his death at a blow,
For all his dreadnought breast and braids of thew:
They could tell him for hours, dandled the to and fro
 Through the cobbled foam-fleece, what could he do
With the burl of the fountains of air, buck and the flood of the wave?

They fought with God's cold—
And they could not and fell to the deck
 (Crushed them) or water (and drowned them) or rolled
With the sea-romp over the wreck.
Night roared, with the heart-break hearing a heart-broke rabble,
The woman's wailing, the crying of child without check—
 Till a lioness arose breasting the babble,
A prophetess towered in the tumult, a virginal tongue told.

Ah, touched in your bower of bone
Are you! turned for an exquisite smart,
 Have you! make words break from me here all alone,
Do you!—mother of being in me, heart.
O unteachably after evil, but uttering truth,
Why, tears! is it? tears; such a melting, a madrigal start!
 Never-eldering revel and river of youth,
What can it be, this glee? the good you have there of your own?

Sister, a sister calling
A master, her master and mine!—
 And the inboard seas run swirling and hawling;
The rash smart sloggering brine
Blinds her; but she that weather sees one thing, one;
Has one fetch in her: she rears herself to divine
 Ears, and the call of the tall nun
To the men in the tops and the tackle rode over the storm's brawling.

She was first of a five and came
Of a coifèd sisterhood.

(O Deutschland, double a desperate name!
O world wide of its good!
But Gertrude, lily, and Luther, are two of a town,
Christ's lily and beast of the waste wood:
From life's dawn it is drawn down,
Abel is Cain's brother and breasts they have sucked the same.)

Loathed for a love men knew in them,
Banned by the land of their birth,
Rhine refused them. Thames would ruin them;
Surf, snow, river and earth
Gnashed: but thou art above, thou Orion of light;
Thy unchancelling poising palms were weighing the worth,
Thou martyr-master: in thy sight
Storm flakes were scroll-leaved flowers, lily showers—sweet heaven was
astrew in them.

Five! The finding and sake
And cipher of suffering Christ.
Mark, the mark is of man's make
And the word of it Sacrificed.
But he scores it in scarlet himself on his own bespoken,
Before-time-taken, dearest prizèd and priced—
Stigma, signal, cinquefoil token
For lettering of the lamb's fleece, ruddying of the rose-flake.

Joy fall to thee, father Francis,
Drawn to the Life that died;
With the gnarls of the nails in thee, niche of the lance, his
Lovescape crucified
And seal of his seraph-arrival! and these thy daughters
And five-livèd and leavèd favour and pride,
Are sisterly sealed in wild waters,
To bathe in his fall-gold mercies, to breathe in his all-fire glances.

Away in the loveable west,
On a pastoral forehead of Wales,
I was under a roof here, I was at rest,
And they the prey of the gales;
She to the black-about air, to the breaker, the thickly
Falling flakes, to the throng that catches and quails
Was calling "O Christ, Christ, come quickly":
The cross to her she calls Christ to her, christens her wild-worst Best.

The majesty! what did she mean?
Breathe, arch and original Breath.
Is it love in her of the being as her lover had been?
Breathe, body of lovely Death.
They were else-minded then, altogether, the men
Woke thee with a *We are perishing* in the weather of Gennesareth.
Or is it that she cried for the crown then,
The keener to come at the comfort for feeling the combating keen?

For how to the heart's cheering
The down-dugged ground-hugged grey
Hovers off, the jay-blue heavens appearing
Of pied and peeled May!
Blue-beating and hoary-glow height; or night, still higher,
With belled fire and the moth-soft Milky Way,
What by your measure is the heaven of desire,
The treasure never eyesight got, nor was ever guessed what for the
hearing?

No, but it was not these.
The jading and jar of the cart,
Time's tasking, it is fathers that asking for ease
Of the sodden-with-its-sorrowing heart,
Not danger, electrical horror; then further it finds
The appealing of the Passion is tenderer in prayer apart:
Other, I gather, in measure her mind's
Burden, in wind's burly and beat of endragonèd seas.

But how shall I . . . make me room there:
Reach me a . . . Fancy, come faster—
Strike you the sight of it? look at it loom there,
Thing that she . . . there then! the Master,
Ipse, the only one, Christ, King, Head:
He was to cure the extremity where he had cast her;
Do, deal, lord it with living and dead;
Let him ride, her pride, in his triumph, despatch and have done with
his doom there.

Ah! there was a heart right!
There was single eye!
Read the unshapeable shock night
And knew the who and the why;
Wording it how but by him that present and past,
Heaven and earth are word of, worded by?—

The Simon Peter of a soul! to the blast
Tarpeïan-fast, but a blown beacon of light.

Jesu, heart's light,
Jesu, maid's son,
What was the feast followed the night
Thou hadst glory of this nun?—
Feast of the one woman without stain.
For so conceivèd, so to conceive thee is done;
But here was heart-throe, birth of a brain,
Word, that heard and kept thee and uttered thee outright.

Well, she has thee for the pain, for the
Patience; but pity of the rest of them!
Heart, go and bleed at a bitterer vein for the
Comfortless unconfessed of them—
No not uncomforted: lovely-felicitous Providence
Finger of a tender of, O of a feathery delicacy, the breast of the
Maiden could obey so, be a bell to, ring of it, and
Startle the poor sheep back! is the shipwrack then a harvest, does tem-
pest carry the grain for thee?

I admire thee, master of the tides,
Of the Yore-flood, of the year's fall;
The recurb and the recovery of the gulf's sides,
The girth of it and the wharf of it and the wall;
Stanching, quenching ocean of a motionable mind;
Ground of being, and granite of it: past all
Grasp God, throned behind
Death with a sovereignty that heeds but hides, bodes but abides;

With a mercy that outrides
The all of water, an ark
For the listener; for the lingerer with a love glides
Lower than death and the dark;
A vein for the visiting of the past-prayer, pent in prison,
The-last-breath penitent spirits—the uttermost mark
Our passion-plungèd giant risen,
The Christ of the Father compassionate, fetched in the storm of his
strides.

Now burn, new born to the world,
Doubled-naturèd name,
The heaven-flung, heart-fleshed, maiden-furled

> Miracle-in-Mary-of-flame,
> Mid-numberèd he in three of the thunder-throne!
> Not a dooms-day dazzle in his coming nor dark as he came;
> Kind, but royally reclaiming his own;
> A released shower, let flash to the shire, not a lightning of fire hard-
> hurled.

> Dame, at our door
> Drowned, and among our shoals,
> Remember us in the roads, the heaven-haven of the Reward:
> Our King back, oh, upon English souls!
> Let him easter in us, be a dayspring to the dimness of us, be a
> crimson-cresseted east,
> More brightening her, rare-dear Britain, as his reign rolls,
> Pride, rose, prince, hero of us, high-priest,
> Our hearts' charity's hearth's fire, our thoughts' chivalry's throng's Lord.
> *(1875, 1918)*

GOD'S GRANDEUR

The world is charged with the grandeur of God.
  It will flame out, like shining from shook foil;
  It gathers to a greatness, like the ooze of oil
Crushed. Why do men then now not reck his rod?
Generations have trod, have trod, have trod;
  And all is seared with trade; bleared, smeared with toil;
  And wears man's smudge and shares man's smell: the soil
Is bare now, nor can foot feel, being shod.

And for all this, nature is never spent;
  There lives the dearest freshness deep down things;
And though the last lights off the black West went
  Oh, morning, at the brown brink eastward, springs—
Because the Holy Ghost over the bent
  World broods with warm breast and with ah! bright wings.
(1877, 1918)

THE LANTERN OUT OF DOORS

Sometimes a lantern moves along the night,
  That interests our eyes. And who goes there?
  I think; where from and bound, I wonder, where,
With, all down darkness wide, his wading light?

Men go by me whom either beauty bright
  In mould or mind or what not else makes rare:
  They rain against our much-thick and marsh air
Rich beams, till death or distance buys them quite.

Death or distance soon consumes them: wind
  What most I may eye after, be in at the end
  I cannot, and out of sight is out of mind.

Christ minds: Christ's interest, what to avow or amend
  There, éyes them, heart wánts, care haúnts, foot fóllows kínd,
Their ránsom, théir rescue, ánd first, fást, last friénd. (*1877, 1918*)

THE WINDHOVER
To Christ Our Lord

I caught this morning morning's minion, king-
  dom of daylight's dauphin, dapple-dawn-drawn Falcon, in his riding
  Of the rolling level underneath him steady air, and striding
High there, how he rung upon the rein of a wimpling wing
In his ecstasy! then off, off forth on swing,
  As a skate's heel sweeps smooth on a bow-bend: the hurl and gliding
  Rebuffed the big wind. My heart in hiding
Stirred for a bird,—the achieve of, the mastery of the thing!

Brute beauty and valour and act, oh, air, pride, plume, here
  Buckle! AND the fire that breaks from thee then, a billion
Times told lovelier, more dangerous, O my chevalier!

  No wonder of it: shéer plód makes plough down sillion
Shine, and blue-bleak embers, ah my dear,
  Fall, gall themselves, and gash gold-vermilion. (*1877, 1918*)

PIED BEAUTY

  Glory be to God for dappled things—
    For skies of couple-colour as a brinded cow;
      For rose-moles all in stipple upon trout that swim;
  Fresh-firecoal chestnut-falls; finches' wings;
    Landscape plotted and pieced—fold, fallow, and plough;
      And áll trádes, their gear and tackle and trim.
  All things counter, original, spare, strange;
    Whatever is fickle, freckled (who knows how?)

With swift, slow; sweet, sour; adazzle, dim;
He fathers-forth whose beauty is past change:
Praise him. (1877, 1918)

HURRAHING IN HARVEST

Summer ends now; now, barbarous in beauty, the stooks rise
Around; up above, what wind-walks! what lovely behaviour
Of silk-sack clouds! has wilder, wilful-wavier
Meal-drift moulded ever and melted across skies?

I walk, I lift up, I lift up heart, eyes,
Down all that glory in the heavens to glean our Saviour;
And, éyes, héart, what looks, what lips yet gave you a
Rapturous love's greeting of realer, of rounder replies?

And the azurous hung hills are his world-wielding shoulder
Majestic—as a stallion stalwart, very-violet-sweet!—
These things, these things were here and but the beholder
Wanting; which two when they once meet,
The heart rears wings bold and bolder
And hurls for him, O half hurls earth for him off under his feet.
(1877, 1918)

THE CAGED SKYLARK

As a dare-gale skylark scanted in a dull cage
   Man's mounting spirit in his bone-house, mean house, dwells—
   That bird beyond the remembering his free fells;
This in drudgery, day-labouring-out life's age.

Though aloft on turf or perch or poor low stage,
   Both sing sometímes the sweetest, sweetest spells,
   Yet both droop deadly sómetimes in their cells
Or wring their barriers in bursts of fear or rage.

Not that the sweet-fowl, song-fowl, needs no rest—
Why, hear him, hear him babble and drop down to his nest,
   But his own nest, wild nest, no prison.

Man's spirit will be flesh-bound when found at best,
But uncumbered: meadow-down is not distressed
   For a rainbow footing it nor he for his bónes rísen. (1877, 191

SPRING AND FALL
to a young child

Márgarét, are you gríeving
Over Goldengrove unleaving?
Léaves, líke the things of man, you
With your fresh thoughts care for, can you?
Ah! ás the heart grows older
It will come to such sights colder
By and by, nor spare a sigh
Though worlds of wanwood leafmeal lie;
And yet you wíll weep and know why.
Now no matter, child, the name:
Sórrow's spríngs áre the same.
Nor mouth had, no nor mind, expressed
What heart heard of, ghost guessed:
It ís the blight man was born for,
It is Margaret you mourn for. (*1880, 1918*)

SPELT FROM SIBYL'S LEAVES

Earnest, earthless, equal attuneable, | vaulty, voluminous, . . stupendous
Evening strains to be tíme's vást, | womb-of-all, home-of-all, hearse-of-
all night.
Her fond yellow hornlight wound to the west, | her wild hollow hoar-
light hung to the height
Waste; her earliest stars, earl-stars, | stárs principal, overbend us,
Fíre-féaturing heaven. For earth | her being has unbound; her dapple
is at an end, as-
tray or aswarm, all throughther, in throngs; | self ín self steepèd and
páshed—qúite
Disremembering, dísmémbering | áll now. Heart, you round me right
With: Óur évening is over us; óur night | whélms, whélms, ánd will
end us.
Only the beak-leaved boughs dragonish | damask the tool-smooth bleak
light; black,
Ever so black on it. Óur tale, O óur oracle! | Lét life, wáned, ah lét life
wind
Off hér once skéined stained véined varíety | upon, áll on twó spools;
párt, pen, páck
Now her áll in twó flocks, twó folds--black, white; | right, wrong;
reckon but, reck but, mind

But thése two; wáre of a wórld where bút these ǀ twó tell, each off the
   óther; of a rack
Where, selfwrung selfstrung, sheathe-and-shelterless ǀ thóughts agaínst
   thoughts ín in groans grínd. *(1918)*

INVERSNAID

This darksome burn, horseback brown,
His rollrock highroad roaring down,
In coop and in comb the fleece of his foam
Flutes and low to the lake falls home.

A windpuff-bonnet of fáwn-fróth
Turns and twindles over the broth
Of a pool so pitchblack, féll-frówning,
It rounds and rounds Despair to drowning.

Degged with dew, dappled with dew
Are the groins of the braes that the brook treads through,
Wiry heathpacks, flitches of fern,
And the beadbonny ash that sits over the burn.

What would the world be, once bereft
Of wet and of wildness? Let them be left,
O let them be left, wildness and wet;
Long live the weeds and the wilderness yet. *(1881, 1918)*

[AS KINGFISHERS CATCH FIRE]

As kingfishers catch fire, dragonflies draw flame;
    As tumbled over rim in roundy wells
      Stones ring; like each tucked string tells, each hung bell's
Bow swung finds tongue to fling out broad its name;
Each mortal thing does one thing and the same:
    Deals out that being indoors each one dwells;
    Selves—goes itself; *myself* it speaks and spells;
Crying *What I do is me: for that I came.*

Í say more: the just man justices;
    Keeps gráce: thát keeps all his goings graces;
Acts in God's eye what in God's eye he is—
    Chríst—for Christ plays in ten thousand places,
Lovely in limbs, and lovely in eyes not his
    To the Father through the features of men's faces.
                        (1882, 1918)

THE LEADEN ECHO AND THE GOLDEN ECHO

(Maiden's Song from St. Winefred's Well)

THE LEADEN ECHO

How to kéep—is there ány any, is there none such, nowhere known
    some, bow or brooch or braid or brace, láce, latch or catch or key to
    keep
Back beauty, keep it, beauty, beauty, beauty, . . . from vanishing away?
Ó is there no frowning of these wrinkles, rankèd wrinkles deep,
Dówn? no waving off of these most mournful messengers, still mes-
    sengers, sad and stealing messengers of grey?
No there's none, there's none, O no there's none,
Nor can you long be, what you now are, called fair,
Do what you may do, what, do what you may,
And wisdom is early to despair:
Be beginning; since, no, nothing can be done
To keep at bay
Age and age's evils, hoar hair,
Ruck and wrinkle, drooping, dying, death's worst, winding sheets,
    tombs and worms and tumbling to decay;
So be beginning, be beginning to despair.
O there's none; no no no there's none:
Be beginning to despair, to despair,
Despair, despair, despair, despair.

THE GOLDEN ECHO

              Spare!
There ís one, yes I have one (Hush there!),
Only not within seeing of the sun.
Not within the singeing of the strong sun,
Tall sun's tingeing, or treacherous the tainting of the earth's air,
Somewhere elsewhere there is ah well where! one,
Óne. Yes I cán tell such a key, I dó know such a place,
Where whatever's prizèd and passes of us, everything that's fresh and
    fast flying of us, seems to us sweet of us and swiftly away with, done
    away with, undone,
Undone, done with, soon done with, and yet dearly and dangerously
    sweet
Of us, the wimpled-water-dimpled, not-by-morning-matchèd face,
The flower of beauty, fleece of beauty, too too apt to, ah! to fleet,
Never fleets móre, fastened with the tenderest truth
To its own best being and its loveliness of youth: it is an everlastingness
    of, O it is an all youth!

Come then, your ways and airs and looks, locks, maidengear, gallantry
    and gaiety and grace,
Winning ways, airs innocent, maiden manners, sweet looks, loose locks,
    long locks, lovelocks, gaygear, going gallant, girlgrace—
Resign them, sign them, seal them, send them, motion them with breath,
And with sighs soaring, soaring síghs deliver
Them; beauty-in-the-ghost, deliver it, early now, long before death
Give beauty back, beauty, beauty, beauty, back to God, beauty's self
    and beauty's giver.
See; not a hair is, not an eyelash, not the least lash lost; every hair
Is, hair of the head, numbered.
Nay, what we had lighthanded left in surly the mere mould
Will have waked and have waxed and have walked with the wind what
    while we slept,
This side, that side hurling a heavyheaded hundredfold
What while we, while we slumbered.
O then, weary then whý should we tread? O why are we so haggard at
    the heart, so care-coiled, care-killed, so fagged, so fashed, so cogged,
    so cumbered,
When the thing we freely fórfeit is kept with fonder a care,
Fonder a care kept than we could have kept it, kept
Far with fonder a care (and we, we should have lost it) finer, fonder
A care kept.—Where kept? Do but tell us where kept, where.—
Yonder.—What high as that! We follow, now we follow.—Yonder, yes
    yonder, yonder,
Yonder. *(1882, 1918)*

[NO WORST, THERE IS NONE]

No worst, there is none. Pitched past pitch of grief,
More pangs will, schooled at forepangs, wilder wring.
Comforter, where, where is your comforting?
Mary, mother of us, where is your relief?
My cries heave, herds-long; huddle in a main, a chief-
woe, world-sorrow; on an age-old anvil wince and sing—
Then lull, then leave off. Fury had shrieked "No ling-
ering! Let me be fell: force I must be brief."
O the mind, mind has mountains; cliffs of fall
Frightful, sheer, no-man-fathomed. Hold them cheap
May who ne'er hung there. Nor does long our small
Durance deal with that steep or deep. Here! creep,
Wretch, under a comfort serves in a whirlwind: all
Life death does end and each day dies with sleep. *(1918)*

[NOT, I'LL NOT, CARRION COMFORT]

Not, I'll not, carrion comfort, Despair, not feast on thee;
Not untwist—slack they may be—these last strands of man
In me ór, most weary, cry I can no more. I can;
Can something, hope, wish day come, not choose not to be.

But ah, but O thou terrible, why wouldst thou rude on me
Thy wring-world right foot rock? lay a lionlimb against me? scan
With darksome devouring eyes my bruisèd bones? and fan,
O in turns of tempest, me heaped there; me frantic to avoid thee and
    flee?

Why? That my chaff might fly; my grain lie, sheer and clear.
Nay in all that toil, that coil, since (seems) I kissed the rod,
Hand rather, my heart lo! lapped strength, stole joy, would laugh, chéer.
Cheer whom though? the hero whose heaven-handling flung me, fóot
    tród
Me? or me that fought him? O which one? is it each one? That night,
    that year
Of now done darkness I wretch lay wrestling with (my God!) my God.
                                            (1885–87, 1918)

[I WAKE AND FEEL THE FELL OF DARK]

I wake and feel the fell of dark, not day.
What hours, O what black hoürs we have spent
This night! what sights you, heart, saw; ways you went!
And more must, in yet longer light's delay.

With witness I speak this. But where I say
Hours I mean years, mean life. And my lament
Is cries countless, cries like dead letters sent
To dearest him that lives alas! away.

I am gall, I am heartburn. God's most deep decree
Bitter would have me taste: my taste was me;
Bones built in me, flesh filled, blood brimmed the curse.

Selfyeast of spirit a dull dough sours. I see
The lost are like this, and their scourge to be
As I am mine, their sweating selves; but worse.   (c. 1885, 1918)

[THOU ART INDEED JUST, LORD]

Justus quidem tu es, Domine, si disputem tecum: verumtamen justa loquar ad te: Quare via impiorum prosperatur? &c.

Thou are indeed just, Lord, if I contend
With thee; but, sir, so what I plead is just.
Why do sinners' ways prosper? and why must
Disappointment all I endeavor end?

Wert thou my enemy, O thou my friend,
How wouldst thou worse, I wonder, than thou dost
Defeat, thwart me? Oh, the sots and thralls of lust
Do in spare hours more thrive than I that spend,

Sir, life upon thy cause. See, banks and brakes
Now, leavèd how thick! lacèd they are again
With fretty chervil, look, and fresh wind shakes

Them; birds build—but not I build; no, but strain,
Time's eunuch, and not breed one work that wakes.
Mine, O thou lord of life, send my roots rain.   (*1889, 1918*)

TO R. B.

The fine delight that fathers thought; the strong
Spur, live and lancing like the blowpipe flame,
Breathes once and, quenchèd faster than it came,
Leaves yet the mind a mother of immortal song.

Nine months she then, nay years, nine years she long
Within her wears, bears, cares and combs the same:
The widow of an insight lost she lives, with aim
Now known and hand at work now never wrong.

Sweet fire the sire of muse, my soul needs this;
I want the one rapture of an inspiration.
O then if in my lagging lines you miss

The roll, the rise, the carol, the creation,
My winter world, that scarcely breathes that bliss
Now, yields you, with some sighs, our explanation.

(*1889, 1918*)

Robert Bridges
(1844–1930)

[I WILL NOT LET THEE GO]

I will not let thee go.
Ends all our month-long love in this?
   Can it be summed up so,
   Quit in a single kiss?
I will not let thee go.

I will not let thee go.
If thy words' breath could scare thy deeds,
   As the soft south can blow
   And toss the feathered seeds,
Then might I let thee go.

I will not let thee go.
Had not the great sun seen, I might;
   Or were he reckoned slow
   To bring the false to light,
Then might I let thee go.

I will not let thee go.
The stars that crowd the summer skies
   Have watched us so below
   With all their million eyes,
I dare not let thee go.

I will not let thee go.
Have we not chid the changeful moon,
   Now rising late, and now
   Because she set too soon,
And shall I let thee go?

I will not let thee go.
Have not the young flowers been content,
   Plucked ere their buds could blow,

       To seal our sacrament?
       I cannot let thee go.

       I will not let thee go.
    I hold thee by too many bands:
       Thou sayest farewell, and lo!
       I have thee by the hands,
       And will not let thee go.   (1873)

A PASSER-BY

Whither, O splendid ship, thy white sails crowding,
    Leaning across the bosom of the urgent West,
That fearest nor sea rising, nor sky clouding,
    Whither away, fair rover, and what thy quest?
    Ah! soon, when Winter has all our vales opprest,
When skies are cold and misty, and hail is hurling,
    Wilt thou glide on the blue Pacific, or rest
In a summer haven asleep, thy white sails furling.

I there before thee, in the country that well thou knowest,
    Already arrived am inhaling the odorous air:
I watch thee enter unerringly where thou goest,
    And anchor queen of the strange shipping there,
    Thy sails for awnings spread, thy masts bare;
Nor is aught from the foaming reef to the snow-capped, grandest
    Peak, that is over the feathery palms more fair
Than thou, so upright, so stately, and still thou standest.

And yet, O splendid ship, unhailed and nameless,
    I know not if, aiming a fancy, I rightly divine
That thou has a purpose joyful, a courage blameless,
    Thy port assured in a happier land than mine.
    But for all I have given thee, beauty enough is thine,
As thou, aslant with trim tackle and shrouding,
    From the proud nostril curve of a prow's line
In the offing scatterest foam, thy white sails crowding.   (1879)

LONDON SNOW

When men were all asleep the snow came flying,
In large white flakes falling on the city brown,
Stealthily and perpetually settling and loosely lying,
    Hushing the latest traffic of the drowsy town;

Deadening, muffling, stifling its murmurs failing;
Lazily and incessantly floating down and down:
    Silently sifting and veiling road, roof and railing;
Hiding difference, making unevenness even,
Into angles and crevices softly drifting and sailing.
    All night it fell, and when full inches seven
It lay in the depth of its uncompacted lightness,
The clouds blew off from a high and frosty heaven;
    And all woke earlier for the unaccustomed brightness
Of the winter dawning, the strange unheavenly glare:
The eye marvelled—marvelled at the dazzling whiteness;
    The ear hearkened to the stillness of the solemn air;
No sound of wheel rumbling nor of foot falling,
And the busy morning cries came thin and spare.
    Then boys I heard, as they went to school, calling,
They gathered up the crystal manna to freeze
Their tongues with tasting, their hands with snowballing;
    Or rioted in a drift, plunging up to the knees;
Or peering up from under the white-mossed wonder,
"O look at the trees!" they cried, "O look at the trees!"
    With lessened load a few carts creak and blunder,
Following along the white deserted way,
A country company long dispersed asunder:
    When now already the sun, in pale display
Standing by Paul's high dome, spread forth below
His sparkling beams, and awoke the stir of the day.
    For now doors open, and war is waged with the snow;
And trains of somber men, past tale of number
Tread long brown paths, as toward their toil they go:
    But even for them awhile no cares encumber
Their minds diverted; the daily word is unspoken,
The daily thoughts of labour and sorrow slumber
At the sight of the beauty that greets them, for the charm they have
   broken. (*1880*)

ON A DEAD CHILD

Perfect little body, without fault or stain on thee,
    With promise of strength and manhood full and fair!
        Though cold and stark and bare,
The bloom and the charm of life doth awhile remain on thee.

Thy mother's treasure wert thou;—alas! no longer
    To visit her heart with wondrous joy; to be

Thy father's pride;—ah, he
Must gather his faith together, and his strength make stronger.

To me, as I move thee now in the last duty,
    Dost thou with a turn or gesture anon respond;
        Startling my fancy fond
With a chance attitude of the head, a freak of beauty.

Thy hand clasps, as 'twas wont, my finger, and holds it:
    But the grasp is the clasp of Death, heartbreaking and stiff;
        Yet feels to my hand as if
'Twas still thy will, thy pleasure and trust that enfolds it.

So I lay thee there, thy sunken eyelids closing,—
    Go lie thou there in thy coffin, thy last little bed!—
        Propping thy wise, sad head,
Thy firm, pale hands across thy chest disposing.

So quiet! does the change content thee?—Death, whither hath he taken
    thee?
    To a world, do I think, that rights the disaster of this?
        The vision of which I miss,
Who weep for the body, and wish but to warm thee and awaken thee?

Ah! little at best can all our hopes avail us
    To lift this sorrow, or cheer us, when in the dark,
        Unwilling, alone we embark,
And the things we have seen and have known and have heard of,
    fail us. (1880)

[THE EVENING DARKENS OVER]

The evening darkens over
After a day so bright
The windcapt waves discover
That wild will be the night.
There's sound of distant thunder.

The latest sea-birds hover
Along the cliff's sheer height;
As in the memory wander
Last flutterings of delight,
White wings lost on the white.

There's not a ship in sight;
And as the sun goes under
Thick clouds conspire to cover
The moon that should rise yonder.
Thou art alone, fond lover. *(1890)*

[I LOVE ALL BEAUTEOUS THINGS]

I love all beauteous things,
    I seek and adore them;
God hath no better praise,
And man in his hasty days
    Is honoured for them.

I too will something make
    And joy in the making;
Although to-morrow it seem
Like the empty words of a dream
    Remembered on waking. *(1890)*

[I NEVER SHALL LOVE THE SNOW AGAIN]

I never shall love the snow again
    Since Maurice died:
With corniced drift it blocked the lane
And sheeted in a desolate plain
    The country side.

The trees with silvery rime bedight
    Their branches bare.
By day no sun appeared; by night
The hidden moon shed thievish light
    In the misty air.

We fed the birds that flew around
    In flocks to be fed:
No shelter in holly or brake they found.
The speckled thrush on the frozen ground
    Lay frozen and dead.

We skated on stream and pond; we cut
    The crinching snow
To Doric temple or Arctic hut;

We laughed and sang at nightfall, shut
    By the fireside glow.

Yet grudged we our keen delights before
    Maurice should come.
We said, In-door or out-of-door
We shall love life for a month or more,
    When he is home.

They brought him home; 'twas two days late
    For Christmas day:
Wrapped in white, in solemn state,
A flower in his hand, all still and straight
    Our Maurice lay.

And two days ere the year outgave
    We laid him low.
The best of us truly were not brave,
When we laid Maurice down in his grave
    Under the snow. (1893)

NIGHTINGALES

Beautiful must be the mountains whence ye come,
And bright in the fruitful valleys the streams, wherefrom
    Ye learn your song:
Where are those starry woods? O might I wander there,
    Among the flowers, which in that heavenly air
    Bloom the year long!

Nay, barren are those mountains and spent the streams:
Our song is the voice of desire, that haunts our dreams,
    A throe of the heart,
Whose pining visions dim, forbidden hopes profound,
    No dying cadence nor long sigh can sound,
    For all our art.

Alone, aloud in the raptured ear of men
We pour our dark nocturnal secret; and then,
    As night is withdrawn
From these sweet-springing meads and bursting boughs of May,
    Dream, while the innumerable choir of day
    Welcome the dawn. (1893)

[WHO HAS NOT WALKED UPON THE SHORE]

Who has not walked upon the shore,
And who does not the morning know,
The day the angry gale is o'er,
The hour the wind has ceased to blow?

The horses of the strong southwest
Are pastured round his tropic tent,
Careless how long the ocean's breast
Sob on and sigh for passion spent.

The frightened birds, that fled inland
To house in rock and tower and tree,
Are gathering on the peaceful strand,
To tempt again the sunny sea;

Whereon the timid ships steal out
And laugh to find their foe asleep,
That lately scattered them about,
And drave them to the fold like sheep.

The snow-white clouds he northward chased
Break into phalanx, line, and band:
All one way to the south they haste,
The south, their pleasant fatherland.

From distant hills their shadows creep,
Arrive in turn and mount the lea,
And flit across the downs, and leap
Sheer off the cliff upon the sea;

And sail and sail far out of sight.
But still I watch their fleecy trains,
That piling all the south with light,
Dapple in France the fertile plains. *(1873, 1894)*

[MY DELIGHT AND THY DELIGHT]

My delight and thy delight
Walking, like two angels white,
In the gardens of the night:

My desire and thy desire
Twining to a tongue of fire,
Leaping live, and laughing higher;
Thro' the everlasting strife
In the mystery of life.

Love, from whom the world begun,
Hath the secret of the sun.

Love can tell, and love alone
Whence the million stars were strewn,
Why each atom knows its own,
How, in spite of woe and death,
Gay is life, and sweet is breath:

This he taught us, this we knew,
Happy in his science true,
Hand in hand as we stood
Neath the shadows of the wood,
Heart to heart as we lay
In the dawning of the day.   (1899)

PATER FILIO

Sense with keenest edge unusèd,
    Yet unsteel'd by scathing fire;
Lovely feet as yet unbruisèd
    On the ways of dark desire;
Sweetest hope that lookest smiling
O'er the wilderness defiling!

Why such beauty, to be blighted
    By the swarm of foul destruction?
Why such innocence delighted,
    When sin stalks to thy seduction?
All the litanies e'er chaunted
Shall not keep thy faith undaunted.

I have pray'd the sainted Morning
    To unclasp her hands to hold thee;
From resignful Eve's adorning
    Stol'n a robe of peace to enfold thee;
With all charms of man's contriving
Arm'd thee for thy lonely striving.

Me too once unthinking Nature
　—Whence Love's timeless mockery took me,—
Fashion'd so divine a creature,
　Yea, and like a beast forsook me.
I forgave, but tell the measure
Of her crime in thee, my treasure.   *(1899)*

EROS

Why hast thou nothing in thy face?
Thou idol of the human race,
Thou tyrant of the human heart,
The flower of lovely youth that art;
Yea, and that standest in thy youth
An image of eternal Truth,
With thy exuberant flesh so fair,
That only Pheidias might compare,
Ere from his chaste marmoreal form
Time had decayed the colours warm;
Like to his gods in thy proud dress,
Thy starry sheen of nakedness.

Surely thy body is thy mind,
For in thy face is nought to find,
Only thy soft unchristen'd smile,
That shadows neither love nor guile,
But shameless will and power immense,
In secret sensuous innocence.

O king of joy, what is thy thought?
I dream thou knowest it is nought,
And wouldst in darkness come, but thou
Makest the light where'er thou go.
Ah yet no victim of thy grace,
None who e'er long'd for thy embrace,
Hath cared to look upon thy face.   *(1899)*

MELANCHOLIA

The sickness of desire, that in dark days
Looks on the imagination of despair,
Forgetteth man, and stinteth God his praise;
Nor but in sleep findeth a cure for care.
　Incertainty that once gave scope to dream

Of laughing enterprise and glory untold,
Is now a blackness that no stars redeem,
A wall of terror in a night of cold.

Fool! thou that hast impossibly desired
And now impatiently despairest, see
How nought is changed: Joy's wisdom is attired
Splendid for others' eyes if not for thee:
Not love or beauty or youth from earth is fled:
If they delight thee not, 'tis thou art dead.   (*1905*)

JOHANNES MILTON, SENEX

SCAZONS

Since I believe in God the Father Almighty,
Man's Maker and Judge, Overruler of Fortune,
'Twere strange should I praise anything and refuse Him praise,
Should love the creature forgetting the Crēator,
Nor unto Him⌄in suff'ring and sorrow turn me:
Nay how coud I withdraw me from⌄His embracing?

But since that I have seen not, and cannot know Him,
Nor in my earthly temple apprehend rightly
His wisdom and the heav'nly purpose ēternal;
Therefore will I be bound to no studied system
Nor argument, nor with delusion enslave me,
Nor seek to pleáse Him in any foolish invention,
Which my spirit within me, that loveth beauty
And hateth evil, hath reprov'd as unworthy:

But I cherish my freedom in loving service,
Gratefully adoring for delight beyond asking
Or thinking, and in hours of anguish and darkness
Confiding always on⌄His excellent greatness.   (*1914*)

LOW BAROMETER

The south-wind strengthens to a gale,
Across the moon the clouds fly fast,
The house is smitten as with a flail,
The chimney shudders to the blast.

On such a night, when Air has loosed
Its guardian grasp on blood and brain,
Old terrors then of god or ghost
Creep from their caves to life again;

And Reason kens he herits in
A haunted house. Tenants unknown
Assert their squalid lease of sin
With earlier title than his own.

Unbodied presences, the pack'd
Pollution and remorse of Time,
Slipp'd from oblivion reënact
The horrors of unhouseld crime.

Some men would quell the thing with prayer
Whose sightless footsteps pad the floor,
Whose fearful trespass mounts the stair
Or bursts the lock'd forbidden door.

Some have seen corpses long interr'd
Escape from hallowing control,
Pale charnel forms—nay ev'n have heard
The shrilling of a troubled soul,

That wanders till the dawn hath cross'd
The dolorous dark, or Earth hath wound
Closer her storm-spredd cloke, and thrust
The baleful phantoms underground.   (*1925*)

A. E. Housman
(1859–1936)

[INTO MY HEART AN AIR THAT KILLS]

Into my heart an air that kills
　From yon far country blows:
What are those blue remembered hills,
　What spires, what farms are those?

That is the land of lost content,
　I see it shining plain,
The happy highways where I went
　And cannot come again.　*(c. 1890, 1896)*

[WITH RUE MY HEART IS LADEN]

With rue my heart is laden
　For golden friends I had,
For many a rose-lipt maiden
　And many a lightfoot lad.

By brooks too broad for leaping
　The lightfoot boys are laid;
The rose-lipt girls are sleeping
　In fields where roses fade.　*(August 1893, 1896)*

[FROM FAR, FROM EVE AND MORNING]

From far, from eve and morning
　And yon twelve-winded sky,
The stuff of life to knit me
　Blew hither: here am I.

Now—for a breath I tarry
　Nor yet disperse apart—
Take my hand quick and tell me,
　What have you in your heart.

Speak now, and I will answer;
    How shall I help you, say;
Ere to the wind's twelve quarters
    I take my endless way. *(c. 1893, 1896)*

[WHITE IN THE MOON THE LONG ROAD LIES]

White in the moon the long road lies,
    The moon stands blank above;
White in the moon the long road lies
    That leads me from my love.

Still hangs the hedge without a gust,
    Still, still the shadows stay:
My feet upon the moonlit dust
    Pursue the ceaseless way.

The world is round, so travellers tell,
    And straight though reach the track,
Trudge on, trudge on, 'twill all be well,
    The way will guide one back.

But ere the circle homeward hies
    Far, far must it remove:
White in the moon the long road lies
    That leads me from my love. *(1894, 1896)*

[FAREWELL TO BARN AND STACK AND TREE]

"Farewell to barn and stack and tree,
    Farewell to Severn shore.
Terence, look your last at me,
    For I come home no more.

"The sun burns on the half-mown hill,
    By now the blood is dried;
And Maurice amongst the hay lies still
    And my knife is in his side.

"My mother thinks us long away;
    'Tis time the field were mown.
She had two sons at rising day,
    To-night she'll be alone.

"And here's a bloody hand to shake,
  And oh, man, here's good-bye;
We'll sweat no more on scythe and rake,
  My bloody hands and I.

"I wish you strength to bring you pride,
  And a love to keep you clean,
And I wish you luck, come Lammastide,
  At racing on the green.

"Long for me the rick will wait,
  And long will wait the fold,
And long will stand the empty plate,
  And dinner will be cold."   *(August 1894, 1896)*

[WHEN I WAS ONE-AND-TWENTY]

When I was one-and-twenty
  I heard a wise man say,
"Give crowns and pounds and guineas
  But not your heart away;
Give pearls away and rubies
  But keep your fancy free."
But I was one-and-twenty,
  No use to talk to me.

When I was one-and-twenty
  I heard him say again,
"The heart out of the bosom
  Was never given in vain;
'Tis paid with sighs a plenty
  And sold for endless rue."
And I am two-and-twenty,
  And oh, 'tis true, 'tis true.   *(January 1895, 1896)*

REVEILLE

Wake: the silver dusk returning
  Up the beach of darkness brims,
And the ships of sunrise burning
  Strands upon the eastern rims.

Wake: the vaulted shadow shatters,
  Trampled to the floor it spanned,

And the tent of night in tatters
    Straws the sky-pavilioned land.

Up, lad, up, 'tis late for lying:
    Hear the drums of morning play;
Hark, the empty highways crying
    "Who'll beyond the hills away?"

Towns and countries woo together,
    Forelands beacon, belfries call;
Never lad that trod on leather
    Lived to feast his heart with all.

Up, lad: thews that lie and cumber
    Sunlit pallets never thrive;
Morns abed and daylight slumber
    Were not meant for man alive.

Clay lies still, but blood's a rover;
    Breath's a ware that will not keep.
Up, lad: when the journey's over
    There'll be time enough to sleep.

                     (January 1895, 1896)

[ON MOONLIT HEATH AND LONESOME BANK]

On moonlit heath and lonesome bank
    The sheep beside me graze;
And yon the gallows used to clank
    Fast by the four cross ways.

A careless shepherd once would keep
    The flocks by moonlight there,
And high amongst the glimmering sheep
    The dead man stood on air.

They hang us now in Shrewsbury jail:
    The whistles blow forlorn,
And trains all night groan on the rail
    To men that die at morn.

There sleeps in Shrewsbury jail to-night,
    Or wakes, as may betide,

A better lad, if things went right,
   Than most that sleep outside.

And naked to the hangman's noose
   The morning clocks will ring
A neck God made for other use
   Than strangling in a string.

And sharp the link of life will snap,
   And dead on air will stand
Heels that held up as straight a chap
   As treads upon the land.

So here I'll watch the night and wait
   To see the morning shine,
When he will hear the stroke of eight
   And not the stroke of nine;

And wish my friend as sound a sleep
   As lads' I did not know,
That shepherded the moonlit sheep
   A hundred years ago. *(February 1895, 1896)*

[WHEN I WATCH THE LIVING MEET]

When I watch the living meet,
   And the moving pageant file
Warm and breathing through the street
   Where I lodge a little while,

If the heats of hate and lust
   In the house of flesh are strong
Let me mind the house of dust
   Where my sojourn shall be long.

In the nation that is not
   Nothing stands that stood before;
There revenges are forgot,
   And the hater hates no more;

Lovers lying two and two
   Ask not whom they sleep beside,

And the bridegroom all night through
   Never turns him to the bride.
                   (c. February 1895, 1896)

[OTHERS, I AM NOT THE FIRST]

Others, I am not the first,
Have willed more mischief than they durst:
If in the breathless night I too
Shiver now, 'tis nothing new.

More than I, if truth were told,
Have stood and sweated hot and cold,
And through their reins in ice and fire
Fear contended with desire.

Agued once like me were they,
But I like them shall win my way
Lastly to the bed of mold
Where there's neither heat nor cold.

But from my grave across my brow
Plays no wind of healing now,
And fire and ice within me fight
Beneath the suffocating night.   *(1896)*

TO AN ATHLETE DYING YOUNG

The time you won your town the race
We chaired you through the market-place;
Man and boy stood cheering by,
And home we brought you shoulder-high.

To-day, the road all runners come,
Shoulder-high we bring you home,
And set you at your threshold down,
Townsman of a stiller town.

Smart lad, to slip betimes away
From fields where glory does not stay
And early though the laurel grows
It withers quicker than the rose.

Eyes the shady night has shut
Cannot see the record cut,
And silence sounds no worse than cheers
After earth has stopped the ears:

Now you will not swell the rout
Of lads that wore their honours out,
Runners whom renown outran
And the name died before the man.

So set, before its echoes fade,
The fleet foot on the sill of shade,
And hold to the low lintel up
The still-defended challenge-cup.

And round that early-laurelled head
Will flock to gaze the strengthless dead,
And find unwithered on its curls
The garland briefer than a girl's.   (c. March 1895, 1896)

[LOVELIEST OF TREES]

Loveliest of trees, the cherry now
Is hung with bloom along the bough,
And stands about the woodland ride
Wearing white for Eastertide.

Now, of my threescore years and ten,
Twenty will not come again,
And take from seventy springs a score,
It only leaves me fifty more.

And since to look at things in bloom
Fifty springs are little room,
About the woodlands I will go
To see the cherry hung with snow.

(c. May 1895, 1896)

[IS MY TEAM PLOUGHING]

"Is my team ploughing,
   That I was used to drive
And hear the harness jingle
   When I was a man alive?"

Ay, the horses trample,
  The harness jingles now;
No change though you lie under
  The land you used to plough.

"Is football playing
  Along the river shore,
With lads to chase the leather,
  Now I stand up no more?"

Ay, the ball is flying,
  The lads play heart and soul;
The goal stands up, the keeper
  Stands up to keep the goal.

"Is my girl happy,
  That I thought hard to leave,
And has she tired of weeping
  As she lies down at eve?"

Ay, she lies down lightly,
  She lies not down to weep:
Your girl is well contented.
  Be still, my lad, and sleep.

"Is my friend hearty,
  Now I am thin and pine,
And has he found to sleep in
  A better bed than mine?"

Yes, lad, I lie easy,
  I lie as lads would choose;
I cheer a dead man's sweetheart,
  Never ask me whose.   *(May–autumn 1895, 1896)*

[THINK NO MORE, LAD]

Think no more, lad; laugh, be jolly:
  Why should men make haste to die?
Empty heads and tongues a-talking
Make the rough road easy walking,
And the feather pate of folly
  Bears the falling sky.

Oh, 'tis jesting, dancing, drinking
   Spins the heavy world around.
If young hearts were not so clever,
Oh, they would be young for ever:
Think no more; 'tis only thinking
   Lays lads underground. *(c. September 1895, 1896)*

[TERENCE, THIS IS STUPID STUFF]

"Terence, this is stupid stuff:
You eat your victuals fast enough;
There can't be much amiss, 'tis clear,
To see the rate you drink your beer.
But oh, good Lord, the verse you make,
It gives a chap the belly-ache.
The cow, the old cow, she is dead;
It sleeps well, the hornèd head:
We poor lads, 'tis our turn now
To hear such tunes as killed the cow.
Pretty friendship 'tis to rhyme
Your friends to death before their time
Moping melancholy mad:
Come, pipe a tune to dance to, lad."

Why, if 'tis dancing you would be,
There's brisker pipes than poetry.
Say, for what were hop-yards meant,
Or why was Burton built on Trent?
Oh, many a peer of England brews
Livelier liquor than the Muse,
And malt does more than Milton can
To justify God's ways to man.
Ale, man, ale's the stuff to drink
For fellows whom it hurts to think:
Look into the pewter pot
To see the world as the world's not.
And faith, 'tis pleasant till 'tis past:
The mischief is that 'twill not last.
Oh, I have been to Ludlow fair
And left my necktie God knows where,
And carried half-way home, or near,
Pints and quarts of Ludlow beer:
Then the world seemed none so bad,

And I myself a sterling lad;
And down in lovely muck I've lain,
Happy till I woke again.
Then I saw the morning sky:
Heigho, the tale was all a lie;
The world, it was the old world yet,
I was I, my things were wet,
And nothing now remained to do
But begin the game anew.

Therefore, since the world has still
Much good, but much less good than ill,
And while the sun and moon endure
Luck's a chance, but trouble's sure,
I'd face it as a wise man would,
And train for ill and not for good.
'Tis true, the stuff I bring for sale
Is not so brisk a brew as ale:
Out of a stem that scored the hand
I wrung it in a weary land.
But take it: if the smack is sour,
The better for the embittered hour;
It should do good to heart and head
When your soul is in my soul's stead;
And I will friend you, if I may,
In the dark and cloudy day.

There was a king reigned in the East:
There, when kings will sit to feast,
They get their fill before they think
With poisoned meat and poisoned drink.
He gathered all that springs to birth
From the many-venomed earth;
First a little, thence to more,
He sampled all her killing store;
And easy, smiling, seasoned sound,
Sate the king when healths went round.
They put arsenic in his meat
And stared aghast to watch him eat;
They poured strychnine in his cup
And shook to see him drink it up:
They shook, they stared as white's their shirt:
Them it was their poison hurt.

—I tell the tale that I heard told.
Mithridates, he died old.   (c. *September 1895, 1986*)

[YONDER SEE THE MORNING BLINK]

Yonder see the morning blink:
   The sun is up, and up must I,
To wash and dress and eat and drink
And look at things and talk and think
   And work, and God knows why.

Oh, often have I washed and dressed
   And what's to show for all my pain?
Let me lie abed and rest:
Ten thousand times I've done my best
   And all's to do again.   (*December 1895, 1922*)

[THE CHESTNUT CASTS HIS FLAMBEAUX]

The chestnut casts his flambeaux, and the flowers
   Stream from the hawthorn on the wind away,
The doors clap to, the pane is blind with showers.
   Pass me the can, lad; there's an end of May.

There's one spoilt spring to scant our mortal lot,
   One season ruined of our little store.
May will be fine next year as like as not:
   Oh ay, but then we shall be twenty-four.

We for a certainty are not the first
   Have sat in taverns while the tempest hurled
Their hopeful plans to emptiness, and cursed
   Whatever brute and blackguard made the world.

It is in truth iniquity on high
   To cheat our sentenced souls of aught they crave,
And mar the merriment as you and I
   Fare on our long fool's-errand to the grave.

Iniquity it is; but pass the can.
   My lad, no pair of kings our mothers bore;
Our only portion is the estate of man:
   We want the moon, but we shall get no more.

If here to-day the cloud of thunder lours
    To-morrow it will hie on far behests;
The flesh will grieve on other bones than ours
    Soon, and the soul will mourn in other breasts.

The troubles of our proud and angry dust
    Are from eternity, and shall not fail.
Bear them we can, and if we can we must.
    Shoulder the sky, my lad, and drink your ale.
                            (*1896–1922, 1922*)

[NOW DREARY DAWNS THE EASTERN LIGHT]

Now dreary dawns the eastern light,
    And fall of eve is drear,
And cold the poor man lies at night,
    And so goes out the year.

Little is the luck I've had,
    And oh, 'tis comfort small
To think that many another lad
    Has had no luck at all.   (*1896–1922, 1922*)

[AS I GIRD ON FOR FIGHTING]

As I gird on for fighting
    My sword upon my thigh,
I think on old ill fortunes
    Of better men than I.

Think I, the round world over,
    What golden lads are low
With hurts not mine to mourn for
    And shames I shall not know.

What evil luck soever
    For me remains in store,
'Tis sure much finer fellows
    Have fared much worse before.

So here are things to think on
    That ought to make me brave,
As I strap on for fighting
    My sword that will not save. (*c. 1900, 1922*)

[THE RAIN, IT STREAMS ON STONE]

The rain, it streams on stone and hillock,
　The boot clings to the clay.
Since all is done that's due and right
Let's home; and now, my lad, good-night,
　For I must turn away.

Good-night, my lad, for nought's eternal;
　No league of ours, for sure.
To-morrow I shall miss you less,
And ache of heart and heaviness
　Are things that time should cure.

Over the hill the highway marches
　And what's beyond is wide:
Oh, soon enough will pine to nought
Remembrance and the faithful thought
　That sits the grave beside.

The skies, they are not always raining
　Nor grey the twelvemonth through;
And I shall meet good days and mirth,
And range the lovely lands of earth
　With friends no worse than you.

But oh, my man, the house is fallen
　That none can build again;
My man, how full of joy and woe
Your mother bore you years ago
　To-night to lie in the rain.   (*1902–22, 1922*)

EIGHT O'CLOCK

He stood, and heard the steeple
　Sprinkle the quarters on the morning town.
One, two, three, four, to market-place and people
　It tossed them down.

Strapped, noosed, nighing his hour,
　He stood and counted them and cursed his luck;
And then the clock collected in the tower
　Its strength, and struck.   (*1922*)

[WAKE NOT FOR THE WORLD-HEARD THUNDER]

Wake not for the world-heard thunder
  Nor the chime that earthquakes toll.
Star may plot in heaven with planet,
Lightning rive the rock of granite,
Tempest tread the oakwood under:
  Fear not you for flesh nor soul.
Marching, fighting, victory past,
Stretch your limbs in peace at last.

Stir not for the soldiers drilling
  Nor the fever nothing cures:
Throb of drum and timbal's rattle
Call but man alive to battle,
And the fife with death-notes filling
  Screams for blood but not for yours.
Times enough you bled your best;
Sleep on now, and take your rest.

Sleep, my lad; the French are landed,
  London's burning, Windsor's down;
Clasp your cloak of earth about you,
We must man the ditch without you,
March unled and fight short-handed,
  Charge to fall and swim to drown.
Duty, friendship, bravery o'er,
Sleep away, lad; wake no more.   *(March 1922, 1922)*

EPITAPH ON AN ARMY OF MERCENARIES

These, in the day when heaven was falling,
  The hour when earth's foundations fled,
Followed their mercenary calling
  And took their wages and are dead.

Their shoulders held the sky suspended;
  They stood, and earth's foundations stay;
What God abandoned, these defended,
  And saved the sum of things for pay.
                    (March 1922, 1922)

[THE NIGHT IS FREEZING FAST]

The night is freezing fast,
  To-morrow comes December;
    And winterfalls of old
Are with me from the past;
  And chiefly I remember
    How Dick would hate the cold.

Fall, winter, fall; for he,
  Prompt hand and headpiece clever,
    Has woven a winter robe,
And made of earth and sea
  His overcoat for ever,
    And wears the turning globe.   *(April 1922, 1922)*

FOR MY FUNERAL

O thou that from thy mansion
  Through time and place to roam,
Dost send abroad thy children,
  And then dost call them home,

That men and tribes and nations
  And all thy hand hath made
May shelter them from sunshine
  In thine eternal shade:

We now to peace and darkness
  And earth and thee restore
Thy creature that thou madest
  And wilt cast forth no more. *(1925, 1936)*

W. B. Yeats
(1865–1939)

THE STOLEN CHILD

Where dips the rocky highland
Of Sleuth Wood in the lake,
There lies a leafy island
Where flapping herons wake
The drowsy water-rats;
There we've hid our faery vats,
Full of berries
And of reddest stolen cherries.
Come away, O human child!
To the waters and the wild
With a faery, hand in hand,
For the world's more full of weeping than you can understand.

Where the wave of moonlight glosses
The dim grey sands with light,
Far off by furthest Rosses
We foot it all the night,
Weaving olden dances,
Mingling hands and mingling glances
Till the moon has taken flight;
To and fro we leap
And chase the frothy bubbles,
While the world is full of troubles
And is anxious in its sleep.
Come away, O human child!
To the waters and the wild
With a faery, hand in hand,
For the world's more full of weeping than you can understand.

Where the wandering water gushes
From the hills above Glen-Car,
In pools among the rushes

That scarce could bathe a star,
We seek for slumbering trout
And whispering in their ears
Give them unquiet dreams;
Leaning softly out
From ferns that drop their tears
Over the young streams.
Come away, O human child!
To the waters and the wild
With a faery, hand in hand,
For the world's more full of weeping than you can understand.

Away with us he's going,
The solemn-eyed:
He'll hear no more the lowing
Of the calves on the warm hillside
Or the kettle on the hob
Sing peace into his breast,
Or see the brown mice bob
Round and round the oatmeal-chest.
For he comes, the human child,
To the waters and the wild
With a faery, hand in hand,
From a world more full of weeping than he can understand.

(1889)

DOWN BY THE SALLEY GARDENS

Down by the salley gardens my love and I did meet;
She passed the salley gardens with little snow-white feet.
She bid me take love easy, as the leaves grow on the tree;
But I, being young and foolish, with her would not agree.

In a field by the river my love and I did stand,
And on my leaning shoulder she laid her snow-white hand.
She bid me take life easy, as the grass grows on the weirs;
But I was young and foolish, and now am full of tears. (1889)

THE ROSE OF THE WORLD

Who dreamed that beauty passes like a dream?
For these red lips, with all their mournful pride,
Mournful that no new wonder may betide,

Troy passed away in one high funeral gleam,
And Usna's children died.

We and the labouring world are passing by:
Amid men's souls, that waver and give place
Like the pale waters in their wintry race,
Under the passing stars, foam of the sky,
Lives on this lonely face.

Bow down, archangels, in your dim abode:
Before you were, or any hearts to beat,
Weary and kind, one lingered by His seat;
He made the world to be a grassy road
Before her wandering feet. (*1893*)

THE LAKE ISLE OF INNISFREE

I will arise and go now, and go to Innisfree,
And a small cabin build there, of clay and wattles made:
Nine bean-rows will I have there, a hive for the honey-bee,
And live alone in the bee-loud glade.

And I shall have some peace there, for peace comes dropping slow,
Dropping from the veils of the morning to where the cricket sings;
There midnight's all a glimmer, and noon a purple glow,
And evening full of the linnet's wings.

I will arise and go now, for always night and day
I hear lake water lapping with low sounds by the shore;
While I stand on the roadway, or on the pavements grey,
I hear it in the deep heart's core. (*1890, 1893*)

THE PITY OF LOVE

A pity beyond all telling
Is hid in the heart of love:
The folk who are buying and selling,
The clouds on their journey above,
The cold wet winds ever blowing,
And the shadowy hazel grove
Where mouse-grey waters are flowing,
Threaten the head that I love. (*1893*)

WHEN YOU ARE OLD

[handwritten: FAILED ROMANCE]

[handwritten left margin: HE LOVED HER THROUGH CHANGES & SORROWS OF LIFE - NOT ONLY WHEN SHE WAS YOUNG & BEAUTIFUL -]

When you are old and grey and full of sleep,
And nodding by the fire, take down this book,
And slowly read, and dream of the soft look
Your eyes had once, and of their shadows deep;

How many loved your moments of glad grace,
And loved your beauty with love false or true,
But one man loved the pilgrim soul in you,
And loved the sorrows of your changing face;

[handwritten right margin: HIS LOVE IS MORE ENDURING THAN A MAN'S]

And bending down beside the glowing bars,
Murmur, a little sadly, how Love fled
And paced upon the mountains overhead
And hid his face amid a crowd of stars.   (*1893*)

WHO GOES WITH FERGUS?

Who will go drive with Fergus now,
And pierce the deep wood's woven shade,
And dance upon the level shore?
Young man, lift up your russet brow,
And lift your tender eyelids, maid,
And brood on hopes and fear no more.

And no more turn aside and brood
Upon love's bitter mystery;
For Fergus rules the brazen cars,
And rules the shadows of the wood,
And the white breast of the dim sea
And all dishevelled wandering stars.   (*1891, 1893*)

THE MAN WHO DREAMED OF FAERYLAND

He stood among a crowd at Dromahair;
His heart hung all upon a silken dress,
And he had known at last some tenderness,
Before earth took him to her stony care;
But when a man poured fish into a pile,
It seemed they raised their little silver heads,
And sang what gold morning or evening sheds
Upon a woven world-forgotten isle

Where people love beside the ravelled seas;
That Time can never mar a lover's vows
Under that woven changeless roof of boughs:
The singing shook him out of his new ease.

He wandered by the sands of Lissadell;
His mind ran all on money cares and fears,
And he had known at last some prudent years
Before they heaped his grave under the hill;
But while he passed before a plashy place,
A lug-worm with its grey and muddy mouth
Sang that somewhere to north or west or south
There dwelt a gay, exulting, gentle race
Under the golden or the silver skies;
That if a dancer stayed his hungry foot
It seemed the sun and moon were in the fruit:
And at that singing he was no more wise.

He mused beside the well of Scanavin,
He mused upon his mockers: without fail
His sudden vengeance were a country tale,
When earthy night had drunk his body in;
But one small knot-grass growing by the pool
Sang where—unnecessary cruel voice—
Old silence bids its chosen race rejoice,
Whatever ravelled waters rise and fall
Or stormy silver fret the gold of day,
And midnight there enfold them like a fleece
And lover there by lover be at peace.
The tale drove his fine angry mood away.

He slept under the hill of Lugnagall;
And might have known at last unhaunted sleep
Under that cold and vapour-turbaned steep,
Now that the earth had taken man and all:
Did not the worms that spired about his bones
Proclaim with that unwearied, reedy cry
That God has laid His fingers on the sky,
That from those fingers glittering summer runs
Upon the dancer by the dreamless wave.
Why should those lovers that no lovers miss
Dream, until God burn Nature with a kiss?
The man has found no comfort in the grave.   (1893)

HE WISHES FOR THE CLOTHS OF HEAVEN

Had I the heavens' embroidered cloths,
Enwrought with golden and silver light,
The blue and the dim and the dark cloths
Of night and light and the half-light,
I would spread the cloths under your feet:
But I, being poor, have only my dreams;
I have spread my dreams under your feet;
Tread softly because you tread on my dreams. *(1899)*

THE LOVER TELLS OF THE ROSE IN HIS HEART

All things uncomely and broken, all things worn out and old,
The cry of a child by the roadway, the creak of a lumbering cart,
The heavy steps of the ploughman, splashing the wintry mould,
Are wronging your image that blossoms a rose in the deeps of my heart.

The wrong of unshapely things is a wrong too great to be told;
I hunger to build them anew and sit on a green knoll apart,
With the earth and the sky and the water, remade, like a casket of gold
For my dreams of your image that blossoms a rose in the deeps of my
  heart. *(1899)*

THE SONG OF WANDERING AENGUS

I went out to the hazel wood,
Because a fire was in my head,
And cut and peeled a hazel wand,
And hooked a berry to a thread;
And when white moths were on the wing,
And moth-like stars were flickering out,
I dropped the berry in a stream
And caught a little silver trout.

When I had laid it on the floor
I went to blow the fire aflame,
But something rustled on the floor,
And some one called me by my name:
It had become a glimmering girl
With apple blossom in her hair
Who called me by my name and ran
And faded through the brightening air.

Though I am old with wandering
Through hollow lands and hilly lands,
I will find out where she has gone,
And kiss her lips and take her hands;
And walk among long dappled grass,
And pluck till time and times are done
The silver apples of the moon,
The golden apples of the sun. (*1899*)

RED HANRAHAN'S SONG ABOUT IRELAND

The old brown thorn-trees break in two high over Cummen Strand,
Under a bitter black wind that blows from the left hand;
Our courage breaks like an old tree in a black wind and dies,
But we have hidden in our hearts the flame out of the eyes
Of Cathleen, the daughter of Houlihan.

The wind has bundled up the clouds high over Knocknarea,
And thrown the thunder on the stones for all that Maeve can say.
Angers that are like noisy clouds have set our hearts abeat;
But we have all bent low and low and kissed the quiet feet
Of Cathleen, the daughter of Houlihan.

The yellow pool has overflowed high up on Clooth-na-Bare,
For the wet winds are blowing out of the clinging air;
Like heavy flooded waters our bodies and our blood;
But purer than a tall candle before the Holy Rood
Is Cathleen, the daughter of Houlihan. (*1903*)

IN THE SEVEN WOODS

I have heard the pigeons of the Seven Woods
Make their faint thunder, and the garden bees
Hum in the lime-tree flowers; and put away
The unavailing outcries and the old bitterness
That empty the heart. I have forgot awhile
Tara uprooted, and new commonness
Upon the throne and crying about the streets
And hanging its paper flowers from post to post,
Because it is alone of all things happy.
I am contented, for I know that Quiet
Wanders laughing and eating her wild heart
Among pigeons and bees, while that Great Archer,

Who but awaits His hour to shoot, still hangs
A cloudy quiver over Pairc-na-lee. (*August 1902, 1903*)

NEVER GIVE ALL THE HEART

Never give all the heart, for love
Will hardly seem worth thinking of
To passionate women if it seem
Certain, and they never dream
That it fades out from kiss to kiss;
For everything that's lovely is
But a brief, dreamy, kind delight.
O never give the heart outright,
For they, for all smooth lips can say,
Have given their hearts up to the play.
And who could play it well enough
If deaf and dumb and blind with love?
He that made this knows all the cost,
For he gave all his heart and lost. (*1903*)

ADAM'S CURSE

We sat together at one summer's end,
That beautiful mild woman, your close friend,
And you and I, and talked of poetry.
I said: "A line will take us hours maybe;
Yet if it does not seem a moment's thought,
Our stitching and unstitching has been naught.
Better go down upon your marrow-bones
And scrub a kitchen pavement, or break stones
Like an old pauper, in all kinds of weather;
For to articulate sweet sounds together
Is to work harder than all these, and yet
Be thought an idler by the noisy set
Of bankers, schoolmasters, and clergymen
The martyrs call the world."

                                And thereupon
That beautiful mild woman for whose sake
There's many a one shall find out all heartache
On finding that her voice is sweet and low
Replied: "To be born woman is to know—
Although they do not talk of it at school—
That we must labour to be beautiful."

I said: "It's certain there is no fine thing
Since Adam's fall but needs much labouring.
There have been lovers who thought love should be
So much compounded of high courtesy
That they would sigh and quote with learned looks
Precedents out of beautiful old books;
Yet now it seems an idle trade enough."

We sat grown quiet at the name of love;
We saw the last embers of daylight die,
And in the trembling blue-green of the sky
A moon, worn as if it had been a shell
Washed by time's waters as they rose and fell
About the stars and broke in days and years.

I had a thought for no one's but your ears:
That you were beautiful, and that I strove
To love you in the old high way of love;
That it had all seemed happy, and yet we'd grown
As weary-hearted as that hollow moon.   *(1902, 1903)*

THE OLD MEN ADMIRING THEMSELVES IN THE WATER

I heard the old, old men say,
"Everything alters,
And one by one we drop away."
They had hands like claws, and their knees
Were twisted like the old thorn-trees
By the waters.
I heard the old, old men say,
"All that's beautiful drifts away
Like the waters."   *(1902, 1903)*

NO SECOND TROY

Why should I blame her that she filled my days
With misery, or that she would of late
Have taught to ignorant men most violent ways,
Or hurled the little streets upon the great,
Had they but courage equal to desire?
What could have made her peaceful with a mind
That nobleness made simple as a fire,
With beauty like a tightened bow, a kind
That is not natural in an age like this,
Being high and solitary and most stern?

Why, what could she have done, being what she is?
Was there another Troy for her to burn? (1908, 1910)

UPON A HOUSE SHAKEN BY THE LAND AGITATION

How should the world be luckier if this house,
Where passion and precision have been one
Time out of mind, became too ruinous
To breed the lidless eye that loves the sun?
And the sweet laughing eagle thoughts that grow
Where wings have memory of wings, and all
That comes of the best knit to the best? Although
Mean roof-trees were the sturdier for its fall,
How should their luck run high enough to reach
The gifts that govern men, and after these
To gradual Time's last gift, a written speech
Wrought of high laughter, loveliness and ease? (1909, 1910)

ALL THINGS CAN TEMPT ME

All things can tempt me from this craft of verse:
One time it was a woman's face, or worse—
The seeming needs of my fool-driven land;
Now nothing but comes readier to the hand
Than this accustomed toil. When I was young,
I had not given a penny for a song
Did not the poet sing it with such airs
That one believed he had a sword upstairs;
Yet would be now, could I but have my wish,
Colder and dumber and deafer than a fish. (1910)

BROWN PENNY

I whispered, "I am too young."
And then, "I am old enough";
Wherefore I threw a penny
To find out if I might love.
"Go and love, go and love, young man,
If the lady be young and fair."
Ah, penny, brown penny, brown penny,
I am looped in the loops of her hair.

O love is the crooked thing,
There is nobody wise enough

To find out all that is in it,
For he would be thinking of love
Till the stars had run away
And the shadows eaten the moon.
Ah, penny, brown penny, brown penny,
One cannot begin it too soon. (*1910*)

SEPTEMBER *1913*

What need you, being come to sense,
But fumble in a greasy till
And add the halfpence to the pence
And prayer to shivering prayer, until
You have dried the marrow from the bone?
For men were born to pray and save:
Romantic Ireland's dead and gone,
It's with O'Leary in the grave.

Yet they were of a different kind,
The names that stilled your childish play,
They have gone about the world like wind,
But little time had they to pray
For whom the hangman's rope was spun,
And what, God help us, could they save?
Romantic Ireland's dead and gone,
It's with O'Leary in the grave.

Was it for this the wild geese spread
The grey wing upon every tide;
For this that all that blood was shed,
For this Edward Fitzgerald died,
And Robert Emmet and Wolfe Tone,
All that delirium of the brave?
Romantic Ireland's dead and gone,
It's with O'Leary in the grave.

Yet could we turn the years again,
And call those exiles as they were
In all their loneliness and pain,
You'd cry, "Some woman's yellow hair
Has maddened every mother's son":
They weighed so lightly what they gave.
But let them be, they're dead and gone,
They're with O'Leary in the grave. (*1913, 1914*)

WHEN HELEN LIVED

We have cried in our despair
That men desert,
For some trivial affair
Or noisy, insolent sport,
Beauty that we have won
From bitterest hours;
Yet we, had we walked within
Those topless towers
Where Helen walked with her boy,
Had given but as the rest
Of the men and women of Troy,
A word and a jest.   *(1913, 1914)*

THE THREE HERMITS

Three old hermits took the air
By a cold and desolate sea,
First was muttering a prayer,
Second rummaged for a flea;
On a windy stone, the third,
Giddy with his hundredth year,
Sang unnoticed like a bird:
"Though the Door of Death is near
And what waits behind the door,
Three times in a single day
I, though upright on the shore,
Fall asleep when I should pray."
So the first, but now the second:
"We're but given what we have earned
When all thoughts and deeds are reckoned,
So it's plain to be discerned
That the shades of holy men
Who have failed, being weak of will,
Pass the Door of Birth again,
And are plagued by crowds, until
They've the passion to escape."
Moaned the other, "They are thrown
Into some most fearful shape."
But the second mocked his moan:
"They are not changed to anything,
Having loved God once, but maybe

To a poet or a king
Or a witty lovely lady."
While he'd rummaged rags and hair,
Caught and cracked his flea, the third,
Giddy with his hundredth year,
Sang unnoticed like a bird. *(1914)*

BEGGAR TO BEGGAR CRIED

"Time to put off the world and go somewhere
And find my health again in the sea air,"
Beggar to beggar cried, being frenzy-struck,
"And make my soul before my pate is bare."

"And get a comfortable wife and house
To rid me of the devil in my shoes,"
Beggar to beggar cried, being frenzy-struck,
"And the worse devil that is between my thighs."

"And though I'd marry with a comely lass,
She need not be too comely—let it pass,"
Beggar to beggar cried, being frenzy-struck,
"But there's a devil in a looking-glass."

"Nor should she be too rich, because the rich
Are driven by wealth as beggars by the itch,"
Beggar to beggar cried, being frenzy-struck,
"And cannot have a humorous happy speech."

"And there I'll grow respected at my ease,
And hear amid the garden's nightly peace,"
Beggar to beggar cried, being frenzy-struck,
"The wind-blown clamour of the barnacle-geese."

(1913, 1914)

THE MAGI

Now as at all times I can see in the mind's eye,
In their stiff, painted clothes, the pale unsatisfied ones
Appear and disappear in the blue depth of the sky
With all their ancient faces like rain-beaten stones,
And all their helms of silver hovering side by side,
And all their eyes still fixed, hoping to find once more,
Being by Calvary's turbulence unsatisfied,
The uncontrollable mystery on the bestial floor. *(1913, 1914)*

THE DOLLS

A doll in the doll-maker's house
Looks at the cradle and bawls:
"That is an insult to us."
But the oldest of all the dolls,
Who had seen, being kept for show,
Generations of his sort,
Out-screams the whole shelf: "Although
There's not a man can report
Evil of this place,
The man and the woman bring
Hither, to our disgrace,
A noisy and filthy thing."
Hearing him groan and stretch
The doll-maker's wife is aware
Her husband has heard the wretch,
And crouched by the arm of his chair,
She murmurs into his ear,
Head upon shoulder leant:
"My dear, my dear, O dear,
It was an accident." *(1913, 1914)*

A COAT

I made my song a coat
Covered with embroideries
Out of old mythologies
From heel to throat;
But the fools caught it,
Wore it in the world's eyes
As though they'd wrought it.
Song, let them take it,
For there's more enterprise
In walking naked. *(1912, 1914)*

THE WILD SWANS AT COOLE

The trees are in their autumn beauty,
The woodland paths are dry,
Under the October twilight the water
Mirrors a still sky;
Upon the brimming water among the stones
Are nine-and-fifty swans.

The nineteenth autumn has come upon me
Since I first made my count;
I saw, before I had well finished,
All suddenly mount
And scatter wheeling in great broken rings
Upon their clamorous wings.

I have looked upon those brilliant creatures,
And now my heart is sore.
All's changed since I, hearing at twilight,
The first time on this shore,
The bell-beat of their wings above my head,
Trod with a lighter tread.

Unwearied still, lover by lover,
They paddle in the cold
Companionable streams or climb the air;
Their hearts have not grown old;
Passion or conquest, wander where they will,
Attend upon them still.

But now they drift on the still water,
Mysterious, beautiful;
Among what rushes will they build,
By what lake's edge or pool
Delight men's eyes when I awake some day
To find they have flown away? *(1916, 1919)*

SOLOMON TO SHEBA

Sang Solomon to Sheba,
And kissed her dusky face,
"All day long from mid-day
We have talked in the one place,
All day long from shadowless noon
We have gone round and round
In the narrow theme of love
Like an old horse in a pound."

To Solomon sang Sheba,
Planted on his knees,
"If you had broached a matter
That might the learned please,

You had before the sun had thrown
Our shadows on the ground
Discovered that my thoughts, not it,
Are but a narrow pound."

Sang Solomon to Sheba,
And kissed her Arab eyes,
"There's not a man or woman
Born under the skies
Dare match in learning with us two,
And all day long we have found
There's not a thing but love can make
The world a narrow pound."   (1918, 1919)

TO A YOUNG BEAUTY

Dear fellow-artist, why so free
With every sort of company,
With every Jack and Jill?
Choose your companions from the best;
Who draws a bucket with the rest
Soon topples down the hill.

You may, that mirror for a school,
Be passionate, not bountiful
As common beauties may,
Who were not born to keep in trim
With old Ezekiel's cherubim
But those of Beauvarlet.

I know what wages beauty gives,
How hard a life her servant lives,
Yet praise the winters gone:
There is not a fool can call me friend,
And I may dine at journey's end
With Landor and with Donne.   (1918, 1919)

THE SCHOLARS

Bald heads forgetful of their sins,
Old, learned, respectable bald heads
Edit and annotate the lines
That young men, tossing on their beds,

Rhymed out in love's despair
To flatter beauty's ignorant ear.

All shuffle there; all cough in ink;
All wear the carpet with their shoes;
All think what other people think;
All know the man their neighbour knows.
Lord, what would they say
Did their Catullus walk that way? *(1915, 1919)*

TOM O'ROUGHLEY

"Though logic-choppers rule the town,
And every man and maid and boy
Has marked a distant object down,
An aimless joy is a pure joy,"
Or so did Tom O'Roughley say
That saw the surges running by,
"And wisdom is a butterfly
And not a gloomy bird of prey.

"If little planned is little sinned
But little need the grave distress.
What's dying but a second wind?
How but in zig-zag wantonness
Could trumpeter Michael be so brave?"
Or something of that sort he said,
"And if my dearest friend were dead
I'd dance a measure on his grave." *(1918, 1919)*

ON WOMAN

May God be praised for woman
That gives up all her mind,
A man may find in no man
A friendship of her kind
That covers all he has brought
As with her flesh and bone,
Nor quarrels with a thought
Because it is not her own.

Though pedantry denies,
It's plain the Bible means

That Solomon grew wise
While talking with his queens,
Yet never could, although
They say he counted grass,
Count all the praises due
When Sheba was his lass,
When she the iron wrought, or
When from the smithy fire
It shuddered in the water:
Harshness of their desire
That made them stretch and yawn,
Pleasure that comes with sleep,
Shudder that made them one.
What else He give or keep
God grant me—no, not here,
For I am not so bold
To hope a thing so dear
Now I am growing old,
But when, if the tale's true,
The Pestle of the moon
That pounds up all anew
Brings me to birth again—
To find what once I had
And know what once I have known,
Until I am driven mad,
Sleep driven from my bed,
By tenderness and care,
Pity, an aching head,
Gnashing of teeth, despair;
And all because of some one
Perverse creature of chance,
And live like Solomon
That Sheba led a dance. (1914, 1919)

THE FISHERMAN

Although I can see him still,
The freckled man who goes
To a grey place on a hill
In grey Connemara clothes
At dawn to cast his flies,
It's long since I began
To call up to the eyes
This wise and simple man.

All day I'd looked in the face
What I had hoped 'twould be
To write for my own race
And the reality;
The living men that I hate,
The dead man that I loved,
The craven man in his seat,
The insolent unreproved,
And no knave brought to book
Who has won a drunken cheer,
The witty man and his joke
Aimed at the commonest ear,
The clever man who cries
The catch-cries of the clown,
The beating down of the wise
And great Art beaten down.

Maybe a twelvemonth since
Suddenly I began,
In scorn of this audience,
Imagining a man,
And his sun-freckled face,
And grey Connemara cloth,
Climbing up to a place
Where stone is dark under froth,
And the down-turn of his wrist
When the flies drop in the stream;
A man who does not exist,
A man who is but a dream;
And cried, "Before I am old
I shall have written him one
Poem maybe as cold
And passionate as the dawn." (*1914, 1919*)

THE PEOPLE

"What have I earned for all that work," I said,
"For all that I have done at my own charge?
The daily spite of this unmannerly town,
Where who has served the most is most defamed,
The reputation of his lifetime lost
Between the night and morning. I might have lived,
And you know well how great the longing has been,
Where every day my footfall should have lit

In the green shadow of Ferrara wall;
Or climbed among the images of the past—
The unperturbed and courtly images—
Evening and morning, the steep street of Urbino
To where the duchess and her people talked
The stately midnight through until they stood
In their great window looking at the dawn;
I might have had no friend that could not mix
Courtesy and passion into one like those
That saw the wicks grow yellow in the dawn;
I might have used the one substantial right
My trade allows: chosen my company,
And chosen what scenery had pleased me best."
Thereon my phoenix answered in reproof,
"The drunkards, pilferers of public funds,
All the dishonest crowd I had driven away,
When my luck changed and they dared meet my face,
Crawled from obscurity, and set upon me
Those I had served and some that I had fed;
Yet never have I, now nor any time,
Complained of the people."

                   All I could reply
Was: "You, that have not lived in thought but deed,
Can have the purity of a natural force,
But I, whose virtues are the definitions
Of the analytic mind, can neither close
The eye of the mind nor keep my tongue from speech."
And yet, because my heart leaped at her words,
I was abashed, and now they come to mind
After nine years, I sink my head abashed. *(1915, 1919)*

A DEEP-SWORN VOW

Others because you did not keep
That deep-sworn vow have been friends of mine;
Yet always when I look death in the face,
When I clamber to the heights of sleep,
Or when I grow excited with wine,
Suddenly I meet your face. *(1915, 1919)*

EGO DOMINUS TUUS

Hic. On the grey sand beside the shallow stream
   Under your old wind-beaten tower, where still

A lamp burns on beside the open book
That Michael Robartes left, you walk in the moon,
And, though you have passed the best of life, still trace,
Enthralled by the unconquerable delusion,
Magical shapes.

Ille.   By the help of an image
   I call to my own opposite, summon all
   That I have handled least, least looked upon.

Hic. And I would find myself and not an image.

Ille. That is our modern hope, and by its light
   We have lit upon the gentle, sensitive mind,
   And lost the old nonchalance of the hand;
   Whether we have chosen chisel, pen or brush,
   We are but critics, or half create,
   Timid, entangled, empty and abashed,
   Lacking the countenance of our friends.

Hic.   And yet
   The chief imagination of Christendom,
   Dante Alighieri, so utterly found himself
   That he has made that hollow face of his
   More plain to the mind's eye than any face
   But that of Christ.

Ille.   And did he find himself,
   Or was the hunger that had made it hollow
   A hunger for the apple on the bough
   Most out of reach? and is that spectral image
   The man that Lapo and that Guido knew?
   I think he fashioned from his opposite
   An image that might have been a stony face
   Staring upon a Bedouin's horse-hair roof
   From doored and windowed cliff, or half upturned
   Among the coarse grass and the camel-dung.
   He set his chisel to the hardest stone.
   Being mocked by Guido for his lecherous life,
   Derided and deriding, driven out
   To climb that stair and eat that bitter bread,
   He found the unpersuadable justice, he found
   The most exalted lady loved by a man.

Hic. Yet surely there are men who have made their art
    Out of no tragic war, lovers of life,
    Impulsive men that look for happiness
    And sing when they have found it.

Ille.   No, not sing,
    For those that love the world serve it in action,
    Grow rich, popular and full of influence,
    And should they paint or write still it is action:
    The struggle of the fly in marmalade.
    The rhetorician would deceive his neighbors,
    The sentimentalist himself; while art
    Is but a vision of reality.
    What portion in the world can the artist have
    Who has awakened from the common dream
    But dissipation and despair?

Hic.   And yet
    No one denies to Keats love of the world;
    Remember his deliberate happiness.

Ille. His art is happy, but who knows his mind?
    I see a schoolboy when I think of him,
    With face and nose pressed to a sweet-shop window,
    For certainly he sank into his grave
    His senses and his heart unsatisfied,
    And made—being poor, ailing and ignorant,
    Shut out from all the luxury of the world,
    The coarse-bred son of a livery-stable keeper—
    Luxuriant song.

Hic.   Why should you leave the lamp
    Burning alone beside an open book,
    And trace these characters upon the sands?
    A style is found by sedentary toil
    And by the imitation of great masters.

Ille. Because I seek an image, not a book.
    Those men that in their writings are most wise
    Own nothing but their blind, stupefied hearts.
    I call to the mysterious one who yet
    Shall walk the wet sands by the edge of the stream
    And look most like me, being indeed my double,
    And prove of all imaginable things

The most unlike, being my anti-self,
And, standing by these characters, disclose
All that I seek; and whisper it as though
He were afraid the birds, who cry aloud
Their momentary cries before it is dawn,
Would carry it away to blasphemous men. *(1915, 1919)*

THE CAT AND THE MOON

The cat went here and there
And the moon spun round like a top,
And the nearest kin of the moon,
The creeping cat, looked up.
Black Minnaloushe stared at the moon,
For, wander and wail as he would,
The pure cold light in the sky
Troubled his animal blood.
Minnaloushe runs in the grass
Lifting his delicate feet.
Do you dance, Minnaloushe, do you dance?
When two close kindred meet,
What better than call a dance?
Maybe the moon may learn,
Tired of that courtly fashion,
A new dance turn.
Minnaloushe creeps through the grass
From moonlit place to place,
The sacred moon overhead
Has taken a new phase.
Does Minnaloushe know that his pupils
Will pass from change to change,
And that from round to crescent,
From crescent to round they range?
Minnaloushe creeps through the grass
Alone, important and wise,
And lifts to the changing moon
            His changing eyes. *(1917, 1919)*

TWO SONGS OF A FOOL

1

A speckled cat and a tame hare
Eat at my hearthstone
And sleep there;

And both look up to me alone
For learning and defence
As I look up to Providence.

I start out of my sleep to think
Some day I may forget
Their food and drink;
Or, the house door left unshut,
The hare may run till it's found
The horn's sweet note and the tooth of the hound.

I bear a burden that might well try
Men that do all by rule,
And what can I
That am a wandering-witted fool
But pray to God that He ease
My great responsibilities?

2

I slept on my three-legged stool by the fire,
The speckled cat slept on my knee;
We never thought to enquire
Where the brown hare might be,
And whether the door were shut.
Who knows how she drank the wind
Stretched up on two legs from the mat,
Before she had settled her mind
To drum with her heel and to leap?
Had I but awakened from sleep
And called her name, she had heard,
It may be, and had not stirred,
That now, it may be, has found
The horn's sweet note and the tooth of the hound.

(1918, 1919)

EASTER 1916

I have met them at close of day
Coming with vivid faces
From counter or desk among grey
Eighteenth-century houses.
I have passed with a nod of the head
Or polite meaningless words,
Or have lingered awhile and said

Polite meaningless words,
And thought before I had done
Of a mocking tale or a gibe
To please a companion
Around the fire at the club,
Being certain that they and I
But lived where motley is worn:
All changed, changed utterly:
A terrible beauty is born.

That woman's days were spent
In ignorant good-will,
Her nights in argument
Until her voice grew shrill.
What voice more sweet than hers
When, young and beautiful,
She rode to harriers?
This man had kept a school
And rode our wingèd horse;
This other his helper and friend
Was coming into his force;
He might have won fame in the end,
So sensitive his nature seemed,
So daring and sweet his thought.
This other man I had dreamed
A drunken, vainglorious lout.
He had done most bitter wrong
To some who are near my heart,
Yet I number him in the song;
He, too, has resigned his part
In the casual comedy;
He, too, has been changed in his turn,
Transformed utterly:
A terrible beauty is born.

Hearts with one purpose alone
Through summer and winter seem
Enchanted to a stone
To trouble the living stream.
The horse that comes from the road,
The rider, the birds that range
From cloud to tumbling cloud,
Minute by minute they change;

A shadow of cloud on the stream
Changes minute by minute;
A horse-hoof slides on the brim,
And a horse plashes within it;
The long-legged moor-hens dive,
And hens to moor-cocks call;
Minute by minute they live:
The stone's in the midst of all.

Too long a sacrifice
Can make a stone of the heart.
O when may it suffice?
That is Heaven's part, our part
To murmur name upon name,
As a mother names her child
When sleep at last has come
On limbs that had run wild.
What is it but nightfall?
No, no, not night but death;
Was it needless death after all?
For England may keep faith
For all that is done and said.
We know their dream; enough
To know they dreamed and are dead;
And what if excess of love
Bewildered them till they died?
I write it out in a verse—
MacDonagh and MacBride
And Connolly and Pearse
Now and in time to be,
Wherever green is worn,
Are changed, changed utterly:
A terrible beauty is born.   (*September 25, 1916; 1921*)

THE ROSE TREE

"O words are lightly spoken,"
Said Pearse to Connolly,
"Maybe a breath of politic words
Has withered our Rose Tree;
Or maybe but a wind that blows
Across the bitter sea."

"It needs to be but watered,"
James Connolly replied,
"To make the green come out again
And spread on every side,
And shake the blossom from the bud
To be the garden's pride."

"But where can we draw water,"
Said Pearse to Connolly,
"When all the wells are parched away?
O plain as plain can be
There's nothing but our own red blood
Can make a right Rose Tree." *(1917, 1921)*

THE SECOND COMING

Turning and turning in the widening gyre
The falcon cannot hear the falconer;
Things fall apart; the centre cannot hold;
Mere anarchy is loosed upon the world,
The blood-dimmed tide is loosed, and everywhere
The ceremony of innocence is drowned;
The best lack all conviction, while the worst
Are full of passionate intensity.

Surely some revelation is at hand;
Surely the Second Coming is at hand.
The Second Coming! Hardly are those words out
When a vast image out of *Spiritus Mundi*
Troubles my sight: somewhere in sands of the desert
A shape with lion body and the head of a man,
A gaze blank and pitiless as the sun,
Is moving its slow thighs, while all about it
Reel shadows of the indignant desert birds.
The darkness drops again; but now I know
That twenty centuries of stony sleep
Were vexed to nightmare by a rocking cradle,
And what rough beast, its hour come round at last,
Slouches towards Bethlehem to be born? *(1919, 1921)*

A PRAYER FOR MY DAUGHTER

Once more the storm is howling, and half hid
Under this cradle-hood and coverlid

My child sleeps on. There is no obstacle
But Gregory's wood and one bare hill
Whereby the haystack- and roof-levelling wind,
Bred on the Atlantic, can be stayed;
And for an hour I have walked and prayed
Because of the great gloom that is in my mind.

I have walked and prayed for this young child an hour
And heard the sea-wind scream upon the tower,
And under the arches of the bridge, and scream
In the elms above the flooded stream;
Imagining in excited reverie
That the future years had come,
Dancing to a frenzied drum,
Out of the murderous innocence of the sea.

May she be granted beauty and yet not
Beauty to make a stranger's eye distraught,
Or hers before a looking-glass, for such,
Being made beautiful overmuch,
Consider beauty a sufficient end,
Lose natural kindness and maybe
The heart-revealing intimacy
That chooses right, and never find a friend.

Helen being chosen found life flat and dull
And later had much trouble from a fool,
While that great Queen, that rose out of the spray,
Being fatherless could have her way
Yet chose a bandy-leggèd smith for man.
It's certain that fine women eat
A crazy salad with their meat,
Whereby the Horn of Plenty is undone.

In courtesy I'd have her chiefly learned;
Hearts are not had as a gift but hearts are earned
By those that are not entirely beautiful;
Yet many, that have played the fool
For beauty's very self, has charm made wise,
And many a poor man that has roved,
Loved and thought himself beloved,
From a glad kindness cannot take his eyes.

May she become a flourishing hidden tree
That all her thoughts may like the linnet be,
And have no business but dispensing round
Their magnanimities of sound,
Nor but in merriment begin a chase,
Nor but in merriment a quarrel.
Oh, may she live like some green laurel
Rooted in one dear perpetual place.

My mind, because the minds that I have loved,
The sort of beauty that I have approved,
Prosper but little, has dried up of late,
Yet knows that to be choked with hate
May well be of all evil chances chief.
If there's no hatred in a mind
Assault and battery of the wind
Can never tear the linnet from the leaf.

WORK BECOMING MORE INTELLECTUAL

An intellectual hatred is the worst,
So let her think opinions are accursed.
Have I not seen the loveliest woman born
Out of the mouth of Plenty's horn,
Because of her opinionated mind
Barter that horn and every good
By quiet natures understood
For an old bellows full of angry wind?

Considering that, all hatred driven hence,
The soul recovers radical innocence
And learns at last that it is self-delighting,
Self-appeasing, self-affrighting,
And that its own sweet will is Heaven's will;
She can, though every face should scowl
And every windy quarter howl
Or every bellows burst, be happy still.

And may her bridegroom bring her to a house
Where all's accustomed, ceremonious;
For arrogance and hatred are the wares
Peddled in the thoroughfares.
How but in custom and in ceremony
Are innocence and beauty born?
Ceremony's a name for the rich horn,
And custom for the spreading laurel tree.   *(June 1919, 1921)*

✗ SAILING TO BYZANTIUM

That is no country for old men. The young
In one another's arms, birds in the trees
—Those dying generations—at their song,
The salmon-falls, the mackerel-crowded seas,
Fish, flesh, or fowl, commend all summer long
Whatever is begotten, born, and dies.
Caught in that sensual music all neglect
Monuments of unaging intellect.

An aged man is but a paltry thing,
A tattered coat upon a stick, unless
Soul clap its hands and sing, and louder sing
For every tatter in its mortal dress,
Nor is there singing school but studying
Monuments of its own magnificence;
And therefore I have sailed the seas and come
To the holy city of Byzantium.

O sages standing in God's holy fire
As in the gold mosaic of a wall,
Come from the holy fire, perne in a gyre,
And be the singing-masters of my soul.
Consume my heart away; sick with desire
And fastened to a dying animal
It knows not what it is; and gather me
Into the artifice of eternity.

Once out of nature I shall never take
My bodily form from any natural thing,
But such a form as Grecian goldsmiths make
Of hammered gold and gold enamelling
To keep a drowsy emperor awake;
Or set upon a golden bough to sing
To lords and ladies of Byzantium
Of what is past, or passing, or to come.   (*1926, 1928*)

THE TOWER

1

What shall I do with this absurdity—
O heart, O troubled heart—this caricature,

Decrepit age that has been tied to me
As to a dog's tail?
          Never had I more
Excited, passionate, fantastical
Imagination, nor an ear and eye
That more expected the impossible—
No, not in boyhood when with rod and fly,
Or the humbler worm, I climbed Ben Bulben's back
And had the livelong summer day to spend.
It seems that I must bid the Muse go pack,
Choose Plato and Plotinus for a friend
Until imagination, ear and eye,
Can be content with argument and deal
In abstract things; or be derided by
A sort of battered kettle at the heel.

2

I pace upon the battlements and stare
On the foundations of a house, or where
Tree, like a sooty finger, starts from the earth;
And send imagination forth
Under the day's declining beam, and call
Images and memories
From ruin or from ancient trees,
For I would ask a question of them all.

Beyond that ridge lived Mrs. French, and once
When every silver candlestick or sconce
Lit up the dark mahogany and the wine,
A serving-man, that could divine
That most respected lady's every wish,
Ran and with the garden shears
Clipped an insolent farmer's ears
And brought them in a little covered dish.

Some few remembered still when I was young
A peasant girl commended by a song,
Who'd lived somewhere upon that rocky place,
And praised the colour of her face,
And had the greater joy in praising her,
Remembering that, if walked she there,
Farmers jostled at the fair
So great a glory did the song confer.

And certain men, being maddened by those rhymes,
Or else by toasting her a score of times,
Rose from the table and declared it right
To test their fancy by their sight;
But they mistook the brightness of the moon
For the prosaic light of day—
Music had driven their wits astray—
And one was drowned in the great bog of Cloone.

Strange, but the man who made the song was blind;
Yet, now I have considered it, I find
That nothing strange; the tragedy began
With Homer that was a blind man,
And Helen has all living hearts betrayed.
O may the moon and sunlight seem
One inextricable beam,
For if I triumph I must make men mad.

And I myself created Hanrahan
And drove him drunk or sober through the dawn
From somewhere in the neighbouring cottages.
Caught by an old man's juggleries
He stumbled, tumbled, fumbled to and fro
And had but broken knees for hire
And horrible splendour of desire;
I thought it all out twenty years ago:

Good fellows shuffled cards in an old bawn;
And when that ancient ruffian's turn was on
He so bewitched the cards under his thumb
That all but the one card became
A pack of hounds and not a pack of cards,
And that he changed into a hare.
Hanrahan rose in frenzy there
And followed up those baying creatures towards—

O towards I have forgotten what—enough!
I must recall a man that neither love
Nor music nor an enemy's clipped ear
Could, he was so harried, cheer;
A figure that has grown so fabulous
There's not a neighbour left to say
When he finished his dog's day:
An ancient bankrupt master of this house.

Before that ruin came, for centuries,
Rough men-at-arms, cross-gartered to the knees
Or shod in iron, climbed the narrow stairs,
And certain men-at-arms there were
Whose images, in the Great Memory stored,
Come with loud cry and panting breast
To break upon a sleeper's rest
While their great wooden dice beat on the board.

As I would question all, come all who can;
Come old, necessitous, half-mounted man;
And bring beauty's blind rambling celebrant;
The red man the juggler sent
Through God-forsaken meadows; Mrs. French,
Gifted with so fine an ear;
The man drowned in a bog's mire,
When mocking Muses chose the country wench.

Did all old men and women, rich and poor,
Who trod upon these rocks or passed this door,
Whether in public or in secret rage
As I do now against old age?
But I have found an answer in those eyes
That are impatient to be gone;
Go therefore; but leave Hanrahan,
For I need all his mighty memories.

Old lecher with a love on every wind,
Bring up out of that deep considering mind
All that you have discovered in the grave,
For it is certain that you have
Reckoned up every unforeknown, unseeing
Plunge, lured by a softening eye,
Or by a touch or a sigh,
Into the labyrinth of another's being;

Does the imagination dwell the most
Upon a woman won or a woman lost?
If on the lost, admit you turned aside
From a great labyrinth out of pride,
Cowardice, some silly over-subtle thought
Or anything called conscience once;
And that if memory recur, the sun's
Under eclipse and the day blotted out.

3

It is time that I wrote my will;
I choose upstanding men
That climb the streams until
The fountain leap, and at dawn
Drop their cast at the side
Of dripping stone; I declare
They shall inherit my pride,
The pride of people that were
Bound neither to Cause nor to State,
Neither to slaves that were spat on,
Nor to the tyrants that spat,
The people of Burke and of Grattan
That gave, though free to refuse—
Pride, like that of the morn,
When the headlong light is loose,
Or that of the fabulous horn,
Or that of the sudden shower
When all streams are dry,
Or that of the hour
When the swan must fix his eye
Upon a fading gleam,
Float out upon a long
Last reach of glittering stream
And there sing his last song.
And I declare my faith:
I mock Plotinus' thought
And cry in Plato's teeth,
Death and life were not
Till man made up the whole,
Made lock, stock and barrel
Out of his bitter soul,
Aye, sun and moon and star, all,
And further add to that
That, being dead, we rise,
Dream and so create
Translunar Paradise.
I have prepared my peace
With learned Italian things
And the proud stones of Greece,
Poet's imaginings
And memories of love,
Memories of the words of women,

All those things whereof
Man makes a superhuman
Mirror-resembling dream.

As at the loophole there
The daws chatter and scream,
And drop twigs layer upon layer.
When they have mounted up,
The mother bird will rest
On their hollow top,
And so warm her wild nest.

I leave both faith and pride
To young upstanding men
Climbing the mountain-side,
That under bursting dawn
They may drop a fly;
Being of that metal made
Till it was broken by
This sedentary trade.

Now shall I make my soul,
Compelling it to study
In a learned school
Till the wreck of body,
Slow decay of blood,
Testy delirium
Or dull decrepitude,
Or what worse evil come—
The death of friends, or death
Of every brilliant eye
That made a catch in the breath—
Seem but the clouds of the sky
When the horizon fades;
Or a bird's sleepy cry
Among the deepening shades.   (*1925, 1928*)

TWO SONGS FROM A PLAY

1

I saw a staring virgin stand
Where holy Dionysus died,
And tear the heart out of his side,

And lay the heart upon her hand
And bear that beating heart away;
And then did all the Muses sing
Of Magnus Annus at the spring,
As though God's death were but a play.

Another Troy must rise and set,
Another lineage feed the crow,
Another Argo's painted prow
Drive to a flashier bauble yet.
The Roman Empire stood appalled:
It dropped the reigns of peace and war
When that fierce virgin and her Star
Out of the fabulous darkness called.

2

In pity for man's darkening thought
He walked that room and issued thence
In Galilean turbulence;
The Babylonian starlight brought
A fabulous, formless darkness in;
Odour of blood when Christ was slain
Made all Platonic tolerance vain
And vain all Doric discipline.

Everything that man esteems
Endures a moment or a day.
Love's pleasure drives his love away,
The painter's brush consumes his dreams;
The herald's cry, the soldier's tread
Exhaust his glory and his might:
Whatever flames upon the night
Man's own resinous heart has fed.   (1928)

LEDA AND THE SWAN

A sudden blow: the great wings beating still
Above the staggering girl, her thighs caressed
By the dark webs, her nape caught in his bill,
He holds her helpless breast upon his breast.

How can those terrified vague fingers push
The feathered glory from her loosening thighs?

And how can body, laid in that white rush,
But feel the strange heart beating where it lies?

A shudder in the loins engenders there
The broken wall, the burning roof and tower
And Agamemnon dead.
                Being so caught up,
So mastered by the brute blood of the air,
Did she put on his knowledge with his power
Before the indifferent beak could let her drop?

(1923, 1928)

AMONG SCHOOL CHILDREN

I walk through the long schoolroom questioning;
A kind old nun in a white hood replies;
The children learn to cipher and to sing,
To study reading-books and history,
To cut and sew, be neat in everything
In the best modern way—the children's eyes
In momentary wonder stare upon
A sixty-year-old smiling public man.

I dream of a Ledæan body, bent
Above a sinking fire, a tale that she
Told of a harsh reproof, or trivial event
That changed some childish day to tragedy—
Told, and it seemed that our two natures blent
Into a sphere from youthful sympathy,
Or else, to alter Plato's parable,
Into the yolk and white of the one shell.

And thinking of that fit of grief or rage
I look upon one child or t'other there
And wonder if she stood so at that age—
For even daughters of the swan can share
Something of every paddler's heritage—
And had that colour upon cheek or hair,
And thereupon my heart is driven wild:
She stands before me as a living child.

Her present image floats into the mind—
Did Quattrocento finger fashion it

Hollow of cheek as though it drank the wind
And took a mess of shadows for its meat?
And I though never of Ledæan kind
Had pretty plumage once—enough of that,
Better to smile on all that smile, and show
There is a comfortable kind of old scarecrow.

What youthful mother, a shape upon her lap
Honey of generation had betrayed,
And that must sleep, shriek, struggle to escape
As recollection or the drug decide,
Would think her son, did she but see that shape
With sixty or more winters on its head,
A compensation for the pang of his birth,
Or the uncertainty of his setting forth?

Plato thought nature but a spume that plays
Upon a ghostly paradigm of things;
Solider Aristotle played the taws
Upon the bottom of a king of kings;
World-famous golden-thighed Pythagoras
Fingered upon a fiddle stick or strings
What a star sang and careless Muses heard:
Old clothes upon old sticks to scare a bird.

Both nuns and mothers worship images,
But those the candles light are not as those
That animate a mother's reveries,
But keep a marble or a bronze repose.
And yet they too break hearts—O Presences
That passion, piety or affection knows,
And that all heavenly glory symbolise—
O self-born mockers of man's enterprise;

Labour is blossoming or dancing where
The body is not bruised to pleasure soul,
Nor beauty born out of its own despair,
Nor blear-eyed wisdom out of midnight oil.
O chestnut-tree, great-rooted blossomer,
Are you the leaf, the blossom or the bole?
O body swayed to music, O brightening glance,
How can we know the dancer from the dance?   (1926, 1928)

A DIALOGUE OF SELF AND SOUL

1

My Soul. I summon to the winding ancient stair;
    Set all your mind upon the steep ascent,
    Upon the broken, crumbling battlement,
    Upon the breathless starlit air,
    Upon the star that marks the hidden pole;
    Fix every wandering thought upon
    That quarter where all thought is done:
    Who can distinguish darkness from the soul?

My Self. The consecrated blade upon my knees
    Is Sato's ancient blade, still as it was,
    Still razor-keen, still like a looking-glass
    Unspotted by the centuries;
    That flowering, silken, old embroidery, torn
    From some court-lady's dress and round
    The wooden scabbard bound and wound,
    Can, tattered, still protect, faded adorn.

My Soul. Why should the imagination of a man
    Long past his prime remember things that are
    Emblematical of love and war?
    Think of ancestral night that can,
    If but imagination scorn the earth
    And intellect its wandering
    To this and that and t'other thing,
    Deliver from the crime of death and birth.

My Self. Montashigi, third of his family, fashioned it
    Five hundred years ago, about it lie
    Flowers from I know not what embroidery—
    Heart's purple—and all these I set
    For emblems of the day against the tower
    Emblematical of the night,
    And claim as by a soldier's right
    A charter to commit the crime once more.

My Soul. Such fullness in that quarter overflows
    And falls into the basin of the mind
    That man is stricken deaf and dumb and blind,

For intellect no longer knows
Is from the *Ought,* or *Knower* from the *Known*—
That is to say, ascends to Heaven;
Only the dead can be forgiven;
But when I think of that my tongue's a stone.

2

My Self. A living man is blind and drinks his drop.
What matter if the ditches are impure?
What matter if I live it all once more?
Endure that toil of growing up;
The ignominy of boyhood; the distress
Of boyhood changing into man;
The unfinished man and his pain
Brought face to face with his own clumsiness;

The finished man among his enemies?—
How in the name of Heaven can he escape
That defiling and disfigured shape
The mirror of malicious eyes
Casts upon his eyes until at last
He thinks that shape must be his shape?
And what's the good of an escape
If honour find him in the wintry blast?

I am content to live it all again
And yet again, if it be life to pitch
Into the frog-spawn of a blind man's ditch,
A blind man battering blind men;
Or into that most fecund ditch of all,
The folly that man does
Or must suffer, if he woos
A proud woman not kindred of his soul.

I am content to follow to its source
Every event in action or in thought;
Measure the lot; forgive myself the lot!
When such as I cast out remorse
So great a sweetness flows into the breast
We must laugh and we must sing,
We are blest by everything,
Everything we look upon is blest.   (*1927, 1933*)

THREE MOVEMENTS

Shakespearean fish swam the sea, far away from land;
Romantic fish swam in nets coming to the hand;
What are all those fish that lie gasping on the strand?

(1932, 1933)

COOLE PARK AND BALLYLEE, 1931

Under my window-ledge the waters race,
Otters below and moor-hens on the top,
Run for a mile undimmed in Heaven's face
Then darkening through "dark" Raftery's "cellar" drop,
Run underground, rise in a rocky place
In Coole demesne, and there to finish up
Spread to a lake and drop into a hole.
What's water but the generated soul?

Upon the border of that lake's a wood
Now all dry sticks under a wintry sun,
And in a copse of beeches there I stood,
For Nature's pulled her tragic buskin on
And all the rant's a mirror of my mood:
At sudden thunder of the mounting swan
I turned about and looked where branches break
The glittering reaches of the flooded lake.

Another emblem there! That stormy white
But seems a concentration of the sky;
And, like the soul, it sails into the sight
And in the morning's gone, no man knows why;
And is so lovely that it sets to right
What knowledge or its lack had set awry,
So arrogantly pure, a child might think
It can be murdered with a spot of ink.

Sound of a stick upon the floor, a sound
From somebody that toils from chair to chair;
Beloved books that famous hands have bound,
Old marble heads, old pictures everywhere;
Great rooms where travelled men and children found
Content or joy; a last inheritor

Where none has reigned that lacked a name and fame
Or out of folly into folly came.

A spot whereon the founders lived and died
Seemed once more dear than life; ancestral trees,
Or gardens rich in memory glorified
Marriages, alliances, and families,
And every bride's ambition satisfied.
Where fashion or mere fantasy decrees
We shift about—all that great glory spent—
Like some poor Arab tribesman and his tent.

We were the last romantics—chose for theme
Traditional sanctity and loveliness;
Whatever's written in what poets name
The book of the people; whatever most can bless
The mind of man or elevate a rhyme;
But all is changed, that high horse riderless,
Though mounted in that saddle Homer rode
Where the swan drifts upon a darkening flood.   (1931, 1933)

FOR ANNE GREGORY

"Never shall a young man,
Thrown into despair
By those great honey-coloured
Ramparts at your ear,
Love you for yourself alone
And not your yellow hair."

"But I can get a hair-dye
And set such colour there,
Brown, or black, or carrot,
That young men in despair
May love me for myself alone
And not my yellow hair."

"I heard an old religious man
But yesternight declare
That he had found a text to prove
That only God, my dear,
Could love you for yourself alone
And not your yellow hair."   (1930, 1933)

SWIFT'S EPITAPH

Swift had sailed into his rest;
Savage indignation there
Cannot lacerate his breast.
Imitate him if you dare,
World-besotted traveller; he
Served human liberty. *(1933)*

THE CHOICE

The intellect of man is forced to choose
Perfection of the life, or of the work,
And if it take the second must refuse
A heavenly mansion, raging in the dark.
When all that story's finished, what's the news?
In luck or out the toil has left its mark:
That old perplexity an empty purse,
Or the day's vanity, the night's remorse. *(1933)*

BYZANTIUM

The unpurged images of day recede;
The Emperor's drunken soldiery are abed;
Night resonance recedes, night-walker's song
After great cathedral gong;
A starlit or a moonlit dome disdains
All that man is,
All mere complexities,
The fury and the mire of human veins.

Before me floats an image, man or shade,
Shade more than man, more image than a shade;
For Hades' bobbin bound in mummy-cloth
May unwind the winding path;
A mouth that has no moisture and no breath
Breathless mouths may summon;
I hail the superhuman;
I call it death-in-life and life-in-death.

Miracle, bird or golden handiwork,
More miracle than bird or handiwork,

Planted on the star-lit golden bough,
Can like the cocks of Hades crow,
Or, by the moon embittered, scorn aloud
In glory of changeless metal
Common bird or petal
And all complexities of mire or blood.

At midnight on the Emperor's pavement flit
Flames that no faggot feeds, nor steel has lit,
Nor storm disturbs, flames begotten of flame,
Where blood-begotten spirits come
And all complexities of fury leave,
Dying into a dance,
An agony of trance,
An agony of flame that cannot singe a sleeve.

Astraddle on the dolphin's mire and blood,
Spirit after spirit! The smithies break the flood,
The golden smithies of the Emperor!
Marbles of the dancing floor
Break bitter furies of complexity,
Those images that yet
Fresh images beget,
That dolphin-torn, that gong-tormented sea. (1930, 1933)

From WORDS FOR MUSIC PERHAPS

1

CRAZY JANE AND THE BISHOP

Bring me to the blasted oak
That I, midnight upon the stroke,
(*All find safety in the tomb.*)
May call down curses on his head
Because of my dear Jack that's dead.
Coxcomb was the least he said:
The solid man and the coxcomb.

Nor was he Bishop when his ban
Banished Jack the Journeyman,
(*All find safety in the tomb.*)
Nor so much as parish priest,
Yet he, an old book in his fist,

Cried that we lived like beast and beast:
The solid man and the coxcomb.

The Bishop has a skin, God knows,
Wrinkled like the foot of a goose,
(*All find safety in the tomb.*)
Nor can he hide in holy black
The heron's hunch upon his back,
But a birch-tree stood my Jack:
The solid man and the coxcomb.

Jack had my virginity,
And bids me to the oak, for he
(*All find safety in the tomb.*)
Wanders out into the night
And there is shelter under it,
But should that other come, I spit:
The solid man and the coxcomb.

2

CRAZY JANE REPROVED

I care not what the sailors say:
All those dreadful thunder-stones,
All that storm that blots the day
Can but show that Heaven yawns;
Great Europa played the fool
That changed a lover for a bull.
Fol de rol, fol de rol.

To round that shell's elaborate whorl,
Adorning every secret track
With the delicate mother-of-pearl,
Made the joints of Heaven crack:
So never hang your heart upon
A roaring, ranting journeyman.
Fol de rol, fol de rol.

3

CRAZY JANE ON THE DAY OF JUDGMENT

"Love is all
Unsatisfied
That cannot take the whole

Body and soul";
And that is what Jane said.

"Take the sour
If you take me,
I can scoff and lour
And scold for an hour."
"That's certainly the case," said he.

"Naked I lay,
The grass my bed;
Naked and hidden away,
That black day";
And that is what Jane said.

"What can be shown?
What true love be?
All could be known or shown
If Time were but gone."
"That's certainly the case," said he.

4

CRAZY JANE AND JACK THE JOURNEYMAN

I know, although when looks meet
I tremble to the bone,
The more I leave the door unlatched
The sooner love is gone,
For love is but a skein unwound
Between the dark and dawn.

A lonely ghost the ghost is
That to God shall come;
I—love's skein upon the ground,
My body in the tomb—
Shall leap into the light lost
In my mother's womb.

But were I left to lie alone
In an empty bed,
The skein so bound us ghost to ghost
When he turned his head
Passing on the road that night,
Mine must walk when dead.

5

CRAZY JANE ON GOD

That lover of a night
Came when he would,
Went in the dawning light
Whether I would or no;
Men come, men go,
All things remain in God.

Banners choke the sky;
Men-at-arms tread;
Armoured horses neigh
Where the great battle was
In the narrow pass:
All things remain in God.

Before their eyes a house
That from childhood stood
Uninhabited, ruinous,
Suddenly lit up
From door to top:
All things remain in God.

I had wild Jack for a lover;
Though like a road
That men pass over
My body makes no moan
But sings on;
All things remain in God.

6

CRAZY JANE TALKS WITH THE BISHOP

I met the Bishop on the road
And much said he and I.
"Those breasts are flat and fallen now,
Those veins must soon be dry;
Live in a heavenly mansion,
Not in some foul sty."

"Fair and foul are near of kin,
And fair needs foul," I cried.

"My friends are gone, but that's a truth
Nor grave nor bed denied,
Learned in bodily lowliness
And in the heart's pride.

"A woman can be proud and stiff
When on love intent;
But Love has pitched his mansion in
The place of excrement;
For nothing can be sole or whole
That has not been rent."

7

CRAZY JANE GROWN OLD LOOKS AT THE DANCERS

I found that ivory image there
Dancing with her chosen youth,
But when he wound her coal-black hair
As though to strangle her, no scream
Or bodily movement did I dare,
Eyes under eyelids did so gleam;
Love is like the lion's tooth.

When she, and though some said she played
I said that she had danced heart's truth,
Drew a knife to strike him dead,
I could but leave him to his fate;
For no matter what is said
They had all that had their hate;
Love is like the lion's tooth.

Did he die or did she die?
Seemed to die or died they both?
God be with the times when I
Cared not a thraneen for what chanced
So that I had the limbs to try
Such a dance as there was danced—
Love is like the lion's tooth.

17

AFTER LONG SILENCE

Speech after long silence; it is right,
All other lovers being estranged or dead,
Unfriendly lamplight hid under its shade,

The curtains drawn upon unfriendly night,
That we descant and yet again descant
Upon the supreme theme of Art and Song:
Bodily decrepitude is wisdom; young
We loved each other and were ignorant.

20

"I AM OF IRELAND"

"I am of Ireland,
And the Holy Land of Ireland,
And time runs on," cried she.
"Come out of charity,
Come dance with me in Ireland."

One man, one man alone
In that outlandish gear,
One solitary man
Of all that rambled there
Had turned his stately head.
"That is a long way off,
And time runs on," he said,
"And the night grows rough."

"I am of Ireland,
And the Holy Land of Ireland,
And time runs on," cried she.
"Come out of charity,
And dance with me in Ireland."

"The fiddlers are all thumbs,
Or the fiddle-string accursed,
The drums and the kettledrums
And the trumpets all are burst,
And the trombone," cried he,
"The trumpet and trombone,"
And cocked a malicious eye,
"But time runs on, runs on."

"I am of Ireland,
And the Holy Land of Ireland,
And time runs on," cried she.
"Come out of charity,
And dance with me in Ireland."   (1929, 1931, 1933)

From A WOMAN YOUNG AND OLD

6

CHOSEN

The lot of love is chosen. I learnt that much
Struggling for an image on the track
Of the whirling Zodiac.
Scarce did he my body touch,
Scarce sank he from the west
Or found a subterranean rest
Of the maternal midnight of my breast
Before I had marked him on his northern way,
And seemed to stand although in bed I lay.

I struggled with the horror of daybreak,
I chose it for my lot! If questioned on
My utmost pleasure with a man
By some new-married bride, I take
That stillness for a theme
Where his heart my heart did seem
And both adrift on the miraculous stream
Where—wrote a learned astrologer—
The Zodiac is changed into a sphere.

9

A LAST CONFESSION

What lively lad most pleasured me
Of all that with me lay?
I answer that I gave my soul
And loved in misery,
But had great pleasure with a lad
That I loved bodily.

Flinging from his arms I laughed
To think his passion such
He fancied that I gave a soul
Did but our bodies touch,
And laughed upon his breast to think
Beast gave beast as much.

I gave what other women gave
That stepped out of their clothes,

But when this soul, its body off,
Naked to naked goes,
He it has found shall find therein
What none other knows,

And give his own and take his own
And rule in his own right;
And though it loved in misery
Close and cling so tight,
There's not a bird of day that dare
Extinguish that delight.   (*1933*)

CHURCH AND STATE

Here is fresh matter, poet,
Matter for old age meet;
Might of the Church and the State,
Their mobs put under their feet.
O but heart's wine shall run pure,
Mind's bread grow sweet.

That were a cowardly song,
Wander in dreams no more;
What if the Church and the State
Are the mob that howls at the door!
Wine shall run thick to the end,
Bread taste sour.   (*August 1934, 1935*)

LAPIS LAZULI

I have heard that hysterical women say
They are sick of the palette and fiddle-bow,
Of poets that are always gay,
For everybody knows or else should know
That if nothing drastic is done
Aeroplane and Zeppelin will come out,
Pitch like King Billy bomb-balls in
Until the town lie beaten flat.

All perform their tragic play,
There struts Hamlet, there is Lear,
That's Ophelia, that Cordelia;
Yet they, should the last scene be there,
The great stage curtain about to drop,

If worthy their prominent part in the play,
Do not break up their lines to weep.
They know that Hamlet and Lear are gay;
Gaiety transfiguring all that dread.
All men have aimed at, found and lost;
Black out; Heaven blazing into the head:
Tragedy wrought to its uttermost.
Though Hamlet rambles and Lear rages,
And all the drop-scenes drop at once
Upon a hundred thousand stages,
It cannot grow by an inch or an ounce.

On their own feet they came, or on shipboard,
Camel-back, horse-back, ass-back, mule-back,
Old civilisations put to the sword.
Then they and their wisdom went to rack:
No handiwork of Callimachus,
Who handled marble as if it were bronze,
Made draperies that seemed to rise
When sea-wind swept the corner, stands;
His long lamp-chimney shaped like the stem
Of a slender palm, stood but a day;
All things fall and are built again,
And those that build them again are gay.

Two Chinamen, behind them a third,
Are carved in lapis lazuli,
Over them flies a long-legged bird,
A symbol of longevity;
The third, doubtless a serving-man,
Carries a musical instrument.

Every discoloration of the stone,
Every accidental crack or dent,
Seems a water-course or an avalanche,
Or lofty slope where it still snows
Though doubtless plum or cherry-branch
Sweetens the little half-way house
Those Chinamen climb towards, and I
Delight to imagine them seated there;
There, on the mountain and the sky,
On all the tragic scene they stare.
One asks for mournful melodies;
Accomplished fingers begin to play.

Their eyes mid many wrinkles, their eyes,
Their ancient, glittering eyes, are gay.   *(1936, 1938)*

AN ACRE OF GRASS

Picture and book remain,
An acre of green grass
For air and exercise,
Now strength of body goes;
Midnight, an old house
Where nothing stirs but a mouse.

My temptation is quiet.
Here at life's end
Neither loose imagination,
Nor the mill of the mind
Consuming its rag and bone,
Can make the truth known.

Grant me an old man's frenzy,
Myself must I remake
Till I am Timon and Lear
Or that William Blake
Who beat upon the wall
Till Truth obeyed his call;

A mind Michael Angelo knew
That can pierce the clouds,
Or inspired by frenzy
Shake the dead in their shrouds;
Forgotten else by mankind,
An old man's eagle mind.   *(1938)*

WHAT THEN?

His chosen comrades thought at school
He must grow a famous man;
He thought the same and lived by rule,
All his twenties crammed with toil;
"What then?" sang Plato's ghost. "What then?"

Everything he wrote was read,
After certain years he won
Sufficient money for his need,

Friends that have been friends indeed;
"What then?" sang Plato's ghost. "What then?"

All his happier dreams came true—
A small old house, wife, daughter, son,
Grounds where plum and cabbage grew,
Poets and Wits about him drew;
"What then?" sang Plato's ghost. "What then?"

"The work is done," grown old he thought,
"According to my boyish plan;
Let the fools rage, I swerved in naught,
Something to perfection brought;"
But louder sang that ghost, "What then?"   *(1938)*

THE WILD OLD WICKED MAN

"Because I am mad about women
I am mad about the hills,"
Said that wild old wicked man
Who travels where God wills.
"Not to die on the straw at home,
Those hands to close these eyes,
That is all I ask, my dear,
From the old man in the skies.
          Daybreak and a candle-end.

"Kind are all your words, my dear,
Do not the rest withhold.
Who can know the year, my dear,
When an old man's blood grows cold?
I have what no young man can have
Because he loves too much.
Words I have that can pierce the heart,
But what can he do but touch?"
          Daybreak and a candle-end.

Then said she to that wild old man,
His stout stick under his hand,
"Love to give or to withhold
Is not at my command.
I gave it all to an older man:
That old man in the skies.

Hands that are busy with His beads
Can never close those eyes."
                    Daybreak and a candle-end.

"Go your ways, O go your ways,
I choose another mark,
Girls down on the seashore
Who understand the dark;
Bawdy talk for the fishermen;
A dance for the fisher-lads;
When dark hangs upon the water
They turn down their beds.
                    Daybreak and a candle-end.

"A young man in the dark am I,
But a wild old man in the light,
That can make a cat laugh, or
Can touch by mother wit
Things hid in their marrow-bones
From time long passed away,
Hid from all those warty lads
That by their bodies lay.
                    Daybreak and a candle-end.

"All men live in suffering,
I know as few can know,
Whether they take the upper road
Or stay content on the low,
Rower bent in his row-boat
Or weaver bent at his loom,
Horseman erect upon horseback
Or child hid in the womb.
                    Daybreak and a candle-end.

"That some stream of lightning
From the old man in the skies
Can burn out that suffering
No right-taught man denies.
But a coarse old man am I,
I choose the second-best,
I forget it all awhile
Upon a woman's breast."
                    Daybreak and a candle-end. (1938)

THE GREAT DAY

Hurrah for revolution and more cannon-shot!
A beggar upon horseback lashes a beggar on foot.
Hurrah for revolution and cannon come again!
The beggars have changed places, but the lash goes on.

(1937, 1938)

PARNELL

Parnell came down the road, he said to a cheering man:
"Ireland shall get her freedom and you still break stone."

(1937, 1938)

A MODEL FOR THE LAUREATE

On thrones from China to Peru
All sorts of kings have sat
That men and women of all sorts
Proclaimed both good and great;
And what's the odds if such as these
For reason of the State
Should keep their lovers waiting,
    Keep their lovers waiting?

Some boast of beggar-kings and kings
Of rascals black and white
That rule because a strong right arm
Puts all men in a fright,
And drunk or sober live at ease
Where none gainsay their right,
And keep their lovers waiting,
    Keep their lovers waiting.

The Muse is mute when public men
Applaud a modern throne:
Those cheers that can be bought or sold,
That office fools have run,
That waxen seal, that signature,
For things like these what decent man
Would keep his lover waiting,
    Keep his lover waiting?   (1938)

THOSE IMAGES

What if I bade you leave
The cavern of the mind?
There's better exercise
In the sunlight and wind.

I never bade you go
To Moscow or to Rome.
Renounce that drudgery,
Call the Muses home.

Seek those images
That constitute the wild,
The lion and the virgin,
The harlot and the child.

Find in middle air
An eagle on the wing,
Recognise the five
That makes the Muses sing.   (1937, 1938)

NEWS FOR THE DELPHIC ORACLE

1

There all the golden codgers lay,
There the silver dew,
And the great water sighed for love,
And the wind sighed too.
Man-picker Niamh leant and sighed
By Oisin on the grass;
There sighed amid his choir of love
Tall Pythagoras.
Plotinus came and looked about,
The salt-flakes on his breast,
And having stretched and yawned awhile
Lay sighing like the rest.

2

Straddling each a dolphin's back
And steadied by a fin,
Those Innocents re-live their death,

Their wounds open again.
The ecstatic waters laugh because
Their cries are sweet and strange,
Through their ancestral patterns dance,
And the brute dolphins plunge
Until, in some cliff-sheltered bay
Where wades the choir of love
Proffering its sacred laurel crowns,
They pitch their burdens off.

3

Slim adolescence that a nymph has stripped,
Peleus on Thetis stares.
Her limbs are delicate as an eyelid,
Love has blinded him with tears;
But Thetis' belly listens.
Down the mountain walls
From where Pan's cavern is
Intolerable music falls.
Foul goat-head, brutal arm appear,
Belly, shoulder, bum,
Flash fishlike; nymphs and satyrs
Copulate in the foam.   (*1939*)

LONG-LEGGED FLY

That civilisation may not sink,
Its great battle lost,
Quiet the dog, tether the pony
To a distant post;
Our master Caesar is in the tent
Where the maps are spread,
His eyes fixed upon nothing,
A hand under his head.
Like a long-legged fly upon the stream
His mind moves upon silence.

That the topless towers be burnt
And men recall that face,
Move most gently if move you must
In this lonely place.
She thinks, part woman, three parts a child,
That nobody looks; her feet
Practice a tinker shuffle

Picked up on a street.
Like a long-legged fly upon the stream
Her mind moves upon silence.

That girls at puberty may find
The first Adam in their thought,
Shut the door of the Pope's chapel,
Keep those children out.
There on that scaffolding reclines
Michael Angelo.
With no more sound than the mice make
His hand moves to and fro.
Like a long-legged fly upon the stream
His mind moves upon silence.   (*1937, 1939*)

JOHN KINSELLA'S LAMENT FOR MRS. MARY MOORE

A bloody and a sudden end,
    Gunshot or a noose,
For Death who takes what man would keep,
    Leaves what man would lose.
He might have had my sister,
    My cousins by the score,
But nothing satisfied the fool
    But my dear Mary Moore,
None other knows what pleasures man
    At table or in bed.
What shall I do for pretty girls
    Now my old bawd is dead?

Though stiff to strike a bargain,
    Like an old Jew man,
Her bargain struck we laughed and talked
    And emptied many a can;
And O! but she had stories,
    Though not for the priest's ear,
To keep the soul of man alive,
    Banish age and care,
And being old she put a skin
    On everything she said.
What shall I do for pretty girls
    Now my old bawd is dead?

The priests have got a book that says
    But for Adam's sin

Eden's Garden would be there
    And I there within.
No expectation fails there,
    No pleasing habit ends,
No man grows old, no girl grows cold,
    But friends walk by friends.
Who quarrels over halfpennies
    That plucks the trees for bread?
What shall I do for pretty girls
    Now my old bawd is dead?   (1938, 1939)

THE APPARITIONS

Because there is safety in derision
I talked about an apparition,
I took no trouble to convince,
Or seem plausible to a man of sense,
Distrustful of that popular eye
Whether it be bold or sly.
Fifteen apparitions have I seen;
The worst a coat upon a coat-hanger.

I have found nothing half so good
As my long-planned half solitude,
Where I can sit up half the night
With some friend that has the wit
Not to allow his looks to tell
When I am unintelligible.
Fifteen apparitions have I seen;
The worst a coat upon a coat-hanger.

When a man grows old his joy
Grows more deep day after day,
His empty heart is full at length,
But he has need of all that strength
Because of the increasing Night
That opens her mystery and fright.
Fifteen apparitions have I seen;
The worst a coat upon a coat-hanger.   (1939)

THE STATESMAN'S HOLIDAY

I lived among great houses,
Riches drove out rank,

Base drove out the better blood,
And mind and body shrank.
No Oscar ruled the table,
But I'd a troop of friends
That knowing better talk had gone
Talked of odds and ends.
Some knew what ailed the world
But never said a thing,
So I have picked a better trade
And night and morning sing:
Tall dames go walking in grass-green Avalon.

Am I a great Lord Chancellor
That slept upon the Sack?
Commanding officer that tore
The khaki from his back?
Or am I de Valéra,
Or the King of Greece,
Or the man that made the motors?
Ach, call me what you please!
Here's a Montenegrin lute,
And its old sole string
Makes me sweet music
And I delight to sing:
Tall dames go walking in grass-green Avalon.

With boys and girls about him,
With any sort of clothes,
With a hat out of fashion,
With old patched shoes,
With a ragged bandit cloak,
With an eye like a hawk,
With a stiff straight back,
With a strutting turkey walk,
With a bag full of pennies,
With a monkey on a chain,
With a great cock's feather,
With an old foul tune.
Tall dames go walking in grass-green Avalon.   (1938, 1939)

CRAZY JANE ON THE MOUNTAIN

I am tired of cursing the Bishop,
(Said Crazy Jane)

Nine books or nine hats
Would not make him a man.
I have found something worse
To meditate on.
A King had some beautiful cousins,
But where are they gone?
Battered to death in a cellar,
And he stuck to his throne.
Last night I lay on the mountain,
(Said Crazy Jane)
There in a two-horsed carriage
That on two wheels ran
Great-bladdered Emer sat,
Her violent man
Cuchulain sat at her side;
Thereupon,
Propped upon my two knees,
I kissed a stone;
I lay stretched out in the dirt
And I cried tears down.   (1939)

THE CIRCUS ANIMALS' DESERTION

1

I sought a theme and sought for it in vain,
I sought it daily for six weeks or so.
Maybe at last, being but a broken man,
I must be satisfied with my heart, although
Winter and summer till old age began
My circus animals were all on show,
Those stilted boys, that burnished chariot,
Lion and woman and the Lord knows what.

2

What can I but enumerate old themes?
First that sea-rider Oisin led by the nose
Through three enchanted islands, allegorical dreams,
Vain gaiety, vain battle, vain repose,
Themes of the embittered heart, or so it seems,
That might adorn old songs or courtly shows;
But what cared I that set him on to ride,
I, starved for the bosom of his faery bride?

And then a counter-truth filled out its play,
The Countess Cathleen was the name I gave it;
She, pity-crazed, had given her soul away,
But masterful Heaven had intervened to save it.
I thought my dear must her own soul destroy,
So did fanaticism and hate enslave it,
And this brought forth a dream and soon enough
This dream itself had all my thought and love.

And when the Fool and Blind Man stole the bread
Cuchulain fought the ungovernable sea;
Heart-mysteries there, and yet when all is said
It was the dream itself enchanted me:
Character isolated by a deed
To engross the present and dominate memory.
Players and painted stage took all my love,
And not those things that they were emblems of.

3

Those masterful images because complete
Grew in pure mind, but out of what began?
A mound of refuse or the sweeping of a street,
Old kettles, old bottles, and a broken can,
Old iron, old bones, old rags, that raving slut
Who keeps the till. Now that my ladder's gone,
I must lie down where all the ladders start,
In the foul rag-and-bone shop of the heart. (*1939*)

POLITICS

"In our time the destiny of man presents its meaning in political terms."
—Thomas Mann

How can I, that girl standing there,
My attention fix
On Roman or on Russian
Or on Spanish politics?
Yet here's a travelled man that knows
What he talks about,
And there's a politician
That has read and thought,
And maybe what they say is true
Of war and war's alarms,

But O that I were young again
And held her in my arms! *(1938, 1939)*

CUCHULAIN COMFORTED

A man that had six mortal wounds, a man
Violent and famous, strode among the dead;
Eyes stared out of the branches and were gone.

Then certain Shrouds that muttered head to head
Came and were gone. He leant upon a tree
As though to meditate on wounds and blood.

A Shroud that seemed to have authority
Among those bird-like things came, and let fall
A bundle of linen. Shrouds by two and three

Came creeping up because the man was still.
And thereupon that linen-carrier said:
"Your life can grow much sweeter if you will

"Obey our ancient rule and make a shroud;
Mainly because of what we only know
The rattle of those arms makes us afraid.

"We thread the needles' eyes, and all we do
All must together do." That done, the man
Took up the nearest and began to sew.

"Now must we sing and sing the best we can,
But first you must be told our character:
Convicted cowards all, by kindred slain

"Or driven from home and left to die in fear."
They sang, but had nor human tunes nor words,
Though all was done in common as before;

They had changed their throats and had the throats of birds.
(1938–1939, 193

THE BLACK TOWER

Say that the men of the old black tower,
Though they but feed as the goatherd feeds,

Their money spent, their wine gone sour,
Lack nothing that a soldier needs,
That all are oath-bound men:
Those banners come not in.

There in the tomb stand the dead upright,
But winds come up from the shore:
They shake when the winds roar,
Old bones upon the mountain shake.

Those banners come to bribe or threaten,
Or whisper that a man's a fool
Who, when his own right king's forgotten,
Cares what king sets up his rule.
If he died long ago
Why do you dread us so?

There in the tomb drops the faint moonlight,
But wind comes up from the shore:
They shake when the winds roar,
Old bones upon the mountain shake.

The tower's old cook that must climb and clamber
Catching small birds in the dew of the morn
When we hale men lie stretched in slumber
Swears that he hears the king's great horn.
But he's a lying hound:
Stand we on guard oath-bound!

There in the tomb the dark grows blacker,
But wind comes up from the shore:
They shake when the winds roar,
Old bones upon the mountain shake.   (1939)

UNDER BEN BULBEN

1

Swear by what the sages spoke
Round the Mareotic Lake
That the Witch of Atlas knew,
Spoke and set the cocks a-crow.

Swear by those horsemen, by those women
Complexion and form prove superhuman,
That pale, long-visaged company
That air in immortality
Completeness of their passions won;
Now they ride the wintry dawn
Where Ben Bulben sets the scene.

Here's the gist of what they mean.

2

Many times man lives and dies
Between his two eternities,
That of race and that of soul,
And ancient Ireland knew it all.
Whether man die in his bed
Or the rifle knocks him dead,
A brief parting from those dear
Is the worst man has to fear.
Though grave-diggers' toil is long,
Sharp their spades, their muscles strong,
They but thrust their buried men
Back in the human mind again.

3

You that Mitchel's prayer have heard,
"Send war in our time, O Lord!"
Know that when all words are said
And a man is fighting mad,
Something drops from eyes long blind,
He completes his partial mind,
For an instant stands at ease,
Laughs aloud, his heart at peace.
Even the wisest man grows tense
With some sort of violence
Before he can accomplish fate,
Know his work or choose his mate.

4

Poet and sculptor, do the work,
Nor let the modish painter shirk
What his great forefathers did,
Bring the soul of man to God,

Make him fill the cradles right.

Measurement began our might:
Forms a stark Egyptian thought,
Forms that gentler Phidias wrought.
Michael Angelo left a proof
On the Sistine Chapel roof,
Where but half-awakened Adam
Can disturb globe-trotting Madam
Till her bowels are in heat,
Proof that there's a purpose set
Before the secret working mind:
Profane perfection of mankind.

Quattrocento put in paint
On backgrounds for a God or Saint
Gardens where a soul's at ease;
Where everything that meets the eye,
Flowers and grass and cloudless sky,
Resemble forms that are or seem
When sleepers wake and yet still dream,
And when it's vanished still declare,
With only bed and bedstead there,
That heavens had opened.
                              Gyres run on;
When that greater dream had gone
Calvert and Wilson, Blake and Claude,
Prepared a rest for the people of God,
Palmer's phrase, but after that
Confusion fell upon our thought.

5

Irish poets, learn your trade,
Sing whatever is well made,
Scorn the sort now growing up
All out of shape from toe to top,
Their unremembering hearts and heads
Base-born products of base beds.
Sing the peasantry, and then
Hard-riding country gentlemen,
The holiness of monks, and after
Porter-drinkers' randy laughter;
Sing the lords and ladies gay

That were beaten into the clay
Through seven heroic centuries;
Cast your mind on other days
That we in coming days may be
Still the indomitable Irishry.

6

Under bare Ben Bulben's head
In Drumcliff churchyard Yeats is laid.
An ancestor was rector there
Long years ago, a church stands near,
By the road an ancient cross.
No marble, no conventional phrase;
On limestone quarried near the spot
By his command these words are cut:

> *Cast a cold eye*
> *On life, on death.*
> *Horseman, pass by!*

(*September 4, 1938, 1939*)

PURGATORY

PERSONS IN THE PLAY

A Boy   An Old Man

[*Scene: a ruined house and a bare tree in the back-ground.*

BOY. Half-door, hall door,
   Hither and thither, day and night,
   Hill or hollow, shouldering this pack,
   Hearing you talk.
OLD MAN.   Study that house.
   I think about its jokes and stories;
   I try to remember what the butler
   Said to a drunken gamekeeper
   In mid-October, but I cannot.
   If I cannot, none living can.
   Where are the jokes and stories of a house,
   Its threshold gone to patch a pig-sty?
BOY.   So you have come this path before?

OLD MAN. The moonlight falls upon the path,
  The shadow of a cloud upon the house,
  And that's symbolical; study that tree,
  What is it like?
BOY.   A silly old man.
OLD MAN. It's like—no matter what it's like.
  I saw it a year ago stripped bare as now,
  So I chose a better trade.
  I saw it fifty years ago
  Before the thunderbolt had riven it,
  Green leaves, ripe leaves, leaves thick as butter,
  Fat, greasy life. Stand there and look,
  Because there is somebody in that house.

> *[The Boy puts down pack and stands in the door-
> way.*

BOY. There's nobody here.
OLD MAN.   There's somebody there.
BOY. The floor is gone, the window's gone,
  And where there should be roof there's sky,
  And here's a bit of an egg-shell thrown
  Out of a jackdaw's nest.
OLD MAN.   But there are some
  That do not care what's gone, what's left:
  The souls in Purgatory that come back
  To habitations and familiar spots.
BOY. Your wits are out again.
OLD MAN.   Re-live
  Their transgressions, and that not once
  But many times; they know at last
  The consequence of those transgressions
  Whether upon others or upon themselves;
  Upon others, others may bring help,
  For when the consequence is at an end
  The dream must end; if upon themselves,
  There is no help but in themselves
  And in the mercy of God.
BOY.   I have had enough!
  Talk to the jackdaws, if talk you must.
OLD MAN. Stop! Sit there upon that stone.
  That is the house where I was born.
BOY. The big old house that was burnt down?

OLD MAN.   My mother that was your grand-dam owned it,
 This scenery and this countryside,
 Kennel and stable, horse and hound—
 She had a horse at the Curragh, and there met
 My father, a groom in a training stable,
 Looked at him and married him.
 Her mother never spoke to her again,
 And she did right.
BOY.   What's right and wrong?
 My grand-dad got the girl and the money.
OLD MAN.   Looked at him and married him,
 And he squandered everything she had.
 She never knew the worst, because
 She died in giving birth to me,
 But now she knows it all, being dead.
 Great people lived and died in this house;
 Magistrates, colonels, members of Parliament,
 Captains and Governors, and long ago
 Men that had fought at Aughrim and the Boyne.
 Some that had gone on Government work
 To London or to India came home to die,
 Or came from London every spring
 To look at the may-blossom in the park.
 They had loved the trees that he cut down
 To pay what he had lost at cards
 Or spent on horses, drink and women;
 Had loved the house, had loved all
 The intricate passages of the house,
 But he killed the house; to kill a house
 Where great men grew up, married, died,
 I here declare a capital offence.
BOY.   My God, but you had luck! Grand clothes,
 And maybe a grand horse to ride.
OLD MAN.   That he might keep me upon his level
 He never sent me to school, but some
 Half-loved me for my half of her:
 A gamekeeper's wife taught me to read,
 A Catholic curate taught me Latin.
 There were old books and books made fine
 By eighteenth-century French binding, books
 Modern and ancient, books by the ton.
BOY.   What education have you given me?
OLD MAN.   I gave the education that befits

A bastard that a pedlar got
Upon a tinker's daughter in a ditch.
When I had come to sixteen years old
My father burned down the house when drunk.
BOY. But that is my age, sixteen years old,
At the Puck Fair.
OLD MAN.   And everything was burnt;
Books, library, all were burnt.
BOY. Is what I have heard upon the road the truth,
That you killed him in the burning house?
OLD MAN. There's nobody here but our two selves?
BOY. Nobody, Father.
OLD MAN.   I stuck him with a knife,
That knife that cuts my dinner now,
And after that I left him in the fire.
They dragged him out, somebody saw
The knife-wound but could not be certain
Because the body was all black and charred.
Then some that were his drunken friends
Swore they would put me upon trial,
Spoke of quarrels, a threat I had made.
The gamekeeper gave me some old clothes,
I ran away, worked here and there
Till I became a pedlar on the roads,
No good trade, but good enough
Because I am my father's son,
Because of what I did or may do.
Listen to the hoof-beats! Listen, listen!
BOY. I cannot hear a sound.
OLD MAN.   Beat! Beat!
This night is the anniversary
Of my mother's wedding night,
Or of the night wherein I was begotten.
My father is riding from the public-house,
A whiskey-bottle under his arm.

                    [*A window is lit showing a young girl.*

Look at the window; she stands there
Listening, the servants are all in bed,
She is alone, he has stayed late
Bragging and drinking in the public-house.
BOY. There's nothing but an empty gap in the wall.
You have made it up. No, you are mad!

You are getting madder every day.

OLD MAN.   It's louder now because he rides
Upon a gravelled avenue
All grass to-day. The hoof-beat stops,
He has gone to the other side of the house,
Gone to the stable, put the horse up.
She has gone down to open the door.
This night she is no better than her man
And does not mind that he is half drunk,
She is mad about him. They mount the stairs,
She brings him into her own chamber.
And that is the marriage-chamber now.
The window is dimly lit again.

Do not let him touch you! It is not true
That drunken men cannot beget,
And if he touch he must beget
And you must bear his murderer.
Deaf! Both deaf! If I should throw
A stick or a stone they would not hear;
And that's a proof my wits are out.
But there's a problem: she must live
Through everything in exact detail,
Driven to it by remorse, and yet
Can she renew the sexual act
And find no pleasure in it, and if not,
If pleasure and remorse must both be there,
Which is the greater?
                         I lack schooling.
Go fetch Tertullian; he and I
Will ravel all that problem out
Whilst those two lie upon the mattress
Begetting me.
                 Come back! Come back!
And so you thought to slip away,
My bag of money between your fingers,
And that I could not talk and see!
You have been rummaging in the pack.

        [*The light in the window has faded out.*

BOY.   You never gave me my right share.
OLD MAN.   And had I given it, young as you are,
You would have spent it upon drink.

BOY.   What if I did? I had a right
  To get it and spend it as I chose.
OLD MAN.   Give me that bag and no more words.
BOY.   I will not.
OLD MAN.   I will break your fingers.

> [*They struggle for the bag. In the struggle it drops,
> scattering the money. The Old Man staggers but
> does not fall. They stand looking at each other. The
> window is lit up. A man is seen pouring whiskey
> into a glass.*]

BOY.   What if I killed you? You killed my grand-dad,
  Because you were young and he was old.
  Now I am young and you are old.
OLD MAN.   [*staring at window*] Better-looking, those sixteen years—
BOY.   What are you muttering?
OLD MAN.   Younger—and yet
  She should have known he was not her kind.
BOY.   What are you saying? Out with it! [*Old man points to window.*]
  My God! The window is lit up
  And somebody stands there, although
  The floorboards are all burnt away.
OLD MAN.   The window is lit up because my father
  Has come to find a glass for his whiskey.
  He leans there like some tired beast.
BOY.   A dead, living, murdered man!
OLD MAN.   "Then the bride-sleep fell upon Adam":
  Where did I read those words?
              And yet
  There's nothing leaning in the window
  But the impression upon my mother's mind;
  Being dead she is alone in her remorse.
BOY.   A body that was a bundle of old bones
  Before I was born. Horrible! Horrible! [*He covers his eyes.*]
OLD MAN.   That beast there would know nothing, being nothing,
  If I should kill a man under the window
  He would not even turn his head. [*He stabs the* BOY.]
  My father and my son on the same jack-knife!
  That finishes—there—there—there—

> [*He stabs again and again. The window grows
> dark.*

"Hush-a-bye baby, thy father's a knight,

Thy mother a lady, lovely and bright."
No, that is something that I read in a book,
And if I sing it must be to my mother,
And I lack rhyme.

[*The stage has grown dark except where the tree
stands in white light.*

Study that tree.
It stands there like a purified soul,
All cold, sweet, glistening light.
Dear mother, the window is dark again,
But you are in the light because
I finished all that consequence.
I killed that lad because had he grown up
He would have struck a woman's fancy,
Begot, and passed pollution on.
I am a wretched foul old man
And therefore harmless. When I have stuck
This old jack-knife into a sod
And pulled it out all bright again,
And picked up all the money that he dropped,
I'll to a distant place, and there
Tell my old jokes among new men.

[*He cleans the knife and begins to pick up money.*

Hoof-beats! Dear God,
How quickly it returns—beat—beat—!

Her mind cannot hold up that dream.
Twice a murderer and all for nothing,
And she must animate that dead night
Not once but many times!
                    O God,
Release my mother's soul from its dream!
Mankind can do no more. Appease
The misery of the living and the remorse of the dead.
                    THE END

                                        (1939)

Walter de la Mare
(1873–1956)

THE SILVER PENNY

"Sailorman, I'll give to you
  My bright silver penny,
If out to sea you'll sail me
  And my dear sister Jenny."

"Get in, young sir, I'll sail ye
  And your dear sister Jenny,
But pay she shall her golden locks
  Instead of your penny."

They sail away, they sail away,
  O fierce the winds blew!
The foam flew in clouds,
  And dark the night grew!

And all the wild sea-water
  Climbed steep into the boat;
Back to the shore again
  Sail will they not.

Drowned is the sailorman,
  Drowned is sweet Jenny,
And drowned in the deep sea
  A bright silver penny.   *(1902)*

THE FUNERAL

They dressed us up in black,
Susan and Tom and me;
And, walking through the fields
All beautiful to see,
With branches high in the air

And daisy and buttercup,
We heard the lark in the clouds,—
In black dressed up.

They took us to the graves,
Susan and Tom and me,
Where the long grasses grow
And the funeral tree:
We stood and watched; and the wind
Came softly out of the sky
And blew in Susan's hair,
As I stood close by.

Back through the fields we came,
Tom and Susan and me,
And we sat in the nursery together,
And had our tea.
And, looking out of the window,
I heard the thrushes sing;
But Tom fell asleep in his chair.
He was so tired, poor thing. (*1902*)

THE THREE CHERRY TREES

There were three cherry trees once,
  Grew in a garden all shady;
And there for delight of so gladsome a sight,
  Walked a most beautiful lady,
  Dreamed a most beautiful lady.

Birds in those branches did sing,
  Blackbird and throstle and linnet,
But she walking there was by far the most fair—
  Lovelier than all else within it,
  Blackbird and throstle and linnet.

But blossoms to berries do come,
  All hanging on stalks light and slender:
And one long summer's day charmed that lady away,
  With vows sweet and merry and tender;
  A lover with voice low and tender.

Moss and lichen the green branches deck;
Weeds nod in its paths green and shady:

Yet a light footstep seems there to wander in dreams,
    The ghost of that beautiful lady,
    That happy and beautiful lady. *(1912)*

OLD SUSAN

When Susan's work was done, she'd sit,
With one fat guttering candle lit,
And window opened wide to win
The sweet night air to enter in.
There, with a thumb to keep her place,
She'd read, with stern and wrinkled face,
Her mild eyes gliding very slow
Across the letters to and fro,
While wagged the guttering candle flame
In the wind that through the window came.
And sometimes in the silence she
Would mumble a sentence audibly,
Or shake her head as if to say,
"You silly souls, to act this way!"
And never a sound from night I'd hear,
Unless some far-off cock crowed clear;
Or her old shuffling thumb should turn
Another page; and rapt and stern,
Through her great glasses bent on me,
She'd glance into reality;
And shake her round old silvery head,
With—"You!—I thought you was in bed!"—
Only to tilt her book again,
And rooted in Romance remain. *(1912)*

MISS LOO

When thin-strewn memory I look through,
I see most clearly poor Miss Loo;
Her tabby cat, her cage of birds,
Her nose, her hair, her muffled words,
And how she'd open her green eyes,
As if in some immense surprise,
Whenever as we sat at tea
She made some small remark to me.

It's always drowsy summer when
From out the past she comes again;

The westering sunshine in a pool
Floats in her parlour still and cool;
While the slim bird its lean wires shakes,
As into piercing song it breaks;

Till Peter's pale-green eyes ajar
Dream, wake; wake, dream, in one brief bar.
And I am sitting, dull and shy,
And she with gaze of vacancy,
And large hands folded on the tray,
Musing the afternoon away;
Her satin bosom heaving slow
With sighs that softly ebb and flow,
And her plain face in such dismay,
It seems unkind to look her way:
Until all cheerful back will come
Her gentle gleaming spirit home:
And one would think that poor Miss Loo
Asked nothing else, if she had you. (*1912*)

THE LISTENERS

"Is there anybody there?" said the Traveller,
    Knocking on the moonlit door;
And his horse in the silence champed the grasses
    Of the forest's ferny floor:
And a bird flew up out of the turret,
    Above the Traveller's head:
And he smote upon the door again a second time;
    "Is there anybody there?" he said.
But no one descended to the Traveller;
    No head from the leaf-fringed sill
Leaned over and looked into his grey eyes,
    Where he stood perplexed and still.
But only a host of phantom listeners
    That dwelt in the lone house then
Stood listening in the quiet of the moonlight
    To that voice from the world of men:
Stood thronging the faint moonbeams on the dark stair,
    That goes down to the empty hall,
Hearkening in an air stirred and shaken
    By the lonely Traveller's call.
And he felt in his heart their strangeness,
    Their stillness answering his cry,

While his horse moved, cropping the dark turf,
   'Neath the starred and leafy sky;
For he suddenly smote on the door, even
   Louder, and lifted his head:—
"Tell them I came, and no one answered,
   That I kept my word," he said.
Never the least stir made the listeners,
   Though every word he spake
Fell echoing through the shadowiness of the still house
   From the one man left awake:
Ay, they heard his foot upon the stirrup,
   And the sound of iron on stone,
And how the silence surged softly backward,
   When the plunging hoofs were gone. *(1912)*

THE SONG OF THE SHADOWS

Sweep thy faint strings, Musician,
   With thy long lean hand;
Downward the starry tapers burn,
   Sinks soft the waning sand;
The old hound whimpers couched in sleep,
   The embers smoulder low;
Across the walls the shadows
      Come, and go.

Sweep softly thy strings, Musician,
   The minutes mount to hours;
Frost on the windless casement weaves
   A labyrinth of flowers;
Ghosts linger in the darkening air,
   Hearken at the open door;
Music hath called them, dreaming,
      Home once more. *(1913)*

THE GHOST

"Who knocks?" "I, who was beautiful,
   Beyond all dreams to restore,
I, from the roots of the dark thorn am hither,
   And knock on the door."

"Who speaks?" "I—once was my speech
   Sweet as the bird's on the air,

When echo lurks by the waters to heed;
   'Tis I speak thee fair."

"Dark is the hour!" "Ay, and cold."
   "Lone is my house." "Ah, but mine?"
"Sight, touch, lips, eyes yearned in vain."
   "Long dead these to thine . . ."

Silence. Still faint on the porch
   Brake the flames of the stars.
In gloom groped a hope-wearied hand
   Over keys, bolts, and bars.

A face peered. All the grey night
   In chaos of vacancy shone;
Nought but vast sorrow was there—
   The sweet cheat gone.   *(1918)*

THE SCRIBE

What lovely things
   Thy hand hath made:
The smooth-plumed bird
   In its emerald shade,
The seed of the grass,
   The speck of stone
Which the wayfaring ant
   Stirs—and hastes on!

Though I should sit
   By some tarn in thy hills,
Using its ink
   As the spirit wills
To write of Earth's wonders,
   Its live, willed things,
Flit would the ages
   On soundless wings
Ere unto Z
   My pen drew nigh;
Leviathan told,
   And the honey-fly:
And still would remain
   My wit to try—
My worn reeds broken,

The dark tarn dry,
All words forgotten—
Thou, Lord, and I. *(1918)*

THE HOLLY

The sturdiest of forest trees
With acorns is inset;
Wan white blossoms the elder brings
To fruit as black as jet;
But O, in all green English woods
Is aught so fair to view
As the sleek, sharp, dark-leaved holly tree
And its berries burning through?

Towers the ash; and dazzling green
The larch her tassels wears;
Wondrous sweet are the clots of may
The tangled hawthorn bears;
But O, in heath or meadow or wold
Springs aught beneath the blue
As brisk and trim as the holly-tree bole
With its berries burning through?

When hither, thither, falls the snow,
And blazes small the frost,
Naked amid the winter stars
The elm's vast boughs are tossed;
But O, of all that summer showed
What now to winter's true
As the prickle-beribbed dark holly tree,
With berries burning through! *(1930)*

LUCY

Strange—as I sat brooding here,
While memory plied her quiet thread,
Your once-loved face came back, my dear,
    Amid the distant dead.

That pleasant cheek, hair smooth and brown.
Clear brows, and wistful eyes—yet gay:
You stand, in your alpaca gown,
    And ghost my heart away.

I was a child then; nine years old—
And you a woman. Well, stoop close,
To heed a passion never told
　　Under how faded a rose!

Do you remember? Few my pence:
I hoarded them with a miser's care,
And bought you, in passionate innocence,
　　A birthday maidenhair.

I see its fronds. Again I sit,
Hunched up in bed, in the dark, alone,
Crazed with those eyes that, memory-lit,
　　Now ponder on my own.

You gave me not a thought, 'tis true—
Precocious, silly child; and yet,
Perhaps of all you have loved—loved you,
　　I may the last forget.

And though no single word of this
You heed—a lifetime gone—at rest;
I would that all remembrances
　　As gently pierced my breast! *(1931)*

A ROBIN

Ghost-grey the fall of night,
　　Ice-bound the lane,
Lone in the dying light
　　Flits he again;
Lurking where shadows steal,
Perched in his coat of blood.
Man's homestead at his heel,
　　Death-still the wood.

Odd restless child; it's dark;
　　All wings are flown
But this one wizard's—hark!—
　　Stone clapped on stone.
Changeling and solitary,
Secret and sharp and small,
Flits he from tree to tree,
　　Calling on all. *(1933)*

SOLITUDE

Ghosts there must be with me in this old house,
Deepening its midnight as the clock beats on.
Whence else upwelled—strange, sweet, yet ominous—
That moment of happiness, and then was gone?

Nimbler than air-borne music, heart may call
A speechless message to the inward ear,
As secret even as that which then befell,
Yet nought that listening could make more clear.

Delicate, subtle senses, instant, fleet!—
But oh, how near the verge at which they fail!
In vain, self hearkens for the fall of feet
Soft as its own may be, beyond the pale.   *(1938)*

THE LAST CHAPTER

I am living more alone now than I did;
This life tends inward, as the body ages;
And what is left of its strange book to read
Quickens in interest with the last few pages.

Problems abound. Its authorship? A sequel?
Its hero-villain, whose ways so little mend?
The plot? still dark. The style? a shade unequal.
And what of the dénouement? And, the end?

No, no, have done! Lay the thumbed thing aside;
Forget its horrors, folly, incitements, lies;
In silence and in solitude abide,
And con what yet may bless your inward eyes.

Pace, still, for pace with you, companion goes;
Though now, through dulled and inattentive ear,
No more—as when a child's—your sick heart knows
His infinite energy and beauty near.

His, too, a World, though viewless save in glimpse;
He, too, a book of imagery bears;
And as your halting foot beside him limps,
Mark you whose badge and livery he wears.   *(1938)*

THE OLD SUMMERHOUSE

This blue-washed, old, thatched summerhouse—
Paint scaling, and fading from its walls—
How often from its hingeless door
I have watched—dead leaf, like the ghost of a mouse,
Rasping the worn brick floor—
The snows of the weir descending below,
And their thunderous waterfall.

Fall—fall: dark, garrulous rumour,
Until I could listen no more.
Could listen no more—for beauty with sorrow
Is a burden hard to be borne:
The evening light on the foam, and the swans, there;
That music, remote, forlorn.   (*1938*)

John Masefield
(1878–1967)

CARGOES

Quinquireme of Nineveh from distant Ophir,
Rowing home to haven in sunny Palestine,
With a cargo of ivory,
And apes and peacocks,
Sandalwood, cedarwood, and sweet white wine.

Stately Spanish galleon coming from the Isthmus,
Dipping through the Tropics by the palm-green shores,
With a cargo of diamonds,
Emeralds, amethysts,
Topazes, and cinnamon, and gold moidores.

Dirty British coaster with a salt-cake smoke stack,
Butting through the Channel in the mad March days,
With a cargo of Tyne coal,
Road-rails, pig-lead,
Firewood, iron-ware, and cheap tin trays.   *(1903)*

From *DAUBER (SECTION 6)*

All through the windless night the clipper rolled
In a great swell with oily gradual heaves
Which rolled her down until her time-bells tolled,
Clang, and the weltering water moaned like beeves.
The thundering rattle of slatting shook the sheaves,
Startles of water made the swing ports gush,
The sea was moaning and sighing and saying "Hush!"

It was all black and starless. Peering down
Into the water, trying to pierce the gloom,
One saw a dim, smooth, oily glitter of brown
Heaving and dying away and leaving room

For yet another. Like the march of doom
Came those great powers of marching silences;
Then fog came down, dead-cold, and hid the seas.

They set the Dauber to the foghorn. There
He stood upon the poop, making to sound
Out of the Pump the sailor's nasal blare,
Listening lest ice should make the note resound.
She bayed there like a solitary hound
Lost in a covert; all the watch she bayed.
The fog, come closelier down, no answer made.

Denser it grew, until the ship was lost.
The elemental hid her; she was merged
In mufflings of dark death, like a man's ghost,
New to the change of death, yet thither urged.
Then from the hidden waters something surged—
Mournful, despairing, great, greater than speech,
A noise like one slow wave on a still beach.

Mournful, and then again mournful, and still
Out of the night that mighty voice arose;
The Dauber at his foghorn felt the thrill.
Who rode that desolate sea? What forms were those?
Mournful, from things defeated, in the throes
Of memory of some conquered hunting-ground,
Out of the night of death arose the sound.

"Whales!" said the Mate. They stayed there all night long
Answering the horn. Out of the night they spoke,
Defeated creatures who had suffered wrong,
But were still noble underneath the stroke.
They filled the darkness when the Dauber woke;
The men came peering to the rail to hear,
And the sea sighed, and the fog rose up sheer.

A wall of nothing at the world's last edge,
Where no life came except defeated life.
The Dauber felt shut in within a hedge,
Behind which form was hidden and thought was rife,
And that a blinding flash, a thrust, a knife
Would sweep the hedge away and make all plain,
Brilliant beyond all words, blinding the brain.

So the night passed, but then no morning broke—
Only a something showed that night was dead.
A sea-bird, cackling like a devil, spoke,
And the fog drew away and hung like lead.
Like mighty cliffs it shaped, sullen and red;
Like glowering gods at watch it did appear,
And sometimes drew away, and then drew near.

Like islands, and like chasms, and like hell,
But always mighty and red, gloomy and ruddy,
Shutting the visible sea in like a well;
Slow heaving in vast ripples, blank and muddy,
Where the sun should have risen it streaked bloody.
The day was still-born; all the sea-fowl scattering
Splashed the still water, mewing, hovering, clattering.

Then Polar snow came down little and light,
Till all the sky was hidden by the small,
Most multitudinous drift of dirty white
Tumbling and wavering down and covering all—
Covering the sky, the sea, the clipper tall,
Furring the ropes with white, casing the mast,
Coming on no known air, but blowing past.

And all the air seemed full of gradual moan,
As though in those cloud-chasms the horns were blowing
The mort for gods cast out and overthrown,
Or for the eyeless sun plucked out and going.
Slow the low gradual moan came in the snowing;
The Dauber felt the prelude had begun.
The snowstorm fluttered by; he saw the sun

Show and pass by, gleam from one towering prison
Into another, vaster and more grim,
Which in dull crags of darkness had arisen
To muffle-to a final door on him.
The gods upon the dull crags lowered dim,
The pigeons chattered, quarrelling in the track.
In the south-west the dimness dulled to black.

Then came the cry of "Call all hands on deck!"
The Dauber knew its meaning; it was come:
Cape Horn, that tramples beauty into wreck,

And crumples steel and smites the strong man dumb.
Down clattered flying kites and staysails: some
Sang out in quick, high calls: the fair-leads skirled,
And from the south-west came the end of the world.

"Caught in her ball-dress," said the Bosun, hauling;
"Lee-ay, lee-ay!" quick, high, come the men's call;
It was all wallop of sails and startled calling.
"Let fly!" "Let go!" "Clew up!" and "Let go all!"
"Now up and make them fast!" "Here, give us a haul!"
"Now up and stow them! Quick! By God! we're done!"
The blackness crunched all memory of the sun.

"Up!" said the Mate. "Mizen top-gallants. Hurry!"
The Dauber ran, the others ran, the sails
Slatted and shook; out of the black a flurry
Whirled in fine lines, tattering the edge to trails.
Painting and art and England were old tales
Told in some other life to that pale man,
Who struggled with white fear and gulped and ran.

He struck a ringbolt in his haste and fell—
Rose, sick with pain, half-lamed in his left knee;
He reached the shrouds where clambering men pell-mell
Hustled each other up and cursed him; he
Hurried aloft with them: then from the sea
Came a cold, sudden breath that made the hair
Stiff on the neck, as though Death whispered there.

A man below him punched him in the side.
"Get up, you Dauber, or let me get past."
He saw the belly of the skysail skied,
Gulped, and clutched tight, and tried to go more fast.
Sometimes he missed his ratline and was grassed,
Scraped his shin raw against the rigid line;
The clamberers reached the futtock-shrouds' incline.

Cursing they came; one, kicking out behind,
Kicked Dauber in the mouth, and one below
Punched at his calves; the futtock-shrouds inclined;
It was a perilous path for one to go.
"Up, Dauber, up!" A curse followed a blow.
He reached the top and gasped, then on, then on.
And one voice yelled "Let go!" and one "All gone!"

Fierce clamberers, some in oilskins, some in rags,
Hustling and hurrying up, up the steep stairs.
Before the windless sails were blown to flags,
And whirled like dirty birds athwart great airs,
Ten men in all, to get this mast of theirs
Snugged to the gale in time. "Up! Damn you, run!"
The mizzen topmast head was safely won.

"Lay out!" the Bosun yelled. The Dauber laid
Out on the yard, gripping the yard and feeling
Sick at the mighty space of air displayed
Below his feet, where mewing birds were wheeling.
A giddy fear was on him; he was reeling.
He bit his lip half through, clutching the jack.
A cold sweat glued the shirt upon his back.

The yard was shaking, for a brace was loose.
He felt that he would fall; he clutched, he bent,
Clammy with natural terror to the shoes
While idiotic promptings came and went.
Snow fluttered on a wind-flaw and was spent;
He saw the water darken. Someone yelled,
"Frap it; don't stay to furl! Hold on!" He held.

Darkness came down—half darkness—in a whirl;
The sky went out, the waters disappeared.
He felt a shocking pressure of blowing hurl
The ship upon her side. The darkness speared
At her with wind; she staggered, she careered,
Then down she lay. The Dauber felt her go;
He saw his yard tilt downwards. Then the snow

Whirled all about—dense, multitudinous, cold—
Mixed with the wind's one devilish thrust and shriek,
Which whiffled out men's tears, deafened, took hold,
Flattening the flying drift against the cheek.
The yards buckled and bent, man could not speak.
The ship lay on her broadside; the wind's sound
Had devilish malice at having got her downed.

*   *   *

How long the gale had blown he could not tell,
Only the world had changed, his life had died.
A moment now was everlasting hell.

Nature, an onslaught from the weather side,
A withering rush of death, a frost that cried,
Shrieked, till he withered at the heart; a hail
Plastered his oilskins with an icy mail.

"Cut!" yelled his mate. He looked—the sail was gone,
Blown into rags in the first furious squall;
The tatters drummed the devil's tattoo. On
The buckling yard a block thumped like a mall.
The ship lay—the sea smote her, the wind's bawl
Came, "loo, loo, loo!" The devil cried his hounds
On to the poor spent stag strayed in his bounds.

"Cut! Ease her!" yelled his mate; the Dauber heard.
His mate wormed up the tilted yard and slashed,
A rag of canvas skimmed like a darting bird.
The snow whirled, the ship bowed to it, the gear lashed,
The sea-tops were cut off and flung down smashed;
Tatters of shouts were flung, the rags of yells—
And clang, clang, clang, below beat the two bells.

"O God!" the Dauber moaned. A roaring rang,
Blasting the royals like a cannonade;
The backstays parted with a crackling clang,
The upper spars were snapped like twigs decayed—
Snapped at their heels, their jagged splinters splayed,
Like white and ghastly hairs erect with fear.
The Mate yelled, "Gone, by God, and pitched them clear!"

"Up" yelled the Bosun; "up and clear the wreck!"
The Dauber followed where he led: below
He caught one giddy glimpsing of the deck
Filled with white water, as though heaped with snow.
He saw the streamers of the rigging blow
Straight out like pennons from the splintered mast,
Then, all sense dimmed, all was an icy blast

Roaring from nether hell and filled with ice,
Roaring and crashing on the jerking stage,
An utter bridle given to utter vice,
Limitless power mad with endless rage
Withering the soul; a minute seemed an age.
He clutched and hacked at ropes, at rags of sail,
Thinking that comfort was a fairy-tale

Told long ago—long, long ago—long since
Heard of in other lives—imagined, dreamed—
There where the basest beggar was a prince
To him in torment where the tempest screamed,
Comfort and warmth and ease no longer seemed
Things that a man could know: soul, body, brain,
Knew nothing but the wind, the cold, the pain.

"Leave that!" the Bosun shouted; "Crojick save!"
The splitting crojick, not yet gone to rags,
Thundered below, beating till something gave,
Bellying between its buntlines into bags.
Some birds were blown past, shrieking: dark, like shags,
Their backs seemed, looking down. "Leu, leu!" they cried.
The ship lay, the seas thumped her; she had died.

They reached the crojick yard, which buckled, buckled
Like a thin whalebone to the topsail's strain.
They laid upon the yard and heaved and knuckled,
Pounding the sail, which jangled and leapt again.
It was quite hard with ice, its rope like chain,
Its strength like seven devils; it shook the mast.
They cursed and toiled and froze: a long time passed.

Two hours passed, then a dim lightening came.
Those frozen ones upon the yard could see
The mainsail and the foresail still the same,
Still battling with the hands and blowing free,
Rags tattered where the staysails used to be.
The lower topsails stood; the ship's lee deck
Seethed with four feet of water filled with wreck.

An hour more went by; the Dauber lost
All sense of hands and feet, all sense of all
But of a wind that cut him to the ghost,
And of a frozen fold he had to haul,
Of heavens that fell and never ceased to fall,
And ran in smoky snatches along the sea,
Leaping from crest to wave-crest, yelling. He

Lost sense of time; no bells went, but he felt
Ages go over him. At last, at last
They frapped the cringled crojick's icy pelt;
In frozen bulge and bunt they made it fast.

Then, scarcely live, they laid in to the mast.
The Captain's speaking trumpet gave a blare,
"Make fast the topsail, Mister, while you're there."

Some seamen cursed, but up they had to go—
Up to the topsail yard to spend an hour
Stowing a topsail in a blinding snow,
Which made the strongest man among them cower.
More men came up, the fresh hands gave them power,
They stowed the sail; then with a rattle of chain
One half the crojick burst its bonds again.

* * *

They stowed the sail, frapping it round with rope,
Leaving no surface for the wind, no fold,
Then down the weather shrouds, half dead, they grope;
That struggle with the sail had made them old.
They wondered if the crojick furl would hold.
"Lucky," said one, "it didn't spring the spar."
"Lucky!" the Bosun said, "Lucky! We are!

She came within two shakes of turning top
Or stripping all her shroud-screws, that first quiff.
Now fish those wash-deck buckets out of the slop.
Here's Dauber says he doesn't like Cape Stiff.
This isn't wind, man, this is only a whiff.
Hold on, all hands, hold on!" a sea, half seen,
Paused, mounted, burst, and filled the main-deck green.

The Dauber felt a mountain of water fall.
It covered him deep, deep, he felt it fill,
Over his head, the deck, the fife-rails, all,
Quieting the ship, she trembled and lay still.
Then with a rush and shatter and clanging shrill
Over she went; he saw the water cream
Over the bitts; he saw the half-deck stream.

Then in the rush he swirled, over she went;
Her lee-rail dipped, he struck, and something gave;
His legs went through a port as the roll spent;
She paused, then rolled, and back the water drave.
He drifted with it as a part of the wave,
Drowning, half-stunned, exhausted, partly frozen,
He struck the booby hatchway; then the Bosun

Leaped, seeing his chance, before the next sea burst,
And caught him as he drifted, seized him, held,
Up-ended him against the bitts, and cursed.
"This ain't the George's Swimming Baths," he yelled;
"Keep on your feet!" Another grey-back felled
The two together, and the Bose, half-blind,
Spat: "One's a joke," he cursed, "but two's unkind."

"Now, damn it, Dauber!" said the Mate. "Look out,
Or you'll be over the side!" The water freed;
Each clanging freeing-port became a spout.
The men cleared up the decks as there was need.
The Dauber's head was cut, he felt it bleed
Into his oilskins as he clutched and coiled.
Water and sky were devil's brews which boiled,

Boiled, shrieked, and glowered; but the ship was saved.
Snugged safely down, though fourteen sails were split.
Out of the dark a fiercer fury raved.
The grey-backs died and mounted, each crest lit
With a white toppling gleam that hissed from it
And slid, or leaped, or ran with whirls of cloud,
Mad with inhuman life that shrieked aloud.

The watch was called; Dauber might go below.
"Splice the main brace!" the Mate called. All laid aft
To get a gulp of momentary glow
As some reward for having saved the craft.
The steward ladled mugs, from which each quaff'd
Whisky, with water, sugar, and lime-juice, hot,
A quarter of a pint each made the tot.

Beside the lamp-room door the steward stood
Ladling it out, and each man came in turn,
Tipped his sou'-wester, drank it, grunted "Good!"
And shambled forward, letting it slowly burn:
When all were gone the Dauber lagged astern,
Torn by his frozen body's lust for heat,
The liquor's pleasant smell, so warm, so sweet,

And by a promise long since made at home
Never to taste strong liquor. Now he knew
The worth of liquor; now he wanted some.

His frozen body urged him to the brew;
Yet it seemed wrong, an evil thing to do
To break that promise. "Dauber," said the Mate,
"Drink, and turn in, man; why the hell d'ye wait?"

"Please, sir, I'm temperance." "Temperance are you, hey?
That's all the more for me! So you're for slops?
I thought you'd had enough slops for to-day.
Go to your bunk and ease her when she drops.
And—damme, steward! you brew with too much hops!
Stir up the sugar, man!—and tell your girl
How kind the Mate was teaching you to furl."

Then the Mate drank the remnants, six men's share,
And ramped into his cabin, where he stripped
And danced unclad, and was uproarious there.
In waltzes with the cabin cat he tripped,
Singing in tenor clear that he was pipped—
That "he who strove the tempest to disarm,
Must never first embrail the lee yard-arm,"

And that his name was Ginger. Dauber crept
Back to the round-house, gripping by the rail.
The wind howled by; the passionate water leapt;
The night was all one roaring with the gale.
Then at the door he stopped, uttering a wail;
His hands were perished numb and blue as veins,
He could not turn the knob for both the Spains.

A hand came shuffling aft, dodging the seas,
Singing "her nut-brown hair" between his teeth;
Taking the ocean's tumult at his ease
Even when the wash about his thighs did seethe.
His soul was happy in its happy sheath;
"What, Dauber, won't it open? Fingers cold?
You'll talk of this time, Dauber, when you're old."

He flung the door half open, and a sea
Washed them both in, over the splashboard, down;
"You silly, salt miscarriage!" sputtered he.
"Dauber, pull out the plug before we drown!
That's spoiled my laces and my velvet gown.
Where is the plug?" Groping in pitch dark water,
He sang between his teeth "The Farmer's Daughter."

It was pitch dark within there; at each roll
The chests slid to the slant; the water rushed,
Making full many a clanging tin pan bowl
Into the black below-bunks as it gushed.
The dog-tired men slept through it; they were hushed.
The water drained, and then with matches damp
The man struck heads off till he lit the lamp.

"Thank you," the Dauber said; the seaman grinned.
"This is your first foul weather?" "Yes." "I thought
Up on the yard you hadn't seen much wind.
Them's rotten sea-boots, Dauber, that you brought.
Now I must cut on deck before I'm caught."
He went; the lamp-flame smoked; he slammed the door;
A film of water loitered across the floor.

The Dauber watched it come and watched it go;
He had had revelation of the lies
Cloaking the truth men never choose to know;
He could bear witness now and cleanse their eyes.
He had beheld in suffering; he was wise;
This was the sea, this searcher of the soul—
This never-dying shriek fresh from the Pole.

He shook with cold; his hands could not undo
His oilskin buttons, so he shook and sat,
Watching his dirty fingers, dirty blue,
Hearing without the hammering tackle slat,
Within, the drops from dripping clothes went pat,
Running in little patters, gentle, sweet,
And "Ai, ai!" went the wind, and the seas beat.

His bunk was sopping wet; he clambered in,
None of his clothes were dry: his fear recurred.
Cramps bunched the muscles underneath his skin.
The great ship rolled until the lamp was blurred.
He took his Bible and tried to read a word;
Trembled at going aloft again, and then
Resolved to fight it out and show it to men.

Faces recurred, fierce memories of the yard,
The frozen sail, the savage eyes, the jests,
The oaths of one great seaman, syphilis-scarred,
The tug of leeches jammed beneath their chests,

The buntlines bellying bunts out into breasts,
The deck so desolate-grey, the sky so wild.
He fell asleep, and slept like a young child.

But not for long; the cold awoke him soon,
The hot-ache and the skin-cracks and the cramp,
The seas thundering without, the gale's wild tune,
The sopping misery of the blankets damp.
A speaking-trumpet roared; a sea-boot's stamp
Clogged at the door. A man entered to shout:
"All hands on deck! Arouse here! Tumble out!"

The caller raised the lamp; his oilskins clicked
As the thin ice upon them cracked and fell.
"Rouse out!" he said. "This lamp is frozen wick'd.
Rouse out!" His accent deepened to a yell.
"We're among ice; it's blowing up like hell.
We're going to hand both topsails. Time, I guess,
We're sheeted up. Rouse out! Don't stay to dress!"

"Is it cold on deck?" said Dauber. "Is it cold?
We're sheeted up, I tell you, inches thick!
The fo'c'sle's like a wedding-cake, I'm told.
Now tumble out, my sons; on deck here, quick!
Rouse out, away, and come and climb the stick.
I'm going to call the half-deck. Bosun! Hey!
Both topsails coming in. Heave out! Away!"

He went; the Dauber tumbled from his bunk,
Clutching the side. He heard the wind go past,
Making the great ship wallow as if drunk.
There was a shocking tumult up the mast.
"This is the end," he muttered, "come at last!
I've got to go aloft, facing this cold.
I can't. I can't. I'll never keep my hold.

"I cannot face the topsail yard again.
I never guessed what misery it would be."
The cramps and hot-ache made him sick with pain,
The ship stopped suddenly from a devilish sea,
Then, with a triumph of wash, a rush of glee,
The door burst in, and in the water rolled,
Filling the lower bunks, black, creaming, cold.

The lamp sucked out. "Wash!" went the water back,
Then in again, flooding; the Bosun swore.
"You useless thing! You Dauber! You lee slack!
Get out, you heekapoota! Shut the door!
You coo-ilyaira, what are you waiting for?
Out of my way, you thing—you useless thing!"
He slammed the door indignant, clanging the ring.

And then he lit the lamp, drowned to the waist:
"Here's a fine house! Get at the scupper-holes"—
He bent against it as the water raced—
"And pull them out to leeward when she rolls.
They say some kinds of landsmen don't have souls.
I well believe. A Port Mahon baboon
Would make more soul then you got with a spoon."

Down in the icy water Dauber groped
To find the plug; the racing water sluiced
Over his head and shoulders as she sloped.
Without, judged by the sound, all hell was loosed.
He felt cold Death about him tightly noosed.
That Death was better than the misery there
Iced on the quaking foothold high in air.

And then the thought came: "I'm a failure. All
My life has been a failure. They were right.
It will not matter if I go and fall;
I should be free then from this hell's delight.
I'll never paint. Best let it end to-night.
I'll slip over the side. I've tried and failed."
So in the ice-cold in the night he quailed.

Death would be better, death, than this long hell
Of mockery and surrender and dismay—
This long defeat of doing nothing well,
Playing the part too high for him to play.
"O Death! who hides the sorry thing away,
Take me; I've failed. I cannot play these cards."
There came a thundering from the topsail yards.

And then he bit his lips, clenching his mind,
And staggered out to muster, beating back
The coward frozen self of him that whined.

Come what cards might he meant to play the pack.
"Ai!" screamed the wind; the topsail sheet went clack;
Ice filled the air with spikes; the grey-backs burst.
"Here's Dauber," said the Mate, "on deck the first.

"Why, holy sailor, Dauber, you're a man!
I took you for a soldier. Up now, come!"
Up on the yards already they began
That battle with a gale which strikes men dumb.
The leaping topsail thundered like a drum.
The frozen snow beat in the face like shots.
The wind spun whipping wave-crests into clots.

So up upon the topsail yard again,
In the great tempest's fiercest hour, began
Probation to the Dauber's soul, of pain
Which crowds a century's torment in a span.
For the next month the ocean taught this man,
And he, in that month's torment, while she wested,
Was never warm nor dry, nor full nor rested.

But still it blew, or, if it lulled, it rose
Within the hour and blew again; and still
The water as it burst aboard her froze.
The wind blew off an ice-field, raw and chill,
Daunting man's body, tampering with his will;
But after thirty days a ghostly sun
Gave sickly promise that the storms were done.   (1912)

[THERE IS NO GOD, AS I WAS TAUGHT]

There is no God, as I was taught in youth,
Though each, according to his stature, builds
Some covered shrine for what he thinks the truth,
Which day by day his reddest heart-blood gilds.
There is no God; but death, the clasping sea,
In which we move like fish, deep over deep
Made of men's souls that bodies have set free,
Floods to a Justice though it seems asleep.
There is no God, but still, behind the veil,
The hurt thing works, out of its agony.
Still, like a touching of a brimming Grail,
Return the pennies given to passers by.

There is no God, but we, who breathe the air,
Are God ourselves and touch God everywhere. *(1916)*

From *REYNARD THE FOX*

Ock Gurney and old Pete were there,
Riding their bonny cobs and swearing.
Ock's wife had giv'n them both a fairing,
A horse-rosette, red, white, and blue.
Their cheeks were brown as any brew,
And every comer to the meet
Said "Hello, Ock" or "Morning, Pete;
Be you a going to a wedding?"
"Why, noa," they said, "we'm going a bedding;
Now ben't us, uncle, ben't us, Ock?"
Pete Gurney was a lusty cock
Turned sixty-three, but bright and hale,
A dairy-farmer in the vale,
Much like a robin in the face,
Much character in little space,
With little eyes like burning coal.
His mouth was like a slit or hole
In leather that was seamed and lined.
He had the russet-apple mind
That betters as the weather worsen.
He was a manly English person,
Kind to the core, brave, merry, true;
One grief he had, a grief still new,
That former Parson joined with Squire
In putting down the Playing Quire,
In church, and putting organ in.
"Ah, boys, that was a pious din
That Quire was; a pious praise
The noise was that we used to raise;
I and my serpent, George with his'n,
On Easter Day in 'He is Risen,'
Or blessed Christmas in 'Venite';
And how the trombone came in mighty,
In Alleluias from the heart.
Pious, for each man played his part,
Not like 'tis now." Thus he, still sore
For changes forty years before,

When all (that could) in time and tune,
Blew trumpets to the newë moon.
He was a bachelor, from choice.
He and his nephew farmed the Boyce,
Prime pasture land for thirty cows.
Ock's wife, Selina Jane, kept house,
And jolly were the three together.

Ock had a face like summer weather,
A broad red sun, split by a smile.
He mopped his forehead all the while,
And said "By damn," and "Ben't us, Unk?"
His eyes were close and deeply sunk.
He cursed his hunter like a lover,
"Now blast your soul, my dear, give over.
Woa, now, my pretty, damn your eyes."
Like Pete he was of middle size,
Dean-oak-like, stuggy, strong in shoulder,
He stood a wrestle like a boulder,
He had a back for pitching hay,
His singing voice was like a bay.
In talk he had a sideways spit,
Each minute, to refresh his wit.
He cracked Brazil nuts with his teeth.
He challenged Cobbett of the Heath
(Weight-lifting champion) once, but lost.
Hunting was what he loved the most,
Next to his wife and Uncle Pete.
With beer to drink and cheese to eat,
And rain in May to fill the grasses,
This life was not a dream that passes
To Ock, but like the summer flower.   (*1919*)

ON GROWING OLD

Be with me, Beauty, for the fire is dying,
My dog and I are old, too old for roving.
Man, whose young passion sets the spindrift flying,
Is soon too lame to march, too cold for loving.
I take the book and gather to the fire,
Turning old yellow leaves; minute by minute,
The clock ticks to my heart; a withered wire

Moves a thin ghost of music in the spinet.
I cannot sail your seas, I cannot wander
Your cornland, nor your hill-land nor your valleys,
Ever again, nor share the battle yonder
Where the young knight the broken squadron rallies.
Only stay quiet while my mind remembers
The beauty of fire from the beauty of embers.

Beauty, have pity, for the strong have power,
The rich their wealth, the beautiful their grace,
Summer of man its sunlight and its flower,
Spring time of man all April in a face.
Only, as in the jostling in the Strand,
Where the mob thrusts or loiters or is loud,
The beggar with the saucer in his hand
Asks only a penny from the passing crowd,
So, from this glittering world with all its fashion,
Its fire and play of men, its stir, its march,
Let me have wisdom, Beauty, wisdom and passion,
Bread to the soul, rain where the summers parch.
Give me but these, and though the darkness close
Even the night will blossom as the rose. *(1919)*

THE LEMMINGS

Once in a hundred years the Lemmings come
Westward, in search of food, over the snow,
Westward, until the salt sea drowns them dumb,
Westward, till all are drowned, those Lemmings go.
Once, it is thought, there was a westward land
(Now drowned) where there was food for those starved things,
And memory of the place has burnt its brand
In the little brains of all the Lemming Kings.
Perhaps, long since, there was a land beyond
Westward from death, some city, some calm place,
Where one could taste God's quiet and be fond
With the little beauty of a human face;
But now the land is drowned, yet still we press
Westward, in search, to death, to nothingness. *(1920)*

James Stephens
(1882–1950)

WHAT TOMAS SAID IN A PUB

I saw God! Do you doubt it?
Do you dare to doubt it?
I saw the Almighty Man! His hand
Was resting on a mountain! And
He looked upon the World, and all about it:
I saw Him plainer than you see me now
—You mustn't doubt it!

He was not satisfied!
His look was all dissatisfied!
His beard swung on a wind, far out of sight
Behind the world's curve! And there was light
Most fearful from His forehead! And He sighed
—That star went always wrong, and from the start
I was dissatisfied!—

He lifted up His hand!
I say He heaved a dreadful hand
Over the spinning earth! Then I said,—Stay,
You must not strike it, God! I'm in the way!
And I will never move from where I stand!—
He said,—Dear child, I feared that you were dead,—
... And stayed His hand! (1909)

THE SHELL

1

And then I pressed the shell
Close to my ear,
And listened well.

And straightway, like a bell,
Came low and clear
The slow, sad murmur of far distant seas

196-I

Whipped by an icy breeze
Upon a shore
Wind-swept and desolate.

It was a sunless strand that never bore
The footprint of a man,
Nor felt the weight

Since time began
Of any human quality or stir,
Save what the dreary winds and wave incur.

2

And in the hush of waters was the sound
Of pebbles, rolling round;
For ever rolling, with a hollow sound:

And bubbling sea-weeds, as the waters go,
Swish to and fro
Their long cold tentacles of slimy grey;

There was no day;
Nor ever came a night
Setting the stars alight

To wonder at the moon:
Was twilight only, and the frightened croon,
Smitten to whimpers, of the dreary wind

And waves that journeyed blind . . .
And then I loosed my ear.—Oh, it was sweet
To hear a cart go jolting down the street! *(1909)*

WHY TOMAS CAM WAS GRUMPY

If I were rich what would I do?
I'd leave the horse just ready to shoe;
I'd leave the pail beside the cow;
I'd leave the furrow beneath the plough;
I'd leave the ducks, tho' they should quack:
"Our eggs will be stolen before you're back";
I'd buy a diamond brooch, a ring,
A chain of gold that I would fling
Around her neck. . . . Ah, what an itch,
If I were rich!

What would I do if I were wise?
I would not debate about the skies;
Nor would I try a book to write;
Or find the wrong in the tangled right;
I would not debate with learned men
Of how, and what, and why, and when;
—I'd train my tongue to a linnet's song,
I'd learn the words that couldn't go wrong—
And then I'd say ... And win the prize,
If I were wise!

But I'm not that nor t'other, I bow
My back to the work that's waiting now:
I'll shoe the horse that's standing ready;
I'll milk the cow if she'll be steady;
I'll follow the plough that turns the loam;
I'll watch the ducks don't lay from home:
—And I'll curse, and curse, and curse again
Till the devil joins in with his big amen;
And none but he and I will wot
When the heart within me starts to rot;
To fester and churn its ugly brew
... Where's my spade! I've work to do!   (1912)

WHAT THE DEVIL SAID

It was night-time! God, the Father Good,
Weary of praises, on a sudden stood
From His great Throne, and leaned upon the sky:
For He had heard a sound; a little cry,
Thin as a whisper, climbing up the Steep.

And so He looked to where the Earth, asleep,
Rocked with the moon: He saw the whirling sea
Swing round the world in surgent energy,
Tangling the moonlight in its netted foam;
And, nearer, saw the white and fretted dome
Of the ice-capped pole spin back again a ray
To whistling stars, bright as a wizard's day.

But these He passed, with eyes intently wide,
Till, closer still, the mountains He espied
Squatting tremendous on the broad-backed Earth,

Each nursing twenty rivers at a birth!
And then, minutely, sought He for the cry
That had climbed the slant of space so hugely high.

He found it in a ditch outside a town:
A tattered hungry woman, crouching down
By a dead babe—So there was nought to do,
For what is done is done! And sad He drew
Back to His Heaven of ivory and gold:
And, as He sat, all suddenly there rolled,
From where the woman wept upon the sod,
Satan's deep voice—*O thou unhappy God!*   (*1912*)

SWEET APPLE

At the end of the bough!
At the top of the tree!
—As fragrant, as high,
And as lovely, as thou—
One sweet apple reddens,
Which all men may see,
—At the end of the bough!

Swinging full to the view!
Though the harvesters now
Overlook it, repass it,
And pass busily:
Overlook it!
Nay, pluck it!
They do not know how!

For it swings out of reach
Like a cloud! And as free
As a star; or thy beauty,
That seems too, I vow,
Remote as the sweet apple swinging
—Ah me!
At the end of the bough!   (*1913*)

DEIRDRE

Do not let any woman read this verse!
It is for men, and after them their sons,
And their sons' sons!

The time comes when our hearts sink utterly;
When we remember Deirdre, and her tale,
And that her lips are dust.

Once she did tread the earth: men took her hand;
They looked into her eyes and said their say,
And she replied to them.

More than two thousand years it is since she
Was beautiful: she trod the waving grass;
She saw the clouds.

Two thousand years! The grass is still the same;
The clouds as lovely as they were that time
When Deirdre was alive.

But there has been again no woman born
Who was so beautiful; not one so beautiful
Of all the women born.

Let all men go apart and mourn together!
No man can ever love her! Not a man
Can dream to be her lover!

No man can bend before her! No man say—
What could one say to her? There are no words
That one could say to her!

Now she is but a story that is told
Beside the fire! No man can ever be
The friend of that poor queen!   (*1915*)

THE SNARE

I hear a sudden cry of pain!
There is a rabbit in a snare:
Now I hear the cry again,
But I cannot tell from where.

But I cannot tell from where
He is calling out for aid!
Crying on the frightened air,
Making everything afraid!

Making everything afraid!
Wrinkling up his little face!
As he cries again for aid;
—And I cannot find the place!

And I cannot find the place
Where his paw is in the snare!
Little One! Oh, Little One!
I am searching everywhere! *(1915)*

A GLASS OF BEER

The lanky hank of a she in the inn over there
Nearly killed me for asking the loan of a glass of beer;
May the devil grip the whey-faced slut by the hair,
And beat bad manners out of her skin for a year.

That parboiled ape, with the toughest jaw you will see
On virtue's path, and a voice that would rasp the dead,
Came roaring and raging the minute she looked at me,
And threw me out of the house on the back of my head!

If I asked her master he'd give me a cask a day;
But she, with the beer at hand, not a gill would arrange!
May she marry a ghost and bear him a kitten, and may
The High King of Glory permit her to get the mange. *(1918)*

D. H. Lawrence
(1885–1930)

LOVE ON THE FARM

What large, dark hands are those at the window
Grasping in the golden light
Which weaves its way through the evening wind
   At my heart's delight?

Ah, only the leaves! But in the west
I see a redness suddenly come
Into the evening's anxious breast—
   'Tis the wound of love goes home!

The woodbine creeps abroad
Calling low to her lover:
   The sun-lit flirt who all the day
   Has poised above her lips in play
   And stolen kisses, shallow and gay
   Of pollen, now has gone away—
   She woos the moth with her sweet, low word;
And when above her his moth-wings hover
Then her bright breast she will uncover
And yield her honey-drop to her lover.

Into the yellow, evening glow
Saunters a man from the farm below;
Leans, and looks in at the low-built shed
Where the swallow has hung her marriage bed.
   The bird lies warm against the wall.
   She glances quick her startled eyes
   Towards him, then she turns away
   Her small head, making warm display
   Of red upon the throat. Her terrors sway
   Her out of the nest's warm, busy ball,
   Whose plaintive cry is heard as she flies

In one blue swoop from out of the sties
Into the twilight's empty hall.

Oh, water-hen, beside the rushes
Hide your quaintly scarlet blushes,
Still your quick tail, lie still as dead,
Till the distance folds over his ominous tread!

The rabbit presses back her ears,
Turns back her liquid, anguished eyes
And crouches low; then with wild spring
Spurts from the terror of *his* oncoming;
To be choked back, the wire ring
Her frantic effort throttling:
    Piteous brown ball of quivering fears!
Ah, soon in his large, hard hands she dies,
And swings all loose from the swing of his walk!
Yet calm and kindly are his eyes
And ready to open in brown surprise
Should I not answer to his talk
Or should he my tears surmise.

I hear his hand on the latch, and rise from my chair
Watching the door open; he flashes bare
His strong teeth in a smile, and flashes his eyes
In a smile like triumph upon me; then careless-wise
He flings the rabbit soft on the table board
And comes toward me: ah! the uplifted sword
Of his hand against my bosom! and oh, the broad
Blade of his glance that asks me to applaud
His coming! With his hand he turns my face to him
And caresses me with his fingers that still smell grim
Of rabbit's fur! God, I am caught in a snare!
I know not what fine wire is round my throat;
I only know I let him finger there
My pulse of life, and let him nose like a stoat
Who sniffs with joy before he drinks the blood.

And down his mouth comes to my mouth! and down
His bright dark eyes come over me, like a hood
Upon my mind! his lips meet mine, and a flood
Of sweet fire sweeps across me, so I drown
Against him, die, and find death good.   *(1913)*

LIGHTNING

I felt the lurch and halt of her heart
    Next my breast, where my own heart was beating;
And I laughed to feel it plunge and bound,
And strange in my blood-swept ears was the sound
    Of the words I kept repeating,
Repeating with tightened arms, and the hot blood's blindfold art.

Her breath flew warm against my neck,
    Warm as a flame in the close night air;
And the sense of her clinging flesh was sweet
Where her arms and my neck's thick pulse could meet.
    Holding her thus, could I care
That the black night hid her from me, blotted out every speck?

I leaned in the darkness to find her lips
    And claim her utterly in a kiss,
When the lightning flew across her face
And I saw her for the flaring space
    Of a second, like snow that slips
From a roof, inert with death, weeping "Not this! Not this!"

A moment there, like snow in the dark
    Her face lay pale against my breast,
Pale love lost in a thaw of fear
And melted in an icy tear,
    And open lips, distressed;
A moment; then darkness shut the lid of the sacred ark.

And I heard the thunder, and felt the rain,
    And my arms fell loose, and I was dumb.
Almost I hated her, sacrificed;
Hated myself and the place, and the iced
    Rain that burnt on my rage; saying: Come
Home, come home, the lightning has made it too plain! (1913)

RELEASE

Helen, had I known yesterday
That you could discharge the ache
    Out of the wound,

Had I known yesterday you could take
The turgid electric ache away,
   Drink it up in the ground
Of your soft white body, as lightning
Is drunk from an agonised sky by the earth,
   I should have hated you, Helen.

But since my limbs gushed full of fire,
Since from out of my blood and bone
   Poured a heavy flame
To you, earth of my atmosphere, stone
Of my steel, lovely white flint of desire,
   You have no name.
Earth of my swaying atmosphere,
Substance of my inconsistent breath,
   I cannot but cleave to you, Helen.

Since you have drunken up the drear
Death-darkened storm, and death
   Is washed from the blue
Of my eyes, I see you beautiful, and dear.
Beautiful, passive and strong, as the breath
   Of my yearning blows over you.
I see myself as the winds that hover
Half substanceless, and without grave worth.
   But you
   Are the earth I hover over. *(1916)*

HYMN TO PRIAPUS

My love lies underground
With her face upturned to mine,
And her mouth unclosed in a last long kiss
That ended her life and mine.

I danced at the Christmas party
Under the mistletoe
Along with a ripe, slack country lass
Jostling to and fro.

The big, soft country lass,
Like a loose sheaf of wheat
Slipped through my arms on the threshing floor
At my feet.

The warm, soft country lass,
Sweet as an armful of wheat
At threshing-time broken, was broken
For me, and ah, it was sweet!

Now I am going home
Fulfilled and alone,
I see the great Orion standing
Looking down.

He's the star of my first beloved
Love-making.
The witness of all that bitter-sweet
Heart-aching.

Now he sees this as well,
This last commission.
Nor do I get any look
Of admonition.

He can add the reckoning up
I suppose, between now and then,
Having walked himself in the thorny, difficult
Ways of men.

He has done as I have done
No doubt:
Remembered and forgotten
Turn and about.

My love lies underground
With her face upturned to mine,
And her mouth unclosed in the last long kiss
That ended her life and mine.

She fares in the stark immortal
Fields of death;
I in these goodly, frozen
Fields beneath.

Something in me remembers
And will not forget.

The stream of my life in the darkness
Deathward set!

And something in me has forgotten,
Has ceased to care.
Desire comes up, and contentment
Is debonair.

I, who am worn and careful,
How much do I care?
How is it I grin then, and chuckle
Over despair?

Grief, grief, I suppose and sufficient
Grief makes us free
To be faithless and faithful together
As we have to be. *(1917)*

SPRING MORNING

Ah, through the open door
Is there an almond tree
Aflame with blossom!
   —Let us fight no more.

Among the pink and blue
Of the sky and the almond flowers
A sparrow flutters.
   —We have come through,

It is really spring!—See,
When he thinks himself alone
How he bullies the flowers.
   —Ah, you and me

How happy we'll be!—See him?
He clouts the tufts of flowers
In his impudence
   —But, did you dream

It would be so bitter? Never mind,
It is finished, the spring is here.
And we're going to be summer-happy
   And summer-kind.

We have died, we have slain and been slain,
We are not our old selves any more.
I feel new and eager
　　To start again.

It is gorgeous to live and forget.
And to feel quite new.
See the bird in the flowers?—he's making
　　A rare to-do!

He thinks the whole blue sky
Is much less than the bit of blue egg
He's got in his nest—we'll be happy,
　　You and I, I and you.

With nothing to fight any more—
In each other, at least.
See, how gorgeous the world is
　　Outside the door! *(San Gaudenzio, 1917)*

THE SONG OF A MAN WHO HAS COME THROUGH

Not I, not I, but the wind that blows through me!
A fine wind is blowing the new direction of Time.
If only I let it bear me, carry me, if only it carry me!
If only I am sensitive, subtle, oh, delicate, a winged gift!
If only, most lovely of all, I yield myself and am borrowed
By the fine, fine wind that takes its course through the chaos of the
　　world
Like a fine, an exquisite chisel, a wedge-blade inserted;
If only I am keen and hard like the sheer tip of a wedge
Driven by invisible blows,
The rock will split, we shall come at the wonder, we shall find the
　　Hesperides.

Oh, for the wonder that bubbles into my soul,
I would be a good fountain, a good well-head,
Would blur no whisper, spoil no expression.

What is the knocking?
What is the knocking at the door in the night?
It is somebody wants to do us harm.

No, no, it is the three strange angels.
Admit them, admit them.   *(1917)*

GLOIRE DE DIJON

When she rises in the morning
I linger to watch her;
Spreads the bath-cloth underneath the window
And the sunbeams catch her
Glistening white on the shoulders,
While down her sides the mellow
Golden shadow glows as
She stoops to the sponge, and the swung breasts
Sway like full-blown yellow
Gloire de Dijon roses.

She drips herself with water, and the shoulders
Glisten as silver, they crumple up
Like wet and falling roses, and I listen
For the sluicing of their rain-dishevelled petals.
In the window full of sunlight
Concentrates her golden shadow
Fold on fold, until it glows as
Mellow as the glory roses.   *(Icking, 1917)*

RIVER ROSES

By the Isar, in the twilight
We were wandering and singing,
By the Isar, in the evening
We climbed the huntsman's ladder and sat swinging
In the fir-tree overlooking the marshes,
While river met with river, and the ringing
Of their pale-green glacier water filled the evening.

By the Isar, in the twilight
We found the dark wild roses
Hanging red at the river; and simmering
Frogs were singing, and over the river closes
Was savour of ice and of roses; and glimmering
Fear was abroad. We whispered: "No one knows us.
Let it be as the snake disposes
Here in this simmering marsh."   *(Kloster Schaeftlarn, 1917)*

NEW HEAVEN AND EARTH

1

And so I cross into another world
shyly and in homage linger for an invitation
from this unknown that I would trespass on.

I am very glad, and all alone in the world,
all alone, and very glad, in a new world
where I am disembarked at last.

I could cry with joy, because I am in the new world, just ventured in.
I could cry with joy, and quite freely, there is nobody to know.

And whosoever the unknown people of this unknown world may be
they will never understand my weeping for joy to be adventuring among
    them
because it will still be a gesture of the old world I am making
which they will not understand, because it is quite, quite foreign to
    them.

2

I was so weary of the world,
I was so sick of it,
everything was tainted with myself,
skies, trees, flowers, birds, water,
people, houses, streets, vehicles, machines,
nations, armies, war, peace-talking,
work, recreation, governing, anarchy,
it was all tainted with myself, I knew it all to start with
because it was all myself.

When I gathered flowers, I knew it was myself plucking my own flow-
    ering.
When I went in a train, I knew it was myself travelling by my own
    invention.
When I heard the cannon of the war, I listened with my own ears to
    my own destruction.
When I saw the torn dead, I knew it was my own torn dead body.
It was all me, I had done it all in my own flesh.

3

I shall never forget the maniacal horror of it all in the end
when everything was me, I knew it all already, I anticipated it all in
   my soul.
because I was the author and the result
I was the God and the creation at once;
creator, I looked at my creation;
created, I looked at myself, the creator:
it was a maniacal horror in the end.

I was a lover, I kissed the woman I loved,
And God of horror, I was kissing also myself.
I was a father and a begetter of children,
And oh, oh horror, I was begetting and conceiving in my own body.

4

At last came death, sufficiency of death,
and that at last relieved me, I died.
I buried my beloved; it was good, I buried myself and was gone.
War came, and every hand raised to murder;
very good, very good, every hand raised to murder!
Very good, very good, I am a murderer!
It is good, I can murder and murder, and see them fall,
the mutilated, horror-struck youths, a multitude
one on another, and then in clusters together
smashed, all oozing with blood, and burned in heaps
going up in a foetid smoke to get rid of them,
the murdered bodies of youths and men in heaps
the heaps and heaps and horrible reeking heaps
till it is almost enough, till I am reduced perhaps;
thousands and thousands of gaping, hideous foul dead
that are youths and men and me
being burned with oil, and consumed in corrupt thick smoke, that rolls
and taints and blackens the sky, till at last it is dark, dark as night, or
   death, or hell
and I am dead, and trodden to nought in the smoke-sodden tomb;
dead and trodden to nought in the sour black earth
of the tomb; dead and trodden to nought, trodden to nought.

5

God, but it is good to have died and been trodden out,
trodden to nought in sour, dead earth,

quite to nought,
absolutely to nothing
nothing
nothing
nothing.

For when it is quite, quite nothing, then it is everything.
When I am trodden quite out, quite, quite out,
every vestige gone, then I am here
risen, accomplishing a resurrection
risen, not born again, but risen, body the same as before,
new beyond knowledge of newness, alive beyond life,
proud beyond inkling or furthest conception of pride,
living where life was never yet dreamed of, nor hinted at,
here, in the other world, still terrestrial
myself, the same as before, yet unaccountably new.

6

I, in the sour black tomb, trodden to absolute death
I put out my hand in the night, one night, and my hand
touched that which was verily not me,
verily it was not me.
Where I had been was a sudden blaze,
a sudden flaring blaze!
So I put my hand out further, a little further
and I felt that which was not I,
it verily was not I,
it was the unknown.

Ha, I was a blaze leaping up!
I was a tiger bursting into sunlight.
I was greedy, I was mad for the unknown.
I, new-risen, resurrected, starved from the tomb,
starved from a life of devouring always myself,
now here was I, new-awakened, with my hand stretching out
and touching the unknown, the real unknown, the unknown unknown.

My God, but I can only say
I touch, I feel the unknown!
I am the first comer!
Cortes, Pisarro, Columbus, Cabot, they are nothing, nothing!
I am the first comer!

I am the discoverer!
I have found the other world!

The unknown, the unknown!
I am thrown upon the shore.
I am covering myself with the sand.
I am filling my mouth with the earth.
I am burrowing my body into the soil.
The unknown, the new world!

7

It was the flank of my wife
I touched with my hand, I clutched with my hand,
rising, new-awakened from the tomb!
It was the flank of my wife
whom I married years ago
at whose side I have lain for over a thousand nights
and all that previous while, she was I, she was I;
I touched her, it was I who touched and I who was touched.

Yet rising from the tomb, from the black oblivion
stretching out my hand, my hand flung like a drowned man's hand on a
    rock,
I touched her flank and knew I was carried by the current in death
over to the new world, and was climbing out on the shore,
risen, not to the old world, the old, changeless I, the old life,
wakened not to the old knowledge
but to a new earth, a new I, a new knowledge, a new world of time.

Ah no, I cannot tell you what it is, the new world.
I cannot tell you the mad, astounded rapture of its discovery.
I shall be mad with delight before I have done,
and whosoever comes after will find me in the new world
a madman in rapture.

8

Green streams that flow from the innermost continent of the new world,
what are they?
Green and illumined and travelling for ever
dissolved with the mystery of the innermost heart of the continent,
mystery beyond knowledge or endurance, so sumptuous
out of the well-heads of the new world.—
The other, she too has strange green eyes!

White sands and fruits unknown and perfumes that never
can blow across the dark seas to our usual world!
And land that beats with a pulse!
And valleys that draw close in love!
And strange ways where I fall into oblivion of uttermost living!—
Also she who is the other has strange-mounded breasts and strange sheer
  slopes, and white levels.

Sightless and strong oblivion in utter life takes possession of me!
The unknown, strong current of life supreme
drowns me and sweeps me away and holds me down
to the sources of mystery, in the depths,
extinguishes there my risen resurrected life
and kindles it further at the core of utter mystery. *(Greatham, 1917)*

PIANO

Softly, in the dusk, a woman is singing to me;
Taking me back down the vista of years, till I see
A child sitting under the piano, in the boom of the tingling strings
And pressing the small, poised feet of a mother who smiles as she sings.

In spite of myself, the insidious mastery of song
Betrays me back, till the heart of me weeps to belong
To the old Sunday evenings at home, with winter outside
And hymns in the cosy parlour, the tinkling piano our guide.

So now it is vain for the singer to burst into clamour
With the great black piano appassionato. The glamour
Of childish days is upon me, my manhood is cast
Down in the flood of remembrance, I weep like a child for the past.
                                                                (1918)

PASSING VISIT TO HELEN

Returning, I find her just the same,
At just the same old delicate game.

Still she says: "Nay, loose no flame
To lick me up and do me harm!
Be all yourself!—for oh, the charm
Of your heart of fire in which I look!
Oh, better there than in any book

Glow and enact the dramas and dreams
I love for ever!—there it seems
You are lovelier than life itself, till desire
Comes licking through the bars of your lips,
And over my face the stray fire slips,
Leaving a burn and an ugly smart
That will have the oil of illusion. Oh, heart
Of fire and beauty, loose no more
Your reptile flames of lust; ah, store
Your passion in the basket of your soul,
Be all yourself, one bonny, burning coal
That stays with steady joy of its own fire!
For in the firing all my porcelain
Of flesh does crackle and shiver and break in pain,
My ivory and marble black with stain,
My veil of sensitive mystery rent in twain,
My altars sullied, I, bereft, remain
A priestess execrable, taken in vain—"

   So the refrain
Sings itself over, and so the game
Restarts itself wherein I am kept
Like a glowing brazier faintly blue of flame,
So that the delicate love-adept
Can warm her hands and invite her soul,
Sprinkling incense and salt of words
And kisses pale, and sipping the toll
Of incense-smoke that rises like birds.

Yet I've forgotten in playing this game,
Things I have known that shall have no name;
Forgetting the place from which I came
I watch her ward away the flame
Yet warm herself at the fire—then blame
Me that I flicker in the basket;
Me that I glow not with content
To have my substance so subtly spent;
Me that I interrupt her game . . .
I ought to be proud that she should ask it
Of me to be her fire-opal. . . .

   It is well
Since I am here for so short a spell

Not to interrupt her?—Why should I
Break in by making any reply! *(1918)*

BABY TORTOISE

You know what it is to be born alone,
Baby tortoise!

The first day to heave your feet little by little from the shell,
Not yet awake,
And remain lapsed on earth,
Not quite alive.

A tiny, fragile, half-animate bean.

To open your tiny beak-mouth, that looks as if it would never open,
Like some iron door;
To lift the upper hawk-beak from the lower base
And reach your skinny little neck
And take your first bite at some dim bit of herbage,
Alone, small insect,
Tiny bright-eye,
Slow one.

To take your first solitary bite
And move on your slow, solitary hunt.
Your bright, dark little eye,
Your eye of a dark disturbed night,
Under its slow lid, tiny baby tortoise,
So indomitable.

No one ever heard you complain.

You draw your head forward, slowly, from your little wimple
And set forward, slow-dragging, on your four-pinned toes,
Rowing slowly forward.
Whither away, small bird?
Rather like a baby working its limbs,
Except that you make slow, ageless progress
And a baby makes none.

The touch of sun excites you,
And the long ages, and the lingering chill

Make you pause to yawn,
Opening your impervious mouth,
Suddenly beak-shaped, and very wide, like some suddenly gaping
    pincers;
Soft red tongue, and hard thin gums,
Then close the wedge of your little mountain front,
Your face, baby tortoise.

Do you wonder at the world, as slowly you turn your head in its wimple
And look with laconic, black eyes?
Or is sleep coming over you again,
The non-life?

You are so hard to wake.

Are you able to wonder?
Or is it just your indomitable will and pride of the first life
Looking round
And slowly pitching itself against the inertia
Which had seemed invincible?

The vast inanimate,
And the fine brilliance of your so tiny eye,
Challenger.

Nay, tiny shell-bird,
What a huge vast inanimate it is, that you must row against,
What an incalculable inertia.

Challenger,
Little Ulysses, fore-runner,
No bigger than my thumb-nail,
Buon viaggio.

All animate creation on your shoulder,
Set forth, little Titan, under your battle-shield.

The ponderous, preponderate,
Inanimate universe;
And you are slowly moving, pioneer, you alone.

How vivid your travelling seems now, in the troubled sunshine,
Stoic, Ulyssean atom;
Suddenly hasty, reckless, on high toes.

Voiceless little bird,
Resting your head half out of your wimple
In the slow dignity of your eternal pause.
Alone, with no sense of being alone,
And hence six times more solitary;
Fulfilled of the slow passion of pitching through **immemorial ages**
Your little round house in the midst of chaos.

Over the garden earth,
Small bird,
Over the edge of all things.

Traveller,
With your tail tucked a little on one side
Like a gentleman in a long-skirted coat.

All life carried on your shoulder,
Invincible fore-runner. *(1921)*

TORTOISE-SHELL

The Cross, the Cross
Goes deeper in than we know,
Deeper into life;
Right into the marrow
And through the bone.

Along the back of the baby tortoise
The scales are locked in an arch like a bridge,
Scale-lapping, like a lobster's sections
Or a bee's.
Then crossways down his sides
Tiger-stripes and wasp-bands.

Five, and five again, and five again,
And round the edges twenty-five little ones,
The sections of the baby tortoise shell.

Four, and a keystone;
Four, and a keystone;
Four, and a keystone;
Then twenty-four, and a tiny little keystone.

It needed Pythagoras to see life placing her counters on the living back
Of the baby tortoise;
Life establishing the first eternal mathematical tablet
Not in stone, like the Judean Lord, or bronze, but in life-clouded, life-
    rosy tortoise-shell.

The first little mathematical gentleman
Stepping, wee mite, in his loose trousers
Under all the eternal dome of mathematical law.

Fives, and tens,
Threes and fours and twelves,
All the *volte face* of decimals,
The whirligig of dozens and the pinnacle of seven.

Turn him on his back,
The kicking little beetle,
And there again, on his shell-tender, earth-touching belly,
The long cleavage of division, upright of the eternal cross
And on either side count five,
On each side, two above, on each side, two below
The dark bar horizontal.

The Cross!
It goes right through him, the sprottling insect,
Through his cross-wise cloven psyche,
Through his five-fold complex-nature.

So turn him over on his toes again;
Four pin-point toes, and a problematical thumb-piece,
Four rowing limbs, and one wedge-balancing head,
Four and one makes five, which is the clue to all mathematics.

The Lord wrote it all down on the little slate
Of the baby tortoise.
Outward and visible indication of the plan within,
The complex, manifold involvedness of an individual creature
Plotted out
On this small bird, this rudiment,
This little dome, this pediment
Of all creation,
This slow one. *(1921)*

TORTOISE GALLANTRY

Making his advances
He does not look at her, nor sniff at her,
No, not even sniff at her, his nose is blank.

Only he senses the vulnerable folds of skin
That work beneath her while she sprawls along
In her ungainly pace,
Her folds of skin that work and row
Beneath the earth-soiled hovel in which she moves.

And so he strains beneath her housey walls
And catches her trouser-legs in his beak
Suddenly, or her skinny limb,
And strange and grimly drags at her
Like a dog,
Only agelessly silent, with a reptile's awful persistency.

Grim, gruesome gallantry, to which he is doomed.
Dragged out of an eternity of silent isolation
And doomed to partiality, partial being,
Ache, and want of being,
Want,
Self-exposure, hard humiliation, need to add himself on to her.

Born to walk alone,
Fore-runner,
Now suddenly distracted into this mazy side-track,
This awkward, harrowing pursuit,
This grim necessity from within.

Does she know
As she moves eternally slowly away?
Or is he driven against her with a bang, like a bird flying in the dark
   against a window,
All knowledgeless?

The awful concussion,
And the still more awful need to persist, to follow, follow, continue,

Driven, after aeons of pristine, fore-god-like singleness and oneness,
At the end of some mysterious, red-hot iron,

Driven away from himself into her tracks,
Forced to crash against her.

Stiff, gallant, irascible, crook-legged reptile,
Little gentleman,
Sorry plight,
We ought to look the other way.

Save that, having come with you so far,
We will go on to the end. *(1921)*

SNAKE

A snake came to my water-trough
On a hot, hot day, and I in pyjamas for the heat,
To drink there.

In the deep, strange-scented shade of the great dark carob-tree
I came down the steps with my pitcher
And must wait, must stand and wait, for there he was at the trough
    before me.

He reached down from a fissure in the earth-wall in the gloom
And trailed his yellow-brown slackness soft-bellied down, over the edge
    of the stone trough
And rested his throat upon the stone bottom,
And where the water had dripped from the tap, in a small clearness,
He sipped with his straight mouth,
Softly drank through his straight gums, into his slack long body,
Silently.

Someone was before me at my water-trough,
And I, like a second comer, waiting.

He lifted his head from his drinking, as cattle do,
And looked at me vaguely, as drinking cattle do,
And flickered his two-forked tongue from his lips, and mused a moment,
And stooped and drank a little more,
Being earth-brown, earth-golden from the burning bowels of the earth
On the day of Sicilian July, with Etna smoking.

The voice of my education said to me
He must be killed,
For in Sicily the black, black snakes are innocent, the gold are
    venomous.

And voices in me said, If you were a man
You would take a stick and break him now, and finish him off.

But must I confess how I liked him,
How glad I was he had come like a guest in quiet, to drink at my
    water-trough
And depart peaceful, pacified, and thankless,
Into the burning bowels of this earth?

Was it cowardice, that I dared not kill him?
Was it perversity, that I longed to talk to him?
Was it humility, to feel so honoured?
I felt so honoured.

And yet those voices:
If you were not afraid, you would kill him!

And truly I was afraid, I was most afraid,
But even so, honoured still more
That he should seek my hospitality
From out the dark door of the secret earth.

He drank enough
And lifted his head, dreamily, as one who has drunken,
And flickered his tongue like a forked night on the air, so black;
Seeming to lick his lips,
And looked around like a god, unseeing, into the air,
And slowly turned his head,
And slowly, very slowly, as if thrice adream,
Proceeded to draw his slow length curving round
And climb again the broken bank of my wall-face.

And as he put his head into that dreadful hole,
And as he slowly drew up, snake-easing his shoulders, and entered
    farther,
A sort of horror, a sort of protest against his withdrawing into that
    horrid black hole,
Deliberately going into the blackness, and slowly drawing himself after,
Overcame me now his back was turned.

I looked around, I put down my pitcher,
I picked up a clumsy log
And threw it at the water-trough with a clatter.

I think I did not hit him,
But suddenly that part of him that was left behind convulsed in undig-
  nified haste,
Writhed like lightning, and was gone
Into the black hole, the earth-lipped fissure in the wall-front,
At which, in the intense still noon, I stared with fascination.

And immediately I regretted it.
I thought how paltry, how vulgar, what a mean act!
I despised myself and the voices of my accursed human education.

And I thought of the albatross,
And I wished he would come back, my snake.

For he seemed to me again like a king,
Like a king in exile, uncrowned in the underworld,
Now due to be crowned again.

And so, I missed my chance with one of the lords
Of life.
And I have something to expiate;
A pettiness.   *(Taormina, 1923)*

HUMMING-BIRD

I can imagine, in some otherworld
Primeval-dumb, far back
In that most awful stillness, that only gasped and hummed,
Humming-birds raced down the avenues.

Before anything had a soul,
While life was a heave of Matter, half inanimate,
This little bit chipped off in brilliance
And went whizzing through the slow, vast, succulent stems.

I believe there were no flowers then,
In the world where the humming-bird flashed ahead of creation.
I believe he pierced the slow vegetable veins with his long beak.

Probably he was big
As mosses, and little lizards, they say, were once big.
Probably he was a jabbing, terrifying monster.

We look at him through the wrong end of the telescope of Time,
Luckily for us.   (*Española, 1923*)

SORROW

Why does the thin grey strand
Floating up from the forgotten
Cigarette between my fingers,
Why does it trouble me?

Ah, you will understand;
When I carried my mother downstairs,
A few times only, at the beginning
Of her soft-foot malady,

I should find, for a reprimand
To my gaiety, a few long grey hairs
On the breast of my coat; and one by one
I watched them float up the dark chimney.   (*1916*)

BROODING GRIEF

A yellow leaf, from the darkness
Hops like a frog before me;
Why should I start and stand still?

I was watching the woman that bore me
Stretched in the brindled darkness
Of the sick-room, rigid with will
To die: and the quick leaf tore me
Back to this rainy swill
Of leaves and lamps and the city street mingled before me.

(*1916*)

MY WAY IS NOT THY WAY

My way is not thy way, and thine is not mine.
But come, before we part
Let us separately go to the Morning Star,
And meet there.

I do not point you to my road, nor yet
Call: "Oh come!"

But the Star is the same for both of us,
Winsome.

The good ghost of me goes down the distance
To the Holy Ghost.
Oh you, in the tent of the cloven flame
Meet me, you I like most.

Each man his own way forever, but towards
The hoverer between;
Who opens his flame like a tent-flap,
As we slip in unseen.

A man cannot tread like a woman,
Nor a woman step out like a man.
The ghost of each through the leaves of shadow
Moves as it can.

But the Morning Star and the Evening Star
Pitch tents of flame
Where we foregather like gypsies, none knowing
How the other came.

I ask for nothing except to slip
In the tent of the Holy Ghost
And be there in the house of the cloven flame,
Guest of the Host.

Be with me there, my woman,
Be bodily there.
Then let the flame wrap round us
Like a snare.

Be there along with me, oh men!
Reach across the hearth,
And laugh with me while the woman rests
For all we are worth. *(1926)*

WHEN I WENT TO THE CIRCUS

When I went to the circus that had pitched on the waste lot
It was full of uneasy people
Frightened of the bare earth and the temporary canvas

and the smell of horses and other beasts
instead of merely the smell of man.

Monkeys rode rather grey and wizened
on curly plump piebald ponies
and the children uttered a little cry—
and dogs jumped through hoops and turned somersaults
and then the geese scuttled in in a little flock
and round the ring they went to the sound of the whip
then doubled, and back, with a funny up-flutter of wings—
and the children suddenly shouted out.

Then came the hush again, like a hush of fear.

The tight-rope lady, pink and blonde and nude-looking, with a few gold
      spangles
footed cautiously out on the rope, turned prettily, spun round
bowed, and lifted her foot in her hand, smiled, swung her parasol
to another balance, tripped round, poised, and slowly sank
her handsome thighs down, down, till she slept her splendid body on
      the rope.
When she rose, tilting her parasol, and smiled at the cautious people
they cheered, but nervously.

The trapeze man, slim and beautiful and like a fish in the air
swung great curves through the upper space, and came down like a star
—And the people applauded, with hollow, frightened applause.

The elephants, huge and grey, loomed their curved bulk through the
      dusk
and sat up, taking strange postures, showing the pink soles of their feet
and curling their precious live trunks like ammonites
and moving always with a soft slow precision
as when a great ship moves to anchor.
The people watched and wondered, and seemed to resent the mystery
      that lies in beasts.

Horses, gay horses, swirling round and plaiting
in a long line, their heads laid over each other's necks;
they were happy, they enjoyed it;
all the creatures seemed to enjoy the game
in the circus, with their circus people.

But the audience, compelled to wonder
compelled to admire the bright rhythms of moving bodies
compelled to see the delicate skill of flickering human bodies
flesh flamey and a little heroic, even in a tumbling clown,
they were not really happy.
There was no gushing response, as there is at the film.

When modern people see the carnal body dauntless and flickering gay
playing among the elements neatly, beyond competition
and displaying no personality,
modern people are depressed.

Modern people feel themselves at a disadvantage.
They know they have no bodies that could play among the elements.
They have only their personalities, that are best seen flat, on the film,
flat personalities in two dimensions, imponderable and touchless.

And they grudge the circus people the swooping gay weight of limbs
that flower in mere movement,
and they grudge them the immediate, physical understanding they have
    with their circus beasts,
and they grudge them their circus-life altogether.

Yet the strange, almost frightened shout of delight that comes now and
    then from the children
shows that the children vaguely know how cheated they are of their
    birthright
in the bright wild circus flesh.   *(1929)*

SWAN

Far-off
at the core of space
at the quick
of time
beats
and goes still
the great swan upon the waters of all endings
the swan within vast chaos, within the electron.

For us
no longer he swims calmly
nor clacks across the forces furrowing a great gay trail

of happy energy,
nor is he nesting passive upon the atoms,
nor flying north desolative icewards
to the sleep of ice,
nor feeding in the marshes,
nor honking horn-like into the twilight.—

But he stoops, now
in the dark
upon us;
he is treading our women
and we men are put out
as the vast white bird
furrows our fatherless women
with unknown shocks
and stamps his black marsh-feet on their white and marshy flesh.

(1929)

WILLY WET-LEG

I can't stand Willy wet-leg,
can't stand him at any price.
He's resigned, and when you hit him
he lets you hit him twice. (1929)

WHEN THE RIPE FRUIT FALLS

When the ripe fruit falls
its sweetness distils and trickles away into the veins of the earth.

When fulfilled people die
the essential oil of their experience enters
the veins of living space, and adds a glisten
to the atom, to the body of immortal chaos.

For space is alive
and it stirs like a swan
whose feathers glisten
silky with oil of distilled experience. (1929)

WHALES WEEP NOT!

They say the sea is cold, but the sea contains
the hottest blood of all, and the wildest, the most urgent.
All the whales in the wider deeps, hot are they, as they urge

on and on, and dive beneath the ice-bergs.
The right whales, the sperm-whales, the hammer-heads, the killers
there they blow, there they blow, hot wild white breath out of the sea!

And they rock and they rock, through the sensual ageless ages
on the depths of the seven seas,
and through the salt they reel with drunk delight
and in the tropics tremble they with love
and roll with massive, strong desire, like gods.
Then the great bull lies up against his bride
in the blue deep of the sea
as mountain pressing on mountain, in the zest of life:
and out of the inward roaring of the inner red ocean of whale blood
the long tip reaches strong, intense, like the maelstrom-tip, and comes to
    rest
in the clasp and the soft, wild clutch of a she-whale's fathomless body.

And over the bridge of the whale's strong phallus, linking the wonder
    of whales
the burning archangels under the sea keep passing, back and forth,
keep passing archangels of bliss
from him to her, from her to him, great Cherubim
that wait on whales in mid-ocean, suspended in the waves of the sea
great heaven of whales in the waters, old hierarchies.

And enormous mother whales lie dreaming suckling their whale-tender
    young
and dreaming with strange whale eyes wide open in the waters of the
    beginning and the end.

And bull-whales gather their women and whale-calves in a ring
when danger threatens, on the surface of the ceaseless flood
and range themselves like great fierce Seraphim facing the threat
encircling their huddled monsters of love.
and all this happiness in the sea, in the salt
where God is also love, but without words:
and Aphrodite is the wife of whales
most happy, happy she!

and Venus among the fishes skips and is a she-dolphin
she is the gay, delighted porpoise sporting with love and the sea
she is the female tunny-fish, round and happy among the males
and dense with happy blood, dark rainbow bliss in the sea. *(1932)*

BAVARIAN GENTIANS

Not every man has gentians in his house
In soft September, at slow, sad Michaelmas.

Bavarian gentians, tall and dark, but dark
Darkening the day-time torch-like with the smoking blueness of Pluto's
    gloom,
Ribbed hellish flowers erect, with their blaze of darkness spread blue,
Blown into points, by the heavy white draught of the day.

Torch-flowers of the blue-smoking darkness, Pluto's dark blue blaze
Black lamps from the halls of Dis, smoking dark blue
Giving off darkness, blue darkness, upon Demeter's yellow-pale day
Whom have you come for, here in the white-cast day?

Reach me a gentian, give me a torch!
Let me guide myself with the blue, forked torch of a flower
Down the darker and darker stairs, where blue is darkened on blueness
Down the way Persephone goes, just now, in first-frosted September.
To the sightless realm where darkness is married to dark
And Persephone herself is but a voice, as a bride,
A gloom invisible enfolded in the deeper dark
Of the arms of Pluto as he ravishes her once again
And pierces her once more with his passion of the utter dark.
Among the splendour of black-blue torches, shedding fathomless dark-
    ness on the nuptials.

Give me a flower on a tall stem, and three dark flames,
For I will go to the wedding, and be wedding-guest
At the marriage of the living dark.   (1932) [MS. "A"]

THE SHIP OF DEATH

1

Now it is autumn and the falling fruit
and the long journey towards oblivion.

The apples falling like great drops of dew
to bruise themselves an exit from themselves.

And it is time to go, to bid farewell
to one's own self, and find an exit
from the fallen self.

2

Have you built your ship of death, O have you?
O build your ship of death, for you will need it.

The grim frost is at hand, when the apples will fall
thick, almost thundrous, on the hardened earth.

And death is on the air like a smell of ashes!
Ah! can't you smell it?

And in the bruised body, the frightened soul
finds itself shrinking, wincing from the cold
that blows upon it through the orifices.

3

And can a man his own quietus make
with a bare bodkin?

With daggers, bodkins, bullets, man can make
a bruise or break of exit for his life;
but is that a quietus, O tell me, is it quietus?

Surely not so! for how could murder, even self-murder
ever a quietus make?

4

O let us talk of quiet that we know,
that we can know, the deep and lovely quiet
of a strong heart at peace!

How can we this, our own quietus, make?

5

Build then the ship of death, for you must take
the longest journey, to oblivion.

And die the death, the long and painful death
that lies between the old self and the new.

Already our bodies are fallen, bruised, badly bruised,
already our souls are oozing through the exit
of the cruel bruise.

Already the dark and endless ocean of the end
is washing in through the breaches of our wounds,
already the flood is upon us.

O build your ship of death, your little ark
and furnish it with food, with little cakes, and wine
for the dark flight down oblivion.

6

Piecemeal the body dies, and the timid soul
has her footing washed away, as the dark flood rises.

We are dying, we are dying, we are all of us dying
and nothing will stay the death-flood rising within us
and soon it will rise on the world, on the outside world.

We are dying, we are dying, piecemeal our bodies are dying
and our strength leaves us,
and our soul cowers naked in the dark rain over the flood,
cowering in the last branches of the tree of our life.

7

We are dying, we are dying, so all we can do
is now to be willing to die, and to build the ship
of death to carry the soul on the longest journey.

A little ship, with oars and food
and little dishes, and all accoutrements
fitting and ready for the departing soul.

Now launch the small ship, now as the body dies
and life departs, launch out, the fragile soul
in the fragile ship of courage, the ark of faith
with its store of food and little cooking pans
and change of clothes,
upon the flood's black waste
upon the waters of the end
upon the sea of death, where still we sail
darkly, for we cannot steer, and have no port.

There is no port, there is nowhere to go
only the deepening blackness darkening still
blacker upon the soundless, ungurgling flood
darkness at one with darkness, up and down
and sideways utterly dark, so there is no direction any more.
And the little ship is there; yet she is gone.
She is not seen, for there is nothing to see her by.

She is gone! gone! and yet
somewhere she is there.
Nowhere!

8

And everything is gone, the body is gone
completely under, gone, entirely gone.
The upper darkness is heavy as the lower,
between them the little ship
is gone
she is gone

It is the end, it is oblivion.

9

And yet out of eternity a thread
separates itself on the blackness,
a horizontal thread
that fumes a little with pallor upon the dark.

Is it illusion? or does the pallor fume
a little higher?
Ah wait, wait, for there's the dawn,
the cruel dawn of coming back to life
out of oblivion.

Wait, wait, the little ship
drifting, beneath the deathly ashy grey
of a flood-dawn.

Wait, wait! even so, a flush of yellow
and strangely, O chilled wan soul, a flush of rose.

A flush of rose, and the whole thing starts again.

10

The flood subsides, and the body, like a worn sea-shell
emerges strange and lovely.
And the little ship wings home, faltering and lapsing
on the pink flood,
and the frail soul steps out, into the house again
filling the heart with peace.

Swings the heart renewed with peace
even of oblivion.

Oh build your ship of death, oh build it!
for you will need it.
For the voyage of oblivion awaits you.   (1932) [MS. "A"]

TREES IN THE GARDEN

Ah in the thunder air
how still the trees are!

And the lime-tree, lovely and tall, every leaf silent
hardly looses even a last breath of perfume.

And the ghostly, creamy-coloured little tree of leaves
white, ivory white among the rambling greens,
how evanescent, variegated elder, she hesitates on the green grass
as if, in another moment, she would disappear
with all her grace of foam!

And the larch that is only a column, it goes up too tall to see:
and the balsam-pines that are blue with the grey-blue blueness of things
    from the sea,
and the young copper beech, its leaves red-rosy at the ends
how still they are together, they stand so still
in the thunder air, all strangers to one another
as the green grass glows upwards, strangers in the garden.   (1932)

THE GODS! THE GODS!

People were bathing and posturing themselves on the beach
and all was dreary, great robot limbs, robot breasts
robot voices, robot even the gay umbrellas.

But a woman, shy and alone, was washing herself under a tap
and the glimmer of the presence of the gods was like lilies,
and like water-lilies.   (1932)

Siegfried Sassoon
(1886–1967)

"IN THE PINK"

So Davies wrote: "This leaves me in the pink."
Then scrawled his name: "Your loving sweetheart, Willie."
With crosses for a hug. He'd had a drink
Of rum and tea; and, though the barn was chilly,
For once his blood ran warm; he had pay to spend.
Winter was passing; soon the year would mend.

He couldn't sleep that night. Stiff in the dark
He groaned and thought of Sundays at the farm,
When he'd go out as cheerful as a lark
In his best suit to wander arm-in-arm
With brown-eyed Gwen, and whisper in her ear
The simple, silly things she liked to hear.

And then he thought: tomorrow night we trudge
Up to the trenches, and my boots are rotten.
Five miles of stodgy clay and freezing sludge,
And everything but wretchedness forgotten.
Tonight he's in the pink; but soon he'll die.
And still the war goes on; *he* don't know why.   *(1917)*

A WORKING PARTY

Three hours ago he blundered up the trench,
Sliding and poising, groping with his boots;
Sometimes he tripped and lurched against the walls
With hands that pawed the sodden bags of chalk.
He couldn't see the man who walked in front;
Only he heard the drum and rattle of feet
Stepping along the trench-boards,—often splashing
Wretchedly where the sludge was ankle-deep.

Voices would grunt, "Keep to your right,—make way!"
When squeezing past the men from the front-line:
White faces peered, puffing a point of red;
Candles and braziers glinted through the chinks
And curtain-flaps of dug-outs; then the gloom
Swallowed his sense of sight; he stooped and swore
Because a sagging wire had caught his neck.
A flare went up; the shining whiteness spread
And flickered upward, showing nimble rats,
And mounds of glimmering sand-bags, bleached with rain;
Then the slow, silver moment died in dark.
The wind came posting by with chilly gusts
And buffeting at corners, piping thin
And dreary through the crannies; rifle-shots
Would split and crack and sing along the night,
And shells came calmly through the drizzling air
To burst with hollow bang below the hill.

Three hours ago he stumbled up the trench;
Now he will never walk that road again:
He must be carried back, a jolting lump
Beyond all need of tenderness and care;
A nine-stone corpse with nothing more to do.

He was a young man with a meagre wife
And two pale children in a Midland town;
He showed the photograph to all his mates;
And they considered him a decent chap
Who did his work and hadn't much to say,
And always laughed at other people's jokes
Because he hadn't any of his own.

That night when he was busy at his job
Of piling bags along the parapet,
He thought how slow time went, stamping his feet,
And blowing on his fingers, pinched with cold.
He thought of getting back by half-past twelve,
And tot of rum to send him warm to sleep
In draughty dug-out frowsty with the fumes
Of coke, and full of snoring, weary men.

He pushed another bag along the top,
Craning his body outward; then a flare
Gave one white glimpse of No Man's Land and wire;

And as he dropped his head the instant split
His startled life with lead, and all went out.   *(1917)*

"BLIGHTERS"

The House is crammed: tier beyond tier they grin
And cackle at the Show, while prancing ranks
Of harlots shrill the chorus, drunk with din;
"We're sure the Kaiser loves the dear old Tanks!"

I'd like to see a Tank come down the stalls,
Lurching to ragtime tunes, or "Home, Sweet Home,"—
And there'd be no more jokes in Music-halls
To mock the riddled corpses round Bapaume.   *(1917)*

"THEY"

The Bishop tells us: "When the boys come back
They will not be the same; for they'll have fought
In a just cause: they lead the last attack
On Anti-Christ; their comrade's blood has bought
New right to breed an honorable race.
They have challenged Death and dared him face to face."

"We're none of us the same!" the boys reply.
"For George lost both his legs; and Bill's stone blind;
Poor Jim's shot through the lungs and like to die;
And Bert's gone syphilitic: you'll not find
A chap who's served that hasn't found *some* change."
And the bishop said: "The ways of God are strange!"   *(1917)*

THE ONE-LEGGED MAN

Propped on a stick he viewed the August weald;
Squat orchard trees and oasts with painted cowls;
A homely, tangled hedge, a corn-stooked field,
With sound of barking dogs and farmyard fowls.

And he'd come home again to find it more
Desirable than ever it was before.
How right it seemed that he should reach the span
Of comfortable years allowed to man!
Splendid to eat and sleep and choose a wife,

Safe with his wound, a citizen of life.
He hobbled blithely through the garden gate,
And thought: "Thank God they had to amputate!" (1917)

HAUNTED

Evening was in the wood, louring with storm.
A time of drought had sucked the weedy pool
And baked the channels; birds had done with song.
Thirst was a dream of fountains in the moon,
Or willow-music blown across the water
Leisurely sliding on by weir and mill.

Uneasy was the man who wandered, brooding,
His face a little whiter than the dusk.
A drone of sultry wings flicker'd in his head.

The end of sunset burning thro' the boughs
Died in a smear of red; exhausted hours
Cumber'd, and ugly sorrows hemmed him in.

He thought: "Somewhere there's thunder," as he strove
To shake off dread; he dared not look behind him,
But stood, the sweat of horror on his face.

He blundered down a path, trampling on thistles,
In sudden race to leave the ghostly trees.
And: "Soon I'll be in open fields," he thought,
And half-remembered starlight on the meadows,
Scent of mown grass and voices of tired men,
Fading along the field-paths; home and sleep
And cool-swept upland spaces, whispering leaves,
And far off the long churring night-jar's note.

But something in the wood, trying to daunt him,
Led him confused in circles through the brake.
He was forgetting his old wretched folly,
And freedom was his need; his throat was choking;
Barbed brambles gripped and clawed him round his legs,
And he floundered over snags and hidden stumps.
Mumbling: "I will get out! I must get out!"
Butting and thrusting up the baffling gloom,
Pausing to listen in a space 'twixt thorns,

He peers around with boding, frantic eyes.
An evil creature in the twilight looping,
Flapped blindly in his face. Beating it off,
He screeched in terror, and straightway something clambered
Heavily from an oak, and dropped, bent double,
To shamble at him zigzag, squat and bestial.

Headlong he charges down the wood, and falls
With roaring brain—agony—the snap't spark—
And blots of green and purple in his eyes.
Then the slow fingers groping on his neck,
And at his heart the strangling clasp of death. *(1917)*

THE TROOPS

Dim, gradual thinning of the shapeless gloom
Shudders to drizzling daybreak that reveals
Disconsolate men who stamp their sodden boots
And turn dulled, sunken faces to the sky
Haggard and hopeless. They, who have beaten down
The stale despair of night, must now renew
Their desolation in the truce of dawn,
Murdering the livid hours that grope for peace.

Yet these, who cling to life with stubborn hands,
Can grin through storms of death and find a gap
In the clawed, cruel tangles of his defence.
They march from safety, and the bird-sung joy
Of grass-green thickets, to the land where all
Is ruin, and nothing blossoms but the sky
That hastens over them where they endure
Sad, smoking, flat horizons, reeking woods,
And foundered trench-lines volleying doom for doom.

O my brave brown companions, when your souls
Flock silently away, and the eyeless dead
Shame the wild beast of battle on the ridge,
Death will stand grieving in that field of war
Since your unvanquished hardihood is spent.
And through some mooned Valhalla there will pass
Battalions and battalions, scarred from hell;
The unreturning army that was youth;
The legions who have suffered and are dust. *(1918)*

THE GENERAL

"Good-morning; good-morning!" the General said
When we met him last week on our way to the line.
Now the soldiers he smiled at are most of 'em dead,
And we're cursing his staff for incompetent swine.
"He's a cheery old card," grunted Harry to Jack
As they slogged up to Arras with rifle and pack.

*　　*　　*

But he did for them both by his plan of attack.　(1918)

REPRESSION OF WAR EXPERIENCE

Now light the candles; one; two; there's a moth;
What silly beggars they are to blunder in
And scorch their wings with glory, liquid flame—
No, no, not that,—it's bad to think of war,
When thoughts you've gagged all day come back to scare you;
And it's been proved that soldiers don't go mad
Unless they lose control of ugly thoughts
That drive them out to jabber among the trees.

Now light your pipe; look, what a steady hand.
Draw a deep breath; stop thinking, count fifteen,
And you're as right as rain. . . .
　　　　　　　　　Why won't it rain? .
I wish there'd be a thunder-storm tonight,
With bucketsful of water to sluice the dark,
And make the roses hang their dripping heads.
Books; what a jolly company they are,
Standing so quiet and patient on their shelves,
Dressed in dim brown, and black, and white, and green,
And every kind of colour. Which will you read?
Come on; O *do* read something; they're so wise.
I tell you all the wisdom of the world
Is waiting for you on those shelves; and yet
You sit and gnaw your nails, and let your pipe out,
And listen to the silence: on the ceiling
There's one big, dizzy moth that bumps and flutters;
And in the breathless air outside the house
The garden waits for something that delays.
There must be crowds of ghosts among the trees,—

Not people killed in battle,—they're in France,—
But horrible shapes in shrouds—old men who died
Slow, natural deaths,—old men with ugly souls,
Who wore their bodies out with nasty sins.

*   *   *

You're quiet and peaceful, summering safe at home;
You'd never think there was a bloody war on! . . .
O yes, you would . . . why, you can hear the guns.
Hark! Thud, thud, thud,—quite soft . . . they never cease—
Those whispering guns—O Christ, I want to go out
And screech at them to stop—I'm going crazy;
I'm going stark, staring mad because of the guns. *(1918)*

PICTURE-SHOW

And still they come and go: and this is all I know—
That from the gloom I watch an endless picture-show,
Where wild or listless faces flicker on their way,
With glad or grievous hearts I'll never understand
Because Time spins so fast, and they've no time to stay
Beyond the moment's gesture of a lifted hand.

And still, between the shadow and the blinding flame,
The brave despair of men flings onward, ever the same
As in those doom-lit years that wait them, and have been . . .
And life is just the picture dancing on a screen. *(1919)*

AT THE GRAVE OF HENRY VAUGHAN

Above the voiceful windings of a river
An old green slab of simply graven stone
Shuns notice, overshadowed by a yew.
Here Vaughan lies dead, whose name flows on for ever
Through pastures of the spirit washed with dew
And starlit with eternities unknown.

Here sleeps the Silurist; the loved physician;
The face that left no portraiture behind;
The skull that housed white angels and had vision
Of daybreak through the gateways of the mind.
Here faith and mercy, wisdom and humility
(Whose influence shall prevail for evermore)

Shine. And this lowly grave tells Heaven's tranquillity.
And here stand I, a suppliant at the door.   (1927)

DECEMBER STILLNESS

December stillness, teach me through your trees
That loom along the west, one with the land,
The veiled evangel of your mysteries.
  While nightfall, sad and spacious, on the down
Deepens, and dusk imbues me where I stand,
With grave diminishings of green and brown,
Speak, roofless Nature, your instinctive words;
And let me learn your secret from the sky,
Following a flock of steadfast-journeying birds
In lone remote migration beating by.
December stillness, crossed by twilight roads,
Teach me to travel far and bear my loads.   (1934)

VIGILS

Lone heart, learning
By one light burning,
Slow discerning of worldhood's worth;
Soul, awaking
By night and taking
Roads forsaking enchanted earth:
Man, unguided
And self-divided,
Clocked by silence which tells decay;
You that keep
In a land asleep
One light burning till break of day:
You whose vigil
Is deed and sigil,
Bond and service of lives afar—
Seek, in seeing
Your own blind being,
Peace, remote in the morning star.   (1934)

Edwin Muir
(1887–1959)

CHILDHOOD

Long time he lay upon the sunny hill,
  To his father's house below securely bound.
Far off the silent, changing sound was still,
  With the black islands lying thick around.

He saw each separate height, each vaguer hue,
  Where the massed islands rolled in mist away,
And though all ran together in his view
  He knew that unseen straits between them lay.

Often he wondered what new shores were there.
  In thought he saw the still light on the sand,
The shallow water clear in tranquil air,
  And walked through it in joy from strand to strand.

Over the sound a ship so slow would pass
  That in the black hill's gloom it seemed to lie.
The evening sound was smooth like sunken glass,
  And time seemed finished ere the ship passed by.

Grey tiny rocks slept round him where he lay,
  Moveless as they, more still as evening came,
The grasses threw straight shadows far away,
  And from the house his mother called his name. *(1925)*

HORSES

Those lumbering horses in the steady plough,
On the bare field—I wonder why, just now,
They seemed terrible, so wild and strange,
Like magic power on the stony grange.

Perhaps some childish hour has come again,
When I watched fearful, through the blackening rain,
Their hooves like pistons in an ancient mill
Move up and down, yet seem as standing still.

Their conquering hooves which trod the stubble down
Were ritual that turned the field to brown,
And their great hulks were seraphim of gold,
Or mute ecstatic monsters on the mould.

And oh the rapture, when, one furrow done,
They marched broad-breasted to the sinking sun!
The light flowed off their bossy sides in flakes;
The furrows rolled behind like struggling snakes.

But when at dusk with steaming nostrils home
They came, they seemed gigantic in the gloam,
And warm and glowing with mysterious fire
That lit their smouldering bodies in the mire.

Their eyes as brilliant and as wide as night
Gleamed with a cruel apocalyptic light.
Their manes the leaping ire of the wind
Lifted with rage invisible and blind.

Ah, now it fades! it fades! and I must pine
Again for that dread country crystalline,
Where the blank field and the still-standing tree
Were bright and fearful presences to me. (1925)

THE ROAD

There is a road that turning always
    Cuts off the country of Again.
Archers stand there on every side
    And as it runs time's deer is slain,
    And lies where it has lain.

That busy clock shows never an hour.
    All flies and all in flight must tarry.
The hunter shoots the empty air
    Far on before the quarry,
    Which falls though nothing's there to parry.

The lion crouching in the centre
   With mountain head and sunset brow
Rolls down the everlasting slope
   Bones picked an age ago,
   And the bones rise up and go.

There the beginning finds the end
   Before the beginning ever can be,
And the great runner never leaves
   The starting and the finishing tree,
   The budding and the fading tree.

There the ship sailing safe in harbour
   Long since in many a sea was drowned.
The treasure burning in her hold
   So near will never be found,
   Sunk past all sound.

There a man on a summer evening
   Reclines at ease upon his tomb
And is his mortal effigy.
   And there within the womb,
   The cell of doom,

The ancestral deed is thought and done,
   And in a million Edens fall
A million Adams drowned in darkness,
   For small is great and great is small,
   And a blind seed all.   *(1937)*

TROY

He all that time among the sewers of Troy
Scouring for scraps. A man so venerable
He might have been Priam's self, but Priam was dead,
Troy taken. His arms grew meagre as a boy's,
And all that flourished in that hollow famine
Was his long, white, round beard. Oh, sturdily
He swung his staff and sent the bold rats skipping
Across the scurfy hills and worm-wet valleys,
Crying: "Achilles, Ajax, turn and fight!
Stop cowards!" Till his cries, dazed and confounded,
Flew back at him with: "Coward, turn and fight!"

And the wild Greeks yelled round him.
Yet he withstood them, a brave, mad old man,
And fought the rats for Troy. The light was rat-grey,
The hills and dells, the common drain, his Simois,
Rat-grey. Mysterious shadows fell
Affrighting him whenever a cloud offended
The sun up in the other world. The rat-hordes,
Moving, were grey dust shifting in grey dust.
Proud history has such sackends. He was taken
At last by some chance robber seeking treasure
Under Troy's riven roots. Dragged to the surface.
And there he saw Troy like a burial ground
With tumbled walls for tombs, the smooth sward wrinkled
As Time's last wave had long since passed that way,
The sky, the sea, Mount Ida and the islands,
No sail from edge to edge, the Greeks clean gone.
They stretched him on a rock and wrenched his limbs,
Asking: "Where is the treasure?" till he died.   (1937)

THE TOWN BETRAYED

Our homes are eaten out by time,
  Our lawns strewn with our listless sons,
Our harlot daughters lean and watch
  The ships crammed down with shells and guns.

Like painted prows far out they lean:
  A world behind, a world before.
The leaves are covering up our hills,
  Neptune has locked the shore.

Our yellow harvests lie forlorn
  And there we wander like the blind,
Returning from the golden field
  With famine in our mind.

Far inland now the glittering swords
  In order rise, in order fall,
In order on the dubious field
  The dubious trumpets call.

Yet here there is no word, no sign
  But quiet murder in the street.

Our leaf-light lives are spared or taken
  By men obsessed and neat.

We stand beside our windows, see
  In order dark disorder come,
And prentice killers duped by death
  Bring and not know our doom.

Our cattle wander at their will.
  To-day a horse pranced proudly by.
The dogs run wild. Vultures and kites
  Wait in the towers for us to die.

At evening on the parapet
  We sit and watch the sun go down,
Reading the landscape of the dead,
  The sea, the hills, the town.

There our ancestral ghosts are gathered.
  Fierce Agamemnon's form I see,
Watching as if his tents were time
  And Troy eternity.

We must take order, bar our gates,
  Fight off these phantoms. Inland now
Achilles, Siegfried, Lancelot
  Have sworn to bring us low. *(1937)*

THEN

There were no men and women then at all,
But the flesh lying alone,
And angry shadows fighting on a wall
That now and then sent out a groan
Buried in lime and stone,
And sweated now and then like tortured wood
Big drops that looked yet did not look like blood.

And yet as each drop came a shadow faded
And left the wall.
There was a lull
Until another in its shadow arrayed it,
Came, fought and left a blood-mark on the wall;
And that was all; the blood was all.

If there had been women there they might have wept
For the poor blood, unowned, unwanted,
Blank as forgotten script.
The wall was haunted
By mute maternal presences whose sighing
Fluttered the fighting shadows and shook the wall
As if that fury of death itself were dying.   (1943)

THE GATE

We sat, two children, warm against the wall
Outside the towering stronghold of our fathers
That frowned its stern security down upon us.
We could not enter there. That fortress life,
Our safe protection, was too gross and strong
For our unpractised palates. Yet our guardians
Cherished our innocence with gentle hands,
(They, who had long since lost their innocence,)
And in grave play put on a childish mask
Over their tell-tale faces, as in shame
For the fine food that plumped their lusty bodies
And made them strange as gods. We sat that day
With that great parapet behind us, safe
As every day, yet outcast, safe and outcast
As castaways thrown upon an empty shore.
Before us lay our well-worn scene, a hillock
So small and smooth and green, it seemed intended
For us alone and childhood, a still pond
That opened upon no sight a quiet eye,
A little stream that tinkled down the slope.
But suddenly all seemed old
And dull and shrunken, shut within itself
In a sullen dream. We were outside, alone.
And then behind us the huge gate swung open.   (1943)

THE RETURN

The doors flapped open in Ulysses' house,
The lolling latches gave to every hand,
Let traitor, babbler, tout and bargainer in.
The rooms and passages resounded
With ease and chaos of a public market,
The walls mere walls to lean on as you talked,
Spat on the floor, surveyed some newcomer
With an absent eye. There you could be yourself.

Dust in the nooks, weeds nodding in the yard,
The thick walls crumbling. Even the cattle came
About the doors with mild familiar stare
As if this were their place.
All round the island stretched the clean blue sea.

Sole at the house's heart Penelope
Sat at her chosen task, endless undoing
Of endless doing, endless weaving, unweaving,
In the clean chamber. Still her loom ran empty
Day after day. She thought: "Here I do nothing
Or less than nothing, making an emptiness
Amid disorder, weaving, unweaving the lie
The day demands. Ulysses, this is duty,
To do and undo, to keep a vacant gate
Where order and right and hope and peace can enter.
Oh will you ever return? Or are you dead,
And this wrought emptiness my ultimate emptiness?"

She wove and unwove and wove and did not know
That even then Ulysses on the long
And winding road of the world was on his way. *(1943)*

THE ANNUNCIATION

The angel and the girl are met.
Earth was the only meeting place.
For the embodied never yet
Travelled beyond the shore of space.
The eternal spirits in freedom go.

See, they have come together, see,
While the destroying minutes flow,
Each reflects the other's face
Till heaven in hers and earth in his
Shine steady there. He's come to her
From far beyond the farthest star,
Feathered through time. Immediacy
Of strangest strangeness is the bliss
That from their limbs all movement takes.
Yet the increasing rapture brings
So great a wonder that it makes
Each feather tremble on his wings.

Outside the window footsteps fall
Into the ordinary day
And with the sun along the wall
Pursue their unreturning way
That was ordained in eternity.
Sound's perpetual roundabout
Rolls its numbered octaves out
And hoarsely grinds its battered tune.

But through the endless afternoon
These neither speak nor movement make,
But stare into their deepening trance
As if their gaze would never break.   (1956)

THE RETURN

The veteran Greeks came home
Sleepwandering from the war.
We saw the galleys come
Blundering over the bar.
Each soldier with his scar
In rags and tatters came home.

Reading the wall of Troy
Ten years without a change
Was such intense employ
(Just out of the arrows' range),
All the world was strange
After ten years of Troy.

Their eyes knew every stone
In the huge heartbreaking wall
Year after year grown
Till there was nothing at all
But an alley steep and small,
Tramped earth and towering stone.

Now even the hills seemed low
In the boundless sea and land,
Weakened by distance so.
How could they understand
Space empty on every hand
And the hillocks squat and low?

And when they arrived at last
They found a childish scene
Embosomed in the past,
And the war lying between—
A child's preoccupied scene
When they came home at last.

But everything trite and strange
The peace, the parcelled ground
The vinerows—never a change!
The past and the present bound
In one oblivious round
Past thinking trite and strange.

But for their grey-haired wives
And their sons grown shy and tall
They would have given their lives
To raise the battered wall
Again, if this was all
In spite of their sons and wives.

Penelope in her tower
Looked down upon the show
And saw within an hour
Each man to his wife go,
Hesitant, sure and slow:
She, alone in her tower. *(1946)*

THE RIDER VICTORY

The rider Victory reins his horse
Midway across the empty bridge
As if head-tall he had met a wall.
Yet there was nothing there at all,
No bodiless barrier, ghostly ridge
To check the charger in his course
So suddenly, you'd think he'd fall.

Suspended, horse and rider stare,
Leaping on air and legendary.
In front the waiting kingdom lies,
The bridge and all the roads are free;
But halted in implacable air

Rider and horse with stony eyes
Uprear their motionless statuary.   (*1946*)

THE MYTH

My childhood all a myth
Enacted in a distant isle;
Time with his hourglass and his scythe
Stood dreaming on the dial,
And did not move the whole day long
That immobility might save
Continually the dying song,
The flower, the falling wave.
And at each corner of the wood
In which I played the ancient play,
Guarding the traditional day
The faithful watchers stood.

My youth a tragi-comedy,
Ridiculous war of dreams and shames
Waged for a Pyrrhic victory
Of reveries and names,
Which in slow-motion rout were hurled
Before sure-footed flesh and blood
That of its hunger built a world
Advancing rood by rood.
And there in practical clay compressed
The reverie played its useful part,
Fashioning a diurnal mart
Of radiant east and west.

So manhood went. Now past the prime
I see this life contrived to stay
With all its works of labouring time
By time beguiled away.
Consolidated flesh and bone
And its designs grow halt and lame;
Unshakeable arise alone
The reverie and the name.
And at each border of the land,
Like monuments a deluge leaves,
Guarding the invisible sheaves
The risen watchers stand.   (*1946*)

THE LABYRINTH

Since I emerged that day from the labyrinth,
Dazed with the tall and echoing passages,
The swift recoils, so many I almost feared
I'd meet myself returning at some smooth corner,
Myself or my ghost, for all there was unreal
After the straw ceased rustling and the bull
Lay dead upon the straw and I remained,
Blood-splashed, if dead or alive I could not tell
In the twilight nothingness (I might have been
A spirit seeking his body through the roads
Of intricate Hades)—ever since I came out
To the world, the still fields swift with flowers, the trees
All bright with blossom, the little green hills, the sea,
The sky and all in movement under it,
Shepherds and flocks and birds and the young and old,
(I stared in wonder at the young and the old,
For in the maze time had not been with me;
I had strayed, it seemed, past sun and season and change,
Past rest and motion, for I could not tell
At last if I moved or stayed; the maze itself
Revolved around me on its hidden axis
And swept me smoothly to its enemy,
The lovely world)—since I came out that day,
There have been times when I have heard my footsteps
Still echoing in the maze, and all the roads
That run through the noisy world, deceiving streets
That meet and part and meet, and rooms that open
Into each other—and never a final room—
Stairways and corridors and antechambers
That vacantly wait for some great audience,
The smooth sea-tracks that open and close again,
Tracks undiscoverable, indecipherable,
Paths on the earth and tunnels underground,
And bird-tracks in the air—all seemed a part
Of the great labyrinth. And then I'd stumble
In sudden blindness, hasten, almost run,
As if the maze itself were after me
And soon must catch me up. But taking thought,
I'd tell myself, "You need not hurry. This
Is the firm good earth. All roads lie free before you."

But my bad spirit would sneer, "No, do not hurry.
No need to hurry. Haste and delay are equal
In this one world, for there's no exit, none,
No place to come to, and you'll end where you are,
Deep in the centre of the endless maze."

I could not live if this were not illusion.
It is a world, perhaps; but there's another.
For once in a dream or trance I saw the gods
Each sitting on the top of his mountain-isle,
While down below the little ships sailed by,
Toy multitudes swarmed in the harbours, shepherds drove
Their tiny flocks to the pastures, marriage feasts
Went on below, small birthdays and holidays,
Ploughing and harvesting and life and death,
And all permissible, all acceptable,
Clear and secure as in a limpid dream.
But they, the gods, as large and bright as clouds,
Conversed across the sounds in tranquil voices
High in the sky above the untroubled sea,
And their eternal dialogue was peace
Where all these things were woven; and this our life
Was as a chord deep in that dialogue,
As easy utterance of harmonious words,
Spontaneous syllables bodying forth a world.

That was the real world; I have touched it once,
And now shall know it always. But the lie,
The maze, the wild-wood waste of falsehood, roads
That run and run and never reach an end,
Embowered in error—I'd be prisoned there
But that my soul has birdwings to fly free.

Oh these deceits are strong almost as life.
Last night I dreamt I was in the labyrinth,
And woke far on. I did not know the place.   (1949)

THE COMBAT

It was not meant for human eyes,
That combat on the shabby patch
Of clods and trampled turf that lies
Somewhere beneath the sodden skies
For eye of toad or adder to catch.

And having seen it I accuse
The crested animal in his pride,
Arrayed in all the royal hues
Which hide the claws he well can use
To tear the heart out of the side.

Body of leopard, eagle's head
And whetted beak, and lion's mane,
And frost-grey hedge of feathers spread
Behind—he seemed of all things bred.
I shall not see his like again.

As for his enemy, there came in
A soft round beast as brown as clay;
All rent and patched his wretched skin;
A battered bag he might have been,
Some old used thing to throw away.

Yet he awaited face to face
The furious beast and the swift attack.
Soon over and done. That was no place
Or time for chivalry or for grace.
The fury had him on his back.

And two small paws like hands flew out
To right and left as the trees stood by.
One would have said beyond a doubt
This was the very end of the bout,
But that the creature would not die.

For ere the death-stroke he was gone,
Writhed, whirled, huddled into his den,
Safe somehow there. The fight was done,
And he had lost who had all but won.
But oh his deadly fury then.

A while the place lay blank, forlorn,
Drowsing as in relief from pain.
The cricket chirped, the grating thorn
Stirred, and a little sound was born.
The champions took their posts again.

And all began. The stealthy paw
Slashed out and in. Could nothing save

These rags and tatters from the claw?
Nothing. And yet I never saw
A beast so helpless and so brave.

And now, while the trees stand watching, still
The unequal battle rages there.
The killing beast that cannot kill
Swells and swells in his fury till
You'd almost think it was despair.   (1949)

THE INTERROGATION

We could have crossed the road but hesitated.
And then came the patrol;
The leader conscientious and intent,
The men surly, indifferent.
While we stood by and waited
The interrogation began. He says the whole
Must come out now, who, what we are,
Where we have come from, with what purpose, whose
Country or camp we plot for or betray.
Question on question.
We have stood and answered through the standing day
And watched across the road beyond the hedge
The careless lovers in pairs go by,
Hand linked in hand, wandering another star,
So near we could shout to them. We cannot choose
Answer or action here,
Though still the careless lovers saunter by
And the thoughtless field is near.
We are on the very edge,
Endurance almost done,
And still the interrogation is going on.   (1949)

THE GOOD TOWN

Look at it well. This was the good town once,
Known everywhere, with streets of friendly neighbours,
Street friend to street and house to house. In summer
All day the doors stood open; lock and key
Were quaint antiquities fit for museums
With gyves and rusty chains. The ivy grew
From post to post across the prison door.

The yard behind was sweet with grass and flowers,
A place where grave philosophers loved to walk.
Old Time that promises and keeps his promise
Was our sole lord indulgent and severe,
Who gave and took away with gradual hand
That never hurried, never tarried, still
Adding, subtracting. These our houses had
Long fallen into decay but that we knew
Kindness and courage can repair time's faults,
And serving him breeds patience and courtesy
In us, light sojourners and passing subjects.
There is a virtue in tranquillity
That makes all fitting, childhood and youth and age,
Each in its place.
                    Look well. These mounds of rubble,
And shattered piers, half-windows, broken arches
And groping arms were once inwoven in walls
Covered with saints and angels, bore the roof,
Shot up the towering spire. These gaping bridges
Once spanned the quiet river which you see
Beyond that patch of raw and angry earth
Where the new concrete houses sit and stare.
Walk with me by the river. See, the poplars
Still gather quiet gazing on the stream.
The white road winds across the small green hill
And then is lost. These few things still remain.
Some of our houses too, though not what once
Lived there and drew a strength from memory.
Our people have been scattered, or have come
As strangers back to mingle with the strangers
Who occupy our rooms where none can find
The place he knew but settles where he can.
No family now sits at the evening table;
Father and son, mother and child are *out*,
A quaint and obsolete fashion. In our houses
Invaders speak their foreign tongues, informers
Appear and disappear, chance whores, officials
Humble or high, frightened, obsequious,
Sit carefully in corners. My old friends
(Friends ere these great disasters) are dispersed
In parties, armies, camps, conspiracies.
We avoid each other. If you see a man
Who smiles good-day or waves a lordly greeting

Be sure he's a policeman or a spy.
We know them by their free and candid air.

It was not time that brought these things upon us,
But these two wars that trampled on us twice,
Advancing and withdrawing, like a herd
Of clumsy-footed beasts on a stupid errand
Unknown to them or us. Pure chance, pure malice,
Or so it seemed. And when, the first war over,
The armies left and our own men came back
From every point by many a turning road,
Maimed, crippled, changed in body or in mind,
It was a sight to see the cripples come
Out on the fields. The land looked all awry,
The roads ran crooked and the light fell wrong.
Our fields were like a pack of cheating cards
Dealt out at random—all we had to play
In the bad game for the good stake, our life.
We played; a little shrewdness scraped us through.
Then came the second war, passed and repassed,
And now you see our town, the fine new prison,
The house-doors shut and barred, the frightened faces
Peeping round corners, secret police, informers,
And all afraid of all.

                  How did it come?
From outside, so it seemed, an endless source,
Disorder inexhaustible, strange to us,
Incomprehensible. Yet sometimes now
We ask ourselves, we the old citizens:
"Could it have come from us? Was our peace peace?
Our goodness goodness? That old life was easy
And kind and comfortable; but evil is restless
And gives no rest to the cruel or the kind.
How could our town grow wicked in a moment?
What is the answer? Perhaps no more than this,
That once the good men swayed our lives, and those
Who copied them took a while the hue of goodness,
A passing loan; while now the bad are up,
And we, poor ordinary neutral stuff,
Not good nor bad, must ape them as we can,
In sullen rage or vile obsequiousness.
Say there's a balance between good and evil

In things, and it's so mathematical,
So finely reckoned that a jot of either,
A bare preponderance will do all you need,
Make a town good, or make it what you see.
But then, you'll say, only that jot is wanting,
That grain of virtue. No: when evil comes
All things turn adverse, and we must begin
At the beginning, heave the groaning world
Back in its place again, and clamp it there.
Then all is hard and hazardous. We have seen
Good men made evil wrangling with the evil,
Straight minds grown crooked fighting crooked minds.
Our peace betrayed us; we betrayed our peace.
Look at it well. This was the good town once."

These thoughts we have, walking among our ruins.   (*1949*)

THE USURPERS

There is no answer. We do here what we will
And there is no answer. This our liberty
No one has known before, nor could have borne,
For it is rooted in this deepening silence
That is our work and has become our kingdom.
If there were an answer, how could we be free?
It was not hard to still the ancestral voices:
A careless thought, less than a thought could do it.
And the old garrulous ghosts died easily,
The friendly and unfriendly, and are not missed
That once were such proud masters. In this air
Our thoughts are deeds; we dare do all we think,
Since there's no one to check us, here or elsewhere.
All round us stretches nothing; we move through nothing,
Nothing but nothing world without end. We are
Self-guided, self-impelled and self-sustained,
Archer and bow and burning arrow sped
On its wild flight through nothing to tumble down
At last on nothing, our home and cure for all.
Around us is alternate light and darkness.
We live in light and darkness. When night comes
We drop like stones plumb to its ocean ground,
While dreams stream past us upward to the place
Where light meets darkness, place of images,

Forest of ghosts, thicket of muttering voices.
We never seek that place; we are for the day
And for the night alone, at home in both.
But each has its device, and this is night's:
To hide in the very heart of night from night,
Black in its blackness.
                                    For these fluttering dreams,
They'd trouble us if we were credulous,
For all the ghosts that frightened frightened men
Long since were bred in that pale territory.
These we can hold in check, but not forget,
Not quite forget, they're so inconsequent.
Sometimes we've heard in sleep tongues talking so:
"I lean my face far out from eternity
For time to work its work on: time, oh time,
What have you done?" These fancies trouble us.
The day itself sometimes works spells upon us
And then the trees look unfamiliar. Yet
It is a lie that they are witnesses,
That the mountains judge us, brooks tell tales about us.
We have thought sometimes the rocks looked strangely on us.
Have fancied that the waves were angry with us,
Heard dark runes murmuring in the autumn wind,
Muttering and murmuring like old toothless women
That phophesied against us in ancient tongues.

These are imaginations. We are free.   (1949)

OEDIPUS

I, Oedipus, the club-foot, made to stumble,
Who long in the light have walked the world in darkness,
And once in the darkness did that which the light
Found and disowned—too well I have loved the light,
Too dearly have rued the darkness. I am one
Who as in innocent play sought out his guilt,
And now through guilt seeks other innocence,
Beset by evil thoughts, led by the gods.
There was a room, a bed of darkness, once
Known to me, now to all. Yet in that darkness,
Before the light struck, she and I who lay
There without thought of sin and knew each other
Too well, yet were to each other quite unknown

Though fastened mouth to mouth and breast to breast—
Strangers laid on one bed, as children blind,
Clear-eyed and blind as children—did we sin
Then on that bed before the light came on us,
Desiring good to each other, bringing, we thought,
Great good to each other? But neither guilt nor death.

Yet if that darkness had been darker yet,
Buried in endless dark past reach of light
Or eye of the gods, a kingdom of solid darkness
Impregnable and immortal, would we have sinned,
Or lived like the gods in deathless innocence?
For sin is born in the light; therefore we cower
Before the face of the light that none can meet
And all must seek. And when in memory now,
Woven of light and darkness, a stifling web,
I call her back, dear, dreaded, who lay with me,
I see guilt, only guilt, my nostrils choke
With the smell of guilt, and I can scarcely breathe
Here in the guiltless guilt-evoking sun.

And when young Oedipus—for it was Oedipus
And not another—on that long vanished night
Far in my night, at that predestined point
Where three paths like three fates crossed one another,
Tracing the evil figure—when I met
The stranger who menaced me, and flung the stone
That brought him death and me this that I carry,
It was not him but fear I sought to kill,
Fear that, the wise men say, is father of evil,
And was my father in flesh and blood, yet fear,
Fear only, father and fear in one dense body,
So that there was no division, no way past:
Did I sin then, by the gods admonished to sin,
By men enjoined to sin? For it is duty
Of god and man to kill the shapes of fear.

These thoughts recur, vain thoughts. The gods see all
And will what must be willed, which guards us here.
Their will in them was anger, in me was terror
Long since, but now is peace. For I am led
By them in darkness; light is all about me;
My way lies in the light; they know it; I

Am theirs to guide and hold. And I have learned,
Though blind, to see with something of their sight,
Can look into that other world and watch
King Oedipus the just, crowned and discrowned,
As one may see oneself rise in a dream,
Distant and strange. Even so I see
The meeting at the place where three roads crossed,
And who was there and why, and what was done
That had to be done and paid for. Innocent
The deed that brought the guilt of father-murder. Pure
The embrace on the bed of darkness. Innocent
And guilty. I have wrought and thought in darkness,
And stand here now, an innocent mark of shame,
That so men's guilt may be made manifest
In such a walking riddle—their guilt and mine,
For I've but acted out this fable. I have judged
Myself, obedient to the gods' high judgment,
And seen myself with their pure eyes, have learnt
That all must bear a portion of the wrong
That is driven deep into our fathomless hearts
Past sight or thought; that bearing it we may ease
The immortal burden of the gods who keep
Our natural steps and the earth and skies from harm.   (1949)

ONE FOOT IN EDEN

One foot in Eden still, I stand
And look across the other land.
The world's great day is growing late,
Yet strange these fields that we have planted
So long with crops of love and hate.
Time's handiworks by time are haunted,
And nothing now can separate
The corn and tares compactly grown.
The armorial weed in stillness bound
About the stalk; these are our own.
Evil and good stand thick around
In the fields of charity and sin
Where we shall lead our harvest in.

Yet still from Eden springs the root
As clean as on the starting day.
Time takes the foliage and the fruit

And burns the archetypal leaf
To shapes of terror and of grief
Scattered along the winter way.
But famished field and blackened tree
Bear flowers in Eden never known.
Blossoms of grief and charity
Bloom in these darkened fields alone.
What had Eden ever to say
Of hope and faith and pity and love
Until was buried all its day
And memory found its treasure trove?
Strange blessings never in Paradise
Fall from these beclouded skies. *(1956)*

THE ANIMALS

They do not live in the world,
Are not in time and space.
From birth to death hurled
No word do they have, not one
To plant a foot upon,
Were never in any place.

For with names the world was called
Out of the empty air,
With names was built and walled,
Line and circle and square,
Dust and emerald;
Snatched from deceiving death
By the articulate breath.

But these have never trod
Twice the familiar track,
Never never turned back
Into the memoried day.
All is new and near
In the unchanging Here
Of the fifth great day of God,
That shall remain the same,
Never shall pass away.

On the sixth day we came. *(1956)*

THE HORSES

Barely a twelvemonth after
The seven days war that put the world to sleep,
Late in the evening the strange horses came.
By then we had made our covenant with silence,
But in the first few days it was so still
We listened to our breathing and were afraid.
On the second day
The radios failed; we turned the knobs; no answer.
On the third day a warship passed us, heading north,
Dead bodies piled on the deck. On the sixth day
A plane plunged over us into the sea. Thereafter
Nothing. The radios dumb;
And still they stand in corners of our kitchens,
And stand, perhaps, turned on, in a million rooms
All over the world. But now if they should speak,
If on a sudden they should speak again,
If on the stroke of noon a voice should speak,
We would not listen, we would not let it bring
That old bad world that swallowed its children quick
At one great gulp. We would not have it again.
Sometimes we think of the nations lying asleep,
Curled blindly in impenetrable sorrow,
And then the thought confounds us with its strangeness.

The tractors lie about our fields; at evening
They look like dank sea-monsters couched and waiting.
We leave them where they are and let them rust:
"They'll moulder away and be like other loam."
We make our oxen drag our rusty ploughs,
Long laid aside. We have gone back
Far past our fathers' land.
                            And then, that evening
Late in the summer the strange horses came.
We heard a distant tapping on the road,
A deepening drumming; it stopped, went on again
And at the corner changed to hollow thunder.
We saw the heads
Like a wild wave charging and were afraid.
We had sold our horses in our fathers' time
To buy new tractors. Now they were strange to us

As fabulous steeds set on an ancient shield
Or illustrations in a book of knights.
We did not dare go near them. Yet they waited,
Stubborn and shy, as if they had been sent
By an old command to find our whereabouts
And that long-lost archaic companionship.
In the first moment we had never a thought
That they were creatures to be owned and used.
Among them were some half-a-dozen colts
Dropped in some wilderness of the broken world,
Yet new as if they had come from their own Eden.
Since then they have pulled our ploughs and borne our loads,
But that free servitude still can pierce our hearts.
Our life is changed; their coming our beginning.   (1956)

Edith Sitwell
(1887–1964)

AUBADE

Jane, Jane,
Tall as a crane,
The morning light creaks down again;

Comb your cockscomb-ragged hair,
Jane, Jane, come down the stair.

Each dull blunt wooden stalactite
Of rain creaks, hardened by the light,

Sounding like an overtone
From some lonely world unknown.

But the creaking empty light
Will never harden into sight,

Will never penetrate your brain
With overtones like the blunt rain.

The light would show (if it could harden)
Eternities of kitchen garden,

Cockscomb flowers that none will pluck,
And wooden flowers that 'gin to cluck.

In the kitchen you must light
Flames as staring, red and white,

As carrots or as turnips, shining
Where the cold dawn light lies whining.

Cockscomb hair on the cold wind
Hangs limp, turns the milk's weak mind. . . .

Jane, Jane,
Tall as a crane,
The morning light creaks down again! *(1923)*

DARK SONG

The fire was furry as a bear
And the flames purr . . .
The brown bear rambles in his chain
Captive to cruel men
Through the dark and hairy wood . . .
The maid sighed, "All my blood
Is animal. They thought I sat
Like a household cat;
But through the dark woods rambled I . . .
Oh, if my blood would die!"
The fire had a bear's fur;
It heard and knew. . . .
The dark earth, furry as a bear,
Grumbled too! *(1923)*

TWO KITCHEN SONGS

1

The harsh bray and hollow
Of the pot and the pan
Seems Midas defying
The great god Apollo!
The leaves' great golden crowns
Hang on the trees;
The maids in their long gowns
Hunt me through these.
Grand'am, Grand'am,
From the pan I am
Flying . . . country gentlemen
Took flying Psyche for a hen
And aimed at her; then turned a gun
On harmless chicken-me—for fun.
The beggars' dogs howl all together,
Their tails turn to a ragged feather;
Pools, like mirrors hung in garrets,
Show each face as red as a parrot's,
Whistling hair that raises ire
In cocks and hens in the kitchen fire!

Every flame shrieks cockle-doo-doo
(With their cockscombs flaring high too);
The witch's rag-rug takes its flight
Beneath the willows' watery light:
The wells of water seem a-plume—
The old witch sweeps them with her broom—
All are chasing chicken-me. . . .
But Psyche—where, oh where, is she? (1923)

2

Grey as a guinea-fowl is the rain
Squawking down from the boughs again.
    "Anne, Anne,
     Go fill the pail,"
Said the old witch who sat on the rail.
"Though there is a hole in the bucket,
Anne, Anne,
It will fill my pocket;
The water-drops when they cross my doors
Will turn to guineas and gold moidores. . . ."
The well-water hops across the floors;
Whimpering, "Anne," it cries, implores;
And the guinea-fowl-plumaged rain,
Squawking down from the boughs again,
Cried, "Anne, Anne, go fill the bucket,
There is a hole in the witch's pocket—
And the water-drops like gold moidores,
Obedient girl, will surely be yours.
So, Anne, Anne,
Go fill the pail,
Of the old witch who sits on the rail!" (1925)

LULLABY

Though the world has slipped and gone,
Sounds my loud discordant cry
Like the steel birds' song on high:
"Still one thing is left—the Bone."
Then out danced the Babioun.

She sat in the hollow of the sea—
A socket whence the eye's put out—
She sang to the child a lullaby
(The steel birds' nest was thereabout).

"Do, do, do, do—
Thy mother's hied to the vaster race:
The Pterodactyl made its nest
And laid a steel egg in her breast—
Under the Judas-colored sun.
She'll work no more, nor dance, nor moan,
And I am come to take her place.
Do—do."

There's nothing left but earth's low bed—
(The Pterodactyl fouls its nest):
But steel wings fan thee to thy rest,
And wingless truth and larvae lie
And eyeless hope and handless fear—
All these for thee as toys are spread,
"Do—do—"

Red is the bed of Poland, Spain,
And thy mother's breast, who has grown wise
In that fouled nest. If she could rise,
Give birth again,
In wolfish pelt she'd hide thy bones
To shield thee from the world's long cold,
And down on all fours shouldst thou crawl
For thus from no height canst thou fall—
"Do—do."

She'd give no hands: there's nought to hold
And nought to make: there's dust to sift,
But no food for the hands to lift.
Do, do.

Heed my ragged lullaby,
Fear not living, fear not chance;
All is equal—blindness, sight,
There is no depth, there is no height:
Do, do.

The Judas-colored sun is gone,
And with the Ape thou art alone—
Do,
   Do.   (*1940*)

STREET SONG

"Love my heart for an hour, but my bone for a day—
At least the skeleton smiles, for it has a morrow:

But the hearts of the young are now the dark treasure of Death,
And summer is lonely.

"Comfort the lonely light and the sun in its sorrow,
Come like the night, for terrible is the sun
As truth, and the dying light shows only the skeleton's hunger
For peace, under the flesh like the summer rose.

"Come through the darkness of death, as once through the branches
Of youth you came, through the shade like the flowering door
That leads into Paradise, far from the street—you, the unborn
City seen by the homeless, the night of the poor.

"You walk in the city ways, where Man's threatening shadow,
Red-edged by the sun like Cain, has a changing shape—
Elegant like the Skeleton, crouched like the Tiger,
With the age-old wisdom and aptness of the Ape.

"The pulse that beats in the heart is changed to the hammer
That sounds in the Potter's Field where they build a new world
From our Bone, and the carrion-bird days' foul droppings and clamor—
But you are my night, and my peace,—

"The holy night of conception, of rest, the consoling
Darkness when all men are equal,—the wrong and the right,
And the rich and the poor are no longer separate nations,—
They are brothers in night."

This was the song I heard; but the Bone is silent!
Who knows if the sound was that of the dead light calling—
Of Caesar rolling onward his heart, that stone,
Or the burden of Atlas falling? (1942)

TEARS

My tears were Orion's splendor with sextuple suns and the million
Flowers in the fields of the heaven, where solar systems are setting—
The rocks of great diamonds in the midst of the clear wave
By May dews and early light ripened, more diamonds begetting.
I wept for the glories of air, for the millions of dawns
And the splendors within Man's heart with the darkness warring,
I wept for the beautiful queens of the world, like a flower-bed shining,—
Now gathered, some at six, some at seven, but all in Eternity's morning.
But now my tears have shrunk and like hours are falling:

I weep for Venus whose body has changed to a metaphysical city
Whose heart-beat is now the sound of the revolutions,—for love changed
To the hospital mercy, the scientists' hope for the future,
And the darkened Man, that complex multiplicity
Of air and water, plant and animal,
Hard diamond, infinite sun. *(1942)*

THE SWANS

In the green light of water, like the day
Under green boughs, the spray
And air-pale petals of the foam seem flowers—
Dark-leaved arbutus blooms with wax-pale bells
And their faint honey-smells,
The velvety syringa with smooth leaves,
Gloxinia with a green shade in the snow,
Jasmine and moon-clear orange-blossoms and green blooms
Of the wild strawberries from the shade of woods.
Their showers
Pelt the white women under the green trees,
Venusia, Cosmopolita, Pistillarine—
White solar statues, white rose-trees in snow
Flowering for ever, child-women, half stars
Half flowers, waves of the sea, born of a dream.

Their laughter flying through the trees like doves,
These angels come to watch their whiter ghosts
In the air-pale water, archipelagos
Of stars and young thin moons from great wings falling
As ripples widen.
These are their ghosts, their own white angels these!
O great wings spreading—
Your bones are made of amber, smooth and thin
Grown from the amber dust that was a rose
Or nymph in swan-smooth waters.
                              But Time's winter falls
With snows as soft, as soundless.... Then, who knows
Rose-footed swan from snow, or girl from rose? *(1942)*

A SONG AT MORNING

The weeping rose in her dark night of leaves
Sighed, "Dark is my heart, and dark my secret love—

Show not the fire within your heart, its light—
For to behold a rainbow in the night
Shall be the presage of your overthrow."

But morning came, and the great dews; then her philosophies
Of the heart's darkness died. And from the chrysalis of my thin sleep
That lay like light or dew upon my form
I rose and wrapped my wings about me, went
From that porphyrian darkness. Like the rose

I, too, was careless in the morning dews,
Seeing the dead and the dead hour return
To forgive the stain on our hands. I, too, at morning
Am like the rose who shouts of the red joys and redder sorrows
Fallen from young veins and heartsprings that once held
The world's incendiarism and the redness of summer,
The hope of the rose. For soon will come the morrow
When ancient Prudence and her wintery dream
Will be no more than the rose's idleness. . . .
The light of tears shall only seem the rose's light
—Nor sorrow darker than her night of leaves.   (1945)

DIRGE FOR THE NEW SUNRISE

(*Fifteen minutes past eight o'clock, on the morning of Monday, the 6th of August, 1945.*)

Bound to my heart as Ixion to the wheel,
Nailed to my heart as the Thief upon the Cross,
I hang between our Christ and the gap where the world was lost

And watch the phantom Sun in Famine Street—
The ghost of the heart of man . . . red Cain,
And the more murderous brain
Of Man, still redder Nero that conceived the death
Of his mother Earth, and tore
Her womb, to know the place where he was conceived.

But no eyes grieved—
For none were left for tears:
They were blinded as the years
Since Christ was born. Mother or Murderer, you have given or taken
   life—
Now all is one!

There was a morning when the holy Light
Was young. . . . The beautiful First Creature came
To our water-springs, and thought us without blame.

Our hearts seemed safe in our breasts and sang to the Light—
The marrow in the bone
We dreamed was safe . . . the blood in the veins, the sap in the tree
Were springs of Deity.

But I saw the little Ant-men as they ran
Carrying the world's weight of the world's filth
And the filth of the heart of Man—
Compressed till those lusts and greeds had a greater heat than that of
 the Sun.

And the ray from that heat came soundless, shook the sky
As if in search for food, and squeezed the stems
Of all that grows on the earth till they were dry—
And drank the marrow of the bone:
The eyes that saw, the lips that kissed, are gone—
Or black as thunder lie and grin at the murdered Sun.

The living blind and seeing dead together lie
As if in love. . . . There was no more hating then,
And no more love: Gone is the heart of Man. *(1949)*

Hugh MacDiarmid[*]
(1892–   )

SIC TRANSIT GLORIA SCOTIA

I amna' fou' sae muckle as tired—deid dune.
It's gey and hard wark coupin' gless for gless
Wi' Cruivie and Gilsanquhar and the like,
And I'm no' juist as bauld as aince I wes.

The elbuck fankles in the coorse o' time,
The sheckle's no' sae souple, and the thrapple
Grows deef and dour: nae langer up and doun
Gleg as a squirrel speils the Adam's apple.

Forbye, the stuffie's no' the real Mackay,
The sun's sel' aince, as sune as ye began it,
Riz in your vera saul: but what keeks in
Noo is in truth the vilest "saxpenny planet."

And as the worth's gane doun the cost has risen.
Yin canna thow the cockles o' yin's hert
Wi'oot ha'en' cauld feet noo, jalousin' what
The wife'll say (I dinna blame her fur't).

It's robbin' Peter to pey Paul at least. . .
And a' that's Scotch aboot it is the name,
Like a' thing else ca'd Scottish nooadays
—A' destitute o' speerit juist the same.

(To prove my saul is Scots I maun begin
Wi' what's still deemed Scots and the folk expect,
And spire up syne by visible degrees
To heichts whereo' the fules ha'e never recked.

* See Glossary, pp. I-281–282.

But aince I get them there I'll whummle them
And souse the craturs in the nether deeps,
—For it's nae choice, and ony man s'ud wish
To dree the goat's weird tae as weel's the sheep's!)

Heifetz in tartan, and Sir Harry Lauder!
Whaur's Isadora Duncan dancin' noo?
Is Mary Garden in Chicago still
And Duncan Grant in Paris—and me fou'?

Sic transit gloria Scotia—a' the floo'ers
O' the Forest are wede awa'. (A blin' bird's nest
Is aiblins biggin' in the thistle tho'? . . .
And better blin' if'ts brood is like the rest!)

You canna gang to a Burns supper even
Wi'oot some wizened scrunt o' a knock-knee
Chinee turns roon to say "Him Haggis—velly goot!"
And ten to wan the piper is a Cockney.

No' wan in fifty kens a wurd Burns wrote
But misapplied is a'body's property,
And gin there was his like alive the day
They'd be the last a kennin' haund to gi'e—

Croose London Scotties wi' their braw shirt fronts
And a' their fancy freen's, rejoicin'
That similah gatherings in Timbuctoo,
Bagdad—and Hell, nae doot—are voicin'

Burns' sentiments o' universal love,
In pidgin' English or in wild-fowl Scots,
And toastin' ane wha's nocht to them but an
Excuse for faitherin' Genius wi' *their* thochts.

A' *they've* to say was aften said afore
A lad was born in Kyle to blaw aboot.
What unco fate mak's *him* the dumpin'-grun'
For a' the sloppy rubbish they jaw oot?

Mair nonsense has been uttered in his name
Than in ony's barrin' liberty and Christ.
If this keeps spreedin' as the drink declines,
Syne turns to tea, wae's me for the *Zeitgeist!*

Rabbie, wad'st thou were here—the warld hath need,
And Scotland mair sae, o' the likes o' thee!
The whisky that aince moved your lyre's become
A laxative for a' loquacity.

O gin they'd stegh their guts and haud their wheesht
I'd thole it, for "a man's a man," I ken,
But though the feck ha'e plenty o' the "a' that,"
They're nocht but zoologically men.

I'm haverin', Rabbie, but ye understaun'
It gets my dander up to see your star
A bauble in Babel, banged like a saxpence
'Twixt Burbank's Baedeker and Bleistein's cigar.

There's nane sae ignorant but think they can
Expatiate on *you,* if on nae ither.
The sumphs ha'e ta'en you at your wurd, and, fegs!
The foziest o' them claims to be a—Brither!

Syne "Here's the cheenge"—the star o' Rabbie Burns.
Sma' cheenge, "Twinkle, Twinkle." The memory slips
As G. K. Chesterton heaves up to gi'e
"The Immortal Memory" in a huge eclipse,

Or somebody else as famous if less fat.
You left the like in Embro in a scunner
To booze wi' thieveless cronies sic as me.
I'se warrant you'd shy clear o' a' the hunner

Odd Burns Clubs tae, or ninety-nine o' them,
And haud your birthday in a different kip
Whaur your name isna ta'en in vain—as Christ
Gied a' Jerusalem's Pharisees the slip,

—Christ wha'd ha'e been Chief Rabbi gin he'd lik't!—
Wi' publicans and sinners to foregather,
But, losh! the publicans noo are Pharisees,
And I'm no' shair o' maist the sinners either.

But that's aside the point! I've got fair waun'ert.
It's no' that I'm sae fou' as juist deid dune,

And dinna ken as muckle's whar I am
Or hoo I've come to sprawl here 'neth the mune.

That's it! It isna me that's fou' at a',
But the fu' mune, the doited jade, that's led
Me fer agley, or 'mogrified the warld.
—For a' I ken I'm safe in my ain bed.

Jean! Jean! Gin she's no' here it's no' *oor* bed,
Or else I'm dreamin' deep and canna wauken,
But it's a fell queer dream if this is no'
A real hillside—and thae things thistles and bracken!

It's hard work haud'n by a thocht worth ha'en'
And harder speakin't, and no' for ilka man;
Maist Thocht's like whisky—a thoosan' under proof,
And a sair price is pitten on't even than.

As Kirks wi' Christianity ha'e dune,
Burns' Clubs wi' Burns—wi' a' thing it's the same,
The core o' ocht is only for the few,
Scorned by the mony, thrang wi'ts empty name.

And a' the names in History mean nocht
To maist folk but "ideas o' their ain,"
The vera opposite o' onything
The Deid 'ud awn gin they cam' back again.

A greater Christ, a greater Burns, may come.
The maist they'll dae is to gi'e bigger pegs
To folly and conceit to hank their rubbish on.
They'll cheenge folks' talk but no' their nature, fegs!   *(1926)*

LOVE*

A luvin' wumman is a licht
That shows a man his waefu' plicht,
Bleezin' steady on ilka bane,
Wrigglin' sinnen an' twinin' vein,
Or fleerin' quick an' gane again,
And the mair scunnersome the sicht
The mair for love and licht he's fain

* Suggested by the French of Edmond Rocher—Author's note.

Till clear and chitterin' and nesh
Move a' the miseries o' his flesh.... (1926)

O WHA'S THE BRIDE?

O wha's the bride that cairries the bunch
O' thistles blinterin' white?
Her cuckold bridegroom little dreids
What he sall ken this nicht.

For closer than gudeman can come
And closer to'r than hersel',
Wha didna need her maidenheid
Has wrocht his purpose fell.

O wha's been here afore me, lass,
And hoo did he get in?
—*A man that deed or was I born
This evil thing has din.*

*And left, as it were on a corpse,
Your maidenheid to me?
—Nae lass, gudeman, sin' Time began
'S hed ony mair to gi'e.*

*But I can gi'e ye kindness, lad,
And a pair o' willin' hands,
And you sall ha'e my breists like stars,
My limbs like willow wands.*

*And on my lips ye'll heed nae mair,
And in my hair forget,
The seed o' a' the men that in
My virgin womb ha'e met....* (1926)

THE LIGHT OF LIFE

Use, then, my lust for whisky and for thee,
Your function but to be and let me be
And see and let me see.

If in a lesser licht I grope my way,
Or use't for ends that need your different ray
Whelm't in superior day.

Then aye increase and ne'er withdraw your licht.
—Gin it shows either o's in hideous plicht,
What gain to turn't to nicht?

Whisky mak's Heaven or Hell and whiles mells baith,
Disease is but the privy torch o' Daith,
—But sex reveals life, faith!

I need them a' and maun be aye at strife.
Daith and ayont are nocht but pairts o' life.
—Then be life's locht, my wife! ... *(1926)*

THE GLEN OF SILENCE

By this cold shuddering fit of fear
My heart divines a presence here,
Goddess or ghost yclept;
Wrecker of homes. . . .

Where have I heard a silence before
Like this that only a lone bird's cries
And the sound of a brawling burn to-day
Serve in this wide empty glen but to emphasize?

Every doctor knows it—the stillness of foetal death,
The indescribable silence over the abdomen then!
A silence literally "heard" because of the way
It stands out in the auscultation of the abdomen.

Here is an identical silence, picked out
By a bickering burn and a lone bird's wheeple
—The foetal death in this great "cleared" glen
Where the *fear-tholladh nan tighem** has done his foul work
—The tragedy of an unevolved people. *(1943)*

THE SPANISH WAR

Ah, Spain, already your tragic landscapes
And the agony of your War to my mind appear
As tears may come into the eyes of a woman very slowly,
So slowly as to leave them CLEAR!

* Destroyer of homes—AUTHOR'S NOTE.

Spain! The International Brigade! At the moment it seems
As though the pressure of a loving hand had gone,
(Till the next proletarian upsurge!)
The touch under which my close-pressed fingers seemed to thrill,
And the skin to divide up into little zones
Of heat and cold whose position continually changed,
So that the whole of my hand, held in that clasp,
Was in a state of internal movement.
My eyes that were full of pride,
My hands that were full of love,
Are empty again . . . for a while.
                    For a little while! (1957)

BRITISH LEFTISH POETRY, 1930–40

Auden, MacNeice, Day Lewis, I have read them all,
Hoping against hope to hear the authentic call.
"A tragical disappointment. There was I
Hoping to hear old Aeschylus, when the Herald
Called out, 'Theognis, bring your chorus forward.'
Imagine what my feelings must have been!
But then Dexitheus pleased me coming forward
And singing his Bœotian melody:
But next came Chaeris with his music truly
That turned me sick and killed me very nearly.
And never in my lifetime, man nor boy,
Was I so vexed as at the present moment;
To see the Pynx, at this time of the morning,
Quite empty, when the Assembly should be full"*
And know the explanation I must pass is this
—You cannot light a match on a crumbling wall. (1962)

OLD WIFE IN HIGH SPIRITS

IN AN EDINBURGH PUB

An auld wumman cam' in, a mere rickle o' banes, in a faded black dress
And a bonnet wi' beads o' jet rattlin' on it;
A puir-lookin' cratur, you'd think she could haurdly ha'e had less
Life left in her and still lived, but dagonit!

He gied her a stiff whisky—she was nervous as a troot
And could haurdly haud the tumbler, puir cratur;

* Aristophanes, *The Acharnians*—AUTHOR'S NOTE.

Syne he gied her anither, joked wi' her, and anither, and syne
Wild as the whisky up cam' her nature.

The rod that struck water frae the rock in the desert
Was naething to the life that sprang oot o' her;
The dowie auld soul was twinklin' and fizzin' wi' fire;
You never saw ocht sae souple and kir.

Like a sackful o' monkeys she was, and her lauchin'
Loupit up whiles to incredible heights;
Wi' ane owre the eight her temper changed and her tongue
Flew juist as the forkt lichtnin' skites.

The heich skeich auld cat was fair in her element;
Wanton as a whirlwind, and shairly better that way
Than a' crippen thegither wi' laneliness and cauld
Like a foretaste o' the graveyaird clay.

Some folk nae doot'll condemn gie'in a guid spree
To the puir dune body and raither she endit her days
Like some auld tashed copy o' the Bible yin sees
On a street book-barrow's tipenny trays.

A' I ken is weel-fed and weel-put-on though they be
Ninety per cent o' respectable folk never hae
As muckle life in their creeshy carcases frae beginnin' to end
As kythed in that wild auld carline that day!   (*1962*)

GLOSSARY OF SCOTTISH TERMS

aiblins perhaps; *ain owre the eight* one minute after eight; *amna'* am not; *awn* own; *ayont* beyond; *baith* both; *biggin'* being built; *bleezin'* blazing; *blinterin'* gleaming; *braw* splendid; *burn* brook; *chitterin'* shivering; *coupin' gless for gless* downing glass for glass; *creeshy* fattened; *crippen* hunched up; *croose* self-important; *deef* unresponsive; *deid* dead; *doited* mad; *dowie* dispirited; *dree the weird* endure fate; *dune* weary; *elbuck* elbow; *fankles* grows heavy; *feck* majority; *fegs!* faith!; *fell* very; *fer agley* far astray; *forbye* besides; *fou'* drunk; *foziest* stupidest; *gey* great; *gin* if; *gleg* eager; *haverin'* talking foolishly; *heich skeich* wildly gay; *ilka* every; *jalousin'* guessing; *keeks* peers in; *kennin' haund* kindly hand; *kir* wanton; *kythed* appeared; *licht* light; *loupit* leapt; *maun* must; *mells* mixes; *muckle* much; *nesh* nervously alert; *ocht* aught; *pitten* put; *rickle* heap; *sae* so; *sair* sore(ly); *saxpenny* sixpenny; *scunner(some)* disgust(ing); *sel'* self; *shair* sure; *sheckle* wrist; *sinnen* sinew; *speils* plays; *stegh* stuff; *sumphs* idiots; *syne* then; *tashed* ruined; *thole* endure; *thow* thaw; *thrang* busy; *thrapple* gullet; *unco* uncommonly; *waun'ert* wandered (from my topic); *wede* gone; *wheesht* talk (*haud . . . wheesht* be silent); *whummle* overturn.

Wilfred Owen
(1893–1918)

ARMS AND THE BOY

Let the boy try along this bayonet-blade
How cold steel is, and keen with hunger of blood;
Blue with all malice, like a madman's flash;
And thinly drawn with famishing for flesh.

Lend him to stroke these blind, blunt bullet-leads
Which long to nuzzle in the hearts of lads,
Or give him cartridges of fine zinc teeth,
Sharp with the sharpness of grief and death.

For his teeth seem for laughing round an apple.
There lurk no claws behind his fingers supple;
And God will grow no talons at his heels,
Nor antlers through the thickness of his curls. *(1920)*

GREATER LOVE

Red lips are not so red
    As the stained stones kissed by the English dead.
Kindness of wooed and wooer
Seems shame to their love pure.
O Love, your eyes lose lure
    When I behold eyes blinded in my stead!

Your slender attitude
    Trembles not exquisite like limbs knife-skewed,
Rolling and rolling there
Where God seems not to care;
Till the fierce love they bear
    Cramps them in death's extreme decrepitude.

Your voice sings not so soft,—
    Though even as wind murmuring through raftered loft,—

Your dear voice is not dear,
Gentle, and evening clear,
As theirs whom none now hear,
    Now earth has stopped their piteous mouths that coughed.

Heart, you were never hot
    Nor large, nor full like hearts made great with shot;
And though your hand be pale,
Paler are all which trail
Your cross through flame and hail:
    Weep, you may weep, for you may touch them not.   (1920)

INSENSIBILITY

1

Happy are men who yet before they are killed
Can let their veins run cold.
Whom no compassion fleers
Or makes their feet
Sore on the alleys cobbled with their brothers.
The front line withers,
But they are troops who fade, not flowers
For poets' tearful fooling:
Men, gaps for filling:
Losses who might have fought
Longer; but no one bothers.

2

And some cease feeling
Even themselves or for themselves.
Dullness best solves
The tease and doubt of shelling,
And Chance's strange arithmetic
Comes simpler than the reckoning of their shilling.
They keep no check on armies' decimation.

3

Happy are these who lose imagination:
They have enough to carry with ammunition.
Their spirit drags no pack,
Their old wounds save with cold can not more ache.
Having seen all things red,
Their eyes are rid
Of the hurt of the colour of blood for ever.

And terror's first constriction over,
Their senses in some scorching cautery of battle
Now long since ironed,
Can laugh among the dying, unconcerned.

4

Happy the soldier home, with not a notion
How somewhere, every dawn, some men attack,
And many sighs are drained.
Happy the lad whose mind was never trained:
His days are worth forgetting more than not.
He sings along the march
Which we march taciturn, because of dusk,
The long, forlorn, relentless trend
From larger day to huger night.

5

We wise, who with a thought besmirch
Blood over all our soul,
How should we seek our task
But through his blunt and lashless eyes?
Alive, he is not vital overmuch;
Dying, not mortal overmuch;
Nor sad, nor proud,
Nor curious at all.
He cannot tell
Old men's placidity from his.

6

But cursed are dullards whom no cannon stuns,
That they should be as stones;
Wretched are they, and mean
With paucity that never was simplicity.
By choice they made themselves immune
To pity and whatever mourns in man
Before the last sea and the hapless stars;
Whatever mourns when many leave these shores;
Whatever shares
The eternal reciprocity of tears.   *(1920)*

DULCE ET DECORUM EST

Bent double, like old beggars under sacks,
Knock-kneed, coughing like hags, we cursed through sludge,

Till on the haunting flares we turned our backs,
And towards our distant rest began to trudge.
Men marched asleep. Many had lost their boots
But limped on, blood-shod. All went lame; all blind;
Drunk with fatigue; deaf even to the hoots
Of tired, outstripped Five-Nines that dropped behind.

Gas! Gas! Quick, boys!—An ecstasy of fumbling,
Fitting the clumsy helmets just in time,
But someone still was yelling out and stumbling
And flound'ring like a man in fire or lime . . .
Dim through the misty panes and thick green light,
As under a green sea, I saw him drowning.

In all my dreams before my helpless sight,
He plunges at me, guttering, choking, drowning.

If in some smothering dreams you too could pace
Behind the wagon that we flung him in,
And watch the white eyes writhing in his face,
His hanging face, like a devil's sick of sin,
If you could hear, at every jolt, the blood
Come gargling from the froth-corrupted lungs
Obscene as cancer, bitter as the cud
Of vile, incurable sores on innocent tongues,—
My friend, you would not tell with such high zest
To children ardent for some desperate glory,
The old lie: *Dulce et decorum est*
Pro patria mori. (1920)

MENTAL CASES

Who are these? Why sit they here in twilight?
Wherefore rock they, purgatorial shadows,
Drooping tongues from jaws that slob their relish,
Baring teeth that leer like skulls' teeth wicked?
Stroke on stroke of pain,—but what slow panic,
Gouged these chasms round their fretted sockets?
Ever from their hair and through their hands' palms
Misery swelters. Surely we have perished
Sleeping, and walk hell; but who these hellish?

—These are men whose minds the Dead have ravished.
Memory fingers in their hair of murders,

Multitudinous murders they once witnessed.
Wading sloughs of flesh these helpless wander,
Treading blood from lungs that had loved laughter.
Always they must see these things and hear them,
Batter of guns and shatter of flying muscles,
Carnage incomparable, and human squander
Rucked too thick for these men's extrication.

Therefore still their eyeballs shrink tormented
Back into their brains, because on their sense
Sunlight seems a blood-smear; night comes blood-black;
Dawn breaks open like a wound that bleeds afresh.
—Thus their heads wear this hilarious, hideous,
Awful falseness of set-smiling corpses.
—Thus their hands are plucking at each other;
Picking at the rope-knouts of their scourging;
Snatching after us who smote them, brother,
Pawing us who dealt them war and madness.   (1920)

FUTILITY

Move him into the sun—
Gently its touch awoke him once,
At home, whispering of fields unsown.
Always it woke him, even in France,
Until this morning and this snow.
If anything might rouse him now
The kind old sun will know.

Think how it wakes the seeds—
Woke, once, the clays of a cold star.
Are limbs, so dear-achieved, are sides
Full-nerved,—still warm,—too hard to stir?
Was it for this the clay grew tall?
—Oh, what made fatuous sunbeams toil
To break earth's sleep at all?   (1920)

DISABLED

He sat in a wheeled chair, waiting for dark,
And shivered in his ghastly suit of grey,
Legless, sewn short at elbow. Through the park
Voices of boys rang saddening like a hymn,

Voices of play and pleasures after day,
Till gathering sleep had mothered them from him.

    *   *   *

About this time Town used to swing so gay
When glow-lamps budded in the light blue trees,
And girls glanced lovelier as the air grew dim,—
In the old times, before he threw away his knees.
Now he will never feel again how slim
Girls' waists are, or how warm their subtle hands;
All of them touch him like some queer disease.

    *   *   *

There was an artist silly for his face,
For it was younger than his youth, last year.
Now, he is old; his back will never brace;
He's lost his colour very far from here,
Poured it down shell-holes till the veins ran dry,
And half his lifetime lapsed in the hot race,
And leap of purple spurted from his thigh.

    *   *   *

One time he liked a blood-smear down his leg,
After the matches, carried shoulder high.
It was after football, when he'd drunk a peg,
He thought he'd better join.—He wonders why.
Someone had said he'd look a god in kilts,
That's why; and may be, too, to please his Meg;
Aye, that was it, to please the giddy jilts
He asked to join. He didn't have to beg;
Smiling they wrote his lie; aged nineteen years.
Germans he scarcely thought of; all their guilt,
And Austria's, did not move him. And no fears
Of Fear came yet. He thought of jewelled hilts
For daggers in plaid socks; of smart salutes;
And care of arms; and leave; and pay arrears;
Esprit de corps; and hints for young recruits.
And soon he was drafted out with drums and cheers.

    *   *   *

Some cheered him home, but not as crowds cheer Goal.
Only a solemn man who brought him fruits
Thanked him; and then inquired about his soul.

    *   *   *

Now, he will spend a few sick years in Institutes,
And do what things the rules consider wise,
And take whatever pity they may dole.
To-night he noticed how the women's eyes
Passed from him to the strong men that were whole.
How cold and late it is! Why don't they come
And put him into bed? Why don't they come? *(1920)*

ANTHEM FOR DOOMED YOUTH

What passing-bells for these who die as cattle?
　　Only the monstrous anger of the guns.
Only the stuttering rifles' rapid rattle
　　Can patter out their hasty orisons.
No mockeries now for them; no prayers nor bells,
　　Nor any voice of mourning save the choirs,—
The shrill, demented choirs of wailing shells;
　　And bugles calling for them from sad shires.

What candles may be held to speed them all?
　　Not in the hands of boys, but in their eyes
Shall shine the holy glimmers of good-byes.
　　The pallor of girls' brows shall be their pall;
Their flowers the tenderness of patient minds,
And each slow dusk a drawing-down of blinds. *(1920)*

STRANGE MEETING

It seemed that out of battle I escaped
Down some profound dull tunnel, long since scooped
Through granites which titanic wars had groined.
Yet also there encumbered sleepers groaned,
Too fast in thought or death to be bestirred.
Then, as I probed them, one sprang up, and stared
With piteous recognition in fixed eyes,
Lifting distressful hands as if to bless.
And by his smile, I knew that sullen hall,
By his dead smile I knew we stood in Hell.
With a thousand pains that vision's face was grained;
Yet no blood reached there from the upper ground,
And no guns thumped, or down the flues made moan.
"Strange friend," I said, "here is no cause to mourn."
"None," said that other, "save the undone years,

The hopelessness. Whatever hope is yours,
Was my life also; I went hunting wild
After the wildest beauty in the world,
Which lies not calm in eyes, or braided hair,
But mocks the steady running of the hour,
And if it grieves, grieves richlier than here.
For of my glee might many men have laughed,
And of my weeping something had been left,
Which must die now. I mean the truth untold,
The pity of war, the pity war distilled.
Now men will go content with what we spoiled.
Or, discontent, boil bloody, and be spilled.
They will be swift with swiftness of the tigress,
None will break ranks, though nations trek from progress.
Courage was mine, and I had mystery,
Wisdom was mine, and I had mastery:
To miss the march of this retreating world
Into vain citadels that are not walled.
Then, when much blood had clogged their chariot-wheels
I would go up and wash them from sweet wells,
Even with truths that lie too deep for taint.
I would have poured my spirit without stint
But not through wounds; not on the cess of war.
Foreheads of men have bled where no wounds were.
I am the enemy you killed, my friend.
I knew you in this dark; for so you frowned
Yesterday through me as you jabbed and killed.
I parried; but my hands were loath and cold.
Let us sleep now. . . ." (1920)

Robert Graves
(1895–   )

THE PIER-GLASS

Lost manor where I walk continually
A ghost, though yet in woman's flesh and blood.
Up your broad stairs mounting with outspread fingers
And gliding steadfast down your corridors
I come by nightly custom to this room,
And even on sultry afternoons I come
Drawn by a thread of time-sunk memory.

Empty, unless for a huge bed of state
Shrouded with rusty curtains drooped awry
(A puppet theatre where malignant fancy
Peoples the wings with fear). At my right hand
A ravelled bell-pull hangs in readiness
To summon me from attic glooms above
Service of elder ghosts; here, at my left,
A sullen pier-glass, cracked from side to side,
Scorns to present the face (as do new mirrors)
With a lying flush, but shows it melancholy
And pale, as faces grow that look in mirrors.

Is there no life, nothing but the thin shadow
And blank foreboding, never a wainscot rat
Rasping a crust? Or at the window-pane
No fly, no bluebottle, no starveling spider?
The windows frame a prospect of cold skies
Half-merged with sea, as at the first creation—
Abstract, confusing welter. Face about,
Peer rather in the glass once more, take note
Of self, the grey lips and long hair dishevelled,
Sleep-staring eyes. Ah, mirror, for Christ's love
Give me one token that there still abides
Remote—beyond this island mystery,
So be it only this side Hope, somewhere,

In streams, on sun-warm mountain pasturage—
True life, natural breath; not this phantasma. *(1921)*

RICHARD ROE AND JOHN DOE

Richard Roe wished himself Solomon,
Made cuckold, you should know, by one John Doe:
Solomon's neck was firm enough to bear
Some score of antlers more than Roe could wear.

Richard Roe wished himself Alexander,
Being robbed of house and land by the same hand:
Ten thousand acres or a principal town
Would have cost Alexander scarce a frown.

Richard Roe wished himself Job the prophet,
Sunk past reclaim in stinking rags and shame—
However ill Job's plight, his own was worse:
He knew no God to call on or to curse.

He wished himself Job, Solomon, Alexander,
For patience, wisdom, power to overthrow
Misfortune; but with spirit so unmanned
That most of all he wished himself John Doe. *(1923)*

TRAVELLER'S CURSE AFTER MISDIRECTION

(from the Welsh)

May they stumble, stage by stage
On an endless pilgrimage,
Dawn and dusk, mile after mile,
At each and every step, a stile;
At each and every step withal
May they catch their feet and fall;
At each and every fall they take
May a bone within them break;
And may the bone that breaks within
Not be, for variation's sake,
Now rib, now thigh, now arm, now shin,
But always, without fail THE NECK. *(1925)*

WELSH INCIDENT

"But that was nothing to what things came out
From the sea-caves of Criccieth yonder."

"What were they? Mermaids? dragons? ghosts?"
"Nothing at all of any things like that."
"What were they, then?"
                    "All sorts of queer things,
Things never seen or heard or written about,
Very strange, un-Welsh, utterly peculiar
Things. Oh, solid enough they seemed to touch,
Had anyone dared it. Marvellous creation,
All various shapes and sizes and no sizes,
All new, each perfectly unlike his neighbour,
Though all came moving slowly out together."
"Describe just one of them."
                   "I am unable."
"What were their colours?"
                    "Mostly nameless colours,
Colours you'd like to see; but one was puce
Or perhaps more like crimson, but not purplish.
Some had no colour."
               "Tell me, had they legs?"
"Not a leg or foot among them that I saw."
"But did these things come out in any order?
What o'clock was it? What was the day of the week?
Who else was present? How was the weather?"
"I was coming to that. It was half-past three
On Easter Tuesday last. The sun was shining.
The Harlech Silver Band played *Marchog Jesu*
On thirty-seven shimmering instruments,
Collecting for Carnarvon's (Fever) Hospital Fund.
The populations of Pwllheli, Criccieth,
Portmadoc, Borth, Tremadoc, Penrhyndeudraeth,
Were all assembled. Criccieth's mayor addressed them
First in good Welsh and then in fluent English,
Twisting his fingers in his chain of office,
Welcoming the things. They came out on the sand,
Not keeping time to the band, moving seaward
Silently at a snail's pace. But at last
The most odd, indescribable thing of all
Which hardly one man there could see for wonder
Did something recognizably a something."
"Well, what?"
            "It made a noise."
                      "A frightening noise?"
"No, no."
        "A musical noise? A noise of scuffling?"

"No, but a very loud, respectable noise—
Like groaning to oneself on Sunday morning
In Chapel, close before the second psalm."
"What did the mayor do?"
"I was coming to that." (1929)

SICK LOVE

O Love, be fed with apples while you may,
And feel the sun and go in royal array,
A smiling innocent on the heavenly causeway,

Though in what listening horror for the cry
That soars in outer blackness dismally,
The dumb blind beast, the paranoiac fury:

Be warm, enjoy the season, lift your head,
Exquisite in the pulse of tainted blood,
That shivering glory not to be despised.

Take your delight in momentariness,
Walk between dark and dark—a shining space
With the grave's narrowness, though not its peace. (1931)

SAINT

This Blatant Beast was finally overcome
And in no secret tourney: wit and fashion
Flocked out and for compassion
Wept as the Red Cross Knight pushed the blade home.

The people danced and sang the paeans due,
Roasting whole oxen on the public spit;
Twelve mountain peaks were lit
With bonfires; yet their hearts were doubt and rue.

Therefore no grave was deep enough to hold
The Beast, who after days came thrusting out,
Wormy from rump to snout,
His yellow cere-cloth patched with the grave's mould.

Nor could sea hold him: anchored with huge rocks,
He swelled and buoyed them up, paddling ashore

As evident as before
With deep-sea ooze and salty creaking bones.

Lime could not burn him, nor the sulphur fire:
So often as the good Knight bound him there,
With stink of singeing hair
And scorching flesh the corpse rolled from the pyre.

In the city-gutter would the Beast lie
Praising the Knight for all his valorous deeds:
"Aye, on those water-meads
He slew even me. These death-wounds testify."

The Knight governed that city, a man shamed
And shrunken: for the Beast was over-dead,
With wounds no longer red
But gangrenous and loathsome and inflamed.

Not all the righteous judgments he could utter,
Nor mild laws frame, nor public works repair,
Nor wars wage, in despair,
Could bury that same Beast, crouched in the gutter.

A fresh remembrance-banquet to forestall,
The Knight turned hermit, went without farewell
To a far mountain-cell;
But the Beast followed as his seneschal,

And there drew water for him and hewed wood
With vacant howling laughter; else all day
Noisome with long decay
Sunning himself at the cave's entry stood.

Would bawl to pilgrims for a dole of bread
To feed the sick saint who once vanquished him
With spear so stark and grim;
Would set a pillow of grass beneath his head,
Would fetch him fever-wort from the pool's brim—
And crept into his grave when he was dead.   *(1931)*

ULYSSES

To the much-tossed Ulysses, never done
    With woman whether gowned as wife or whore,

Penelope and Circe seemed as one:
She like a whore made his lewd fancies run,
　　And wifely she a hero to him bore.

Their counter-changings terrified his way:
　　They were the clashing rocks, Symplegades,
Scylla and Charybdis too were they;
Now they were storms frosting the sea with spray
　　And now the lotus island's drunken ease.

They multiplied into the Sirens' throng,
　　Forewarned by fear of whom he stood bound fast
Hand and foot helpless to the vessel's mast,
Yet would not stop his ears: daring their song
　　He groaned and sweated till that shore was past.

One, two and many: flesh had made him blind,
　　Flesh had one pleasure only in the act,
Flesh set one purpose only in the mind—
Triumph of flesh and afterwards to find
　　Still those same terrors wherewith flesh was racked.

His wiles were witty and his fame far known,
Every king's daughter sought him for her own,
　　Yet he was nothing to be won or lost.
　　All hands to him with Ithaca: love-tossed
He loathed the fraud, yet would not bed alone.   (*1933*)

DOWN, WANTON, DOWN!

Down, wanton, down! Have you no shame
That at the whisper of Love's name,
Or Beauty's, presto! up you raise
Your angry head and stand at gaze?

Poor bombard-captain, sworn to reach
The ravelin and effect a breach—
Indifferent what you storm or why,
So be that in the breach you die!

Love may be blind, but Love at least
Knows what is man and what mere beast;
Or Beauty wayward, but requires
More delicacy from her squires.

Tell me, my witless, whose one boast
Could be your staunchness at the post,
When were you made a man of parts
To think fine and profess the arts?

Will many-gifted Beauty come
Bowing to your bald rule of thumb,
Or Love swear loyalty to your crown?
Be gone, have done! Down, wanton, down!   *(1933)*

ON DWELLING

Courtesies of good-morning and good-evening
From rustic lips fail as the town encroaches:
Soon nothing passes but the cold quick stare
Of eyes that see ghosts, yet too many for fear.

Here I too walk, silent myself, in wonder
At a town not mine though plainly coextensive
With mine, even in days coincident:
In mine I dwell, in theirs like them I haunt.

And the green country, should I turn again there?
My bumpkin neighbours loom even ghostlier:
Like trees they murmur or like blackbirds sing
Courtesies of good-morning and good-evening.   *(1933)*

OGRES AND PYGMIES

Those famous men of old, the Ogres—
They had long beards and stinking arm-pits,
They were wide-mouthed, long-yarded and great-bellied
Yet not of taller stature, Sirs, than you.
They lived on Ogre-Strand, which was no place
But the churl's terror of their vast extent,
Where every foot was three-and-thirty inches
And every penny bought a whole hog.
Now of their company none survive, not one,
The times being, thank God, unfavourable
To all but nightmare shadows of their fame;
Their images stand howling on the hill
(The winds enforced against those wide mouths),
Whose granite haunches country-folk salute
With May Day kisses, and whose knobbed knees.

So many feats they did to admiration:
With their enormous throats they sang louder
Than ten cathedral choirs, with their grand yards
Stormed the most rare and obstinate maidenheads,
With their strong-gutted and capacious bellies
Digested stones and glass like ostriches.
They dug great pits and heaped huge mounds,
Deflected rivers, wrestled with the bear
And hammered judgements for posterity—
For the sweet-cupid-lipped and tassel-yarded
Delicate-stomached dwellers
In Pygmy Alley, where with brooding on them
A foot is shrunk to seven inches
And twelve-pence will not buy a spare rib.
And who would judge between Ogres and Pygmies—
The thundering text, the snivelling commentary—
Reading between such covers he will marvel
How his own members bloat and shrink again.   *(1933)*

RECALLING WAR

Entrance and exit wounds are silvered clean,
The track aches only when the rain reminds.
The one-legged man forgets his leg of wood,
The one-armed man his jointed wooden arm.
The blinded man sees with his ears and hands
As much or more than once with both his eyes.
Their war was fought these twenty years ago
And now assumes the nature-look of time,
As when the morning traveller turns and views
His wild night-stumbling carved into a hill.

What, then, was war? No mere discord of flags
But an infection of the common sky
That sagged ominously upon the earth
Even when the season was the airiest May.
Down pressed the sky, and we, oppressed, thrust out
Boastful tongue, clenched fist and valiant yard.
Natural infirmities were out of mode,
For Death was young again: patron alone
Of healthy dying, premature fate-spasm.

Fear made fine bed-fellows. Sick with delight
At life's discovered transitoriness,

Our youth became all-flesh and waived the mind.
Never was such antiqueness of romance,
Such tasty honey oozing from the heart.
And old importances came swimming back—
Wine, meat, log-fires, a roof over the head,
A weapon at the thigh, surgeons at call.
Even there was a use again for God—
A word of rage in lack of meat, wine, fire,
In ache of wounds beyond all surgeoning.

War was return of earth to ugly earth,
War was foundering of sublimities,
Extinction of each happy art and faith
By which the world had still kept head in air.
Protesting logic or protesting love,
Until the unendurable moment struck—
The inward scream, the duty to run mad.

And we recall the merry ways of guns—
Nibbling the walls of factory and church
Like a child, piecrust: felling groves of trees
Like a child, dandelions with a switch.
Machine-guns rattle toy-like from a hill,
Down in a row the brave tin-soldiers fall:
A sight to be recalled in elder days
When learnedly the future we devote
To yet more boastful visions of despair. *(1938)*

A JEALOUS MAN

To be homeless is a pride
To the jealous man prowling
Hungry down the night lanes,

Who has no steel at his side,
No drink hot in his mouth,
But a mind dream-enlarged,

Who witnesses warfare,
Man with woman, hugely
Raging from hedge to hedge:

The raw knotted oak-club
Clenched in the raw fist,
The ivy-noose well flung,

The thronged din of battle,
Gaspings of the throat-snared,
Snores of the battered dying,

Tall corpses, braced together,
Fallen in clammy furrows,
Male and female,

Or, among haulms of nettle
Humped, in noisome heaps,
Male and female.

He glowers in the choked roadway
Between twin churchyards,
Like a turnip ghost.

(Here, the rain-worn headstone,
There, the Celtic cross
In rank white marble.)

This jealous man is smitten,
His fear-jerked forehead
Sweats a fine musk;

A score of bats bewitched
By the ruttish odour
Swoop singing at his head;

Nuns bricked up alive
Within the neighbouring wall
Wail in cat-like longing.

Crow, cocks, crow loud,
Reprieve the doomed devil—
Has he not died enough?

Now, out of careless sleep,
She wakes and greets him coldly,
The woman at home,

She, with a private wonder
At shoes bemired and bloody—
His war was not hers. *(1938)*

A LOVE STORY

The full moon easterly rising, furious,
Against a winter sky ragged with red;
The hedges high in snow, and owls raving—
Solemnities not easy to withstand:
A shiver wakes the spine.

In boyhood, having encountered the scene,
I suffered horror: I fetched the moon home,
With owls and snow, to nurse in my head
Throughout the trials of a new spring,
Famine unassuaged.

But fell in love, and made a lodgement
Of love on those chill ramparts.
Her image was my ensign: snows melted,
Hedges sprouted, the moon tenderly shone,
The owls trilled with tongues of nightingale.

These were all lies, though they matched the time,
And brought me less than luck: her image
Warped in the weather, turned beldamish.
Then back came winter on me at a bound,
The pallid sky heaved with a moon-quake.

Dangerous it had been with love-notes
To serenade Queen Famine.
In tears I recomposed the former scene,
Let the snow lie, watched the moon rise, suffered the owls.
Paid homage to them of unevent.   (*1946*)

THE GLUTTON

Beyond the Atlas roams a glutton
Lusty and sleek, a shameless robber,
Sacred to Aethiopian Aphrodite;
The aborigines harry it with darts.
And its flesh is esteemed, though of a fishy tang
Tainting the eater's mouth and lips.

Ourselves once, wandering in mid-wilderness
And by despair drawn to this diet,

Before the meal was over sat apart
Loathing each other's carrion company.   (1946)

THE THIEVES

Lovers in the act dispense
With such meum-teum sense
As might warningly reveal
What they must not pick or steal,
And their nostrum is to say:
"I and you are both away."

After, when they disentwine
You from me and yours from mine,
Neither can be certain who
Was that I whose mine was you.
To the act again they go
More completely not to know.

Theft is theft and raid is raid
Though reciprocally made.
Lovers, the conclusion is
Doubled sighs and jealousies
In a single heart that grieves
For lost honour among thieves.   (1946)

TO JUAN AT THE WINTER SOLSTICE

There is one story and one story only
That will prove worth your telling,
Whether as learned bard or gifted child;
To it all lines or lesser gauds belong
That startle with their shining
Such common stories as they stray into.

Is it of trees you tell, their months and virtues,
Or strange beasts that beset you,
Of birds that croak at you the Triple will?
Or of the Zodiac and how slow it turns
Below the Boreal Crown,
Prison of all true kings that ever reigned?

Water to water, ark again to ark,
From woman back to woman:

So each new victim treads unfalteringly
The never altered circuit of his fate,
Bringing twelve peers as witness
Both to his starry rise and starry fall.

Or is it of the Virgin's silver beauty,
All fish below the thighs?
She in her left hand bears a leafy quince;
When, with her right she crooks a finger, smiling,
How may the King hold back?
Royally then he barters life for love.

Or of the undying snake from chaos hatched,
Whose coils contain the ocean,
Into whose chops with naked sword he springs,
Then in black water, tangled by the reeds,
Battles three days and nights,
To be spewed up beside her scalloped shore?

Much snow is falling, winds roar hollowly,
The owl hoots from the elder,
Fear in your heart cries to the loving-cup:
Sorrow to sorrow as the sparks fly upward.
The log groans and confesses:
There is one story and one story only.

Dwell on her graciousness, dwell on her smiling,
Do not forget what flowers
The great boar trampled down in ivy time.
Her brow was creamy as the crested wave,
Her sea-blue eyes were wild
But nothing promised that is not performed.   *(1946)*

THE PERSIAN VERSION

Truth-loving Persians do not dwell upon
The trivial skirmish fought near Marathon.
As for the Greek theatrical tradition
Which represents that summer's expedition
Not as a mere reconnaissance in force
By three brigades of foot and one of horse
(Their left flank covered by some obsolete
Light craft detached from the main Persian fleet)
But as a grandiose, ill-starred attempt
To conquer Greece—they treat it with contempt;

And only incidentally refute
Major Greek claims, by stressing what repute
The Persian monarch and the Persian nation
Won by this salutary demonstration:
Despite a strong defence and adverse weather
All arms combined magnificently together.   (*1946*)

GROTESQUES

1

My Chinese uncle, gouty, deaf, half-blinded,
And more than a trifle absent-minded,
Astonished all St. James's Square one day
By giving long and unexceptionably exact directions
To a little coolie girl, who'd lost her way.

2

The Lion-faced Boy at the Fair
And the Heir Apparent
Were equally slow at remembering people's faces.
But whenever they met, incognito, in the Brazilian
Pavilion, the Row and such-like places,
They exchanged, it is said, their sternest nods—
Like gods of dissimilar races.

3

Dr. Newman with the crooked pince-nez
Had studied in Vienna and Chicago.
Chess was his only relaxation.
And Dr. Newman remained unperturbed
By every nastier manifestation
Of plutodemocratic civilization:
All that was cranky, corny, ill-behaved,
Unnecessary, askew or orgiastic
Would creep unbidden to his side-door (hidden
Behind a poster in the Tube Station,
Nearly half-way up the moving stairs),
Push its way in, to squat there undisturbed
Among box-files and tubular steel-chairs.

He was once seen at the Philharmonic Hall
Noting the reactions of two patients,
With pronounced paranoiac tendencies,

To old Dutch music. He appeared to recall
A tin of lozenges in his breast-pocket,
Put his hand confidently in—
And drew out a black imp, or sooterkin,
Six inches long, with one ear upside-down,
Licking at a vanilla ice-cream cornet—
Then put it back again with a slight frown.

4

A Royal Duke, with no campaigning medals
To dignify his Orders, he would speak
Nostalgically at times of Mozambique
Where once the ship he cruised in ran aground:
How he drank cocoa, from a sailor's mug,
Poured from the common jug,
While loyal toasts went round.

5

Sir John addressed the Snake God in his temple,
Which was full of bats, not as a votary
But with the somewhat cynical courtesy,
Just short of condescension,
He might have paid the Governor-General
Of a small, hot, backward colony.
He was well versed in primitive religion,
But found this an embarrassing occasion:
The God was immense, noisy and affable,
Began to tickle him with a nervous chuckle,
Unfobbed a great gold clock for him to listen,
Hissed like a snake, and swallowed him at one mouthful.

6

All horses on the racecourse of Tralee
   Have four more legs in gallop than in trot—
   Two pairs fully extended, two pairs not;
And yet no thoroughbred with either three
   Or five legs but is mercilessly shot.
I watched a filly gnaw her fifth leg free,
Warned by a speaking mare since turned silentiary.   *(1946)*

THE SURVIVOR

To die with a forlorn hope, but soon to be raised
By hags, the spoilers of the field; to elude their claws

And stand once more on a well-swept parade-ground,
Scarred and bemedalled, sword upright in fist
At head of a new undaunted company:

Is this joy? to be doubtless alive again,
And the others dead? Will your nostrils gladly savour
The fragrance, always new, of a first hedge-rose?
Will your ears be charmed by the thrush's melody
Sung as though he had himself devised it?

And is this joy: after the double suicide
(Heart against heart) to be restored entire,
To smooth your hair and wash away the life-blood,
And presently seek a young and innocent bride,
Whispering in the dark: "for ever and ever"?   (1951)

THE PORTRAIT

She speaks always in her own voice
Even to strangers; but those other women
Exercise their borrowed, or false, voices
Even on sons and daughters.

She can walk invisibly at noon
Along the high road; but those other women
Gleam phosphorescent—broad hips and gross fingers—
Down every lampless alley.

She is wild and innocent, pledged to love
Through all disaster; but those other women
Decry her for a witch or a common drab
And glare back when she greets them.

Here is her portrait, gazing sidelong at me,
The hair in disarray, the young eyes pleading:
"And you, love? As unlike those other men
As I those other women?"   (1951)

THE BLUE-FLY

Five summer days, five summer nights,
The ignorant, loutish, giddy blue-fly
Hung without motion on the cling peach,

Humming occasionally: "O my love, my fair one!"
    As in the *Canticles.*

Magnified one thousand times, the insect
Looks farcically human; laugh if you will!
Bald head, stage-fairy wings, blear eyes,
A caved-in chest, hairy black mandibles,
    Long spindly thighs.

The crime was detected on the sixth day.
What then could be said or done? By anyone?
It would have been vindictive, mean and what-not
To swat that fly for being a blue-fly,
    For debauch of a peach.

Is it fair, either, to bring a microscope
To bear on the case, even in search of truth?
Nature, doubtless, has some compelling cause
To glut the carriers of her epidemics—
    Nor did the peach complain. *(1953)*

TO CALLIOPE

Permit me here a simple brief aside,
    Calliope,
You who have shown such patience with my pride
    And obstinacy:

Am I not loyal to you? I say no less
    Than is to say;
If more, only from angry-heartedness,
    Not for display.

But you know, I know, and you know I know
    My principal curse:
Shame at the mounting dues I have come to owe
    A devil of verse

Who caught me young, ingenuous and uncouth,
    Prompting me how
To evade the patent clumsiness of truth—
    Which I do now.

No: nothing reads so fresh as I first thought,
    Or as you could wish—
Yet must I, when far worse is eagerly bought,
    Cry stinking fish?   *(1953)*

Austin Clarke
(1896–   )

ANCIENT LIGHTS

When all of us wore smaller shoes
And knew the next world better than
The knots we broke, I used to hurry
On missions of my own to Capel
Street, Bolton Street and Granby Row
To see what man has made. But darkness
Was roomed with fears. Sleep, stripped by woes
I had been taught, beat door, leaped landing,
Lied down the bannisters of naught.

Being sent to penance, come Saturday,
I shuffled slower than my sins should.
My fears were candle-spiked at side-shrines,
Rays lengthened them in stained-glass. Confided
To night again, my grief bowed down,
Heard hand on shutter-knob. Did I
Take pleasure, when alone—how much—
In a bad thought, immodest look
Or worse, unnecessary touch?

Closeted in the confessional,
I put on flesh, so many years
Were added to my own, attempted
In vain to keep Dominican
As much i' the dark as I was, mixing
Whispered replies with his low words;
Then shuddered past the crucifix,
The feet so hammered, daubed-on blood-drip,
Black with lip-scrimmage of the damned.

Once as I crept from the church-steps,
Beside myself, the air opened

On purpose. Nature read in a flutter
An evening lesson above my head.
Atwirl beyond the leadings, corbels,
A cage-bird came among sparrows
(The moral inescapable)
Plucked, roof-mired, all in mad bits. O
The pizzicato of its wires!

Goodness of air can be proverbial:
That day, by the kerb at Rutland Square,
A bronze bird fabled out of trees,
Mailing the spearheads of the railings,
Sparrow at nails, I hailed the skies
To save the tiny dropper, found
Appetite gone. A child of clay
Has blustered it away. Pity
Could raise some littleness from dust.

What Sunday clothes can change us now
Or humble orders in black and white?
Stinking with centuries the act
Of thought. So think, man, as Augustine
Did, dread the ink-bespattered ex-monk,
And keep your name. No, let me abandon
Night's jakes. Self-persecuted of late
Among the hatreds of rent Europe,
Poetry burns at a different stake.

Still, still I remember aweful downpour
Cabbing Mountjoy Street, spun loneliness
Veiling almost the Protestant church,
Two backyards from my very home.
I dared to shelter at locked door.
There, walled by heresy, my fears
Were solved. I had absolved myself:
Feast-day effulgence, as though I gained
For life a plenary indulgence.

The sun came out, new smoke flew up,
The gutters of the Black Church rang
With services. Waste water mocked
The ballcocks: down-pipes sparrowing,
And all around the spires of Dublin
Such swallowing in the air, such cowling

To keep high offices pure: I heard,
From shore to shore, the iron gratings
Take half our heavens with a roar.   *(1955)*

RESPECTABLE PEOPLE

Thought rattles along the empty railings
Of street and square they lived in, years
Ago. I dream of them at night,
Strangers to this artificial light,
Respectable people who gave me sweets,
Talked above my head or unfobbed
The time. I know them by each faded
Smile and their old-fashioned clothes.
But how can I make room for them
In a mind too horrible with life?
This is the last straw in the grave,
Propping the tear in which grief burns
Away. Shame of eternity
Has stripped them of their quiet habits,
Unshovelled them out of the past.
Memory finds beyond that last
Improvidence, their mad remains.   *(1955)*

THE ENVY OF POOR LOVERS

Pity poor lovers who may not do what they please
With their kisses under a hedge, before a raindrop
Unhouses it; and astir from wretched centuries,
Bramble and briar remind them of the saints.

Her envy is the curtain seen at night-time,
Happy position that could change her name.
His envy—clasp of the unmarried whose thoughts can be alike,
Whose nature flows without the blame or shame.

Lying in the grass as if it were a sin
To move, they hold each other's breath, tremble,
Ready to share that ancient dread—kisses begin
Again—of Ireland keeping company with them.

Think, children, of institutions mured above
Your ignorance, where every look is veiled,
State-paid to snatch away the folly of poor lovers
For whom, it seems, the sacraments have failed.   *(1955)*

INTERCESSORS

Our nuns come out to shop in the afternoon,
For holy fashion has decreed hold-alls.
Torchbearers sidle the clergy to their stalls
To share in the dark, huge hug, comic cartoon,
Forget awhile the morning fast in croon
Of saxophone. Free from the pledge of walls,
Passing the beggar-women who still wear shawls,
Capuchin pads in mediaeval shoon.
These are our intercessors. Strange that hotel
Lounge, cinema, shop-window can unbell
Them! Flattered by their numbers and display,
We break their vows with a smile. No rebel guessed
Prayer and retreat would sanctify unrest,
When Britain took the garrisons away.   (1960)

From MNEMOSYNE LAY IN DUST

1

Past the house where he was got
In darkness, terrace, provision shop,
Wing-hidden convent opposite,
Past public-houses at lighting-up
Time, crowds outside them—Maurice Devane
Watched from the taxi window in vain
National stir and gaiety
Beyond himself: St. Patrick's Day,
The spike-ends of the Blue Coat school,
Georgian houses, ribald gloom
Rag-shadowed by gaslight, quiet pavements
    Moon-waiting in Blackhall Place.

For six weeks Maurice had not slept,
Hours pillowed him from right to left side,
Unconsciousness became the pit
Of terror. Void would draw his spirit,
Unself him. Sometimes he fancied that music,
Soft lights in Surrey, Kent, could cure him,
Hypnotic touch, until, one evening,
The death-chill seemed to mount from feet

To shin, to thigh. Life burning in groin
And prostate ached for a distant joy.
But nerves need solitary confinement.
    Terror repeals the mind.

Cabs ranked at Kingsbridge Station, Guinness
Tugs moored at their wooden quay, glinting
Of Liffey mudbank; hidden vats
Brewing intoxication, potstill,
Laddering of distilleries
Ready to sell their jollities,
Delirium tremens. Dublin swayed,
Drenching, drowning the shamrock: unsaintly
Mirth. The high departments were filed,
Yard, store, unlit. Whiskey-all-round,
Beyond the wealth of that square mile,
    Was healthing every round.

The eighteenth century hospital
Established by the tears of Madam
Steevens, who gave birth, people said, to
A monster with a pig's snout, pot-head.
The Ford turned right, slowed down. Gates opened,
Closed with a clang; acetylene glow
Of headlights. How could Maurice Devane
Suspect from weeping-stone, porch, vane,
The classical rustle of the harpies,
Hopping in filth among the trees,
The Mansion of Forgetfulness
    Swift gave us for a jest?

2

Straight-jacketing sprang to every lock
And bolt, shadowy figures shocked,
Wall, ceiling; hat, coat, trousers flung
From him, vest, woollens, Maurice was plunged
Into a steaming bath; half suffocated,
He sank, his assailants gesticulating,
A Keystone reel gone crazier;
The terror-peeling celluloid,
Whirling the figures into vapour,
    Dissolved them. All was void.

Drugged in the dark, delirious,
In vision Maurice saw, heard, struggle
Of men and women, shouting, groans.
In an accident at Westland Row,
Two locomotives with mangle of wheel-spokes,
Colliding: up-scatter of smoke, steel,
Above: the gong of ambulances.
Below, the quietly boiling hiss
Of steam, the winter-sleet of glances,
    The quiet boiling of pistons.

The crowds were noisy. Sudden cries
Of "Murder! Murder!" from a byeway,
The shriek of women with upswollen
Bodies, held down in torment, rolling
And giving birth to foundlings, shriek
After shriek, the blanket lifting unspeakable
Protrusions. The crowds were stumbling backward,
Barefooted cry of "Murder" scurried.
Police batoned eyesight into blackness.
    Bandages were blurred.

Maurice had wakened up. He saw a
Circular peep-hole rimmed with polished
Brass within the door. It gloomed.
A face was glaring into the bed-room
With bulging eyes and fierce moustache.
Quicker than thought, a torchlight flashed
From wall to pillow. Motionless,
It spied until the face had gone.
The sound of sleepers in unrest:
    Still watchful, the peep-hole shone.

What night was it, he heard the creaking
Of boots and tiptoed to the peep-hole?
Four men were carrying a coffin
Upon their shoulders. As they shuffled,
Far in his mind a hollaloo
Echoed: "The Canon of Killaloe . . ."
Death-chill would mount from feet to limbs,
His loins, secretion no longer burn.
Those shoulderers would come for him with
    The shroud, spade, last thud.

Nightly he watched a masquerade
Go by his cell and was afraid
Of one—the stooping, bald-headed madman
Who muttered curse after curse, his hands
Busily knitting, twiddling white reeds:
So huge, he seemed to be the leader.
The others tormented by their folly,
The narrows of the moon, crowded
Together, gibboned his gestures, followed
    That madman knitting reed, brow.

Once, getting out of bed, he peeped
Into the domitory. Sheet
And slip were laundry-white. Dazes
Of electric light came down. Patients
Stirred fitfully. Their fidgetting marred
With scrawls the whiteness of the ward,
Gift of the moon. He wondered who
He was, but memory had hidden
All. Someone sat beside him, drew
    Chair nearer, murmured: "Think!"

One afternoon, he looked in dread
Into the ward outside. The beds
Were empty. Quiet sunshine glowed
On waxed floor and brass. He hurried
Across to the high window, stood
On the hot pipes to see the view.
Below there was a widespread garden,
With shrubberies, walks, summerhouses.
He stared in wonder from his bars,
    Saddened by the boughs.

6

One night he heard heart-breaking sound.
It was a sigh unworlding its sorrow.
Another followed. Slowly he counted
Four different sighs, one after another.
"My mother," he anguished, "and my sisters
Have passed away. I am alone, now,
Lost in myself in a mysterious
Darkness, the victim in a story."

Far whistle of a train, the voice of steam.
Evil was peering through the peep-hole.

Suddenly heart began to beat
Too quickly, too loudly. It clamoured
As if it were stopping. He left the heat
And stumbled forward, hammered
The door, called out that he was dying.
Key turned. Body was picked up, carried
Beyond the ward, the bedwhite row
Of faces, into a private darkness.
Lock turned. He cried out. All was still.
He stood, limbs shivering in the chill.

He tumbled into half the truth:
Burial alive. His breath was shouting:
"Let, let me out." But words were puny.
Fists hushed on a wall of inward-outness.
Knees crept along a floor that stirred
As softly. All was the same chill.
He knew the wall was circular
And air was catchcry in the stillness
For reason had returned to tell him
That he was in a padded cell.

The key had turned again. Blankets
Were flung into blackness as if to mock
The cringer on the floor. He wrapped
The bedclothes around his limbs, shocked back
To sanity. Lo! in memory yet,
Margaret came in a frail night-dress,
Feet bare, her heavy plaits let down
Between her knees, his pale protectress.
Nightly restraint, unwanted semen
Had ended their romantic dream.

Early next morning, he awakened,
Saw only greyness shining down
From a skylight on the grey walls
Of leather, knew, in anguish, his bowels
Had opened. He turned, shivering, all shent.
Wrapping himself in the filthied blankets,
Fearful of dire punishment,

He waited there until a blankness
Enveloped him. . . . When he raised his head up,
Noon-light was gentle in the bedroom.

18

Rememorised, Maurice Devane
Went out, his future in every vein,
The Gate had opened. Down Steeven's Lane
The high wall of the Garden, to right
Of him, the Fountain with a horse-trough,
Illusions had become a story.
There was the departmental storey
Of Guinness's, God-given right
Of goodness in every barrel, tun,
They averaged. Upon that site
Of shares and dividends in sight
Of Watling Street and the Cornmarket,
At Number One in Thomas Street
Shone in the days of the ballad-sheet,
The house in which his mother was born.   *(1966)*

C. Day Lewis
(1904-   )

[NOW I HAVE COME TO REASON]

Now I have to come to reason
And cast my schoolboy clout,
Disorder I see is without,
And the mind must sweat a poison
Keener than Thessaly's brew;
A pus that, discharged not thence,
Gangrenes the vital sense
And makes disorder true.
It is certain we shall attain
No life till we stamp on all
Life the tetragonal
Pure symmetry of brain.

I felt, in my scorning
Of common poet's talk,
As arrogant as the hawk
When he mounts above the morning.
"Behold man's droll appearance,
Faith wriggling upon his hooks,
Chin-deep in Eternal Flux
Angling for reassurance!"
I care not if he retorts—
"Of all that labour and wive
And worship, who would give
A fiddlestick for these thoughts
That sluggishly yaw and bend,
Fat strings of barges drawn
By a tug they have never seen
And never will comprehend?"

I sit in a wood and stare
Up at untroubled branches
Locked together and staunch as

Though girders of the air:
And think, the first wind rising
Will crack that intricate crown
And let the daylight down.
But there is naught surprising
Can explode the single mind:—
Let figs from thistles fall
Or stars from their pedestal,
This architecture will stand. (*1929*)

[DESIRE IS A WITCH]

Desire is a witch
And runs against the clock.
It can unstitch
The decent hem
Where space tacks on to time:
It can unlock
Pandora's privacies.

It puffs in these
Top-gallants of the mind,
And away I stand
On the elemental gale
Into an ocean
That the liar Lucian
Had never dared retail.

When my love leans with all
Her shining breast and shoulder,
I know she is older
Than Ararat the hill,
And yet more young
Than the first daffodil
That ever shews a spring.

When her eyes delay
On me, so deep are they
Tunnelled by love, although
You poured Atlantic
In this one and Pacific
In the other, I know
They would not overflow.

Desire clicks back
Like cuckoo into clock;
Leaves me to explain
Eyes that a tear will drown
And a body where youth
Nor age will long remain
To implicate the truth.

It seems that we must call
Anything truth whose well
Is deep enough;
For the essential
Philosopher-stone, desire,
Needs no other proof
Than its own fire. (1929)

[NOW SHE IS LIKE THE WHITE TREE-ROSE]

Now she is like the white tree-rose
That takes a blessing from the sun:
Summer has filled her veins with light,
And her warm heart is washed with noon.

Or as a poplar, ceaselessly
Gives a soft answer to the wind:
Cool on the light her leaves lie sleeping,
Folding a column of sweet sound.

Powder the stars. Forbid the night
To wear those brilliants for a brooch
So soon, dark death, you may close down
The mines that made this beauty rich.

Her thoughts are pleiads, stooping low
O'er glades where nightingale has flown:
And like the luminous night around her
She has at heart a certain dawn. (1931)

[DO NOT EXPECT AGAIN A PHOENIX HOUR]

Do not expect again a phoenix hour,
The triple-towered sky, the dove complaining,

Sudden the rain of gold and heart's first ease
Tranced under trees by the eldritch light of sundown.

By a blazed trail our joy will be returning:
One burning hour throws light a thousand ways,
And hot blood stays into familiar gestures.
The best years wait, the body's plenitude.

Consider then, my lover, this is the end
Of the lark's ascending, the hawk's unearthly hover:
Spring season is over soon and first heatwave;
Grave-browed with cloud ponders the huge horizon.

Draw up the dew. Swell with pacific violence.
Take shape in silence. Grow as the clouds grew.
Beautiful brood the cornlands, and you are heavy;
Leafy the boughs—they also hide big fruit.   *(1931)*

[LET US NOW PRAISE FAMOUS MEN]

Let us now praise famous men,
Not your earth-shakers, not the dynamiters,
But who in the Home Counties or the Khyber,
Trimming their nails to meet an ill wind,
Facing the Adversary with a clean collar,
Justified the system.
Admire the venerable pile that bred them,
Bones are its foundations,
The pinnacles are stone abstractions,
Whose halls are whispering-galleries designed
To echo voices of the past, dead tongues.
White hopes of England here
Are taught to rule by learning to obey,
Bend over before vested interests,
Kiss the rod, salute the quarter-deck;
Here is no savage discipline
Of peregrine swooping, of fire destroying,
But a civil code; no capital offender
But the cool cad, the man who goes too far.
Ours the curriculum
Neither of building birds nor wasteful waters,
Bound in book not violent in vein:
Here we inoculate with dead ideas

Against blood-epidemics, against
The infection of faith and the excess of life.
Our methods are up to date; we teach
Through head and not by heart,
Language with gramophones and sex with charts,
Prophecy by deduction, prayer by numbers.
For honors see prospectus: those who leave us
Will get a post and pity the poor;
Their eyes glaze at strangeness;
They are never embarrassed, have a word for everything,
Living on credit, dying when the heart stops;
Will wear black armlets and stand a moment in silence
For the passing of an era, at their own funeral.   (1933)

BOMBERS

Through the vague morning, the heart preoccupied,
A deep in air buried grain of sound
Starts and grows, as yet unwarning—
The tremor of baited deepsea line.

Swells the seed, and now tight sound-buds
Vibrate, upholding their paean flowers
To the sun. There are bees in sky-bells droning,
Flares of crimson at the heart unfold.

Children look up, and the elms spring-garlanded
Tossing their heads and marked for the axe.
Gallant or woebegone, alike unlucky—
Earth shakes beneath us: we imagine loss.

Black as vermin, crawling in echelon
Beneath the cloud-floor, the bombers come:
The heavy angels, carrying harm in
Their wombs that ache to be rid of death.

This is the seed that grows for ruin,
The iron embryo conceived in fear.
Soon or late its need must be answered
In fear delivered and screeching fire.

Choose between your child and this fatal embryo.
Shall your guilt bear arms, and the children you want

Be condemned to die by the powers you paid for
And haunt the houses you never built?   *(1938)*

A HAPPY VIEW

... So take a happy view—
This lawn graced with the candle-flames of crocus,
Frail-handed girls under the flowering chestnut,
Or anything will do
That time takes back before it seems untrue:

And, if the truth were told,
You'd count it luck, perceiving in what shallow
Crevices and few crumbling grains of comfort
Man's joy will seed, his cold
And hardy fingers find an eagle's hold.   *(1938)*

From OVERTURES TO DEATH

7

For us, born into a still
Unsweetened world, of sparse
Breathing-room, alleys brackish as hell's pit
And heaven-accusing spires,

You were never far nor fable,
Judgement nor happy end:
We have come to think of you, mister, as
Almost the family friend.

Our kiddies play tag with you often
Among the tornado wheels;
Through fevered nights you sit up with them,
You serve their little meals.

You lean with us at street-corners,
We have met you in the mine;
Your eyes are the foundry's glare, you beckon
From the snake-tooth, sly machine.

Low in the flooded engineroom,
High on the yawing steeple—

Wherever we are, we begin to fancy
That we're your chosen people.

They came to us with charity,
They came to us with whips,
They came with chains behind their back
And freedom on their lips:

Castle and field and city—
Ours is a noble land,
Let us work for its fame together, they said:
But we don't quite understand.

For they took the land and the credit,
Took virtue and double-crossed her;
They left us the scrag-end of the luck
And the brunt of their disaster.

And now like horses they fidget
Smelling death in the air:
But we are your chosen people, and
We've little to lose or fear.

When the time comes for a clearance,
When light brims over the hill,
Mister, you can rely on us
To execute your will.   (1938)

THE COMMITTEE

So the committee met again, and again
Nailed themselves to the never-much-altered agenda,
Making their points as to the manner born,
Hammering them home with the skill of long practice.

These men and women are certainly representative
Of every interest concerned. For example, A. wears
Integrity like a sheriff's badge, while B.
Can grind an axe on either side of a question:
C. happens to have the facts, D. a vocation
For interpreting facts to the greater glory of Dogma:
E. is pompously charming, diffidently earnest,
F. is the acid-drop, the self-patented catalyst.

Our chairman's a prince of procedure, in temporizing
Power a Proteus, and adept in seeming to follow
Where actually he leads—as indeed he must be,
Or the rest would have torn him to pieces a long time ago.
Yet all, in a curious way, are public-spirited,
Groping with their *ad hoc* decisions to find
The missing, presumed omnipotent, directive.

Idly the sun tracing upon their papers
Doodles of plane-leaf shadows and rubbing them out:
The buzz of flies, the gen of the breeze, the river
Endlessly stropping its tides against the embankment:
Seasons revolving with colors like stage armies,
Years going west along the one-way street—
All these they ignore, whose session or obsession
Must do with means, not ends. But who called this meeting
Of irreconcileables? Will they work out some positive
Policy, something more than a *modus vivendi?*
Or be adjourned, *sine die,* their task half done?

So the committee, as usual, reached a compromise—
If reach is the word, denoting, as it ought to,
A destination (though why should destiny not
Favor a compromise, which is only the marriage
For better or worse between two or more incompatibles,
Like any marriage of minds?) and left the table,
There being no further business for today.
And the silent secretary wrote up the minutes,
Putting the leaves in order. For what? the eye
Of higher authority? or the seal of the dust?
Or again, to be dispersed irreparably
When the hinge turns and a brusque new life blows in?
And I regret another afternoon wasted,
And wearily think there is something to be said
For the methods of the dictatorships—I who shall waste
Even the last drops of twilight in self-pity
That I should have to be chairman, secretary,
And all the committee, all the one-man committee. *(1957)*

Patrick Kavanagh
(1905–1967)

FATHER MAT

1

In a meadow
Beside the chapel three boys were playing football.
At the forge door an old man was leaning
Viewing a hunter-hoe. A man could hear
If he listened to the breeze the fall of wings—
How wistfully the sin-birds come home!

It was Confession Saturday, the first
Saturday in May; the May Devotions
Were spread like leaves to quieten
The excited armies of conscience.
The knife of penance fell so like a blade
Of grass that no one was afraid.

Father Mat came slowly walking, stopping to
Stare through gaps at ancient Ireland sweeping
In again with all its unbaptized beauty:
The calm evening,
The whitethorn blossoms,
The smell from ditches that were not Christian.
The dancer that dances in the hearts of men cried:
Look! I have shown this to you before—
The rags of living surprised
The joy in things you cannot forget.

His heavy hat was square upon his head,
Like a Christian Brother's;
His eyes were an old man's watery eyes,
Out of his flat nose grew spiky hairs.
He was a part of the place,
Natural as a round stone in a grass field;

He could walk through a cattle fair
And the people would only notice his odd spirit there.

His curate passed on a bicycle—
He had the haughty intellectual look
Of the man who never reads in brook or book;
A man designed
To wear a mitre,
To sit on committees—
For will grows strongest in the emptiest mind.

The old priest saw him pass
And, seeing, saw
Himself a mediaeval ghost.
Ahead of him went Power,
One who was not afraid when the sun opened a flower,
Who was never astonished
At a stick carried down a stream
Or at the undying difference in the corner of a field.

2

The Holy Ghost descends
At random like the muse
On wise man and fool,
And why should poet in the twilight choose?

Within the dim chapel was the grey
Mumble of prayer
To the Queen of May—
The Virgin Mary with the schoolgirl air.

Two guttering candles on a brass shrine
Raised upon the wall
Monsters of despair
To terrify deep into the soul.

Through the open door the hum of rosaries
Came out and blended with the homing bees.
                    The trees
Heard nothing stranger than the rain or the wind
Or the birds—
But deep in their roots they knew a seed had sinned.

In the graveyard a goat was nibbling at a yew,
The cobbler's chickens with anxious looks
Were straggling home through nettles, over graves.
A young girl down a hill was driving cows
To a corner at the gable-end of a roofless house.

Cows were milked earlier,
The supper hurried,
Hens shut in,
Horses unyoked,
And three men shaving before the same mirror.

3

The trip of iron tips on tile
Hesitated up the middle aisle,
Heads that were bowed glanced up to see
Who could this last arrival be.

Murmur of women's voices from the porch,
Memories of relations in the graveyard.
On the stem
Of memory imaginations blossom.

In the dim
Corners in the side seats faces gather,
Lit up now and then by a guttering candle
And the ghost of day at the window.
A secret lover is saying
Three Hail Marys that she who knows
The ways of women will bring
Cathleen O'Hara (he names her) home to him.
Ironic fate! Cathleen herself is saying
Three Hail Marys to her who knows
The ways of men to bring
Somebody else home to her—
"O may he love me."
What is the Virgin Mary now to do?

4

From a confessional
The voice of Father Mat's absolving
Rises and falls like a briar in the breeze.
As the sins pour in the old priest is thinking

His fields of fresh grass, his horses, his cows,
His earth into the fires of Purgatory.
It cools his mind.
"They confess to the fields," he mused,
"They confess to the fields and the air and the sky,"
And forgiveness was the soft grass of his meadow by the river;
His thoughts were walking through it now.

His human lips talked on:
"My son,
Only the poor in spirit shall wear the crown;
Those down
Can creep in the low door
On to heaven's floor."

The Tempter had another answer ready:
"Ah lad, upon the road of life
'Tis best to dance with Chance's wife
And let the rains that come in time
Erase the footprints of the crime."

The dancer that dances in the hearts of men
Tempted him again:
"Look! I have shown you this before;
From this mountain-top I have tempted Christ
With what you see now
Of beauty—all that's music, poetry, art
In things you can touch every day.
I broke away
And rule all dominions that are rare;
I took with me all the answers to every prayer
That young men and girls pray for: love, happiness, riches—"
O Tempter! O Tempter!

5

As Father Mat walked home
Venus was in the western sky
And there were voices in the hedges:
"God the Gay is not the Wise."

"Take your choice, take your choice,"
Called the breeze through the bridge's eye.
"The domestic Virgin and Her Child
Or Venus with her ecstasy." (*1947*)

IF EVER YOU GO TO DUBLIN TOWN

If ever you go to Dublin town
In a hundred years or so
Inquire for me in Baggot Street
And what I was like to know.
O he was a queer one
Fol dol the di do,
He was a queer one
I tell you.

My great-grandmother knew him well,
He asked her to come and call
On him in his flat and she giggled at the thought
Of a young girl's lovely fall.
O he was dangerous
Fol dol the di do,
He was dangerous
I tell you.

On Pembroke Road look out for my ghost
Dishevelled with shoes untied,
Playing through the railings with little children
Whose children have long since died.
O he was a nice man
Fol dol the di do,
He was a nice man
I tell you.

Go into a pub and listen well
If my voice still echoes there,
Ask the men what their grandsires thought
And tell them to answer fair.
O he was eccentric
Fol dol the di do,
He was eccentric
I tell you.

He had the knack of making men feel
As small as they really were
Which meant as great as God had made them
But as males they disliked his air.

O he was a proud one
Fol dol the di do,
He was a proud one
I tell you.

If ever you go to Dublin town
In a hundred years or so
Sniff for my personality,
Is it vanity's vapour now?
O he was a vain one
Fol dol the di do,
He was a vain one
I tell you.

I saw his name with a hundred others
In a book in the library,
It said he had never fully achieved
His potentiality.
O he was slothful
Fol dol the di do,
He was slothful
I tell you.

He knew that posterity has no use
For anything but the soul,
The lines that speak the passionate heart,
The spirit that lives alone.
O he was a lone one
Fol dol the di do,
Yet he lived happily
I tell you.   (1960)

CANAL BANK WALK

Leafy-with-love banks and the green waters of the canal
Pouring redemption for me, that I do
The will of God, wallow in the habitual, the banal,
Grow with nature again as before I grew.
The bright stick trapped, the breeze adding a third
Party to the couple kissing on an old seat,
And a bird gathering materials for the nest for the Word
Eloquently new and abandoned to its delirious beat.
O unworn world enrapture me, enrapture me in a web

Of fabulous grass and eternal voices by a beech,
Feed the gaping need of my senses, give me ad lib
To pray unselfconsciously with overflowing speech
For this soul needs to be honoured with a new dress woven
From green and blue things and arguments that cannot be proven.

(1960)

LINES WRITTEN ON A SEAT ON THE GRAND CANAL, DUBLIN, "ERECTED TO THE MEMORY OF MRS. DERMOT O'BRIEN"

O commemorate me where there is water,
Canal water preferably, so stilly
Greeny at the heart of summer. Brother
Commemorate me thus beautifully.
Where by a lock Niagariously roars
The falls for those who sit in the tremendous silence
Of mid-July. No one will speak in prose
Who finds his way to these Parnassian islands.
A swan goes by head low with many apologies,
Fantastic light looks through the eyes of bridges—
And look! a barge comes bringing from Athy
And other far-flung towns mythologies.
O commemorate me with no hero-courageous
Tomb—just a canal-bank seat for the passer-by.   (1960)

John Betjeman
(1906–   )

THE ARREST OF OSCAR WILDE AT THE CADOGAN HOTEL

He sipped at a weak hock and seltzer
  As he gazed at the London skies
Through the Nottingham lace of the curtains
  Or was it his bees-winged eyes?

To the right and before him Pont Street
  Did tower in her new built red,
As hard as the morning gaslight
  That shone on his unmade bed.

"I want some more hock in my seltzer,
  And Robbie, please give me your hand—
Is this the end or beginning?
  How can I understand?

"So you've brought me the latest *Yellow Book:*
  And Buchan has got in it now:
Approval of what is approved of
  Is as false as a well-kept vow.

"More hock, Robbie—where is the seltzer?
  Dear boy, pull again at the bell!
They are all little better than *cretins,*
  Though this *is* the Cadogan Hotel.

"One astrakhan coat is at Willis's—
  Another one's at the Savoy:
Do fetch my morocco portmanteau,
  And bring them on later, dear boy."

A thump, and a murmur of voices—
  ("Oh why must they make such a din?")

I-333

As the door of the bedroom swung open
  And TWO PLAIN CLOTHES POLICEMEN came in:

"Mr. Woilde, we 'ave come for tew take yew
  Where felons and criminals dwell:
We must ask yew tew leave with us quoietly
  For this *is* the Cadogan Hotel."

He rose, and he put down *The Yellow Book*.
  He staggered—and, terrible-eyed,
He brushed past the palms on the staircase
  And was helped to a hansom outside. *(1937)*

AN INCIDENT IN THE EARLY LIFE
OF EBENEZER JONES, POET, 1828

"We were together at a well-known boarding-school of that day (1828), situated at the foot of Highgate Hill, and presided over by a dissenting minister, the Rev. John Bickerdike. . . .

We were together, though not on the same form; and on a hot summer afternoon, with about fifty other boys, were listlessly conning our tasks in a large schoolroom built out from the house, which made a cover for us to play under when it was wet. Up the ladder-like stairs from the playground a lurcher dog had strayed into the schoolroom, panting with the heat, his tongue lolling out with thirst. The choleric usher who presided, and was detested by us for his tyranny, seeing this, advanced down the room. Enraged at our attention being distracted from our tasks, he dragged the dog to the top of the stairs, and there lifted him bodily up with the evident intention—and we had known him to do similar things—of hurling the poor creature to the bottom.

'YOU SHALL NOT!' ran through the room, as little Ebby, so exclaiming at the top of his voice, rushed with kindling face to the spot from among all the boys—some of them twice his age.

But even while the words passed his lips, the heavy fall was heard, and the sound seemed to travel through his listening form and face, as, with a strange look of anguish in one so young, he stood still, threw up his arms, and burst into an uncontrollable passion of tears.

With a coarse laugh at this, the usher led him back by his ear to the form; and there he sat, long after his sobbing had subsided, like one dazed and stunned." (*From an account of his brother by Sumner Jones in the 1879 re-issue of Ebenezer Jones's "Studies of Sensation and Event."*)

The lumber of a London-going dray,
The still-new stucco on the London clay,
Hot summer silence over Holloway.

Dissenting chapels, tea-bowers, lovers' lairs,
Neat new-built villas, ample Grecian squares,
Remaining orchards ripening Windsor pears.

Hot silence where the older mansions hide
On Highgate Hill's thick elm-encrusted side,
And Pancras, Hornsey, Islington divide.

June's hottest silence where the hard rays strike
Yon hill-foot house, window and wall alike,
School of the Reverend Mr. Bickerdike,

For sons of Saints, blest with this world's possessions
(Seceders from the Protestant Secessions),
Good grounding in the more genteel professions.

A lurcher dog, which draymen kick and pass,
Tongue lolling, thirsty over shadeless grass,
Leapt up the playground ladder to the class.

The godly usher left his godly seat,
His skin was prickly in the ungodly heat,
The dog lay panting at his godly feet.

The milkman on the road stood staring in.
The playground nettles nodded "Now begin"—
And Evil waited, quivering, for sin.

He lifted it and not a word he spoke,
His big hand tightened. Could he make it choke?
He trembled, sweated, and his temper broke.

"You SHALL NOT!" clear across to Highgate Hill
A boy's voice sounded. Creaking forms were still.
The cat jumped slowly from the window sill.

"You SHALL NOT!" flat against the summer sun,
Hard as the hard sky frowning over one,
Gloat, little boys! enjoy the coming fun!

"GOD DAMNS A CUR. I AM, I AM HIS WORD!"
He flung it, flung it and it never stirrred,
"You shall not!—shall not!" ringing on unheard.

Blind desolation! bleeding, burning rod!
Big, bull-necked Minister of Calvin's God!
Exulting milkman, redfaced, shameless clod,

Look on and jeer! Not Satan's thunder-quake
Can cause the mighty walls of Heaven to shake
As now they do, to hear a boy's heart break.   (1940)

TREBETHERICK

We used to picnic where the thrift
    Grew deep and tufted to the edge;
We saw the yellow foam-flakes drift
    In trembling sponges on the ledge
Below us, till the wind would lift
    Them up the cliff and o'er the hedge.
Sand in the sandwiches, wasps in the tea,
Sun on our bathing-dresses heavy with the wet,
Squelch of the bladder-wrack waiting for the sea,
Fleas round the tamarisk, an early cigarette.

From where the coastguard houses stood
    One used to see, below the hill,
The lichened branches of a wood
    In summer silver-cool and still;
And there the Shade of Evil could
    Stretch out at us from Shilla Mill.
Thick with sloe and blackberry, uneven in the light,
Lonely ran the hedge, the heavy meadow was remote,
The oldest part of Cornwall was the wood as black as night,
And the pheasant and the rabbit lay torn open at the throat.

But when a storm was at its height,
    And feathery slate was black in rain,
And tamarisks were hung with light
    And golden sand was brown again,
Spring tide and blizzard would unite
    And sea came flooding up the lane.
Waves full of treasure then were roaring up the beach,
Ropes round our mackintoshes, waders warm and dry,
We waited for the wreckage to come swirling into reach,
Ralph, Vasey, Alastair, Biddy, John and I.

Then roller into roller curled
    And thundered down the rocky bay,
And we were in a water-world
    Of rain and blizzard, sea and spray,
And one against the other hurled
    We struggled round to Greenaway.
Blesséd be St. Enodoc, blesséd be the wave,
Blesséd be the springy turf, we pray, pray to thee,
Ask for our children all the happy days you gave
To Ralph, Vasey, Alastair, Biddy, John and me. *(1940)*

BRISTOL AND CLIFTON

"Yes, I was only sidesman here when last
You came to Evening Communion.
But now I have retired from the bank
I have more leisure time for church finance.
We moved into a somewhat larger house
Than when you knew us in Manilla Road.
This is the window to my lady wife.
You cannot see it now, but in the day
The greens and golds are truly wonderful."

"How very sad. I do not mean about
The window, but I mean about the death
Of Mrs. Battlecock. When did she die?"

"Two years ago when we had just moved in
To Pembroke Road. I rather fear the stairs
And basement kitchen were too much for her—
Not that, of course, she did the servants' work—
But supervising servants all the day
Meant quite a lot of climbing up and down."

"How very sad. Poor Mrs. Battlecock."
" 'The glory that men do lives after them,'*
And so I gave this window in her name.
It's executed by a Bristol firm;
The lady artist who designed it, made
The figure of the lady on the left
Something like Mrs. Battlecock."
"How nice."

* Shakespeare, of course—AUTHOR'S NOTE.

            "Yes, was it not? We had
A stained glass window on the stairs at home,
In Pembroke Road. But not so good as this.
This window is the glory of the church
At least I think so—and the unstained oak
Looks very chaste beneath it. When I gave
The oak, that brass inscription on your right
Commemorates the fact, the Dorcas Club
Made these blue kneelers, though we do not kneel:
We leave that to the Roman Catholics."
"How very nice, indeed. How very nice."

"Seeing I have some knowledge of finance
Our kind Parochial Church Council made
Me People's Warden, and I'm glad to say
That our collections are still keeping up.
The chancel has been flood-lit, and the stove
Which used to heat the church was obsolete.
So now we've had some radiators fixed
Along the walls and eastward of the aisles;
This last I thought of lest at any time
A Ritualist should be inducted here
And want to put up altars. He would find
The radiators inconvenient.
Our only ritual here is with the Plate;
I think we make it dignified enough.
I take it up myself, and afterwards,
Count the Collection on the vestry safe."

"Forgive me, aren't we talking rather loud?
I think I see a woman praying there."
"Praying? The service is all over now
And here's the verger waiting to turn out
The lights and lock the church up. She cannot
Be Loyal Church of England. Well, good-bye.
Time flies. I must be going. Come again.
There are some pleasant people living here
I know the Inskips very well indeed."   *(1940)*

IN WESTMINSTER ABBEY

    Let me take this other glove off
        As the *vox humana* swells,

And the beauteous fields of Eden
  Bask beneath the Abbey bells.
Here, where England's statesmen lie,
Listen to a lady's cry.

Gracious Lord, oh bomb the Germans.
  Spare their women for Thy Sake,
And if that is not too easy
  We will pardon Thy Mistake.
But, gracious Lord, whate'er shall be,
Don't let anyone bomb me.

Keep our Empire undismembered
  Guide our Forces by Thy Hand,
Gallant blacks from far Jamaica,
  Honduras and Togoland;
Protect them Lord in all their fights,
And, even more, protect the whites.

Think of what our Nation stands for,
  Books from Boots' and country lanes,
Free speech, free passes, class distinction,
  Democracy and proper drains.
Lord, put beneath Thy special care
One-eighty-nine Cadogan Square.

Although dear Lord I am a sinner,
  I have done no major crime;
Now I'll come to Evening Service
  Whensoever I have the time.
So, Lord, reserve for me a crown,
And do not let my shares go down.

I will labour for Thy Kingdom,
  Help our lads to win the war,
Send white feathers to the cowards
  Join the Women's Army Corps,
Then wash the Steps around Thy Throne
In the Eternal Safety Zone.

Now I feel a little better,
  What a treat to hear Thy Word,
Where the bones of leading statesmen,

Have so often been interr'd.
And now, dear Lord, I cannot wait
Because I have a luncheon date. (1940)

THE TOWN CLERK'S VIEWS

"Yes, the Town Clerk will see you." In I went.
He was, like all Town Clerks, from north of Trent;
A man with bye-laws busy in his head
Whose Mayor and Council followed where he led.
His most capacious brain will make us cower,
His only weakness is a lust for power—
And that is not a weakness, people think,
When unaccompanied by bribes or drink.
So let us hear this cool careerist tell
His plans to turn our country into hell.
"I cannot say how shock'd I am to see
The *variations* in our scenery.
Just take for instance, at a casual glance,
Our muddled coastline opposite to France:
Dickensian houses by the Channel tides
With old hipp'd roofs and weather-boarded sides.
I blush to think one corner of our isle
Lacks concrete villas in the modern style.
Straight lines of hops in pale brown earth of Kent,
Yeomen's square houses once, no doubt, content
With willow-bordered horse-pond, oast-house, shed,
Wide orchard, garden walls of browny-red—
All useless now, but what fine sites they'ld be
For workers' flats and some light industry.
Those lumpy church towers, unadorned with spires,
And wavy roofs that burn like smouldering fires
In sharp spring sunlight over ashen flint
Are out of date as some old aquatint.
Then glance below the line of Sussex downs
To stucco terraces of seaside towns
Turn'd into flats and residential clubs
Above the wind-slashed Corporation shrubs.
Such Georgian relics should by now, I feel,
Be all rebuilt in glass and polished steel.
Bournemouth is looking up. I'm glad to say
That modernistic there has come to stay.
I walk the asphalt paths of Branksome Chine

In resin-scented air like strong Greek wine
And dream of cliffs of flats along those heights,
Floodlit at night with green electric lights.
But as for Dorset's flint and Purbeck stone,
Its old thatched farms in dips of down alone—
It should be merged with Hants and made to be
A self-contained and plann'd community.
Like Flint and Rutland, it is much too small
And has no reason to exist at all.
Of Devon one can hardly say the same,
But "South-West Area One" 's a better name
For those red sandstone cliffs that stain the sea
By mid-Victoria's Italy—Torquay.
And "South-West Area Two" could well include
The whole of Cornwall from Land's End to Bude.
Need I retrace my steps through other shires?
Pinnacled Somerset? Northampton's spires?
Burford's broad High Street is descending still
Stone-roofed and golden-walled her elmy hill
To meet the river Windrush. What a shame
Her houses are not brick and all the same.
Oxford is growing up to date at last.
Cambridge, I fear, is living in the past.
She needs more factories, not useless things
Like that great chapel which they keep at King's.
As for remote East Anglia, he who searches
Finds only thatch and vast, redundant churches.
But that's the dark side. I can safely say
A beauteous England's really on the way.
Already our hotels are pretty good
For those who're fond of *very simple food*—
Cod and two veg., free pepper, salt and mustard,
Followed by nice hard plums and lumpy custard,
A pint of bitter beer for one-and-four,
Then coffee in the lounge a shilling more.
In a few years this country will be looking
As uniform and tasty as its cooking.
Hamlets which fail to pass the planners' test
Will be demolished. We'll rebuild the rest
To look like Welwyn mixed with Middle West.
All fields we'll turn to sports grounds, lit at night
From concrete standards by fluorescent light:
And over all the land, instead of trees,

Clean poles and wire will whisper in the breeze.
We'll keep one ancient village just to show
What England once was when the times were slow—
Broadway for me. But here I know I must
Ask the opinion of our National Trust.
And ev'ry old cathedral that you enter
By then will be an Area Culture Centre.
Instead of nonsense about Death and Heaven
Lectures on civic duty will be given;
Eurhythmic classes dancing round the spire,
And economics courses in the choir.
So don't encourage tourists. Stay your hand
Until we've really got the country plann'd." *(1948)*

THE LICORICE FIELDS AT PONTEFRACT

In the licorice fields at Pontefract
    My love and I did meet
And many a burdened licorice bush
    Was blooming round our feet;
Red hair she had and golden skin,
Her sulky lips were shaped for sin,
Her sturdy legs were flannel-slack'd,
The strongest legs in Pontefract.

The light and dangling licorice flowers
    Gave off the sweetest smells;
From various black Victorian towers
    The Sunday evening bells
Came pealing over dales and hills
And tanneries and silent mills
And lowly streets where country stops
And little shuttered corner shops.

She cast her blazing eyes on me
    And plucked a licorice leaf;
I was her captive slave and she
    My red-haired robber chief.
Oh love! for love I could not speak,
It left me winded, wilting, weak
And held in brown arms strong and bare
And wound with flaming ropes of hair. *(1954)*

LATE-FLOWERING LUST

My head is bald, my breath is bad,
    Unshaven is my chin,
I have not now the joys I had
    When I was young in sin.

I run my fingers down your dress
    With brandy-certain aim
And you respond to my caress
    And maybe feel the same.

But I've a picture of my own
    On this reunion night,
Wherein two skeletons are shown
    To hold each other tight;

Dark sockets look on emptiness
    Which once was loving-eyed,
The mouth that opens for a kiss
    Has got no tongue inside.

I cling to you inflamed with fear
    As now you cling to me,
I feel how frail you are my dear
    And wonder what will be—

A week? or twenty years remain?
    And then—what kind of death?
A losing fight with frightful pain
    Or a gasping fight for breath?

Too long we let our bodies cling,
    We cannot hide disgust
At all the thoughts that in us spring
    From this late-flowering lust. *(1954)*

FALSE SECURITY

I remember the dread with which I at a quarter past four
Let go with a bang behind me our house front door
And, clutching a present for my dear little hostess tight,

Sailed out for the children's party into the night
Or rather the gathering night. For still some boys
In the near municipal acres were making a noise
Shuffling in fallen leaves and shouting and whistling
And running past hedges of hawthorn, spikey and bristling.
And black in the oncoming darkness stood out the trees
And pink shone the ponds in the sunset ready to freeze
And all was still and ominous waiting for dark
And the keeper was ringing his closing bell in the park
And the arc lights started to fizzle and burst into mauve
As I climbed West Hill to the great big house in The Grove,
Where the children's party was and the dear little hostess.
But halfway up stood the empty house where the ghost is
I crossed to the other side and under the arc
Made a rush for the next kind lamp-post out of the dark
And so to the next and the next till I reached the top
Where the Grove branched off to the left. Then ready to drop
I ran to the ironwork gateway of number seven
Secure at last on the lamplit fringe of Heaven.
Oh who can say how subtle and safe one feels
Shod in one's children's sandals from Daniel Neal's,
Clad in one's party clothes made of stuff from Heal's?
And who can still one's thrill at the candle shine
On cakes and ices and jelly and blackcurrant wine,
And the warm little feel of my hostess's hand in mine?
Can I forget my delight at the conjuring show?
And wasn't I proud that I was the last to go?
Too overexcited and pleased with myself to know
That the words I heard my hostess's mother employ
To a guest departing, would ever diminish my joy,
I WONDER WHERE JULIA FOUND THAT STRANGE, RATHER COMMON
   LITTLE BOY? (1958)

William Empson
(1906–   )

INVITATION TO JUNO

Lucretius could not credit centaurs;
Such bicycle he deemed asynchronous.
"Man superannuates the horse;
Horse pulses will not gear with ours."

Johnson could see no bicycle would go;
"You bear yourself, and the machine as well."
Gennets for germans sprang not from Othello,
And Ixion rides upon a single wheel.

Courage. Weren't strips of heart culture seen
Of late mating two periodicities?
Could not Professor Charles Darwin
Graft annual upon perennial trees?   *(1935)*

DISSATISFACTION WITH METAPHYSICS

High over Mecca Allah's prophet's corpse
(The empty focus opposite the sun)
Receives homage, centre of the universe.
How smooth his epicycles round him run,
Whose hearth is cold, and all his wives undone.

Two mirrors with Infinity to dine
Drink him below the table when they please.
Adam and Eve breed still their dotted line,
Repeated incest, a plain series.
Their trick is all philosophers' disease.

New safe straight lines are finite though unbounded,
Old epicycles numberless in vain.
Then deeper than e'er plummet, plummet sounded,

Then corpses flew, when God flooded the plain.
He promised Noah not to flood again. (*1935*)

SEA VOYAGE

Re-plyed, extorted, oft transposed, and fleeting,
Tune from plucked cotton, the cat's-cradle pattern
Dances round fingers that would scratch in meeting
And dures and fosters their abandoned kitten.
Drawn taut, this flickering of wit would freeze,
And grave, knot-diamond, its filigrees.

Pillowed on gulfs between exiguous bobbins
The Son of Spiders, crucified to lace,
Suspends a red rag to a thousand dobbins
And sails so powered to a better place.
All his gained ports, thought's inter-reached trapeze,
Map-sail, transport him towards Hercules,

Earth-bound. Blue-sea-bound, the crisp silver foam,
Forbad be crystal, a lace eringo,
Flaps from the haunch seven petticoats at home,
Wards, silk, in ocean overskirt, her rainbow.
Sand-rope, the sodden goblet of the seas
Holds, concentrate, her liquid pedigrees.
We sum in port her banquet of degrees. (*1935*)

CAMPING OUT

And now she cleans her teeth into the lake:
Gives it (God's grace) for her own bounty's sake
What morning's pale and the crisp mist debars:
Its glass of the divine (that Will could break)
Restores, beyond Nature: or lets Heaven take
(Itself being dimmed) her pattern, who half awake
Milks between rocks a straddled sky of stars.

Soap tension the star pattern magnifies.
Smoothly Madonna through-assumes the skies
Whose vaults are opened to achieve the Lord.
No, it is we soaring explore galaxies,
Our bullet boat light's speed by thousands flies.
Who moves so among stars their frame unties;
See where they blur, and die, and are outsoared. (*1935*)

VILLANELLE

It is the pain, it is the pain, endures.
Your chemic beauty burned my muscles through.
Poise of my hands reminded me of yours.

What later purge from this deep toxin cures?
What kindness now could the old salve renew?
It is the pain, it is the pain, endures.

The infection slept (custom or change inures)
And when pain's secondary phase was due
Poise of my hands reminded me of yours.

How safe I felt, whom memory assures,
Rich that your grace safely by heart I knew.
It is the pain, it is the pain, endures.

My stare drank deep beauty that still allures.
My heart pumps yet the poison draught of you.
Poise of my hands reminded me of yours.

You are still kind whom the same shape immures.
Kind and beyond adieu. We miss our cue.
It is the pain, it is the pain, endures.
Poise of my hands reminded me of yours. *(1935)*

THE SCALES

The proper scale would pat you on the head
But Alice showed her pup Ulysses' bough
Well from behind a thistle, wise with dread;

And though your gulf-sprung mountains I allow
(Snow-puppy curves, rose-solemn dado band)
Charming for nurse, I am not nurse just now.

Why pat or stride them, when the train will land
Me high, through climbing tunnels, at your side,
And careful fingers meet through castle sand.

Claim slyly rather that the tunnels hide
Solomon's gems, white vistas, preserved kings,
By jackal sandhole to your air flung wide.

Say (she suspects) to sea Nile only brings
Delta and indecision, who instead
Far back up country does enormous things. *(1935)*

LEGAL FICTION

Law makes long spokes of the short stakes of men.
Your well fenced out real estate of mind
No high flat of the nomad citizen
Looks over, or train leaves behind.

Your rights extend under and above your claim
Without bound; you own land in Heaven and Hell;
Your part of earth's surface and mass the same,
Of all cosmos' volume, and all stars as well.

Your rights reach down where all owners meet, in Hell's
Pointed exclusive conclave, at earth's centre
(Your spun farm's root still on that axis dwells);
And up, through galaxies, a growing sector.

You are nomad yet; the lighthouse beam you own
Flashes, like Lucifer, through the firmament.
Earth's axis varies; your dark central cone
Wavers, a candle's shadow, at the end. *(1935)*

EARTH HAS SHRUNK IN THE WASH

They pass too fast. Ships, and there's time for sighing;
Express and motor, Doug can jump between.
Only dry earth now asteroid her flying
Mates, if they miss her, must flick past unseen;

Or striking breasts that once the air defended
(Bubble of rainbow straddling between twilights,
Mother-of-pearl that with earth's oyster ended)
They crash and burrow and spill all through skylights.

There, airless now, from the bare sun take cancer,
Curve spines as earth and gravitation wane,
Starve on the mirror images of plants, or
Miss diabeatic down odd carbon chain.

One daily tortures the poor Christ anew
(On every planet moderately true)
But has much more to do,
And can so much entail here,
Daily brings rabbits to a new Australia,
New unforeseen, new cataclysmic failure,

And cannot tell. He who all answers brings
May (ever in the great taskmaster's eye)
Dowser be of his candle as of springs,
And pump the valley with the tunnel dry. (1935)

THIS LAST PAIN

This last pain for the damned the Fathers found:
"They knew the bliss with which they were not crowned."
    Such, but on earth, let me foretell,
    Is all, of heaven or of hell.

Man, as the prying housemaid of the soul,
May know her happiness by eye to hole:
    He's safe; the key is lost; he knows
    Door will not open, nor hole close.

"What is conceivable can happen too,"
Said Wittgenstein, who had not dreamt of you;
    But wisely; if we worked it long
    We should forget where it was wrong.

Those thorns are crowns which, woven into knots,
Crackle under and soon boil fool's pots;
    And no man's watching, wise and long,
    Would ever stare them into song.

Thorns burn to a consistent ash, like man;
A splendid cleanser for the frying-pan:
    And those who leap from pan to fire
    Should this brave opposite admire.

All those large dreams by which men long live well
Are magic-lanterned on the smoke of hell;
    This then is real, I have implied,
    A painted, small, transparent slide.

These the inventive can hand-paint at leisure,
Or most emporia would stock or measure;
    And feasting in their dappled shade
    We should forget how they were made.

Feign then what's by a decent tact believed
And act that state is only so conceived,
    And build an edifice of form
    For house where phantoms may keep warm.

Imagine, then, by miracle, with me,
(Ambiguous gifts, as what gods give must be)
    What could not possibly be there,
    And learn a style from a despair. (1935)

HOMAGE TO THE BRITISH MUSEUM

There is a supreme God in the ethnological section;
A hollow toad shape, faced with a blank shield.
He needs his belly to include the Pantheon,
Which is inserted through a hole behind.
At the navel, at the points formally stressed, at the organs of sense,
Lice glue themselves, dolls, local deities,
His smooth wood creeps with all the creeds of the world.

Attending there let us absorb the cultures of nations
And dissolve into our judgement all their codes.
Then, being clogged with a natural hesitation
(People are continually asking one the way out),
Let us stand here and admit that we have no road.
Being everything, let us admit that is to be something
Or give ourselves the benefit of the doubt;
Let us offer our pinch of dust all to this God,
And grant his reign over the entire building. (1935)

IGNORANCE OF DEATH

Then there is this civilizing love of death, by which
Even music and painting tell you what else to love.
Buddhists and Christians contrive to agree about death

Making death their ideal basis for different ideals.
The Communists however disapprove of death
Except when practical. The people who dig up

Corpses and rape them are I understand not reported.
The Freudians regard the death-wish as fundamental,
Though "the clamour of life" proceeds from its rival "Eros."

Whether you are to admire a given case for making less clamour
Is not their story. Liberal hopefulness
Regards death as a mere border to an improving picture.

Because we have neither hereditary nor direct knowledge of death
It is the trigger of the literary man's biggest gun
And we are happy to equate it to any conceived calm.

Heaven me, when a man is ready to die about something
Other than himself, and is in fact ready because of that,
Not because of himself, that is something clear about himself.

Otherwise I feel very blank upon this topic,
And think that though important, and proper for anyone to bring up,
It is one that most people should be prepared to be blank upon.   (1940)

MISSING DATES

Slowly the poison the whole blood stream fills.
It is not the effort nor the failure tires.
The waste remains, the waste remains and kills.

It is not your system or clear sight that mills
Down small to the consequence a life requires;
Slowly the poison the whole blood stream fills.

They bled an old dog dry yet the exchange rills
Of young dog blood gave but a month's desires;
The waste remains, the waste remains and kills.

It is the Chinese tombs and the slag hills
Usurp the soil, and not the soil retires.
Slowly the poison the whole blood stream fills.

Not to have fire is to be a skin that shrills.
The complete fire is death. From partial fires
The waste remains, the waste remains and kills.

It is the poems you have lost, the ills
From missing dates, at which the heart expires.
Slowly the poison the whole blood stream fills.
The waste remains, the waste remains and kills.   *(1940)*

W. H. Auden
(1907–   )

THE WALKING TOUR

To throw away the key and walk away,
Not abrupt exile, the neighbors asking why,
But following a line with left and right
An altered gradient at another rate
Learns more than maps upon the whitewashed wall
The hand put up to ask; and makes us well
Without confession of the ill. All pasts
Are single old past now, although some posts
Are forwarded, held looking on a new view;
The future shall fulfill a surer vow
Not smiling at queen over the glass rim
Nor making gunpowder in the top room,
Not swooping at the surface still like gulls
But with prolonged drowning shall develop gills.

But there are still to tempt; areas not seen
Because of blizzards or an erring sign
Whose guessed-at wonders would be worth alleging,
And lies about the cost of a night's lodging.
Travellers may sleep at inns but not attach,
They sleep one night together, not asked to touch;
Receive no normal welcome, not the pressed lip,
Children to lift, not the assuaging lap.
Crossing the pass descend the growing stream
Too tired to hear except the pulses' strum,
Reach villages to ask for a bed in
Rock shutting out the sky, the old life done. *(1930)*

A FREE ONE

Watch any day his nonchalant pauses, see
His dextrous handling of a wrap as he
Steps after into cars, the beggar's envy.

"There is a free one," many say, but err.
He is not that returning conqueror,
Nor ever the poles' circumnavigator.

But poised between shocking falls on razor-edge
Has taught himself this balancing subterfuge
Of the accosting profile, the erect carriage.

The song, the varied action of the blood,
Would drown the warning from the iron wood,
Would cancel the inertia of the buried:

Travelling by daylight on from house to house
The longest way to the intrinsic peace,
With love's fidelity and with love's weakness.   (1930)

TALLER TO-DAY

OLDER MORE MATURE.

Taller to-day, we remember similar evenings,
Walking together in a windless orchard
Where the brook runs over the gravel, far from the glacier.

Nights come bringing the snow, and the dead howl
Under headlands in their windy dwelling
Because the Adversary put too easy questions
On lonely roads.

But happy now, though no nearer each other,   *FRIENDSHIP WASN'T GROWN.*
We see farms lighted all along the valley;
Down at the mill-shed hammering stops
And men go home.

NEW POSSIBILITIES.

Noises at dawn will bring
Freedom for some, but not this peace
No bird can contradict: passing, but here, sufficient now
For something fulfilled this hour, loved or endured.   (1930)

WHAT DID.   *UNCERTAINTY*

PETITION

PRAYER

SECULAR.   Sir, no man's enemy, forgiving all
But will its negative inversion, be prodigal: *SON - RETURNS*
Send to us power and light, a sovereign touch   *LORDLY.*
Curing the intolerable neural itch,

LUST?

So

The exhaustion of weaning, the liar's quinsy, — *TONSILITIS.*
And the distortions of ingrown virginity.
Prohibit sharply the rehearsed response   *WANTS GOD TO STEP*
And gradually correct the coward's stance;   *IN AND CHANGE THESE*
Cover in time with beams those in retreat   *THINGS.*
That, spotted, they turn though the reverse were great;
Publish each healer that in city lives
Or country houses at the end of drives;—   *UNAVAILABLE.*
Harrow the house of the dead; look shining at
New styles of architecture, a change of heart.   (1930)

THE DECOYS

There are some birds in these valleys
Who flutter round the careless
With intimate appeal,
By seeming kindness trained to snaring,
They feel no falseness.

Under the spell completely
They circle can serenely,
And in the tricky light
The masked hill has a purer greenness.
Their flight looks fleeter.

But fowlers, O, like foxes,
Lie ambushed in the rushes.
Along the harmless tracks
The madman keeper crawls through brushwood,
Axe under oxter.

Alas, the signal given,
Fingers on trigger tighten.
The real unlucky dove
Must smarting fall away from brightness
Its love from living.   (1932)

["O WHERE ARE YOU GOING?"]

"O where are you going?" said reader to rider,
"That valley is fatal when furnaces burn,
Yonder's the midden whose odours will madden,
That gap is the grave where the tall return."

"O do you imagine," said fearer to farer,
"That dusk will delay on your path to the pass,
Your diligent looking discover the lacking
Your footsteps feel from granite to grass?"

"O what was that bird," said horror to hearer,
"Did you see that shape in the twisted trees?
Behind you swiftly the figure comes softly,
The spot on your skin is a shocking disease."

"Out of this house"—said rider to reader,
"Yours never will"—said farer to fearer,
"They're looking for you"—said hearer to horror,
As he left them there, as he left them there.   (1932)

THE WANDERER

Doom is dark and deeper than any sea-dingle.
Upon what man it fall
In spring, day-wishing flowers appearing,
Avalanche sliding, white snow from rock-face,
That he should leave his house,
No cloud-soft hand can hold him, restraint by women;
But ever that man goes
Through place-keepers, through forest trees,
A stranger to strangers over undried sea,
Houses for fishes, suffocating water,
Or lonely on fell as chat,
By pot-holed becks
A bird stone-haunting, an unquiet bird.

There head falls forward, fatigued at evening,
And dreams of home,
Waving from window, spread of welcome,
Kissing of wife under single sheet;
But waking sees
Bird-flocks nameless to him, through doorway voices
Of new men making another love.

Save him from hostile capture,
From sudden tiger's spring at corner;
Protect his house,
His anxious house where days are counted

From thunderbolt protect,
From gradual ruin spreading like a stain;
Converting number from vague to certain,
Bring joy, bring day of his returning,
Lucky with day approaching, with leaning dawn.   (*1934*)

ON THIS ISLAND

Look, stranger, on this island now
The leaping light for your delight discovers,
Stand stable here
And silent be,
That through the channels of the ear
May wander like a river
The swaying sound of the sea.

Here at a small field's ending pause
When the chalk wall falls to the foam and its tall ledges
Oppose the pluck
And knock of the tide,
And the shingle scrambles after the suck-
-ing surf,
And a gull lodges
A moment on its sheer side.

Far off like floating seeds the ships
Diverge on urgent voluntary errands,
And the full view
Indeed may enter
And move in memory as now these clouds do,
That pass the harbour mirror
And all the summer through the water saunter.   (*1936*)

[NOW THE LEAVES ARE FALLING FAST]

Now the leaves are falling fast,
Nurse's flowers will not last,
Nurses to their graves are gone,
But the prams go rolling on.

Whispering neighbours left and right
Daunt us from our true delight,
Able hands are left to freeze
Derelict on lonely knees.

Close behind us on our track,
Dead in hundreds cry Alack,
Arms raised stiffly to reprove
In false attitudes of love.

Scrawny through a plundered wood,
Trolls run scolding for their food,
Owl and nightingale are dumb,
And the angel will not come.

Clear, unscaleable, ahead
Rise the Mountains of Instead,
From whose cold cascading streams
None may drink except in dreams.   (1936)

[FISH IN THE UNRUFFLED LAKES]

Fish in the unruffled lakes
Their swarming colours wear,
Swans in the winter air
A white perfection have,
And the great lion walks
Through his innocent grove;
Lion, fish, and swan
Act, and are gone
Upon Time's toppling wave.

We, till shadowed days are done,
We must weep and sing
Duty's conscious wrong,
The Devil in the clock,
The Goodness carefully worn
For atonement or for luck;
We must lose our loves,
On each beast and bird that moves
Turn an envious look.

Sighs for folly done and said
Twist our narrow days,
But I must bless, I must praise
That you, my swan, who have
All gifts that to the swan
Impulsive Nature gave,

The majesty and pride,
Last night should add
Your voluntary love.   (*1936*)

THE QUARRY

O what is that sound which so thrills the ear
  Down in the valley drumming, drumming?
Only the scarlet soldiers, dear,
  The soldiers coming.

O what is that light I see flashing so clear
  Over the distance brightly, brightly?
Only the sun on their weapons, dear,
  As they step lightly.

O what are they doing with all that gear,
  What are they doing this morning, this morning?
Only their usual manoeuvres, dear,
  Or perhaps a warning.

O why have they left the road down there,
  Why are they suddenly wheeling, wheeling?
Perhaps a change in their orders, dear.
  Why are you kneeling?

O haven't they stopped for the doctor's care,
  Haven't they reined their horses, their horses?
Why, they are none of them wounded, dear,
  None of these forces.

O is it the parson they want, with white hair,
  Is it the parson, is it, is it?
No, they are passing his gateway, dear,
  Without a visit.

O it must be the farmer who lives so near.
  It must be the farmer so cunning, so cunning?
They have passed the farmyard already, dear,
  And now they are running.

O where are you going? Stay with me here!
  Were the vows you swore deceiving, deceiving?

No, I promised to love you, dear,
    But I must be leaving.

O it's broken the lock and splintered the door,
    O it's the gate where they're turning, turning;
Their boots are heavy on the floor
    And their eyes are burning. (*1936*)

From SONNETS FROM CHINA

1

So from the years their gifts were showered: each
Grabbed at the one it needed to survive;
Bee took the politics that suit a hive,
Trout finned as trout, peach moulded into peach,

And were successful at their first endeavour.
The hour of birth their only time in college,
They were content with their precocious knowledge,
To know their station and be right for ever.

Till, finally, there came a childish creature
On whom the years could model any feature,
Fake, as chance fell, a leopard or a dove,

Who by the gentlest wind was rudely shaken,
Who looked for truth but always was mistaken,
And envied his few friends, and chose his love.

2

They wondered why the fruit had been forbidden:
It taught them nothing new. They hid their pride,
But did not listen much when they were chidden:
They knew exactly what to do outside.

They left. Immediately the memory faded
Of all they'd known: they could not understand
The dogs now who before had always aided;
The stream was dumb with whom they'd always planned.

They wept and quarrelled: freedom was so wild.
In front maturity as he ascended
Retired like a horizon from the child,

The dangers and the punishments grew greater,
And the way back by angels was defended
Against the poet and the legislator.

4

He stayed, and was imprisoned in possession:
By turns the seasons guarded his one way,
The mountains chose the mother of his children,
In lieu of conscience the sun ruled his day.

Beyond him, his young cousins in the city
Pursued their rapid and unnatural courses,
Believed in nothing but were easy-going,
Far less afraid of strangers than of horses.

He, though, changed little,
But took his colour from the earth,
And grew in likeness to his fowls and cattle.

The townsman thought him miserly and simple,
Unhappy poets took him for the truth,
And tyrants held him up as an example.

5

His care-free swagger was a fine invention:
Life was too slow, too regular, too grave.
With horse and sword he drew the girls' attention,
A conquering hero, bountiful and brave,

To whom teen-agers looked for liberation:
At his command they left behind their mothers,
Their wits were sharpened by the long migration,
His camp-fires taught them all the horde were brothers.

Till what he came to do was done: unwanted,
Grown seedy, paunchy, pouchy, disappointed,
He took to drink to screw his nerves to murder,

Or sat in offices and stole,
Boomed at his children about Law and Order,
And hated life with heart and soul.

6

He watched the stars and noted birds in flight;
A river flooded or a fortress fell:
He made predictions that were sometimes right;
His lucky guesses were rewarded well.

Falling in love with Truth before he knew Her,
He rode into imaginary lands,
By solitude and fasting hoped to woo Her,
And mocked at those who served Her with their hands.

Drawn as he was to magic and obliqueness,
In Her he honestly believed, and when
At last She beckoned to him he obeyed,

Looked in Her eyes: awe-struck but unafraid,
Saw there reflected every human weakness,
And knew himself as one of many men.

7

He was their servant (some say he was blind),
Who moved among their faces and their things:
Their feeling gathered in him like a wind
And sang. They cried "It is a God that sings,"

And honoured him, a person set apart,
Till he grew vain, mistook for personal song
The petty tremors of his mind or heart
At each domestic wrong.

Lines came to him no more; he had to make them
(With what precision was each strophe planned):
Hugging his gloom as peasants hug their land,

He stalked like an assassin through the town,
And glared at men because he did not like them,
But trembled if one passed him with a frown.

10

So an age ended, and its last deliverer died
In bed, grown idle and unhappy; they were safe:
The sudden shadow of a giant's enormous calf
Would fall no more at dusk across their lawns outside.

They slept in peace: in marshes here and there no doubt
A sterile dragon lingered to a natural death,
But in a year the slot had vanished from the heath;
A kobold's knocking in the mountain petered out.

Only the sculptors and the poets were half-sad,
And the pert retinue from the magician's house
Grumbled and went elsewhere. The vanquished powers were glad

To be invisible and free; without remorse
Struck down the silly sons who strayed into their course,
And ravished the daughters, and drove the fathers mad.

13

Far from a cultural centre he was used:
Abandoned by his general and his lice,
Under a padded quilt he turned to ice
And vanished. He will never be perused

When this campaign is tidied into books:
No vital knowledge perished in that skull;
His jokes were stale; like wartime, he was dull;
His name is lost for ever like his looks.

Though runeless, to instructions from headquarters
He added meaning like a comma when
He joined the dust of China, that our daughters

Might keep their upright carriage, not again
Be shamed before the dogs, that, where are waters,
Mountains and houses, may be also men.   *(1939)*

LAW LIKE LOVE

Law, say the gardeners, is the sun,
Law is the one
All gardeners obey
To-morrow, yesterday, to-day.

Law is the wisdom of the old,
The impotent grandfathers feebly scold;
The grandchildren put out a treble tongue,
Law is the senses of the young.

[handwritten annotations: "NATURAL LAW - SEASONS ETC.", "IMPLIES GROWTH", "EVERYONE MAKES THE LAW WHAT THEY WANT IT TO BE."]

Law, says the priest with a priestly look,
Expounding to an unpriestly people,
Law is the words in my priestly book,
Law is my pulpit and my steeple.

Law, says the judge as he looks down his nose,
Speaking clearly and most severely,
Law is as I've told you before,
Law is as you know I suppose,
Law is but let me explain it once more,
Law is The Law.

Yet law-abiding scholars write:
Law is neither wrong nor right,
Law is only crimes
Punished by places and by times,
Law is the clothes men wear
Anytime, anywhere,
Law is Good morning and Good night.

Others say, Law is our Fate;
Others say, Law is our State;
Others say, others say
Law is no more,
Law has gone away.

And always the loud angry crowd,
Very angry and very loud,
Law is We,
And always the soft idiot softly Me.

If we, dear, know we know no more
Than they about the Law,
If I no more than you
Know what we should and should not do
Except that all agree
Gladly or miserably
That the Law is
And that all know this,
If therefore thinking it absurd
To identify Law with some other word,
Unlike so many men
I cannot say Law is again,

No more than they can we suppress
The universal wish to guess
Or slip out of our own position
Into an unconcerned condition.
Although I can at least confine
Your vanity and mine
To stating timidly
A timid similarity,
We shall boast anyway:
Like love I say.

Like love we don't know where or why,
Like love we can't compel or fly,
Like love we often weep,
Like love we seldom keep.   (1940)

LULLABY

Lay your sleeping head, my love,
Human on my faithless arm;
Time and fevers burn away
Individual beauty from
Thoughtful children, and the grave
Proves the child ephemeral:
But in my arms till break of day
Let the living creature lie,
Mortal, guilty, but to me
The entirely beautiful.

Soul and body have no bounds:
To lovers as they lie upon
Her tolerant enchanted slope
In their ordinary swoon,
Grave the vision Venus sends
Of supernatural sympathy,
Universal love and hope;
While an abstract insight wakes
Among the glaciers and the rocks
The hermit's carnal ecstasy.

Certainty, fidelity
On the stroke of midnight pass
Like vibrations of a bell

And fashionable madmen raise
Their pedantic boring cry:
Every farthing of the cost,
All the dreaded cards foretell,
Shall be paid, but from this night
Not a whisper, not a thought,
Not a kiss nor look be lost.

Beauty, midnight, vision dies:
Let the winds of dawn that blow
Softly round your dreaming head
Such a day of welcome show
Eye and knocking heart may bless,
Find our mortal world enough;
Noons of dryness find you fed
By the involuntary powers,
Nights of insult let you pass
Watched by every human love.   (1937, 1940)

SEPTEMBER 1, 1939

I sit in one of the dives
On Fifty-second Street
Uncertain and afraid
As the clever hopes expire
Of a low dishonest decade:
Waves of anger and fear
Circulate over the bright
And darkened lands of the earth,
Obsessing our private lives;
The unmentionable odour of death
Offends the September night.

Accurate scholarship can
Unearth the whole offence
From Luther until now
That has driven a culture mad,
Find what occurred at Linz,
What huge imago made
A psychopathic god:
I and the public know
What all schoolchildren learn,
Those to whom evil is done
Do evil in return.

Exiled Thucydides knew
All that a speech can say
About Democracy,
And what dictators do,
The elderly rubbish they talk
To an apathetic grave;
Analysed all in his book,
The enlightenment driven away,
The habit-forming pain,
Mismanagement and grief:
We must suffer them all again.

ALL THIS STUFF (IN STANZAS (1&2) IS TIMELESS.

Into this neutral air *— AMERICA*
Where blind skyscrapers use
Their full height to proclaim
The strength of Collective Man,
Each language pours its vain
Competitive excuse:
But who can live for long
In an euphoric dream;
Out of the mirror they stare,
Imperialism's face
And the international wrong.

THESE ARE THE REAL REASONS FOR PROBLEMS.

Faces along the bar
Cling to their average day:
The lights must never go out,
The music must always play,
All the conventions conspire
To make this fort assume
The furniture of home;
Lest we should see where we are,
Lost in a haunted wood,
Children afraid of the night
Who have never been happy or good.

The windiest militant trash
Important Persons shout
Is not so crude as our wish:
What mad Nijinsky wrote
About Diaghilev
Is true of the normal heart;
For the error bred in the bone
Of each woman and each man

Craves what it cannot have,
Not universal love
But to be loved alone.

From the conservative dark ~ SUBWAYS.
Into the ethical life
The dense commuters come,
Repeating their morning vow;
"I *will* be true to the wife,
I'll concentrate more on my work," COMMANDMENTS OF
And helpless governors wake EVERYDAY LIFE.
To resume their compulsory game:
Who can release them now,
Who can reach the deaf,
Who can speak for the dumb?

All I have is a voice
To undo the folded lie,
The romantic lie in the brain
Of the sensual man-in-the-street
And the lie of Authority
Whose buildings grope the sky:
There is no such thing as the State
And no one exists alone;
Hunger allows no choice
To the citizen or the police;
We must love one another or die.

Defenceless under the night
Our world in stupor lies;
Yet, dotted everywhere,
Ironic points of light
Flash out wherever the Just
Exchange their messages:
May I, composed like them
Of Eros and of dust,
Beleaguered by the same
Negation and despair,
Show an affirming flame.   (1940)

MUSÉE DES BEAUX ARTS

About suffering they were never wrong,   GENERAL TO
The Old Masters: how well they understood   SPECIFIC
        PAINTERS

Its human position; *of suffering* how it takes place
While someone else is eating or opening a window or just walking dully
  along; *occurs while others are doing nothing*
How, when the aged are reverently, passionately waiting *special up enjoying themselves*
For the miraculous birth, there always must be
Children who did not specially want it to happen, skating
On a pond at the edge of the wood:
They never forgot — *OLD MASTERS.*
That even the dreadful martyrdom must run its course
Anyhow in a corner, some untidy spot
Where the dogs go on with their doggy life and the torturer's horse
Scratches its innocent behind on a tree.

In Brueghel's *Icarus,* for instance: how everything turns away *Ship & legs are delicate —*
Quite leisurely from the disaster; the ploughman may *should be important*
Have heard the splash, the forsaken cry, *to each other.*
But for him it was not an important failure; the sun shone
As it had to on the white legs disappearing into the green
Water; and the expensive delicate ship that must have seen
Something amazing, a boy falling out of the sky,
Had somewhere to get to and sailed calmly on. (*1940*)

IN MEMORY OF W. B. YEATS

1

He disappeared in the dead of winter:
The brooks were frozen, the airports almost deserted,
And snow disfigured the public statues;
The mercury sank in the mouth of the dying day.
What instruments we have agree
The day of his death was a dark cold day.

Far from his illness
The wolves ran on through the evergreen forests,
The peasant river was untempted by the fashionable quays;
By mourning tongues
The death of the poet was kept from his poems.

But for him it was his last afternoon as himself,
An afternoon of nurses and rumours;
The provinces of his body revolted,
The squares of his mind were empty,
Silence invaded the suburbs,
The current of his feeling failed: he became his admirers.

Now he is scattered among a hundred cities
And wholly given over to unfamiliar affections,
To find his happiness in another kind of wood
And be punished under a foreign code of conscience.
The words of a dead man
Are modified in the guts of the living.

But in the importance and noise of to-morrow
When the brokers are roaring like beasts on the floor of the Bourse,
And the poor have the sufferings to which they are fairly accustomed,
And each in the cell of himself is almost convinced of his freedom,
A few thousand will think of this day
As one thinks of a day when one did something slightly unusual.
What instruments we have agree
The day of his death was a dark cold day.

2

You were silly like us; your gift survived it all:
The parish of rich women, physical decay,
Yourself. Mad Ireland hurt you into poetry.
Now Ireland has her madness and her weather still,
For poetry makes nothing happen: it survives
In the valley of its making where executives
Would never want to tamper; flows on south
From ranches of isolation and the busy griefs,
Raw towns that we believe and die in; it survives,
A way of happening, a mouth.

3

Earth, receive an honoured guest:
William Yeats is laid to rest.
Let the Irish vessel lie
Emptied of its poetry.

In the nightmare of the dark
All the dogs of Europe bark,
And the living nations wait,
Each sequestered in its hate;

Intellectual disgrace
Stares from every human face,
And the seas of pity lie
Locked and frozen in each eye.

Follow, poet, follow right
To the bottom of the night,
With your unconstraining voice
Still persuade us to rejoice;

With the farming of a verse
Make a vineyard of the curse,
Sing of human unsuccess
In a rapture of distress;

In the deserts of the heart
Let the healing fountain start,
In the prison of his days
Teach the free man how to praise.   (1940)

PRIME

Simultaneously, as soundlessly,
  Spontaneously, suddenly
As, at the vaunt of the dawn, the kind
  Gates of the body fly open
To its world beyond, the gates of the mind,
  The horn gate and the ivory gate
Swing to, swing shut, instantaneously
  Quell the nocturnal rummage
Of its rebellious fronde, ill-favoured,
  Ill-natured and second-rate,
Disenfranchised, widowed and orphaned
  By an historical mistake:
Recalled from the shades to be a seeing being,
  From absence to be on display,
Without a name or history I wake
  Between my body and the day.

Holy this moment, wholly in the right,
  As, in complete obedience
To the light's laconic outcry, next
  As a sheet, near as a wall,
Out there as a mountain's poise of stone,
  The world is present, about,
And I know that I am, here, not alone
  But with a world, and rejoice
Unvexed, for the will has still to claim

This adjacent arm as my own.
The memory to name me, resume
Its routine of praise and blame,
And smiling to me is this instant while
Still the day is intact, and I
The Adam sinless in our beginning,
Adam still previous to any act.

I draw breath; that is of course to wish
No matter what, to be wise,
To be different, to die and the cost,
No matter how, is Paradise
Lost of course and myself owing a death:
The eager ridge, the steady sea,
The flat roofs of the fishing village
Still asleep in its bunny,
Though as fresh and sunny still are not friends
But things to hand, this ready flesh
No honest equal, but my accomplice now,
My assassin to be, and my name
Stands for my historical share of care
For a lying self-made city,
Afraid of our living task, the dying
Which the coming day will ask.   (1951)

IN PRAISE OF LIMESTONE

If it form the one landscape that we, the inconstant ones,
Are consistently homesick for, this is chiefly
Because it dissolves in water. Mark these rounded slopes
With their surface fragrance of thyme and, beneath,
A secret system of caves and conduits; hear the springs
That spurt out everywhere with a chuckle,
Each filling a private pool for its fish and carving
Its own little ravine whose cliffs entertain
The butterfly and the lizard; examine this region
Of short distances and definite places:
What could be more like Mother or a fitter background
For her son, the flirtatious male who lounges
Against a rock in the sunlight, never doubting
That for all his faults he is loved; whose works are but
Extensions of his power to charm? From weathered outcrop
To hill-top temple, from appearing waters to

Conspicuous fountains, from a wild to a formal vineyard,
  Are ingenious but short steps that a child's wish
To receive more attention than his brothers, whether
  By pleasing or teasing, can easily take.

Watch, then, the band of rivals as they climb up and down
  Their steep stone gennels in twos and threes, at times
Arm in arm, but never, thank God, in step; or engaged
  On the shady side of a square at midday in
Voluble discourse, knowing each other too well to think
  There are any important secrets, unable
To conceive a god whose temper-tantrums are moral
  And not to be pacified by a clever line
Or a good lay: for, accustomed to a stone that responds,
  They have never had to veil their faces in awe
Of a crater whose blazing fury could not be fixed;
  Adjusted to the local needs of valleys
Where everything can be touched or reached by walking,
  Their eyes have never looked into infinite space
Through the lattice-work of a nomad's comb; born lucky,
  Their legs have never encountered the fungi
And insects of the jungle, the monstrous forms and lives
  With which we have nothing, we like to hope, in common.
So, when one of them goes to the bad, the way his mind works
  Remains comprehensible: to become a pimp
Or deal in fake jewellery or ruin a fine tenor voice
  For effects that bring down the house, could happen to all
But the best and the worst of us . . .
                            That is why, I suppose,
  The best and worst never stayed here long but sought
Immoderate soils where the beauty was not so external,
  The light less public and the meaning of life
Something more than a mad camp. "Come!" cried the granite wastes,
  "How evasive is your humour, how accidental
Your kindest kiss, how permanent is death." (Saints-to-be
  Slipped away sighing.) "Come!" purred the clays and gravels.
"On our plains there is room for armies to drill; rivers
  Wait to be tamed and slaves to construct you a tomb
In the grand manner: soft as the earth is mankind and both
  Need to be altered." (Intendant Caesars rose and
Left, slamming the door.) But the really reckless were fetched
  By an older colder voice, the oceanic whisper:
"I am the solitude that asks and promises nothing;

That is how I shall set you free. There is no love;
There are only the various envies, all of them sad."
    They were right, my dear, all those voices were right
And still are; this land is not the sweet home that it looks,
    Nor its peace the historical calm of a site
Where something was settled once and for all: A backward
    And dilapidated province, connected
To the big busy world by a tunnel, with a certain
    Seedy appeal, is that all it is now? Not quite:
It has a worldly duty which in spite of itself
    It does not neglect, but calls into question
All the Great Powers assume; it disturbs our rights. The poet,
    Admired for his earnest habit of calling
The sun the sun, his mind Puzzle, is made uneasy
    By these marble statues which so obviously doubt
His antimythological myth; and these gamins,
    Pursuing the scientist down the tiled colonnade
With such lively offers, rebuke his concern for Nature's
    Remotest aspects: I, too, am reproached, for what
And how much you know. Not to lose time, not to get caught,
    Not to be left behind, not, please! to resemble
The beasts who repeat themselves, or a thing like water
    Or stone whose conduct can be predicted, these
Are our Common Prayer, whose greatest comfort is music
    Which can be made anywhere, is invisible,
And does not smell. In so far as we have to look forward
    To death as a fact, no doubt we are right: But if
Sins can be forgiven, if bodies rise from the dead,
    These modifications of matter into
Innocent athletes and gesticulating fountains,
    Made solely for pleasure, make a further point:
The blessed will not care what angle they are regarded from,
    Having nothing to hide. Dear, I know nothing of
Either, but when I try to imagine a faultless love
    Or the life to come, what I hear is the murmur
Of underground streams, what I see is a limestone landscape. (1951)

ET IN ARCADIA EGO

Who, now, seeing Her so
Happily married,
Housewife, helpmate to Man,

Can imagine the screeching
Virago, the Amazon,
Earth Mother was?

Her jungle growths
Are abated,
Her exorbitant monsters abashed,

Her soil mumbled,
Where crops, aligned precisely,
Will soon be orient:

Levant or couchant,
Well-daunted thoroughbreds
Graze on mead and pasture,

A church clock subdivides the day,
Up the lane at sundown
Geese podge home.

As for Him:
What has happened to the Brute
Epics and nightmares tell of?

No bishops pursue
Their archdeacons with axes,
In the crumbling lair

Of a robber baron
Sightseers picnic
Who carry no daggers.

I well might think myself
A humanist,
Could I manage not to see

How the autobahn
Thwarts the landscape
In godless Roman arrogance,

The farmer's children
Tiptoe past the shed
Where the gelding knife is kept. (1965)

Louis MacNeice
(1907–1963)

BIRMINGHAM

Smoke from the train-gulf hid by hoardings blunders upward, the
    brakes of cars
Pipe as the policeman pivoting round raises his flat hand, bars
With his figure of a monolith Pharaoh the queue of fidgety machines
(Chromium dogs on the bonnet, faces behind the triplex screens).
Behind him the streets run away between the proud glass of shops,
Cubical scent-bottles artificial legs arctic foxes and electric mops,
But beyond this centre the slumward vista thins like a diagram:
There, unvisited, are Vulcan's forges who doesn't care a tinker's damn.
Splayed outwards through the suburbs houses, houses for rest
Seducingly rigged by the builder, half-timbered houses with lips pressed
So tightly and eyes staring at the traffic through bleary haws
And only a six-inch grip of the racing earth in their concrete claws;
In these houses men as in a dream pursue the Platonic Forms
With wireless and cairn terriers and gadgets approximating to the fickle
    norms
And endeavour to find God and score one over the neighbour
By climbing tentatively upward on jerry-built beauty and sweated
    labour.
The lunch hour: the shops empty, shopgirls' faces relax
Diaphanous as green glass, empty as old almanacs
As incoherent with ticketed gewgaws tiered behind their heads
As the Burne-Jones windows in St. Philip's broken by crawling leads;
Insipid color, patches of emotion, Saturday thrills
(This theatre is sprayed with "June")—the gutter take our old playbills,
Next week-end it is likely in the heart's funfair we shall pull
Strong enough on the handle to get back our money; or at any rate it is
    possible.
On shining lines the trams like vast sarcophagi move
Into the sky, plum after sunset, merging to duck's egg, barred with
    mauve
Zeppelin clouds, and Pentecost-like the cars' headlights bud

Out from sideroads and the traffic signals, crême-de-menthe or bull's
    blood,
Tell one to stop, the engine gently breathing, or to go on
To where like black pipes of organs in the frayed and fading zone
Of the West the factory chimneys on sullen sentry will all night wait
To call, in the harsh morning, sleep-stupid faces through the daily gate.
                                          (1933, 1935)

SNOW

The room was suddenly rich and the great bay-window was
Spawning snow and pink roses against it
Soundlessly collateral and incompatible:
World is suddener than we fancy it.

World is crazier and more of it than we think,
Incorrigibly plural. I peel and portion
A tangerine and spit the pips and feel
The drunkenness of things being various.

And the fire flames with a bubbling sound for world
Is more spiteful and gay than one supposes—
On the tongues on the eyes on the ears in the palms of your hands—
There is more than glass between the snow and the huge roses. *(1935)*

THE SUNLIGHT ON THE GARDEN

        The sunlight on the garden
        Hardens and grows cold,
        We cannot cage the minute
        Within its nets of gold;
        When all is told
        We cannot beg for pardon.

        Our freedom as free lances
        Advances towards its end;
        The earth compels, upon it
        Sonnets and birds descend;
        And soon, my friend,
        We shall have no time for dances.

        The sky was good for flying
        Defying the church bells

And every evil iron
Siren and what it tells:
The earth compels,
We are dying, Egypt, dying

And not expecting pardon,
Hardened in heart anew,
But glad to have sat under
Thunder and rain with you,
And grateful too
For sunlight on the garden.   (1937, 1938)

JUNE THUNDER

The Junes were free and full, driving through tiny
Roads, the mudguards brushing the cowparsley,
Through fields of mustard and under boldly embattled
   Mays and chestnuts

Or between beeches verdurous and voluptuous
Or where broom and gorse beflagged the chalkland—
All the flare and gusto of the unenduring
   Joys of a season

Now returned but I note as more appropriate
To the maturer moods impending thunder
With an indigo sky and the garden hushed except for
   The treetops moving.

Then the curtains in my room blow suddenly inward,
The shrubbery rustles, birds fly heavily homeward,
The white flowers fade to nothing on the trees and rain comes
   Down like a dropscene.

Now there comes the catharsis, the cleansing downpour
Breaking the blossoms of our overdated fancies
Our old sentimentality and whimsicality
      Loves of the morning.

Blackness at half-past eight, the night's precursor,
Clouds like falling masonry and lightning's lavish
Annunciation, the sword of the mad archangel
   Flashed from the scabbard.

If only now you would come and dare the crystal
Rampart of rain and the bottomless moat of thunder,
If only now you would come I should be happy
   Now if now only. *(1937, 1938)*

BAGPIPE MUSIC

It's no go the merrygoround, it's no go the rickshaw,
All we want is a limousine and a ticket for the peepshow.
Their knickers are made of crêpe-de-chine, their shoes are made of
   python,
Their halls are lined with tiger rugs and their walls with heads of bison.

John MacDonald found a corpse, put it under the sofa,
Waited till it came to life and hit it with a poker,
Sold its eyes for souvenirs, sold its blood for whiskey,
Kept its bones for dumb-bells to use when he was fifty.

It's no go the Yogi-Man, it's no go Blavatsky,
All we want is a bank balance and a bit of skirt in a taxi.

Annie MacDougall went to milk, caught her foot in the heather,
Woke to hear a dance record playing of Old Vienna.
It's no go your maidenheads, it's no go your culture,
All we want is a Dunlop tyre and the devil mend the puncture.

The Laird o' Phelps spent Hogmanay declaring he was sober,
Counted his feet to prove the fact and found he had one foot over.
Mrs. Carmichael had her fifth, looked at the job with repulsion,
Said to the midwife "Take it away; I'm through with over-production."

It's no go the gossip column, it's no go the Ceilidh,
All we want is a mother's help and a sugar-stick for the baby.

Willie Murray cut his thumb, couldn't count the damage,
Took the hide of an Ayrshire cow and used it for a bandage.
His brother caught three hundred cran when the seas were lavish,
Threw the bleeders back in the sea and went upon the parish.

It's no go the Herring Board, it's no go the Bible,
All we want is a packet of fags when our hands are idle.

It's no go the picture palace, it's no go the stadium,
It's no go the country cot with a pot of pink geraniums,

It's no go the Government grants, it's no go the elections,
Sit on your arse for fifty years and hang your hat on a pension.

It's no go my honey love, it's no go my poppet;
Work your hands from day to day, the winds will blow the profit.
The glass is falling hour by hour, the glass will fall for ever,
But if you break the bloody glass you won't hold up the weather.

(1937, 1938)

From AUTUMN JOURNAL

3

August is nearly over, the people
   Back from holiday are tanned
With blistered thumbs and a wallet of snaps and a little
   Joie de vivre which is contraband;
Whose stamina is enough to face the annual
   Wait for the annual spree,
Whose memories are stamped with specks of sunshine
   Like faded *fleurs de lys*.
Now the till and the typewriter call the fingers,
   The workman gathers his tools
For the eight-hour day but after that the solace
   Of films or football pools
Or of the gossip or cuddle, the moments of self-glory
   Or self-indulgence, blinkers on the eyes of doubt,
The blue smoke rising and the brown lace sinking
   In the empty glass of stout.
Most are accepters, born and bred to harness,
   And take things as they come,
But some refusing harness and more who are refused it
   Would pray that another and a better Kingdom come,
Which now is sketched in the air or travestied in slogans
   Written in chalk or tar on stucco or plaster-board
But in time may find its body in men's bodies,
   Its law and order in their hearts' accord,
Where skill will no longer languish nor energy be trammelled
   To competition and graft,
Exploited in subservience but not allegiance
   To an utterly lost and daft
System that gives a few at fancy prices
   Their fancy lives

While ninety-nine in the hundred who never attend the banquet
  Must wash the grease of ages off the knives.
And now the tempter whispers "But you also
  Have the slave-owner's mind,
Would like to sleep on a mattress of easy profits,
  To snap your fingers or a whip and find
Servants or houris ready to wince and flatter
  And build with their degradation your self-esteem;
What you want is not a world of the free in function
  But a niche at the top, the skimmings of the cream."
And I answer that that is largely so for habit makes me
  Think victory for one implies another's defeat,
That freedom means the power to order, and that in order
  To preserve the values dear to the élite
The élite must remain a few. It is so hard to imagine
  A world where the many would have their chance without
A fall in the standard of intellectual living
  And nothing left that the highbrow cared about.
Which fears must be suppressed. There is no reason for thinking
  That, if you give a chance to people to think or live,
The arts of thought or life will suffer and become rougher
  And not return more than you could ever give.
And now I relapse to sleep, to dreams perhaps and reaction
  Where I shall play the gangster or the sheikh,
Kill for the love of killing, make the world my sofa,
  Unzip the women and insult the meek.
Which fantasies no doubt are due to my private history,
  Matter for the analyst,
But the final cure is not in his past-dissecting fingers
  But in a future of action, the will and fist
Of those who abjure the luxury of self-pity,
  And prefer to risk a movement without being sure
If movement would be better or worse in a hundred
  Years or a thousand when their heart is pure.
None of our hearts are pure, we always have mixed motives,
  Are self deceivers, but the worst of all
Deceits is to murmur "Lord, I am not worthy"
  And, lying easy, turn your face to the wall.
But may I cure that habit, look up and outwards
  And may my feet follow my wider glance
First no doubt to stumble, then to walk with the others
  And in the end—with time and luck—to dance. (*1938, 1939*)

PROGNOSIS

Goodbye, Winter,
The days are getting longer,
The tea-leaf in the teacup
Is herald of a stranger.

Will he bring me business
Or will be bring me gladness
Or will he come for cure
Of his own sickness?

With a pedlar's burden
Walking up the garden
Will he come to beg
Or will he come to bargain?

Will he come to pester,
To cringe or to bluster,
A promise in his palm
Or a gun in his holster?

Will his name be John
Or will his name be Jonah
Crying to repent
On the Island of Iona?

Will his name be Jason
Looking for a seaman
Or a mad crusader
Without rhyme or reason?

What will be his message—
War or work or marriage?
News as new as dawn
Or an old adage?

Will he give a champion
Answer to my question
Or will his words be dark
And his ways evasion?

Will his name be Love
And all his talk be crazy?
Or will his name be Death
And his message easy?   *(Spring 1939, 1940)*

ENTIRELY

If we could get the hang of it entirely
   It would take too long;
All we know is the splash of words in passing
   And falling twigs of song,
And when we try to eavesdrop on the great
   Presences it is rarely
That by a stroke of luck we can appropriate
   Even a phrase entirely.

If we could find our happiness entirely
   In somebody else's arms
We should not fear the spears of the spring nor the city's
   Yammering fire alarms
But, as it is, the spears each year go through
   Our flesh and almost hourly
Bell or siren banishes the blue
   Eyes of Love entirely.

And if the world were black or white entirely
   And all the charts were plain
Instead of a mad weir of tigerish waters,
   A prism of delight and pain,
We might be surer where we wished to go
   Or again we might be merely
Bored but in brute reality there is no
   Road that is right entirely.   *(1940, 1940)*

IL PICCOLO RIFIUTO

Impatient with cripples, foreigners, children,
As though they were midges or wasps he refused
Jam on his bread or to walk in the shrubbery.
Crutch and giggle and guttural accent
Were left in the air. He was disabused
Of a world not his, his birth certificate
Faded behind his eyes, his eyes

Blinked as the jets dived on the jampot
He had not ordered and harpy-wise
The insect world grew breasts and talons
And wogs and wops kept babbling and mad
Children went on a spacelark and God
Began to limp and deep in the bad
Shrubbery shrubs that should be ever
Green turned brown. He asked for a stone
But the waiter offered him bread in yiddish.
No, he repeated, I never ordered
Jam, God damn you, leave me alone.   (*1961*)

IN LIEU

Roses with the scent bred out,
In lieu of which is a long name on a label.
Dragonflies reverting to grubs,
Tundra and desert overcrowded,
And in lieu of a high altar
Wafers and wine procured by a coin in a slot.

On the podium in lieu of a man
With fallible hands is ensconced
A metal lobster with built-in tempi;
The deep sea fishermen in lieu of
Battling with tunny and cod
Are signing their contracts for processing plankton.

On roof after roof the prongs
Are baited with faces, in saltpan and brainpan
The savour is lost, in deep
Freeze after freeze in lieu of a joint
Are piled the shrunken heads of the past
And the offals of unborn children.

In lieu therefore of choice
Thy Will be undone just as flowers
Fugues, vows and hopes are undone
While the weather is packaged and the spacemen
In endless orbit and in lieu of a flag
The orator hangs himself from the flagpost.   (*1963*)

THE GREY ONES

Crouched beneath a snowbound sky
Three grey sisters share an eye;
Before they lose it and forget
Ask the way to Never Yet,

Which might be Once Upon a Time,
Golden Age or Perfect Crime,
Kingdom Come or Free for All,
No past, no future and no fall.

Bandied round from face to face
One lonely eye in frozen space
Skewers the perspectives of the mind
Till what you wished you fear to find,

Which might be what your childhood swore
Lay shrined beyond the haunted door
Or might be where your mentor seems
To misdirect you to in dreams.

Every such what and where betwixt
Your fact and fancy stays transfixed
By that one unremitting stare
Which cancels what you never were,

Who might have been a prince of Troy,
A lord of song, a roaring boy,
Or might have been an idiot mild
Who meets his match in every child,

For all which persons lacking proof
The three grey sisters wait aloof;
They chew the cud, they pass the eye
And check the client next to die,

Who might be in some mountain cup
Where climbers meet it struggling up
Or might be in some Eastern town
Where most men take it lying down

Sprawled against the Gates of Doom
Whence all kebabs and cockstands come,
On which stands guard for ever more
A beggar with a flaming sore.   (1963)

Stephen Spender
(1909–   )

[ROLLED OVER ON EUROPE]

Rolled over on Europe: the sharp dew frozen to stars
Below us; above our heads, the night
Frozen again to stars; the stars
In pools between our coats; and that charmed moon.
Ah, what supports? What cross draws out our arms,
Heaves up our bodies towards the wind
And hammers us between the mirrored lights?

Only my body is real; which wolves
Are free to oppress and gnaw. Only this rose
My friend laid on my breast, and these few lines
Written from home, are real.   (*1933*)

[WITHOUT THAT ONCE CLEAR AIM]

Without that once clear aim, the path of flight
To follow for a lifetime through white air,
This century chokes me under roots of night.
I suffer like history in Dark Ages, where
Truth lies in dungeons, too deep for whisper.
We hear of towers long broken off from sight
And tortures and wars, smoky and dark with rumour,
But on Mind's buried thought there falls no light.
Watch me who walk through coiling streets where rain
And fog choke every sigh; round corners of day,
Road-drills explore new areas of pain,
Nor trees reach leaf-lit branches down to play.
The city climbs in horror to my brain,
The writings are my only wings away.   (*1933*)

[I THINK CONTINUALLY OF THOSE]

I think continually of those who were truly great.
Who, from the womb, remembered the soul's history

Through corridors of light where the hours are suns,
Endless and singing. Whose lovely ambition
Was that their lips, still touched with fire,
Should tell of the Spirit, clothed from head to foot in song.
And who hoarded from the Spring branches
The desires falling across their bodies like blossoms.

What is precious is never to forget
The essential delight of the blood drawn from ageless springs
Breaking through rocks in worlds before our earth.
Never to deny its pleasure in the morning simple light
Nor its grave evening demand for love.
Never to allow gradually the traffic to smother
With noise and fog the flowering of the Spirit.

Near the snow, near the sun, in the highest fields,
See how these names are fêted by the waving grass
And by the streamers of white cloud
And whispers of wind in the listening sky.
The names of those who in their lives fought for life,
Who wore at their hearts the fire's centre.
Born of the sun, they travelled a short while toward the sun
And left the vivid air signed with their honour.   (1933)

THE FUNERAL

Death is another milestone on their way.
With laughter on their lips and with winds blowing round them
They record simply
How this one excelled all others in making driving belts.

This is festivity, it is the time of statistics,
When they record what one unit contributed:
They are glad as they lay him back in the earth
And thank him for what he gave them.

They walk home remembering the straining red flags,
And with pennons of song still fluttering through their blood
They speak of the World State
With its towns like brain centres and its pulsing arteries.

They think how one life hums, revolves and toils,
One cog in a golden singing hive:

Like spark from fire, its task happily achieved,
It falls away quietly.

No more are they haunted by the individual grief
Nor the crocodile tears of European genius,
The decline of a culture
Mourned by scholars who dream of the ghosts of Greek boys.

(1933)

[NOT PALACES, AN ERA'S CROWN]

Not palaces, an era's crown
Where the mind dwells, intrigues, rests;
Architectural gold-leaved flower
From people ordered like a single mind,
I build. This only what I tell:
It is too late for rare accumulation,
For family pride, for beauty's filtered dusts;
I say, stamping the words with emphasis,
Drink from here energy and only energy,
As from the electric charge of a battery,
To will this Time's change.
Eye, gazelle, delicate wanderer,
Drinker of horizon's fluid line;
Ear that suspends on a chord
The spirit drinking timelessness;
Touch, love, all senses;
Leave your gardens, your singing feasts,
Your dreams of suns circling before our sun,
Of heaven after our world.
Instead, watch images of flashing brass
That strike the outward sense, the polished will
Flag of our purpose which the wind engraves.
No spirit seek here rest. But this: No one
Shall hunger: Man shall spend equally.
Our goal which we compel: Man shall be man.
          That programme of the antique Satan
Bristling with guns on the indented page,
With battleship towering from hilly waves:
For what? Drive of a ruining purpose
Destroying all but its age-long exploiters.
Our programme like this, but opposite,
Death to the killers, bringing light to life. (1933)

THE EXPRESS

After the first powerful plain manifesto
The black statement of pistons, without more fuss
But gliding like a queen, she leaves the station.
Without bowing and with restrained unconcern
She passes the houses which humbly crowd outside,
The gasworks and at last the heavy page
Of death, printed by gravestones in the cemetery.
Beyond the town there lies the open country
Where, gathering speed, she acquires mystery,
The luminous self-possession of ships on ocean.
It is now she begins to sing—at first quite low
Then loud, and at last with a jazzy madness—
The song of her whistle screaming at curves,
Of deafening tunnels, brakes, innumerable bolts.
And always light, aerial, underneath
Goes the elate meter of her wheels.
Steaming through metal landscape on her lines
She plunges new eras of wild happiness
Where speed throws up strange shapes, broad curves
And parallels clean like the steel of guns.
At last, further than Edinburgh or Rome,
Beyond the crest of the world, she reaches night
Where only a low streamline brightness
Of phosphorus on the tossing hills is white.
Ah, like a comet through flames she moves entranced
Wrapt in her music no bird song, no, nor bough
Breaking with honey buds, shall ever equal.   (1933)

ULTIMA RATIO REGUM

The guns spell money's ultimate reason
In letters of lead on the spring hillside.
But the boy lying dead under the olive trees
Was too young and too silly
To have been notable to their important eye.
He was a better target for a kiss.

When he lived, tall factory hooters never summoned him.
Nor did restaurant plate-glass doors revolve to wave him in.
His name never appeared in the papers.
The world maintained its traditional wall

Round the dead with their gold sunk deep as a well,
Whilst his life, intangible as a Stock Exchange rumour, drifted outside.

O too lightly he threw down his cap
One day when the breeze threw petals from the trees.
The unflowering wall sprouted with guns,
Machine-gun anger quickly scythed the grasses;
Flags and leaves fell from hands and branches;
The tweed cap rotted in the nettles.

Consider his life which was valueless
In terms of employment, hotel ledgers, news files.
Consider. One bullet in ten thousand kills a man.
Ask. Was so much expenditure justified
On the death of one so young and so silly
Lying under the olive trees, O world, O death?   *(1939)*

THE BARN

Half-hidden by trees, the sheer roof of the barn
Is warped to a river of tiles
By currents of the sky's weather
Through long damp years.

Under the leaves, a great butterfly's wing
Seems its brilliant red, streaked with dark lines
Of lichen and rust, an underwing
Of winter leaves.

A sapling, with a jet of flaming
Foliage, cancels with its branches
The guttered lower base of the roof, reflecting
The tiles in a cup of green.

Under the crashing vault of sky,
At the side of the road flashing past
With a rumour of smoke and steel,
Hushed by whispers of leaves, and bird song,
The barn from its dark throat
Gurgitates with a gentle booming murmur.

This ghost of a noise suggests a gust
Caught in its rafters aloft long ago,
The turn of a winch, the wood of a wheel.

Tangled in the sound, as in a girl's hair,
Is the enthusiastic scent
Of vivid yellow straw, lit by a sun-beam
Laden with motes, on the boards of a floor.   (1942)

EPILOGUE TO A HUMAN DRAMA

When pavements were blown up, exposing nerves,
And the gas mains burned blue and gold
And stucco houses were smashed to a cloud
Pungent with mice, dust, garlic, anxiety:
When the reverberant façades
Of the palaces of commerce,
Isolated in a vacuum of silence, suddenly
Cracked and roared and fell, and the seven-maned
Golden lions licked the stony fragments:

Then the only voice through deserted streets
Was the Cassandra bell which rang and rang and ran
As if released at last by time
Towards those fires that burst through many walls—
Prophetic doom opened to the nostrils,
Blood and fire streaming from the stones.

The City burned with unsentimental dignity
Of resigned wisdom: those stores and churches
Which had glittered emptily in gold and silk,
Stood near the crowning dome of the cathedral
Like courtiers round the Royal Martyr.
August shadows of night
And bursting days of concentrated light
Dropped from the skies to paint a final scene—
Illuminated agony of frowning stone.
Who can wonder then that every word
In burning London seemed out of a play?

On the stage, there were heroes, maidens, fools,
Victims, a chorus. The heroes were brave,
The rescued appeared passively beautiful,
The fools spat jokes into the skull of death,
The victims waited with the humble patience
Of animals trapped behind a wall
For the pickaxes to break with sun and water.
The chorus assisted, bringing cups of tea,

Praising the heroes, discussing the habits of the wicked,
Underlining the moral, explaining doom and truth. *(1949)*

ONE MORE NEW BOTCHED BEGINNING

Their voices heard, I stumble suddenly,
Choking in undergrowth. I'm torn
Mouth pressed against the thorns,
                              remembering
    Ten years ago here in Geneva,

I walked with Merleau-Ponty by the lake.
Upon his face I saw his intellect.
The energy of the sun-interweaving
Waves, electric, danced on him. His eyes
Smiled with their gay logic through
Black coins thrown down from leaves. He who
Was Merleau-Ponty that day is no more
Irrevocable than the I that day who was
Beside him—I'm still living!

    Also that summer
My son stayed up the valley in the mountains.
One day I went to see him, and he stood
Not seeing me, watching some hens.
Doing so, he was absorbed
In their wire-netted world. He danced
On one leg. Leaning forward, he became
A bird-boy. I am there
Still seeing him. To him,
That moment—unselfknowing even then—
Is drowned in the oblivious earliness . . .

                              Such pasts
Are not diminished distances, perspective
Vanishing points, but doors
Burst open suddenly by gusts
That seek to blow the heart out.
                    Today, I see
Three undergraduates standing talking in
A college quad. They show each other poems—
Louis MacNeice, Bernard Spencer, and I.
Louis caught cold in the rain, Bernard fell

From a train door.
Their lives are now those poems that were
Pointers to the poems to be their lives.
We read there in the college quad, each poem
Is still a new beginning. If
They had been finished though, they would have died
Before they died. Being alive
Is when each moment's a new start, with past
And future shuffled between fingers
For a new game. I'm dealing out
My hand to them, one more new botched beginning
There, where we still stand talking in the quad.   (*1964*)

Dylan Thomas
(1914–1953)

THE FORCE THAT THROUGH THE GREEN FUSE DRIVES THE FLOWER

The force that through the green fuse drives the flower
Drives my green age; that blasts the roots of trees
Is my destroyer.
And I am dumb to tell the crooked rose
My youth is bent by the same wintry fever.

The force that drives the water through the rocks
Drives my red blood; that dries the mouthing streams
Turns mine to wax.
And I am dumb to mouth unto my veins
How at the mountain spring the same mouth sucks.

The hand that whirls the water in the pool
Stirs the quicksand; that ropes the blowing wind
Hauls my shroud sail.
And I am dumb to tell the hanging man
How of my clay is made the hangman's lime.

The lips of time leech to the fountain head;
Love drips and gathers, but the fallen blood
Shall calm her sores.
And I am dumb to tell a weather's wind
How time has ticked a heaven round the stars.

And I am dumb to tell the lover's tomb
How at my sheet goes the same crooked worm.   *(1934)*

LIGHT BREAKS WHERE NO SUN SHINES

Light breaks where no sun shines;
Where no sea runs, the waters of the heart

Push in their tides;
And, broken ghosts with glow-worms in their heads,
The things of light
File through the flesh where no flesh decks the bones.

A candle in the thighs
Warms youth and seed and burns the seeds of age;
Where no seed stirs,
The fruit of man unwrinkles in the stars,
Bright as a fig;
Where no wax is, the candle shows its hairs.

Dawn breaks behind the eyes;
From poles of skull and toe the windy blood
Slides like a sea;
Nor fenced, nor staked, the gushers of the sky
Spout to the rod
Divining in a smile the oil of tears.

Night in the sockets rounds,
Like some pitch moon, the limit of the globes;
Day lights the bone;
Where no cold is, the skinning gales unpin
The winter's robes;
The film of spring is hanging from the lids.

Light breaks on secret lots,
On tips of thought where thoughts smell in the rain;
When logics die,
The secret of the soil grows through the eye,
And blood jumps in the sun;
Above the waste allotments the dawn halts.   *(1934)*

AND DEATH SHALL HAVE NO DOMINION

And death shall have no dominion.
Dead men naked they shall be one
With the man in the wind and the west moon;
When their bones are picked clean and the clean bones gone,
They shall have stars at elbow and foot;
Though they go mad they shall be sane,
Though they sink through the sea they shall rise again;
Though lovers be lost love shall not;
And death shall have no dominion.

And death shall have no dominion.
Under the windings of the sea
They lying long shall not die windily;
Twisting on racks when sinews give way,
Strapped to a wheel, yet they shall not break;
Faith in their hands shall snap in two,
And the unicorn evils run them through;
Split all ends up they shan't crack;
And death shall have no dominion.

And death shall have no dominion.
No more may gulls cry at their ears
Or waves break loud on the seashores;
Where blew a flower may a flower no more
Lift its head to the blows of the rain;
Though they be mad and dead as nails,
Heads of the characters hammer through daisies;
Break in the sun till the sun breaks down,
And death shall have no dominion. (1936)

From ALTARWISE BY OWL-LIGHT

1

Altarwise by owl-light in the half-way house
The gentleman lay graveward with his furies;
Abaddon in the hangnail cracked from Adam,
And, from his fork, a dog among the fairies,
The atlas-eater with a jaw for news,
Bit out the mandrake with tomorrow's scream.
Then, penny-eyed, that gentleman of wounds,
Old cock from nowheres and the heaven's egg,
With bones unbuttoned to the half-way winds,
Hatched from the windy salvage on one leg,
Scraped at my cradle in a walking word
That night of time under the Christward shelter,
I am the long world's gentleman, he said,
And share my bed with Capricorn and Cancer.

2

Death is all metaphors, shape in one history;
The child that sucketh long is shooting up,
The planet-ducted pelican of circles

Weans on an artery the gender's strip;
Child of the short spark in a shapeless country
Soon sets alight a long stick from the cradle;
The horizontal cross-bones of Abaddon,
You by the cavern over the black stairs,
Rung bone and blade, the verticals of Adam,
And, manned by midnight, Jacob to the stars.
Hairs of your head, then said the hollow agent,
Are but the roots of nettles and of feathers
Over these groundworks thrusting through a pavement
And hemlock-headed in the wood of weathers.

3

First there was the lamb on knocking knees
And three dead seasons on a climbing grave
That Adam's wether in the flock of horns,
Butt of the tree-tailed worm that mounted Eve,
Horned down with skullfoot and the skull of toes
On thunderous pavements in the garden time;
Rip of the vaults, I took my marrow-ladle
Out of the wrinkled undertaker's van,
And, Rip Van Winkle from a timeless cradle,
Dipped me breast-deep in the descended bone;
The black ram, shuffling of the year, old winter,
Alone alive among his mutton fold,
We rung our weathering changes on the ladder,
Said the antipodes, and twice spring chimed.

4

What is the metre of the dictionary?
The size of genesis? the short spark's gender?
Shade without shape? the shape of Pharaoh's echo?
(My shape of age nagging the wounded whisper).
Which sixth of wind blew out the burning gentry?
(Questions are hunchbacks to the poker marrow).
What of a bamboo man among your acres?
Corset the boneyards for a crooked boy?
Button your bodice on a hump of splinters,
My camel's eyes will needle through the shroud.
Love's reflection of the mushroom features,
Stills snapped by night in the bread-sided field,
Once close-up smiling in the wall of pictures,
Arc-lamped thrown back upon the cutting flood.

8

This was the crucifixion on the mountain,
Time's nerve in vinegar, the gallow grave
As tarred with blood as the bright thorns I wept;
The world's my wound, God's Mary in her grief,
Bent like three trees and bird-papped through her shift,
With pins for teardrops is the long wound's woman.
This was the sky, Jack Christ, each minstrel angle
Drove in the heaven-driven of the nails
Till the three-coloured rainbow from my nipples
From pole to pole leapt round the snail-waked world.
I by the tree of thieves, all glory's sawbones
Unsex the skeleton this mountain minute,
And by this blowclock witness of the sun
Suffer the heaven's children through my heartbeat.

9

From the oracular archives and the parchment,
Prophets and fibre kings in oil and letter,
The lamped calligrapher, the queen in splints,
Buckle to lint and cloth their natron footsteps,
Draw on the glove of prints, dead Cairo's henna
Pour like a halo on the caps and serpents.
This was the resurrection in the desert,
Death from a bandage, rants the mask of scholars
Gold on such features, and the linen spirit
Weds my long gentleman to dusts and furies;
With priest and pharaoh bed my gentle wound,
World in the sand, on the triangle landscape,
With stones of odyssey for ash and garland
And rivers of the dead around my neck.

10

Let the tale's sailor from a Christian voyage
Atlaswise hold half-way off the dummy bay
Time's ship-racked gospel on the globe I balance:
So shall winged harbours through the rockbirds' eyes
Spot the blown word, and on the seas I imagine
December's thorn screwed in a brow of holly.
Let the first Peter from a rainbow's quayrail
Ask the tall fish swept from the bible east,
What rhubarb man peeled in her foam-blue channel

Has sown a flying garden round that sea-ghost?
Green as beginning, let the garden diving
Soar, with its two bark towers, to that Day
When the worm builds with the gold straws of venom
My nest of mercies in the rude, red tree.   (*1936*)

AFTER THE FUNERAL

(*In memory of Ann Jones*)

After the funeral, mule praises, brays,
Windshake of sailshaped ears, muffle-toed tap
Tap happily of one peg in the thick
Grave's foot, blinds down the lids, the teeth in black,
The spittled eyes, the salt ponds in the sleeves,
Morning smack of the spade that wakes up sleep,
Shakes a desolate boy who slits his throat
In the dark of the coffin and sheds dry leaves,
That breaks one bone to light with a judgment clout,
After the feast of tear-stuffed time and thistles
In a room with a stuffed fox and a stale fern,
I stand, for this memorial's sake, alone
In the snivelling hours with dead, humped Ann
Whose hooded, fountain heart once fell in puddles
Round the parched worlds of Wales and drowned each sun
(Though this for her is a monstrous image blindly
Magnified out of praise; her death was a still drop;
She would not have me sinking in the holy
Flood of her heart's fame; she would lie dumb and deep
And need no druid of her broken body).
But I, Ann's bard on a raised hearth, call all
The seas to service that her wood-tongued virtue
Babble like a bellbuoy over the hymning heads,
Bow down the walls of the ferned and foxy woods
That her love sing and swing through a brown chapel,
Bless her bent spirit with four, crossing birds.
Her flesh was meek as milk, but this skyward statue
With the wild breast and blessed and giant skull
Is carved from her in a room with a wet window
In a fiercely mourning house in a crooked year.
I know her scrubbed and sour humble hands
Lie with religion in their cramp, her threadbare
Whisper in a damp word, her wits drilled hollow,
Her fist of a face died clenched on a round pain;

And sculptured Ann is seventy years of stone.
These cloud-sopped, marble hands, this monumental
Argument of the hewn voice, gesture and psalm,
Storm me forever over her grave until
The stuffed lung of the fox twitch and cry Love
And the strutting fern lay seeds on the black sill.   (1938)

TWENTY-FOUR YEARS

Twenty-four years remind the tears of my eyes.
(Bury the dead for fear that they walk to the grave in labour.)
In the groin of the natural doorway I crouched like a tailor
Sewing a shroud for a journey
By the light of the meat-eating sun.
Dressed to die, the sensual strut begun,
With my red veins full of money,
In the final direction of the elementary town
I advance for as long as forever is.   (1939)

A REFUSAL TO MOURN THE DEATH, BY FIRE,
OF A CHILD IN LONDON

Never until the mankind making
Bird beast and flower
Fathering and all humbling darkness
Tells with silence the last light breaking
And the still hour
Is come of the sea tumbling in harness

And I must enter again the round
Zion of the water bead
And the synagogue of the ear of corn
Shall I let pray the shadow of a sound
Or sow my salt seed
In the least valley of sackcloth to mourn

The majesty and burning of the child's death.
I shall not murder
The mankind of her going with a grave truth
Nor blaspheme down the stations of the breath
With any further
Elegy of innocence and youth.

Deep with the first dead lies London's daughter,
Robed in the long friends,
The grains beyond age, the dark veins of her mother,
Secret by the unmourning water
Of the riding Thames.
After the first death, there is no other.   (1946)

A WINTER'S TALE

It is a winter's tale
That the snow blind twilight ferries over the lakes
And floating fields from the farm in the cup of the vales,
Gliding windless through the hand folded flakes,
The pale breath of cattle at the stealthy sail,

And the stars falling cold,
And the smell of hay in the snow, and the far owl
Warning among the folds, and the frozen hold
Flocked with the sheep white smoke of the farm house cowl
In the river wended vales where the tale was told.

Once when the world turned old
On a star of faith pure as the drifting bread,
As the food and flames of the snow, a man unrolled
The scrolls of fire that burned in his heart and head,
Torn and alone in a farm house in a fold

Of fields. And burning then
In his firelit island ringed by the winged snow
And the dung hills white as wool and the hen
Roosts sleeping chill till the flame of the cock crow
Combs through the mantled yards and the morning men

Stumble out with their spades,
The cattle stirring, the mousing cat stepping shy,
The puffed birds hopping and hunting, the milkmaids
Gentle in their clogs over the fallen sky,
And all the woken farm at its white trades,

He knelt, he wept, he prayed,
By the spit and the black pot in the log bright light
And the cup and the cut bread in the dancing shade,

In the muffled house, in the quick of night,
At the point of love, forsaken and afraid.

He knelt on the cold stones,
He wept from the crest of grief, he prayed to the veiled sky
May his hunger go howling on bare white bones
Past the statues of the stables and the sky roofed sties
And the duck pond glass and the blinding byres alone

Into the home of prayers
And fires where he should prowl down the cloud
Of his snow blind love and rush in the white lairs.
His naked need struck him howling and bowed
Though no sound flowed down the hand folded air

But only the wind strung
Hunger of birds in the fields of the bread of water, tossed
In high corn and the harvest melting on their tongues.
And his nameless need bound him burning and lost
When cold as snow he should run the wended vales among

The rivers mouthed in night,
And drown in the drifts of his need, and lie curled caught
In the always desiring centre of the white
Inhuman cradle and the bride bed forever sought
By the believer lost and the hurled outcast of light.

Deliver him, he cried,
By losing him all in love, and cast his need
Alone and naked in the engulfing bride,
Never to flourish in the fields of the white seed
Or flower under the time dying flesh astride.

Listen. The minstrels sing
In the departed villages. The nightingale,
Dust in the buried wood, flies on the grains of her wings
And spells on the winds of the dead his winter's tale.
The voice of the dust of water from the withered spring

Is telling. The wizened
Stream with bells and baying water bounds. The dew rings
On the gristed leaves and the long gone glistening
Parish of snow. The carved mouths in the rock are wind swept strings.
Time sings through the intricately dead snow drop. Listen.

It was a hand or sound
In the long ago land that glided the dark door wide
And there outside on the bread of the ground
A she bird rose and rayed like a burning bride.
A she bird dawned, and her breast with snow and scarlet downed.

Look. And the dancers move
On the departed, snow bushed green, wanton in moon light
As a dust of pigeons. Exulting, the grave hooved
Horses, centaur dead, turn and tread the drenched white
Paddocks in the farms of birds. The dead oak walks for love.

The carved limbs in the rock
Leap, as to trumpets. Calligraphy of the old
Leaves is dancing. Lines of age on the stones weave in a flock.
And the harp shaped voice of the water's dust plucks in a fold
Of fields. For love, the long ago she bird rises. Look.

And the wild wings were raised
Above her folded head, and the soft feathered voice
Was flying through the house as though the she bird praised
And all the elements of the slow fall rejoiced
That a man knelt alone in the cup of the vales,

In the mantle and calm,
By the spit and the black pot in the log bright light.
And the sky of birds in the plumed voice charmed
Him up and he ran like a wind after the kindling flight
Past the blind barns and byres of the windless farm.

In the poles of the year
When black birds died like priests in the cloaked hedge row
And over the cloth of counties the far hills rode near,
Under the one leaved trees ran a scarecrow of snow
And fast through the drifts of the thickets antlered like deer,

Rags and prayers down the knee-
Deep hillocks and loud on the numbed lakes,
All night lost and long wading in the wake of the she-
Bird through the times and lands and tribes of the slow flakes.
Listen and look where she sails the goose plucked sea,

The sky, the bird, the bride,
The cloud, the need, the planted stars, the joy beyond

The fields of seed and the time dying flesh astride,
The heavens, the heaven, the grave, the burning font.
In the far ago land the door of his death glided wide,

                    And the bird descended.
On a bread white hill over the cupped farm
And the lakes and floating fields and the river wended
Vales where he prayed to come to the last harm
And the homes of prayers and fires, the tale ended.

                    The dancing perishes
On the white, no longer growing green, and, minstrel dead,
The singing breaks in the snow shoed villages of wishes
That once cut the figures of birds on the deep bread
And over the glazed lakes skated the shapes of fishes

                    Flying. The rite is shorn
Of nightingale and centaur dead horse. The springs wither
Back. Lines of age sleep on the stones till trumpeting dawn.
Exultation lies down. Time buries the spring weather
That belled and bounded with the fossil and the dew reborn.

                    For the bird lay bedded
In a choir of wings, as though she slept or died,
And the wings glided wide and he was hymned and wedded,
And through the thighs of the engulfing bride,
The woman breasted and the heaven headed

                    Bird, he was brought low,
Burning in the bride bed of love, in the whirl-
Pool at the wanting centre, in the folds
Of paradise, in the spun bud of the world.
And she rose with him flowering in her melting snow.   (1946)

IN MY CRAFT OR SULLEN ART

In my craft or sullen art
Exercised in the still night
When only the moon rages
And the lovers lie abed
With all their griefs in their arms,
I labour by singing light
Not for ambition or bread
Or the strut and trade of charms

[handwritten margin note: HE'S HARD TO WRITE FOR WORDSWORTH PERHAPS BUT CROWS THAT THEY WILL TWO ONES WHO DON'T LISTEN]

On the ivory stages
But for the common wages
Of their most secret heart.

[handwritten: LOVERS.] *[handwritten: STANDS APART]*

Not for the proud man apart
From the raging moon I write
On these spindrift pages *[handwritten: FROTH ON TOP OF WAVES. LIGHT]*
Nor for the towering dead *[handwritten: KEATS INSUBSTANTIAL]*
With their nightingales and psalms *[handwritten: MILTON]*
But for the lovers, their arms
Round the griefs of the ages, *[handwritten: ORDINARY & HUMAN TIMELESS]*
Who pay no praise or wages
Nor heed my craft or art.   (1946)

[handwritten: DON'T EVEN LISTEN.]

CEREMONY AFTER A FIRE RAID

1

Myselves
The grievers
Grieve
Among the street burned to tireless death
A child of a few hours
With its kneading mouth
Charred on the black breast of the grave
The mother dug, and its arms full of fires.

Begin
With singing
Sing
Darkness kindled back into beginning
When the caught tongue nodded blind,
A star was broken
Into the centuries of the child
Myselves grieve now, and miracles cannot atone.

Forgive
Us forgive
Us your death that myselves the believers
May hold it in a great flood
Till the blood shall spurt,
And the dust shall sing like a bird
As the grains blow, as your death grows, through our heart.

Crying
Your dying
Cry,
Child beyond cockcrow, by the fire-dwarfed
Street we chant the flying sea
In the body bereft.
Love is the last light spoken. Oh
Seeds of sons in the loin of the black husk left.

2

I know not whether
Adam or Eve, the adorned holy bullock
Or the white ewe lamb
Or the chosen virgin
Laid in her snow
On the altar of London,
Was the first to die
In the cinder of the little skull,
O bride and bride groom
O Adam and Eve together
Lying in the lull
Under the sad breast of the head stone
White as the skeleton
Of the garden of Eden.

I know the legend
Of Adam and Eve is never for a second
Silent in my service
Over the dead infants
Over the one
Child who was priest and servants,
Word, singers, and tongue
In the cinder of the little skull,
Who was the serpent's
Night fall and the fruit like a sun,
Man and woman undone,
Beginning crumbled back to darkness
Bare as the nurseries
Of the garden of wilderness.

3

Into the organpipes and steeples
Of the luminous cathedrals,

Into the weathercocks' molten mouths
Rippling in twelve-winded circles,
Into the dead clock burning the hour
Over the urn of sabbaths
Over the whirling ditch of daybreak
Over the sun's hovel and the slum of fire
And the golden pavements laid in requiems,
Into the bread in a wheatfield of flames,
Into the wine burning like brandy,
The masses of the sea
The masses of the sea under
The masses of the infant-bearing sea
Erupt, fountain, and enter to utter for ever
Glory glory glory
The sundering ultimate kingdom of genesis' thunder.   (1946)

FERN HILL

Now as I was young and easy under the apple boughs
About the lilting house and happy as the grass was green,
      The night above the dingle starry,
            Time let me hail and climb
      Golden in the heydays of his eyes,
And honoured among wagons I was prince of the apple towns
And once below a time I lordly had the trees and leaves
            Trail with daisies and barley
      Down the rivers of the windfall light.

And as I was green and carefree, famous among the barns
About the happy yard and singing as the farm was home,
      In the sun that is young once only,
            Time let me play and be
      Golden in the mercy of his means,
And green and golden I was huntsman and herdsman, the calves
Sang to my horn, the foxes on the hills barked clear and cold,
            And the sabbath rang slowly
      In the pebbles of the holy streams.

All the sun long it was running, it was lovely, the hay
Fields high as the house, the tunes from the chimneys, it was air
      And playing, lovely and watery
            And fire green as grass.
      And nightly under the simple stars

As I rode to sleep the owls were bearing the farm away,
All the moon long I heard, blessed among stables, the nightjars
　　Flying with the ricks, and the horses
　　　Flashing into the dark.

And then to awake, and the farm, like a wanderer white
With the dew, come back, the cock on his shoulder: it was all
　　Shining, it was Adam and maiden,
　　　The sky gathered again
　　And the sun grew round that very day.
So it must have been after the birth of the simple light
In the first, spinning place, the spellbound horses walking warm
　　Out of the whinnying green stable
　　　On to the fields of praise.

And honoured among foxes and pheasants by the gay house
Under the new made clouds and happy as the heart was long,
　　In the sun born over and over,
　　　I ran my heedless ways,
　　My wishes raced through the house-high hay
And nothing I cared, at my sky blue trades, that time allows
In all his tuneful turning so few and such morning songs
　　Before the children green and golden
　　　Follow him out of grace.

Nothing I cared, in the lamb white days, that time would take me
Up to the swallow thronged loft by the shadow of my hand,
　　In the moon that is always rising,
　　　Nor that riding to sleep
　　I should hear him fly with the high fields
And wake to the farm forever fled from the childless land.
Oh, as I was young and easy in the mercy of his means,
　　Time held me green and dying
　　Though I sang in my chains like the sea.　(1946)

Philip Larkin
(1922–   )

PLACES, LOVED ONES

No, I have never found
The place where I could say
This is my proper ground,
Here I shall stay;
Nor met that special one
Who has an instant claim
On everything I own
Down to my name;

To find such seems to prove
You want no choice in where
To build, or whom to love;
You ask them to bear
You off irrevocably,
So that it's not your fault
Should the town turn dreary,
The girl a dolt.

Yet, having missed them, you're
Bound, none the less, to act
As if what you settled for
Mashed you, in fact;
And wiser to keep away
From thinking you still might trace
Uncalled-for to this day
Your person, your place.   *(1955)*

DRY-POINT

Endlessly, time-honoured irritant,
A bubble is restively forming at your tip.
Burst it as fast as we can—
It will grow again, until we begin dying.

410-I

Silently it inflates, till we're enclosed
And forced to start the struggle to get out:
Bestial, intent, real.
The wet spark comes, the bright blown walls collapse,

But what sad scapes we cannot turn from then:
What ashen hills! what salted, shrunken lakes!
How leaden the ring looks,
Birmingham magic all discredited,

And how remote that bare and sunscrubbed room,
Intensely far, that padlocked cube of light
We neither define nor prove,
Where you, we dream, obtain no right of entry.   *(1955)*

GOING

There is an evening coming in
Across the fields, one never seen before,
That lights no lamps.

Silken it seems at a distance, yet
When it is drawn up over the knees and breast
It brings no comfort.

Where has the tree gone, that locked
Earth to the sky? What is under my hands,
That I cannot feel?

What loads my hands down?   *(1955)*

CHURCH GOING

Once I am sure there's nothing going on
I step inside, letting the door thud shut.
Another church: matting, seats, and stone,
And little books; sprawlings of flowers, cut
For Sunday, brownish now; some brass and stuff
Up at the holy end; the small neat organ;
And a tense, musty, unignorable silence,
Brewed God knows how long. Hatless, I take off
My cycle-clips in awkward reverence,

Move forward, run my hand around the font.
From where I stand, the roof looks almost new—
Cleaned or restored? Someone would know: I don't.
Mounting the lectern, I peruse a few
Hectoring large-scale verses, and pronounce
"Here endeth" much more loudly than I'd meant.
The echoes snigger briefly. Back at the door
I sign the book, donate an Irish sixpence,
Reflect the place was not worth stopping for.

Yet stop I did: in fact I often do,
And always end much at a loss like this,
Wondering what to look for; wondering, too,
When churches fall completely out of use
What we shall turn them into, if we shall keep
A few cathedrals chronically on show,
Their parchment, plate and pyx in locked cases,
And let the rest rent-free to rain and sheep.
Shall we avoid them as unlucky places?

Or, after dark, will dubious women come
To make their children touch a particular stone;
Pick simples for a cancer; or on some
Advised night see walking a dead one?
Power of some sort or other will go on
In games, in riddles, seemingly at random;
But superstition, like belief, must die,
And what remains when disbelief has gone?
Grass, weedy pavement, brambles, buttress, sky,

A shape less recognisable each week,
A purpose more obscure. I wonder who
Will be the last, the very last, to seek
This place for what it was, one of the crew
That tap and jot and know what rood-lofts were?
Some ruin-bibber, randy for antique,
Or Christmas-addict, counting on a whiff
Of gown-and-bands and organ-pipes and myrrh?
Or will he be my representative,

Bored, uninformed, knowing the ghostly silt
Dispersed, yet tending to this cross of ground
Through suburb scrub because it held unspilt

So long and equably what since is found
Only in separation—marriage, and birth,
And death, and thoughts of these—for whom was built
This special shell? For, though I've no idea
What this accoutred frowsty barn is worth,
It pleases me to stand in silence here;

A serious house on serious earth it is,
In whose blent air all our compulsions meet,
Are recognized, and robed as destinies.
And that much never can be obsolete,
Since someone will forever be surprising
A hunger in himself to be more serious,
And gravitating with it to this ground,
Which, he once heard, was proper to grow wise in,
If only that so many dead lie round.   (*1955*)

AGE

My age fallen away like white swaddling
Floats in the middle distance, becomes
An inhabited cloud. I bend closer, discern
A lighted tenement scuttling with voices.
O you tall game I tired myself with joining!
Now I wade through you like knee-level weeds,

And they attend me, dear translucent bergs:
Silence and space. By now so much has flown
From the nest here of my head that I needs must turn
To know what prints I leave, whether of feet,
Or spoor of pads, or a bird's adept splay.   (*1955*)

MYXOMATOSIS

Caught in the centre of a soundless field
While hot inexplicable hours go by
What trap is this? Where were its teeth concealed?
You seem to ask.
                    I make a sharp reply,
Then clean my stick. I'm glad I can't explain
Just in what jaws you were to suppurate:
You may have thought things would come right again
If you could only keep quite still and wait.   (*1955*)

TOADS

Why should I let the toad *work*
    Squat on my life?
Can't I use my wit as a pitchfork
    And drive the brute off?

Six days of the week it soils
    With its sickening poison—
Just for paying a few bills!
    That's out of proportion.

Lots of folk live on their wits:
    Lecturers, lispers,
Losels, loblolly-men, louts—
    They don't end as paupers;

Lots of folk live up lanes
    With fires in a bucket,
Eat windfalls and tinned sardines—
    They seem to like it.

Their nippers have got bare feet,
    Their unspeakable wives
Are skinny as whippets—and yet
    No one actually *starves*.

Ah, were I courageous enough
    To shout *Stuff your pension!*
But I know, all too well, that's the stuff
    That dreams are made on:

For something sufficiently toad-like
    Squats in me, too;
Its hunkers are heavy as hard luck,
    And cold as snow,

And will never allow me to blarney
    My way to getting
The fame and the girl and the money
    All at one sitting.

I don't say, one bodies the other
   One's spiritual truth;
But I do say it's hard to lose either,
   When you have both.   *(1955)*

POETRY OF DEPARTURES

Sometimes you hear, fifth-hand,
As epitaph:
He chucked up everything
And just cleared off,
And always the voice will sound
Certain you approve
This audacious, purifying,
Elemental move.

And they are right, I think.
We all hate home
And having to be there:
I detest my room,
Its specially-chosen junk,
The good books, the good bed,
And my life, in perfect order:
So to hear it said

He walked out on the whole crowd
Leaves me flushed and stirred,
Like *Then she undid her dress*
Or *Take that you bastard;*
Surely I can, if he did?
And that helps me stay
Sober and industrious.
But I'd go today,

Yes, swagger the nut-strewn roads,
Crouch in the fo'c'sle
Stubbly with goodness, if
It weren't so artificial,
Such a deliberate step backwards
To create an object:
Books; china; a life
Reprehensibly perfect.   *(1955)*

DECEPTIONS

"Of course I was drugged, and so heavily I did not regain my consciousness till the next morning. I was horrified to discover that I had been ruined, and for some days I was inconsolable, and cried like a child to be killed or sent back to my aunt."—Mayhew, *London Labour and the London Poor.*

Even so distant, I can taste the grief,
Bitter and sharp with stalks, he made you gulp.
The sun's occasional print, the brisk brief
Worry of wheels along the street outside
Where bridal London bows the other way,
And light, unanswerable and tall and wide,
Forbids the scar to heal, and drives
Shame out of hiding. All the unhurried day
Your mind lay open like a drawer of knives.

Slums, years, have buried you. I would not dare
Console you if I could. What can be said,
Except that suffering is exact, but where
Desire takes charge, readings will grow erratic?
For you would hardly care
That you were less deceived, out on that bed,
Than he was, stumbling up the breathless stair
To burst into fulfilment's desolate attic. *(1955)*

HERE

Swerving east, from rich industrial shadows
And traffic all night north; swerving through fields
Too thin and thistled to be called meadows,
And now and then a harsh-named halt, that shields
Workmen at dawn; swerving to solitude
Of skies and scarecrows, haystacks, hares and pheasants,
And the widening river's slow presence,
The piled gold clouds, the shining gull-marked mud,

Gathers to the surprise of a large town:
Here domes and statues, spires and cranes cluster
Beside grain-scattered streets, barge-crowded water,
And residents from raw estates, brought down
The dead straight miles by stealing flat-faced trolleys,
Push through plate-glass swing doors to their desires—

Cheap suits, red kitchen-ware, sharp shoes, iced lollies,
Electric mixers, toasters, washers, driers—

A cut-price crowd, urban yet simple, dwelling
Where only salesmen and relations come
Within a terminate and fishy-smelling
Pastoral of ships up streets, the slave museum,
Tattoo-shops, consulates, grim head-scarfed wives;
And out beyond its mortgaged half-built edges
Fast-shadowed wheat-fields, running high as hedges,
Isolate villages, where removed lives

Loneliness clarifies. Here silence stands
Like heat. Here leaves unnoticed thicken,
Hidden weeds flower, neglected waters quicken,
Luminously-peopled air ascends;
And past the poppies bluish neutral distance
Ends the land suddenly beyond a beach
Of shapes and shingle. Here is unfenced existence:
Facing the sun, untalkative, out of reach.   *(1964)*

TOADS REVISITED

Walking around in the park
Should feel better than work:
The lake, the sunshine,
The grass to lie on,

Blurred playground noises
Beyond black-stockinged nurses—
Not a bad place to be.
Yet it doesn't suit me,

Being one of the men
You meet of an afternoon:
Palsied old step-takers,
Hare-eyed clerks with the jitters,

Waxed-fleshed out-patients
Still vague from accidents,
And characters in long coats
Deep in the litter-baskets—

All dodging the toad work
By being stupid or weak.
Think of being them!
Hearing the hours chime,

Watching the bread delivered,
The sun by clouds covered,
The children going home;
Think of being them,

Turning over their failures
By some bed of lobelias,
Nowhere to go but indoors,
No friends but empty chairs—

No, give me my in-tray,
My loaf-haired secretary,
My shall-I-keep-the-call-in-Sir:
What else can I answer,

When the lights come on at four
At the end of another year?
Give me your arm, old toad;
Help me down Cemetery Road. (1964)

Charles Tomlinson
(1927–   )

DISTINCTIONS

The seascape shifts

Between the minutest interstices of time
Blue is blue.

A pine-branch
Tugs at the eye: the eye
Returns to gray-blue, blue-black or indigo
Or it returns, simply,
To blue-after-the-pine-branch.

Here, there is no question of aberrations
Into pinks, golds, or mauves:
This is the variation Pater indicated
But failed to prove.

Art exists at a remove.
Evocation, at two,
Discusses a blue that someone
Heard someone talking about.   *(1958)*

PARING THE APPLE

There are portraits and still-lifes.

And there is paring the apple.

And then? Paring it slowly,
From under cool-yellow
Cold-white emerging. And . . . ?

The spring of concentric peel
Unwinding off white,
The blade hidden, dividing.

There are portraits and still-lifes
And the first, because "human"
Does not excel the second, and
Neither is less weighted
With a human gesture, than paring the apple
With a human stillness.

The cool blade
Severs between coolness, apple-rind
Compelling a recognition.   (1958)

POEM

Upended, it crouches on broken limbs
About to run forward. No longer threatened
But surprised into this vigilance
It gapes enmity from its hollowed core.

Moist woodflesh, softened to a paste
Of marl and white splinter, dangles
Where overhead the torn root
Casts up its wounds in a ragged orchis.

The seasons strip, but do not tame you.
I grant you become more smooth
As you are emptied and where the heart shreds
The gap mouths a more practiced silence.

You would impress, but merely startle. Your accomplice
Twilight is dragging its shadows here
Deliberate and unsocial: I leave you
To your own meaning, yourself alone.   (1958)

FAREWELL TO VAN GOGH

The quiet deepens. You will not persuade
    One leaf of the accomplished, steady, darkening
Chestnut-tower to displace itself
    With more of violence than the air supplies
When, gathering dusk, the pond brims evenly
    And we must be content with stillness.

Unhastening, daylight withdraws from us its shapes
    Into their central calm. Stone by stone

Your rhetoric is dispersed until the earth
   Becomes once more the earth, the leaves
A sharp partition against cooling blue.

Farewell, and for your instructive frenzy
   Gratitude. The world does not end tonight
And the fruit that we shall pick tomorrow
   Await us, weighing the unstripped bough.   *(1958)*

ON THE HALL AT STOWEY

Walking by map, I chose unwonted ground,
   A crooked, questionable path which led
Beyond the margin, then delivered me
   At a turn. Red marl
Had rutted the aimless track
   That firmly withheld the recompense it hid
Till now, close by its end, the day's discoveries
   Began with the dimming night:

A house. The wall-stones, brown.
   The doubtful light, more of a mist than light
Floating at hedge-height through the sodden fields
   Had yielded, or a final glare
Burst there, rather, to concentrate
   Sharp saffron, as the ebbing year—
Or so it seemed, for the dye deepened—poured
   All of its yellow strength through the way I went:

Over grass, garden-space, over the grange
   That jutted beyond, lengthening-down
The house line, tall as it was,
   By tying it to the earth, trying its pride
(Which submitted) under a nest of barns,
   A walled weight of lesser encumbrances—
Few of which worsened it, and none
   As the iron sheds, sealing my own approach.

All stone. I had passed these last, unwarrantable
   Symbols of—no; let me define, rather
The thing they were not, all that we cannot be,
   By the description, simply of that which merits it:
Stone. Why must (as it does at each turn)
   Each day, the mean rob us of patience, distract us

Before even its opposite?—before stone, which
   Cut, piled, mortared, is patience's presence.

The land farmed, the house was neglected: but
   Gashed panes (and there were many) still showed
Into the pride of that presence. I had reached
   Unchallenged, within feet of the door
Ill-painted, but at no distant date—the least
   Our prodigal time could grudge it; paused
To measure the love, to assess its object,
   That trusts for continuance to the mason's hand.

Five centuries—here were (at the least) five—
   In linked love, eager excrescence
Where the door, arched, crowned with acanthus,
   Aimed at a civil elegance, but hit
This sturdier compromise, neither Greek, Gothic
   Nor Strawberry, clumped from the arching-point
And swathing down, like a fist of wheat,
   The unconscious emblem for the house's worth.

Conclusion surrounded it, and the accumulation
   After Lammas growth. Still coming on
Hart's-tongue by maiden-hair
   Thickened beneath the hedges, the corn leveled
And carried, long-since; but the earth
   (Its tint glowed in the house wall)
Out of the reddish dark still thrust up foison
   Through the browning-back of the exhausted year:

Thrust through the unweeded yard, where earth and house
   Debated the terrain. My eye
Caught in those flags a gravestone's fragment
   Set by a careful century. The washed inscription
Still keen, showed only a fragile stem
   A stave, a broken circlet, as
(Unintelligibly clear, craft in the sharp decrepitude)
   A pothook grooved its firm memorial.

Within, wet from the failing roof,
   Walls greened. Each hearth refitted
For a suburban whim, each room
   Denied what it was, diminished thus

To a barbarous mean, had comforted (but for a time)
   Its latest tenant. Angered, I turned to my path
Through the inhuman light, light that a fish might swim
   Stained by the grayness of the smoking fields.

Five centuries. And we? What we had not
   Made ugly, we had laid waste—
Left (I should say) the office to nature
   Whose blind battery, best fitted to perform it
Outdoes us, completes by persistence
   All that our negligence fails in. Saddened,
Yet angered beyond sadness, where the road
   Doubled upon itself I halted, for a moment
Facing the empty house and its laden barns. (1958)

RETURN TO HINTON

Written on the author's return to Hinton Blewett from the United States

Ten years
   and will you be
      a footnote, merely,
England
   of the Bible
      open at Genesis
on the parlour table?
   "God
      saw the light
that it was good."
   It falls
      athwart the book
through window-lace
   whose shadow
      decorates the sheets
of "The Bridal March"—
   a square of white
      above the keyboard
and below
   a text which is a prayer.
      The television box
is one,
   the mullions and flagged floor
      of the kitchen

through an open door
        witness a second
                world in which
beside the hob
        the enormous kettles'
                blackened bellies ride—
as much the tokens of an order as
        the burnished brass.
                You live
between the two
        and, ballasted against
                the merely new, the tide
and shift of time
        you wear
                your widow's silk
your hair
        plaited, as it has been
                throughout those years
whose rime it bears.
        A tractor
                mounts the ramp of stones
into the yard:
        a son surveys
                the scenes
that occupied a father's days.
        Proud of his machine,
                will he transmit
that more than bread
        that leaves you undisquieted?
                This house
is poorer by a death
        than last I saw it
                yet
who may judge
        as poverty that
                sadness without bitterness
those sudden tears
        that your composure
                clears, admonishes?
Your qualities
        are like the land
                —inherited:
but you

have earned
　　your right to them
have given
　　grief its due
　　　　and, on despair,
have closed your door
　　as the gravestones tell you to.
　　　　Speak
your composure and you share
　　the accent of their rhymes
　　　　express
won readiness
　　in a worn dress
　　　　of chapel gospel.
Death's
　　not the enemy
　　　　of you nor of your kind:
a surer death
　　creeps after me
　　　　out of that generous
rich and nervous land
　　where, buried by
　　　　the soft oppression of prosperity,
locality's mere grist
　　to build
　　　　the even bed
of roads that will not rest
　　until they lead
　　　　into a common future
rational
　　and secure
　　　　that we must speed
by means that are not either.
　　　　Narrow
　　　　your farm-bred certainties
I do not hold:
　　I share
　　　　your certain enemy.
For we who write
　　the verse you do not read
　　　　already plead your cause
before
　　that cold tribunal

                        while you're unaware
            they hold their session.
                    Our language is our land
                        that we'll
            not waste or sell
                    against a promised mess
                        of pottage that we may not taste.
            For who has known
                    the seasons' sweet succession
                        and would still
            exchange them for a whim, a wish
                    or swim into
                        a mill-race for an unglimpsed fish?   (1963)

THE CAVERN

Obliterate
mythology as you unwind
this mountain-interior
into the negative-dark mind,
as there
the gypsum's snow
the limestone stair
and boneyard landscape grow
into the identity of flesh.

Pulse of the water-drop,
veils and scales, fins
and flakes of the forming
leprous rock,
how should these
inhuman, turn
human with such chill affinities.

Hard to the hand,
these mosses not of moss,
but nostrils, pits
of eyes, faces
in flight and prints
of feet where no feet ever were,
elude the mind's
hollow that would contain
this canyon within a mountain.

Not far
enough from the familiar,
press
in under a deeper dark until
the curtained sex
the arch, the streaming buttress
have become
the self's unnameable and shaping home.   (*1966*)

Thomas Kinsella
(1928–   )

BAGGOT STREET DESERTA

Lulled, at silence, the spent attack.
The will to work is laid aside.
The breaking-cry, the strain of the rack,
Yield, are at peace. The window is wide
On a crawling arch of stars, and the night
Reacts faintly to the mathematic
Passion of a cello suite
Plotting the quiet of my attic.
A mile away the river toils
Its buttressed fathoms out to sea;
Tucked in the mountains, many miles
Away from its roaring outcome, a shy
Gasp of waters in the gorse
Is sonnetting origins. Dreamers' heads
Lie mesmerised in Dublin's beds
Flashing with images, Adam's morse.

A cigarette, the moon, a sigh
Of educated boredom, greet
A curlew's lingering threadbare cry
Of common loss. Compassionate,
I add my call of exile, half-
Buried longing, half-serious
Anger and the rueful laugh.
We fly into our risk, the spurious.

Versing, like an exile, makes
A virtuoso of the heart,
Interpreting the old mistakes
And discords in a work of Art
For the One, a private masterpiece
Of doctored recollections. Truth

Concedes, before the dew, its place
In the spray of dried forgettings Youth
Collected when they were a single
Furious undissected bloom.
A voice clarifies when the tingle
Dies out of the nerves of time:
Endure and let the present punish.
Looking backward, all is lost;
The past becomes a fairy bog
Alive with fancies, double crossed
By pad of owl and hoot of dog,
Where shaven, serious-minded men
Appear with lucid theses, after
Which they don the mists again
With trackless, cotton-silly laughter;
Secretly a swollen Burke
Assists a decomposing Hare
To cart a body of good work
With midnight mutterings off somewhere;
The goddess who had light for thighs
Grows feet of dung and takes to bed,
Affronting horror-stricken eyes,
The marsh bird that children dread.

I nonetheless inflict, endure,
Tedium, intracordal hurt,
The sting of memory's quick, the drear
Uprooting, burying, prising apart
Of loves a strident adolescent
Spent in doubt and vanity.
All feed a single stream, impassioned
Now with obsessed honesty,
A tugging scruple that can keep
Clear eyes staring down the mile
The thousand fathoms, into sleep.

Fingers cold against the sill
Feel, below the stress of flight,
The slow implosion of my pulse
In a wrist with poet's cramp, a tight
Beat tapping out endless calls
Into the dark, as the alien
Garrison in my own blood

Keeps constant contact with the main
Mystery, not to be understood.
Out where imagination arches
Chilly points of light transact
The business of the border-marches
Of the Real, and I—a fact
That may be countered or may not—
Find their privacy complete.

My quarter-inch of cigarette
Goes flaring down to Baggot Street.   (1958)

IN THE RINGWOOD

As I roved out impatiently
Good Friday with my bride
To drink in the rivered Ringwood
The draughty season's pride
A fell dismay held suddenly
Our feet on the green hill-side.

The Yellow Spring on Vinegar Hill,
The smile of Slaney water,
The wind in the withered Ringwood,
Grew dark with ancient slaughter.
My love cried out and I beheld her
Change to Sorrow's daughter.

"Ravenhair, what rending
Set those red lips a-shriek,
And dealt those locks in black lament
Like blows on your white cheek,
That in your looks outlandishly
Both woe and fury speak?"

As sharp a lance as the fatal heron
There on the sunken tree
Will strike in the stones of the river
Was the gaze she bent on me.
O her robe into her right hand
She gathered grievously.

"Many times the civil lover
Climbed that pleasant place,

Many times despairing
Died in his love's face,
His spittle turned to vinegar,
Blood in his embrace.

Love that is every miracle
Is torn apart and rent.
The human turns awry
The poles of the firmament.
The fish's bright side is pierced
And good again is spent.

Though every stem on Vinegar Hill
And stone on the Slaney's bed
And every leaf in the living Ringwood
Builds till it is dead
Yet heart and hand, accomplished,
Destroy until they dread.

Dread, a grey devourer,
Stalks in the shade of love.
The dark that dogs our feet
Eats what is sickened of.
The End that stalks Beginning
Hurries home its drove."

I kissed three times her shivering lips.
I drank their naked chill.
I watched the river shining
Where the heron wiped his bill.
I took my love in my icy arms
In the Spring on Ringwood Hill.   (1958)

A COUNTRY WALK

Sick of the piercing company of women
I swung the gate shut with a furious sigh,
Rammed trembling hands in pockets and drew in
A breath of river air. A rook's wet wing
Cuffed abruptly upward through the drizzle.

On either hand dead trunks in drapes of creeper,
Strangled softly by horse-mushroom, writhed
In vanished passion, broken down like sponge.

I walked their hushed stations, passion dying,
Each slow footfall a drop of peace returning.

I clapped my gloves. Three cattle turned aside
Their fragrant bodies from a corner gate
And down the sucking chaos of a hedge
Churned land to liquid in their dreamy passage.
Briefly through the beaded grass a path
Led to the holy stillness of a well
And there in the smell of water, stone and leaf
I knelt, baring my hand, and scooped and drank,
Shivering, and inch by inch rejoiced:
Ferocity became intensity.

Or so it seemed as with a lighter step
I turned an ivied corner to confront
The littered fields where summer broke and fled.
Below me, right and left, the valley floor
Tilted in a silence full of storms;
A ruined aqueduct in delicate rigor
Clenched cat-backed, rooted to one horizon;
A vast asylum reared its potent calm
Up from the other through the sodden air,
Tall towers ochre where the gutters dripped;
A steeple; the long yielding of a railway turn
Through thorn and willow; a town endured its place . . .

Joining the two slopes, blocking an ancient way
With crumbled barracks, castle and brewery
It took the running river, wrinkling and pouring
Into its blunt embrace. A line of roofs
Fused in veils of rain and steely light
As the dying sun struck it huge glancing blows.
A strand of idle smoke mounted until
An idler current combed it slowly west,
A hook of shadow dividing the still sky . . .
Mated, like a fall of rock, with time,
The place endured its burden: as a froth
Locked in a swirl of turbulence, a shape
That forms and fructifies and dies, a wisp
That hugs the bridge, an omphalos of scraps.

I moved, my glove-backs glistening, over flesh-
And forest-fed earth; till, skirting a marshy field

Where melancholy brambles scored the mud
By the gapped glitter of a speckled ford,
I shuddered with a visual sweet excitement.

Those murmuring shallows made a trampling place
Apt for death-combat, as the tales agree:
There, the day that Christ hung dying, twin
Brothers armed in hate on either side;
The day darkened but they moved to meet
With crossed swords under a dread eclipse
And mingled their bowels at the saga's end.
There the first Normans massacred my fathers,
Then stroked their armoured horses' necks, disposed
In ceremony, sable on green sward.
Twice more the reeds grew red, the stones obscured;
When knot-necked Cromwell and his fervent sword
Despatched a convent shrieking to their Lover,
And when in peasant fear a rebel host,
Through long retreat grown half hysterical
—Methodical, ludicrous—piked in groups of three
Cromwell's puritan brood, their harmless neighbours,
Forked them half living to the sharp water
And melted into the martyred countryside,
Root eaters, strange as badgers. Pulses calmed;
The racked heroic nerved itself for peace;
Then came harsh winters, motionless waterbirds,
And generations that let welcome fail.

Road and river parted. Now my path
Lay gleaming through the greasy dusk, uphill
Into the final turn. A concrete cross
Low in the ditch grew to the memory
Of one who answered latest the phantom hag,
Tireless Rebellion, when with mouth awry
She hammered at the door, disrupting harvest.
There he bled to death, his line of sight
Blocked by the corner-stone, and did not see
His town ablaze with joy, the grinning foe
Driven in heavy lorries from the field;
And he lay cold in the Hill Cemetery
When freedom burned his comrades' itchy palms,
Too much for flesh and blood, and—armed in hate—
Brother met brother in a modern light.
They turned the bloody corner, knelt and killed,

Who gather still at Easter round his grave,
Our watchful elders. Deep in his crumbled heart
He takes their soil, and chatting they return
To take their town again, that have exchanged
A trenchcoat playground for a gombeen jungle.

Around the corner, in an open square,
I came upon the sombre monuments
That bear their names: MacDonagh & McBride,
Merchants; Connolly's Commercial Arms . . .
Their windows gave me back my stolid self
In attitudes of staring as I paced
Their otherworldly gloom, reflected light
Playing on lens and raincoat stonily.
I turned away. Down the sloping square
A lamp switched on above the urinal;
Across the silent handball alley, eyes
That never looked on lover measured mine
Over the Christian Brothers' frosted glass
And turned away. Out of the neighboring shades
A car plunged soundlessly and disappeared
Pitching downward steeply to the bridge.
I too descended. Naked sycamores,
Gathered dripping near the quay, stood still
And dropped from their combining arms a single
Word upon my upturned face. I trod
The river underfoot; the parapet
Above the central arch received my hands.

Under a darkening and clearing heaven
The hastening river streamed in a slate sheen,
Its face a-swarm. Across the swollen water
(Delicate myriads vanishing in a breath)
Faint ripples winked; a thousand currents broke,
Kissing, dismembering, in threads of foam
Or poured intact over the stony bed
Glass-green and chill; their shallow, shifting world
Slid on in troubled union, forging together
Surfaces that gave and swallowed light;
And grimly the flood divided where it swept
An endless debris through the failing dusk
Under the thudding span beneath my feet.
Venit Hesperus;

In green and golden light; bringing sweet trade.
The inert stirred. Heart and tongue were loosed:
"The waters hurtle through the flooded night . . ." (1962)

MASK OF LOVE

Mask of Love, starting
Aghast out of unreason,
Do you come to us for peace?
Me, flinching from your stare;
Her, whose face you bear!

Remember
How with extreme care
And gentleness we have come,
Aching in heart and throat,
To stand again and again
On peaks of stress, face
To face, wearied with horror,
Yelling in ecstasy
Across the narrow abyss.

Remember
That our very bodies lack peace:
In tiny darknesses,
In accustomed hideousness,
The skin angrily flames,
Nerve gropes for muscle
Across the silent abyss.

You have seen our nocturnal
Suicidal dance,
When the moon hung vast, and seemed
To wet our mocking mouths:
She, turning in despair
Round some tiny mote;
I, doubled in laughter,
Clasping my paunch in grief
For the world in a speck of dust;
Between us, the fuming abyss.

Dumb vapours pour
Where the mask of Love appears,
Reddening, and disappears. (1966)

FIRST LIGHT

A prone couple still sleeps.
Light ascends like a pale gas
Out of the sea: dawn-
Light, reaching across the hill
To the dark garden. The grass
Emerges, soaking with grey dew.

Inside, in silence, an empty
Kitchen takes form, tidied and swept,
Blank with marriage—where shrill
Lover and beloved have kept
Another vigil far
Into the night, and raved and wept.

Upstairs a whimper or sigh
Comes from an open bedroom door
And lengthens to an ugly wail
—A child enduring a dream
That grows, at the first touch of day,
Unendurable. (1966)

RITUAL OF DEPARTURE

A man at the moment of departure, turning
To leave, treasures some stick of furniture
With slowly blazing eyes, or the very door
Broodingly with his hand as it falls shut.

*   *   *

Open the soft string that clasps in series
A dozen silver spoons, and spread them out,
Matched perfectly, one maker and to the year:
                    brilliance in use that fell
Open before the first inheritor.

A stag crest stares from the soft solid silver
And grimaces, with fat cud-lips but jaws
That could crack bones.
                    The stag heart stumbles.
He rears at bay, slavering silver; rattles
A trophied head among the gothic rocks.

*   *   *

Stones of a century and a half ago.
This same city distinct in the same air,
More open in an earlier evening light.
Dublin under the Georges . . .

                    stripped of Parliament,
Lying powerless in sweet-breathing death-ease
                  after forced Union.
Under a theatre of swift-moving cloud
Domes, pillared, in the afterglow—
A portico, beggars moving on the steps—
A horserider locked in soundless greeting,
Bowed among dogs and dung; the panelled vista
Closing on pleasant smoke-blue far-off hills.

             *   *   *

The ground opens. Pale wet potatoes
Break into light. The black soil falls from their flesh,
From the hands that tear them up and spread them out
In fresh disorder, perishable roots to eat.
                  The fields vanish in rain
Among white rock and red bog—saturated
High places traversed by spring sleet
Or thrust up in summer through the thin wind
Into pounding silence. Farther south: cattle,
Wheat, salmon glistening, the sea.
Landscape with ancestral figures . . . names
Settling and intermixing on the earth,
The seed in slow retreat, through time and blood,
Into bestial silence.
              Faces sharpen and grow blank,
With eyes for nothing.
                And their children's children
Venturing to disperse, some came to Dublin
To vanish in the city lanes.
             I saw the light
Enter from the laneway, through the scullery
To the foot of the stairs, creep across grey floorboards,
Sink in plush in the staleness of an inner room.

I scoop at the earth, and sense famine, a first
Sourness in the clay. The roots tear softly.　*(1968)*

Thom Gunn
(1929–   )

ON THE MOVE

"Man, you gotta Go."

The blue jay scuffling in the bushes follows
Some hidden purpose, and the gust of birds
That spurts across the field, the wheeling swallows,
Have nested in the trees and undergrowth.
Seeking their instinct, or their poise, or both,
One moves with an uncertain violence
Under the dust thrown by a baffled sense
Or the dull thunder of approximate words.

On motorcycles, up the road, they come:
Small, black, as flies hanging in the heat, the Boys,
Until the distance throws them forth, their hum
Bulges to thunder held by calf and thigh.
In goggles, donned impersonality,
In gleaming jackets trophied with the dust,
They strap in doubt—by hiding it, robust—
And almost hear a meaning in their noise.

Exact conclusion of their hardiness
Has no shape yet, but from known whereabouts
They ride, direction where the tires press.
They scare a flight of birds across the field:
Much that is natural, to the will must yield.
Men manufacture both machine and soul,
And use what they imperfectly control
To dare a future from the taken routes.

It is a part solution, after all.
One is not necessarily discord
On earth; or damned because, half animal,
One lacks direct instinct, because one wakes

Afloat on movement that divides and breaks.
One joins the movement in a valueless world,
Choosing it, till, both hurler and the hurled,
One moves as well, always toward, toward.

A minute holds them, who have come to go:
The self-defined, astride the created will
They burst away; the towns they travel through
Are home for neither bird nor holiness,
For birds and saints complete their purposes.
At worst, one is in motion; and at best,
Reaching no absolute, in which to rest,
One is always nearer by not keeping still.   *(1957)*

IN SANTA MARIA DEL POPOLO

Waiting for when the sun an hour or less
Conveniently oblique makes visible
The painting on one wall of this recess
By Caravaggio, of the Roman School,
I see how shadow in the painting brims
With a real shadow, drowning all shapes out
But a dim horse's haunch and various limbs,
Until the very subject is in doubt.

But evening gives the act, beneath the horse
And one indifferent groom, I see him sprawl,
Foreshortened from the head, with hidden face,
Where he has fallen, Saul becoming Paul.
O wily painter, limiting the scene
From a cacophony of dusty forms
To the one convulsion, what is it you mean
In that wide gesture of the lifting arms?

No Ananias croons a mystery yet,
Casting the pain out under name of sin.
The painter saw what was, an alternate
Candor and secrecy inside the skin.
He painted, elsewhere, that firm insolent
Young whore in Venus' clothes, those pudgy cheats,
Those sharpers; and was strangled, as things went,
For money, by one such picked off the streets.

I turn, hardly enlightened, from the chapel
To the dim interior of the church instead,
In which there kneel already several people,
Mostly old women: each head closeted
In tiny fists holds comfort as it can.
Their poor arms are too tired for more than this
—For the large gesture of solitary man,
Resisting, by embracing, nothingness.   (1961)

MY SAD CAPTAINS

One by one they appear in
the darkness: a few friends, and
a few with historical
names. How late they start to shine!
but before they fade they stand
perfectly embodied, all

the past lapping them like a
cloak of chaos. They were men
who, I thought, lived only to
renew the wasteful force they
spent with each hot convulsion.
They remind me, distant now.

True, they are not at rest yet,
but now that they are indeed
apart, winnowed from failures,
they withdraw to an orbit
and turn with disinterested
hard energy, like the stars.   (1961)

CONFESSIONS OF THE LIFE ARTIST

1

"Whatever is here, it is
material for my art.

On the extreme shore of land,
and facing the disordered
rhythms of the sea, I taste
a summoning on the air.

I derive from these rocks, which
inhibit the sea's impulse.
But it is a condition,
once accepted, like air: air
haunted by the taste of salt.

2

I think, therefore I cannot
avoid thought of the morrow.
Outside the window, the birds
of the air and the lily
have lost themselves in action.
I think of the birds that sleep
in flight, of the lily's pale
waxy gleaming, of myself,
and of the morrow pending.
The one thing clear is that I
must not lose myself in thought.

3

You control what you can, and
use what you cannot.
                    Heady,
to hover above the winds,
buoyant with a sense of choice.
Circling over a city,
to reject the thousand, and
to select the one. To watch
the goodly people there, to
know that their blood circulates,
that it races as yours does,
live between extremities.

4

But what of the unchosen?

They are as if dead. Their deaths,
now, validate the chosen.

Of course, being left as dead
may lead to the thing itself.
I read about them: and what
could be more fortifying

to one's own identity
than another's suicide?

If there are forbidden arts,
mine must indeed be of them.

5

She is immersed in despair,
but I am here, luckily.
She, become indefinite,
leans on me who am starkly
redefined at each moment,
aware of her need, and trained
to have few needs of my own.

As I support her, so, with
my magnificent control,
I suddenly ask: 'What if
she has the edge over me?'

6

To give way to all passions,
I know, is merely whoring.
Yes, but to give way to none
is to be a whore-master.

I stride through the whore-house
when my girls are off duty,
I load them with chocolates,
but cannot for one moment
possess red hair like hers, fresh
cheeks or bee-stung lips like hers,
or a wasteful heart like hers.

7

I elevate not what I
have, but what I wish to have,
and see myself in others.

There is a girl in the train
who emulates the bee-hive
of the magazine stars of
four years ago.

I blush at
the jibes that grow inside me,
lest someone should utter them.

Why was something evolved so
tender, so open to pain?

8

Here is a famous picture.

It is of a little Jew
in Warsaw, some years ago,
being hustled somewhere. His
mother dressed him that morning
warmly in cap and cloth coat.
He stares at the camera
as he passes. Whatever
those big shining dark eyes have
just looked on, they can see now
no appeal in the wide world.

9

I grow old in the design.

Prophecies become fulfilled,
though never as expected,
almost accidentally,
in fact, as if to conform
to some alien order.

But I am concerned with my
own knowledge that the design
is everywhere ethical
and harmonious: circles
start to close, lines to balance.

10

The art of designing life
is no excuse for that life.

People will forget Shakespeare.
He will lie with George Formby
and me, here where the swine root.

Later, the solar system
will flare up and fall into
space, irretrievably lost.

For the loss, as for the life,
there will be no excuse, there
is no justification."   (1967)

TOUCH

You are already
asleep. I lower
myself in next to
you, my skin slightly
numb with the restraint
of habits, the patina of
self, the black frost
of outsideness, so that even
unclothed it is
a resilient chilly
hardness, a superficially
malleable, dead
rubbery texture.

You are a mound
of bedclothes, where the cat
in sleep braces
its paws against your
calf through the blankets,
and kneads each paw in turn.

Meanwhile and slowly
I feel a is it
my own warmth surfacing or
the ferment of your whole
body that in darkness beneath
the cover is stealing
bit by bit to break
down that chill.
                    You turn and
hold me tightly, do
you know who
I am or am I

your mother or
the nearest human being to
hold on to in a
dreamed pogrom.

What I, now loosened,
sink into is an old
big place, it is
there already, for
you are already
there, and the cat
got there before you, yet
it is hard to locate.
What is more, the place is
not found but seeps
from our touch in
continuous creation, dark
enclosing cocoon round
ourselves alone, dark
wide realm where we
walk with everyone.   (1967)

Ted Hughes
(1930–   )

HAWK ROOSTING

I sit in the top of the wood, my eyes closed.
Inaction, no falsifying dream
Between my hooked head and hooked feet:
Or in sleep rehearse perfect kills and eat.

The convenience of the high trees!
The air's buoyancy and the sun's ray
Are of advantage to me;
And the earth's face upward for my inspection.

My feet are locked upon the rough bark.
It took the whole of Creation
To produce my foot, my each feather:
Now I hold Creation in my foot

Or fly up, and revolve it all slowly—
I kill where I please because it is all mine.
There is no sophistry in my body:
My manners are tearing off heads—

The allotment of death.
For the one path of my flight is direct
Through the bones of the living.
No arguments assert my right:

The sun is behind me.
Nothing has changed since I began.
My eye has permitted no change.
I am going to keep things like this.   (*1957*)

NOVEMBER

The month of the drowned dog. After long rain the land
Was sodden as the bed of an ancient lake,

Treed with iron and birdless. In the sunk lane
The ditch—a seep silent all summer—

Made brown foam with a big voice: that, and my boots
On the lane's scrubbed stones, in the gulleyed leaves,
Against the hill's hanging silence;
Mist silvering the droplets on the bare thorns

Slower than the change of daylight.
In a let of the ditch a tramp was bundled asleep:
Face tucked down into beard, drawn in
Under its hair like a hedgehog's. I took him for dead,

But his stillness separated from the death
Of the rotting grass and the ground. A wind chilled,
And a fresh comfort tightened through him,
Each hand stuffed deeper into the other sleeve.

His ankles, bound with sacking and hairy band,
Rubbed each other, resettling. The wind hardened;
A puff shook a glittering from the thorns,
And again the rains' dragging grey columns

Smudged the farms. In a moment
The fields were jumping and smoking; the thorns
Quivered, riddled with the glassy verticals.
I stayed on under the welding cold

Watching the tramp's face glisten and the drops on his coat
Flash and darken. I thought what strong trust
Slept in him—as the trickling furrows slept,
And the thorn-roots in their grip on darkness;

And the buried stones, taking the weight of winter;
The hill where the hare crouched with clenched teeth.
Rain plastered the land till it was shining
Like hammered lead, and I ran, and in the rushing wood

Shuttered by a black oak leaned.
The keeper's gibbet had owls and hawks
By the neck, weasels, a gang of cats, crows:
Some, stiff, weightless, twirled like dry bark bits

In the drilling rain. Some still had their shape,
Had their pride with it; hung, chins on chests,

Patient to outwait these worst days that beat
Their crowns bare and dripped from their feet.   *(1960)*

PIKE

Pike, three inches long, perfect
Pike in all parts, green tigering the gold.
Killers from the egg: the malevolent aged grin.
They dance on the surface among the flies.

Or move, stunned by their own grandeur,
Over a bed of emerald, silhouette
Of submarine delicacy and horror.
A hundred feet long in their world.

In ponds, under the heat-struck lily pads—
Gloom of their stillness:
Logged on last year's black leaves, watching upwards.
Or hung in an amber cavern of weeds

The jaws' hooked clamp and fangs
Not to be changed at this date;
A life subdued to its instrument;
The gills kneading quietly, and the pectorals.

Three we kept behind glass,
Jungled in weed: three inches, four,
And four and a half: fed fry to them—
Suddenly there were two. Finally one

With a sag belly and the grin it was born with.
And indeed they spare nobody.
Two, six pounds each, over two feet long,
High and dry and dead in the willow-herb—

One jammed past its gills down the other's gullet:
The outside eye stared: as a vice locks—
The same iron in this eye
Though its film shrank in death.

A pond I fished, fifty yards across,
Whose lilies and muscular tench

Had outlasted every visible stone
Of the monastery that planted them—

Stilled legendary depth:
It was as deep as England. It held
Pike too immense to stir, so immense and old
That past nightfall I dared not cast

But silently cast and fished
With the hair frozen on my head
For what might move, for what eye might move.
The still splashes on the dark pond,

Owls hushing the floating woods
Frail on my ear against the dream
Darkness beneath night's darkness had freed,
That rose slowly towards me, watching. *(1960)*

LUPERCALIA

1

The dog loved its churlish life,
Scraps, thefts. Its declined blood
An anarchy of mindless pride.
Nobody's pet, but good enough

To double with a bitch as poor.
It had bitten ears and little stone eyes,
A mouth like an incinerator.
It held man's reasonable ways.

Between its teeth. Received death
Closed eyes and grinning mouth.

2

This woman's as from death's touch: a surviving
Barrenness: she abides; perfect,
But flung from the wheel of the living,
The past killed in her, the future plucked out.

The dead are indifferent underground.
Little the live may learn from them—

A sort of hair and bone wisdom,
A worn witchcraft accoutrement

Of proverbs. Now the brute's quick
Be tinder: Old spark of the blood-heat
And not death's touch engross her bed,
Though that has stripped her stark indeed.

3

Goats, black, not angels, but
Bellies round as filled wine-skins
Slung under carcase bones.
Yet that's no brute light

And no merely mountain light—
Their eyes' golden element.
Rustle of their dry hooves, dry patter,
Wind in the oak-leaves; and their bent

Horns, stamp, sudden reared stare
Startle women. Spirit of the ivy,
Stink of goat, of a rank thriving,
O mountain listener.

4

Over sand that the sun's burned out
Thudding feet of the powerful,
Their oiled bodies brass-bright
In a drift of dust. The earth's crammed full,

Its baked red bellying to the sky's
Electric blue. Their attitudes—
A theorem of flung effort, blades:
Nothing mortal falters their poise

Though wet with blood: the dog has blessed
Their fury. Fresh thongs of goat-skin
In their hands they go bounding past,
And deliberate welts have snatched her in

To the figure of racers. Maker of the world,
Hurrying the lit ghost of man
Age to age while the body hold,
Touch this frozen one.   *(1960)*

AN OTTER

1

Underwater eyes, an eel's
Oil of water body, neither fish nor beast is the otter.
Four-legged yet water-gifted, to outfish fish;
With webbed feet and long ruddering tail
And a round head like an old tomcat.

Brings the legend of himself
From before wars or burials, in spite of hounds and verminpoles;
Does not take root like the badger. Wanders, cries;
Gallops along land he no longer belongs to;
Re-enters the water by melting.

Of neither water nor land. Seeking
Some world lost when first he dived, that he cannot come at since,
Takes his changed body into the holes of lakes;
As if blind, cleaves the stream's push till he licks
The pebbles of the source; from sea

To sea crosses in three nights
Like a king in hiding. Crying to the old shape of the starlit land,
Over sunken farms where the bats go round,
Without answer. Till light and birdsong come
Walloping up roads with the milk wagon.

2

The hunt's lost him. Pads on mud,
Among sedges, nostrils a surface bead,
The otter remains, hours. The air,
Circling the globe, tainted and necessary,

Mingling tobacco-smoke, hounds and parsley,
Comes carefully to the sunk lungs.
So the self under the eye lies,
Attendant and withdrawn. The otter belongs

In double robbery and concealment—
From water that nourishes and drowns, and from land
That gave him his length and the mouth of the hound.
He keeps fat in the limpid integument

Reflections live on. The heart beats thick,
Big trout muscle out of the dead cold;
Blood is the belly of logic; he will lick
The fishbone bare. And can take stolen hold

On a bitch otter in a field full
Of nervous horses, but linger nowhere.
Yanked above hounds, reverts to nothing at all,
To this long pelt over the back of a chair.   (1960)

CADENZA

The violinist's shadow vanishes.

The husk of a grasshopper
Sucks a remote cyclone and rises.

The full, bared throat of a woman walking water,
The loaded estuary of the dead.

And I am the cargo
Of a coffin attended by swallows.

And I am the water
Bearing the coffin that will not be silent.

The clouds are full of surgery and collisions
But the coffin escapes—as a black diamond,

A ruby brimming blood,
An emerald beating its shores,

The sea lifts swallow wings and flings
A summer lake open,

Sips and bewilders its reflection,
Till the whole sky dives shut like a burned land back to its spark—

A bat with a ghost in its mouth
Struck at by lightnings of silence—

Blue with sweat, the violinist
Crashes into the orchestra, which explodes.   (1967)

SONG OF A RAT

1

THE RAT'S DANCE

The rat is in the trap, it is in the trap,
And attacking heaven and earth with a mouthful of screeches like torn
  tin,

An effective gag.
When it stops screeching, it pants

And cannot think
"This has no face, it must be God" or

"No answer is also an answer."
Iron jaws, strong as the whole earth

Are stealing its backbone
For a crumpling of the Universe with screechings,

For supplanting every human brain inside its skull with a rat-body that
  knots and unknots,
A rat that goes on screeching,

Trying to uproot itself into each escaping screech,
But its long fangs bar that exit—

The incisors bared to the night spaces, threatening the constellations,
The glitterers in the black, to keep off,

Keep their distance,
While it works this out.

The rat understands suddenly. It bows and is still,
With a little beseeching of blood on its nose-end.

2

THE RAT'S VISION

The rat hears the wind saying something in the straw
And the night-fields that have come up to the fence, leaning their
  silence,

The widowed land
With its trees that know how to cry

The rat sees the farm bulk of beam and stone
Wobbling like reflection on water.
The wind is pushing from the gulf
Through the old barbed wire, in through the trenched gateway, past the
    gates of the ear, deep into the worked design of days,

Breathes onto the solitary snow crystal

The rat screeches
And "Do not go" cry the dandelions, from their heads of folly
And "Do not go" cry the yard cinders, who have no future, only their
    infernal aftermath
And "Do not go" cries the cracked trough by the gate, fatalist of starlight
    and zero

"Stay" says the arrangement of stars

Forcing the rat's head down into godhead.

3

THE RAT'S FLIGHT

The heaven shudders, a flame unrolled like a whip,
And the stars jolt in their sockets.
And the sleep-souls of eggs
Wince under the shot of shadow—

That was the Shadow of the Rat
Crossing into power
Never to be buried

The horned Shadow of the Rat
Casting here by the door
A bloody gift for the dogs

While it supplants Hell. *(1967)*

BIOGRAPHICAL AND BIBLIOGRAPHICAL NOTES:
POETS OF BRITAIN

The following notes are intended to provide only the most basic identification of the poets represented in this anthology and a highly selective list of their books. Occasionally commentaries on their lives and work are noted, but only when these seem particularly useful to students.

Wystan Hugh Auden (1907–   ). Educated Oxford University. Schoolteacher 1930–1935. Leader of Left poetry movement, with Spender, Day Lewis, and MacNeice in 1930's. Emigrated to U.S. in 1939, naturalized 1946. After teaching in American colleges and universities, elected Professor of Poetry at Oxford, 1956–1961. *Poems*, 1930, 1933, 1934–1935 (three distinct editions); *The Orators*, 1932 (rev. 1966); *On This Island*, 1937; *Selected Poems*, 1938; *The Collected Poetry*, 1945; *The Age of Anxiety*, 1947; *Nones*, 1951; *The Shield of Achilles*, 1955; *Homage to Clio*, 1960; *About the House*, 1965; *Collected Shorter Poems*, 1966; *Collected Longer Poems*, 1968. PROSE: *The Dyer's Hand, and Other Essays*, 1962. COMMENTARY: Richard Hoggart, *Auden, An Introductory Essay*, 1951; Joseph Warren Beach, *The Making of the Auden Canon*, 1957; Monroe K. Spears, *The Poetry of W. H. Auden: The Disenchanted Island*, 1963; *City without Walls*, 1969.

John Betjeman (1906–   ). Educated Oxford University. Former schoolteacher, journalist, authority on English architecture. *Collected Poems*, 1958; *Summoned by Bells*, 1960. COMMENTARY: Derek Stanford, *John Betjeman: A Study*, 1961.

Robert Bridges (1844–1930). Educated Oxford University. Medical studies St. Bartholomew's Hospital. London physician until 1882, thereafter devoting himself to literature. Appointed Poet Laureate 1913. His devotion to church music related to special interest in questions of prosody. *Poetical Works*, 1912; *The Testament of Beauty*, 1929; *Poetical Works*, 1936; *Poems* (ed. W. H. Gardner), 1948. PROSE: *Milton's Prosody*, 1893. COMMENTARY: Albert J. Guérard, *Robert Bridges*, 1965.

Austin Clarke (1896–   ). Former university teacher; playwright, novelist, journalist; a younger associate of Yeats in the Abbey Theatre. *Collected Poems,* 1936; *Later Poems,* 1961; *Flight to Africa,* 1963; *Collected Plays,* 1963; *Mnemosyne Lay in Dust,* 1966; *The Echo at Coole,* 1968. PROSE: *Twice Round the Black Church* (autobiography), 1962.

Walter de la Mare (1873–1956). Educated St. Paul's Cathedral Choir School, London. Clerk, Anglo-American branch of Standard Oil Company 1890–1908, after which government grant and pension enabled him to devote himself to writing. *Poems, 1901–1918* (published in U.S. as *Collected Poems, 1901–1918*), 1920; *Collected Poems,* 1941; *A Choice of de la Mare's Verse* (ed. W. H. Auden), 1963. PROSE: *The Collected Tales,* 1950.

William Empson (1906–   ). Educated Cambridge University. Has taught English literature at Chinese and Japanese universities, and at Sheffield University in England. One of the leading "New Critics." *Poems,* 1935; *The Gathering Storm,* 1940; *Collected Poems,* 1955. CRITICISM: *Seven Types of Ambiguity,* 1930; *Some Versions of Pastoral,* 1935; *The Structure of Complex Words,* 1951; *Milton's God,* 1961 (rev. 1965).

Robert Graves (1895–   ). Son of Irish poet Alfred Percival Graves. Educated Oxford University. First recognition as poet of World War I. Prolific writer of fiction, criticism, literary polemic, mythological studies. Now perhaps best known for *The White Goddess,* 1948, a study of the continuing inspiration of poetry by certain motifs of ancient myth. Elected Professor of Poetry, Oxford, in 1961. *Collected Poems, 1965,* 1965. PROSE: *Good-bye to All That* (autobiography), 1929 (rev. 1958); *I, Claudius* (fiction), 1934; *A Survey of Modernist Poetry* (with Laura Riding), 1927; *A Pamphlet against Anthologies* (with Laura Riding), 1928; *The White Goddess: A Historical Grammar of Poetic Myth,* 1948; *The Common Asphodel: Collected Essays on Poetry,* 1949; *Occupation: Writer,* 1950; *The Crowning Privilege,* 1955; *The Greek Myths,* 1955; *Hebrew Myths* (with Raphael Patai), 1964. COMMENTARY: J. M. Cohen, *Robert Graves,* 1960.

Thom Gunn (1929–   ). Educated Cambridge University. Critic, anthologist; has lived in California and taught at the University of California at Berkeley since 1954. *Fighting Terms,* 1954 (rev. 1959, 1962); *The Sense of Movement,* 1957; *My Sad Captains,* 1961; *Touch,* 1967.

Thomas Hardy (1840–1928). After apprenticeship and formal study to be an architect, turned to poetry, then to fiction, and to poetry again after the indignant reception of his novel *Jude the Obscure*, 1895. *Wessex Poems*, 1898; *Time's Laughingstocks*, 1909; *Satires of Circumstance*, 1914; *The Dynasts*, 1903–1908; *Collected Poems*, 1919 (1st vol. of *The Poetical Works*; expanded in *New Complete American Edition*, 1926, and in *4th Edition*, 1932). FICTION: *Far from the Madding Crowd*, 1874; *The Return of the Native*, 1878; *The Mayor of Casterbridge*, 1886; *Tess of the D'Urbervilles*, 1891. COMMENTARY: Florence Emily Hardy, *The Life of Thomas Hardy, 1840–1928*, 1962 (originally in two volumes, 1928, 1930); *Southern Review*, "Thomas Hardy Memorial Issue," VI, summer 1940; Harvey C. Webster, *On a Darkling Plain: The Art and Thought of Thomas Hardy*, 1947; Albert J. Guérard, *Thomas Hardy*, 1949; C. Day Lewis, *The Lyrical Poetry of Thomas Hardy*, 1951; Albert J. Guérard, ed., *Hardy: A Collection of Critical Essays*, 1963.

Gerard Manley Hopkins (1844–1889). Educated Oxford University. Converted to Catholicism, entered Jesuit priesthood. His correspondence with Robert Bridges and other poets a notable contribution to poetics. Professor of Classics, University College, Dublin. *Poems*, edited 1918 by Robert Bridges, 1930 by Charles Williams, 1948 by W. H. Gardner, 1967 by W. H. Gardner and N. H. MacKenzie. See also *The Letters of Gerard Manley Hopkins to Robert Bridges*, ed. C. C. Abbott, 1935; *The Journals and Papers of Gerard Manley Hopkins*, ed. Humphrey House and Graham Storey, 1959; *The Sermons and Devotional Writings of Gerard Manley Hopkins*, ed. Christopher Devlin, 1959. COMMENTARY: W. H. Gardner, *Gerard Manley Hopkins*, Vol. I, 1944 (rev. 1948) and Vol. II, 1949; *Gerard Manley Hopkins*, by the Kenyon Critics, 1945; Norman Weyand, ed., *Immortal Diamond*, 1949.

A. E. Housman (1859–1936). Educated Oxford University. Employed Patent Office 1882–1892. Professor of Latin, University College, London, 1892–1911; Cambridge University thereafter. An outstanding classical scholar. *A Shropshire Lad*, 1896; *Last Poems*, 1922; *More Poems*, 1936; *Complete Poems*, 1959. PROSE: *Selected Prose*, 1961. COMMENTARY: Oliver Robinson, *Angry Dust: The Poetry of A. E. Housman*, 1950; George L. Watson, *A. E. Housman*, 1957; Tom Burns Haber, *A. E. Housman*, 1967.

Ted Hughes (1930–   ). Educated Cambridge University. Writer for radio, television; former schoolteacher. Married to the American poet

Sylvia Plath until her death in 1963. *The Hawk in the Rain,* 1957; *Lupercal,* 1960; *Wodwo,* 1967.

Patrick Kavanagh (1905–1967). Son of a rural shoemaker in County Monaghan, Ireland; early poverty and the barrenness of peasant life deeply affected his writing as well as his career. Gave up farming in 1939 to live in Dublin, where he had the hard life of a needy writer and freelance journalist and film critic, and was often the center of controversy. For some years associated with a group of Irish and English poets including George Barker and David Wright, editor of the magazine X. *Ploughman and Other Poems,* 1936; *The Great Hunger,* 1942; *A Soul for Sale,* 1947; *Come Dance with Kitty Stobling,* 1960; *Collected Poems,* 1964. PROSE: *Self-Portrait,* 1964; *Collected Prose,* 1967.

Thomas Kinsella (1928–   ). Former Irish civil servant, Department of Finance. Professor of English, Southern Illinois University. *Poems,* 1956; *Another September,* 1958; *Poems and Translations,* 1961; *Downstream,* 1962; *Wormwood,* 1966; *Nightwalker and Other Poems,* 1968.

Philip Larkin (1922–   ). Educated Oxford University. Librarian, University of Hull. A spokesman, in his wry way, for England's postwar literary generation of "angry young men," and the chief representative of "Movement" poetry—restrained, anti-Romantic, formally controlled and emphasizing wit and good sense rather than passion or experiment—as advocated and exemplified in Robert Conquest's *New Lines* anthologies, 1956 and 1963. *The North Ship,* 1945; *The Less Deceived,* 1955; *The Whitsun Weddings,* 1964. FICTION: *Jill,* 1946; *A Girl in Winter,* 1947.

D. H. Lawrence (1885–1930). Son of Nottinghamshire miner. (See autobiographical novel *Sons and Lovers,* 1913, for a picture of Lawrence's early years.) Educated Nottingham Day Training College. Schoolteacher for occasional periods. Noted for fiction and poetry especially, but also for critical and social theory and painting. Traveled Australia, Mexico, Sicily, Sardinia, Italy, United States after leaving England in 1919. Portrayed as Mark Rampion in Aldous Huxley's *Point Counter Point. Look! We Have Come Through!,* 1917; *Birds, Beasts and Flowers,* 1923; *The Collected Poems,* 1928 (American edition 1929); *Pansies,* 1929; *Last Poems,* 1932; *The Ship of Death,* 1933; *Selected Poems,* 1947; *Complete Poems,* ed. Vivian de Sola Pinto and F. Warren Roberts, 1964. NOVELS: *The Rainbow,*

1915; *Women in Love,* 1920; *Aaron's Rod,* 1922; *The Plumed Serpent,* 1926; *Lady Chatterley's Lover,* 1928. OTHER FICTION: *The Prussian Officer,* 1914; *The Ladybird, The Fox, The Captain's Doll,* 1923; *The Man Who Died,* 1931. CRITICISM: *Studies in Classic American Literature,* 1923. TRAVEL: *Twilight in Italy,* 1916; *Sea and Sardinia,* 1921. See also *The Letters,* 1932, ed. Aldous Huxley. COMMENTARY: Horace Gregory, *Pilgrim of the Apocalypse,* 1933; W. Y. Tindall, *D. H. Lawrence and Susan His Cow,* 1939; Frederick J. Hoffman and Harry T. Moore, *The Achievement of D. H. Lawrence,* 1953; Graham Hough, *The Dark Sun: A Study of D. H. Lawrence,* 1957; Edward Nehls, ed., *D. H. Lawrence, A Composite Biography,* 1957–1959; Mark Spilka, ed., *D. H. Lawrence: A Collection of Critical Essays,* 1963.

Cecil Day Lewis (1904–   ). Born Ireland, son of Anglican clergyman. Educated Oxford University. Schoolteacher 1927–1935. Professor of Poetry, Oxford University, 1951–1956. *A Hope for Poetry,* 1934, was outstanding manifesto of Left poetry movements of 1930's. Translator from the classics. Under pseudonym Nicholas Blake author of detective fiction. *Transitional Poem,* 1929; *From Feathers to Iron,* 1931; *The Magnetic Mountain,* 1933; *Collected Poems,* 1954; *Selected Poems,* 1967. PROSE: *The Poetic Image,* 1947; *The Buried Day* (autobiography), 1960. Appointed Poet Laureate of England, 1968.

Hugh MacDiarmid (1892–   ). Pen name of Christopher Murray Grieve. Son of a rural Scottish postman, educated at Langholm Academy and Broughton Junior Student Centre, Edinburgh, where he trained to be a teacher. Became a journalist instead, with a strong interest in political and economic as well as literary questions, which he has pursued as editor, anthologist, and polemicist. Founded Scottish Renaissance Movement and is chiefly responsible for the use of Scots (or "Lallans") in serious modern Scottish poetry. Both a Scottish Nationalist and a Communist, he opposed the Prime Minister in the 1964 general election, standing in the same constituency. *Sangschaw,* 1925; *Penny Wheep,* 1926; *A Drunk Man Looks at the Thistle,* 1926; *To Circumjack Cencrastus,* 1930; *First Hymn to Lenin and Other Poems,* 1931; *Scots Unbound and Other Poems,* 1932; *Stony Limits and Other Poems,* 1934; *Second Hymn to Lenin and Other Poems,* 1935; *Selected Poems,* ed. R. Crombie Saunders, 1944; *Three Hymns to Lenin,* 1957; *Collected Poems,* 1962; (slightly rev. 1967). PROSE: *Scottish Eccentrics,* 1936; *Lucky Poet* (autobiography), 1943. COMMENTARY: Kenneth Buthlay, *Hugh Mac-*

Diarmid (C. M. Grieve), 1964; Duncan Glen, Hugh MacDiarmid and the Scottish Renaissance, 1964.

Louis MacNeice (1907–1963). Born in Belfast, Ireland, son of an Anglican clergyman. Educated Oxford University. Lecturer in Classics at University of Birmingham and other English and American colleges and universities. Translator from the classics. Blind Fireworks, 1929; Poems, 1935; Autumn Journal, 1939; Poems 1925–1940, 1940; Collected Poems, 1949; Ten Burnt Offerings, 1952; Autumn Sequel, 1954; Visitations, 1957; Solstices, 1961; The Burning Perch, 1963; Collected Poems, ed. E. R. Dodds, 1966. PROSE: Modern Poetry, A Personal Essay, 1938; The Strings Are False: An Unfinished Autobiography, 1965.

John Masefield (1878–1967). Trained at first for the merchant marine, he left the service at fifteen and worked at odd jobs before entering the literary world as poet, free-lance writer, and journalist. Appointed Poet Laureate in 1930 at the death of Robert Bridges. Salt-Water Ballads, 1902; The Everlasting Mercy, 1911; The Widow in the Bye Street, 1912; Dauber, 1913; Reynard the Fox, 1919; The Collected Poems of John Masefield, 1923 (new and enlarged revised ed., 1932); Poems, "Complete Edition, with Recent Poems," 1935.

Edwin Muir (1887–1959). Born Orkney Islands. Little formal education, poverty-filled youth in Glasgow which opened him to Socialist thought. Later turned to more mystical and religious views. Editor, critic, translator (with Willa, his wife) of Kafka and other important modern writers in German. Became Director of the British Institute in Prague and in Rome after World War II, and in 1950 Warden of Newbattle Abbey College. First Poems, 1925; Chorus of the Newly Dead, 1926; Variations on a Time Theme, 1934; The Labyrinth, 1949; Collected Poems 1921–1951, 1952; One Foot in Eden, 1956; Collected Poems 1921–1958, 1960 (2nd ed., slightly expanded, 1965). PROSE: Essays on Literature and Society, 1949 (enlarged and rev., 1965); An Autobiography, 1954. COMMENTARY: Peter H. Butter, Edwin Muir, Man and Poet, 1966.

Wilfred Owen (1893–1918). Son of minor railway official in Shropshire. Educated Birkenhead Institute. Killed in action World War I. The most famous of the English war poets, together with Siegfried Sassoon, who first collected his poems in 1920. Poems, 1920; The Poems of Wilfred Owen, " a new edition including many pieces now first published, and notices of his life and work," ed. Edmund

Blunden 1931; *Collected Poems*, ed. C. Day Lewis, 1963. COM-MENTARY: Dennis S. R. Welland, *Wilfred Owen: A Critical Study*, 1960; Harold Owen, *Journey from Obscurity: Memoirs of the Owen Family*, 1963–1965.

Siegfried Sassoon (1886–1967). Educated Cambridge University. Together with Wilfred Owen, the outstanding English war poet, continuing his pacifist writing after the War. *The War Poems of Siegfried Sassoon*, 1919; *Selected Poems*, 1925; *Collected Poems, 1908–1956*, 1961. AUTOBIOGRAPHICAL NOVEL: *Memoirs of George Sherston*, 1967 (originally in three volumes with other titles, 1928, 1930, 1936).

Edith Sitwell (1887–1964). Member of a famous literary family, sister of Osbert and Sacheverell Sitwell. Privately educated. Editor *Wheels*, 1916–1918, 1921, which attacked the formal limitations of the popular Georgian school. Made a Dame in 1954. *Facade*, 1922; *The Sleeping Beauty*, 1924; *The Collected Poems*, 1930, 1954; *Street Songs*, 1942; *The Song of the Cold*, 1945; *The Canticle of the Rose: Poems 1917–1949*, 1949. PROSE: *Aspects of Modern Poetry*, 1934; *Taken Care Of: An Autobiography*, 1965.

Stephen Spender (1909–   ). Educated Oxford University. A member of the "Auden Group" in the thirties. A distinguished critic and literary journalist as well as poet. *Poems*, 1933; *Vienna*, 1934; *Trial of a Judge*, 1938; *The Still Centre*, 1939; *Ruins and Visions*, 1942; *Collected Poems, 1928–1953*, 1959; *Selected Poems*, 1965. PROSE: *The Destructive Element*, 1935; *World Within World* (autobiography), 1951; *The Creative Element*, 1953.

James Stephens (1882–1950). Born Dublin. Childhood in poverty, no formal education. Intense Irish nationalist, reflected in Celtic themes and stylistic mannerisms. *Collected Poems*, 1926 (expanded 1954); *A Selection*, 1962. FICTION: *The Crock of Gold*, 1912; *The Demi-Gods*, 1914; *Deirdre*, 1923.

Dylan Thomas (1914–1953). Born Swansea, Wales. Educated Swansea Grammar School. Distinguished career as broadcaster on B.B.C. His rich speaking voice made his reading tours the most successful of any poet's in this century. (The hectic character of these tours and the self-destructive alcoholism they intensified in Thomas are vividly described in John Malcolm Brinnin, *Dylan Thomas in America: An Intimate Journal*, 1955.) *Eighteen Poems*, 1934; *Twenty-Five Poems*,

1936; *Map of Love: Verse and Prose*, 1939; *New Poems*, 1943; *Selected Writings*, 1946; *Deaths and Entrances*, 1946; *In Country Sleep*, 1952; *The Collected Poems*, 1952. PROSE: *Portrait of the Artist as a Young Dog*, 1940. DRAMA: *Under Milk Wood*, 1954. COMMENTARY: Henry Treece, *Dylan Thomas*, 1949 (rev. 1956). Elder Olson, *The Poetry of Dylan Thomas*, 1954. Caitlin Thomas (MacNamara), *Leftover Life to Kill*, 1957; Constantine Fitzgibbon, *The Life of Dylan Thomas*, 1965.

Charles Tomlinson (1927–   ). Educated Cambridge University. Teaches at Bristol University. Exemplar of the influence of American poetry on younger British writers. *Relations and Contraries*, 1951; *The Necklace*, 1955; *Seeing Is Believing*, 1958; *A Peopled Landscape*, 1963; *American Scenes*, 1966; *The Way of a World*, 1969.

William Butler Yeats (1865–1939). Born Ireland, son of the painter John Butler Yeats. See his *Autobiography*, 1927, for descriptions of the influences of his childhood. No university education, but studied at Erasmus Smith School and the Metropolitan School of Art in Dublin, and private studies in occultism and poetry. His collections of Irish folklore and his early coediting of Blake's works are two instances among many of his capacity to direct his own studies. In the 'nineties, a leading poet both of England and Ireland. Also, a leader of the Irish Renaissance; he helped found the Abbey Theatre. Senator, Irish Free State, 1922–1928. Nobel Prize for Literature, 1923. Dramatist, critic, mystical thinker (see *A Vision*, 1925 [enlarged revised edition 1937, 1956]; the ideas of this work are extremely important in Yeats's later writings). *The Wanderings of Oisin*, 1889; *The Wind among the Reeds*, 1899; *In the Seven Woods*, 1903; *The Green Helmet*, 1910; *Responsibilities*, 1914; *The Wild Swans at Coole*, 1917; *Michael Robartes and the Dancer*, 1920; *The Tower*, 1928; *The Winding Stair*, 1933; *The Collected Poems*, 1933 (enlarged edition, 1951; "Definitive Edition," 1956); *Last Poems and Plays*, 1940; *The Variorum Edition of the Poems*, ed. Peter Allt and Russell K. Alspach, 1957; *Selected Poems and Two Plays*, ed. M. L. Rosenthal, 1962. DRAMA: *The Collected Plays*, 1953 ("New edition, with five additional plays"). PROSE: *Essays*, 1924; *The Letters*, ed. Allan Wade, 1955; *The Autobiography of William Butler Yeats*, 1927 (as *Autobiographies*), 1958; *Mythologies*, 1959; *Essays and Introductions*, 1961. COMMENTARY: Joseph M. Hone, *Life of William Butler Yeats*, 1942; T. R. Henn, *The Lonely Tower*, 1950; Allan Wade, *A Bibliography of the Writings of W. B. Yeats*, 1951; A. Norman Jeffares, *W. B. Yeats, Man and Poet*, 1949;

Richard Ellmann, *Yeats: The Man and the Masks*, 1948, and *The Identity of Yeats*, 1954; Thomas Parkinson, *W. B. Yeats, Self-Critic*, 1951, and *W. B. Yeats: The Later Poetry*, 1964; Frank Kermode, *Romantic Image*, 1957; F. A. C. Wilson, *W. B. Yeats and Tradition*, 1958, and *Yeats's Iconography*, 1961; A. G. Stock, *W. B. Yeats: His Poetry and Thought*, 1961; John Unterrecker, ed., *Yeats: A Collection of Critical Essays*, 1963; Jon Stallworthy, *Between the Lines*, 1963, and *Vision and Revision in Yeats's Last Poems*, 1969; Curtis Bradford, *Yeats at Work*, 1965.

INDEX

of authors, titles, and first lines

Titles are in italics, first lines in roman type. When a title and first line
are the same, usually only the first line is indexed. *A, an,* or *the* at the
beginning of a title is placed at the end, but in first lines these words are
indexed in their normal order. When first lines are long, only the first few
words may be given.

- IRISH NAT'LIST SENTIMENTS
- FASCINATED BY ELEGANCE + REFINEMENT OF
WEALTHY.

EARLY POEMS - HIS OWN SENSE OF
LOSS ETC - LATER ONES MORE
UNIVERSAL.

"I" IS SAME PERSON THROUGH WHICH
PAST SPEAKS - LENDS DISTANCE.

LATE WORKS - EFFORT TO FIND
PATTERNS & RELATIONSHIPS IN LIFE